D0840782

PIMLICO

265

ROGER CASEMENT'S DIARIES

In 1864, Roger Casement was born into the Irish
landed gentry, the fourth and last child of a Protestant
father and a Roman Catholic mother. By the age of 13
he was an orphan, boarding at a school which later
became Ballymena Academy, and spending his holidays mainly at the family seat, Magherintemple, or
with the Bannisters – his maternal aunt's family – in
Liverpool.

On leaving school Casement started working for
the Elder Dempster Shipping Company, and in 1883
became purser on board one of the company's ships
trading with West Africa. This led to a number of
adventurous African posts, initially in the Congo Free
State.

Casement's primary career began with his employment by the Foreign Office in what is now Nigeria.
His performance there led to his joining the British
consular service, and a succession of African appoint-
ments followed. After an interlude of 'special service'
during the Boer War, his last African post as consul
was in the Congo. There he became famous as an
emancipator, in the cause of the rubber-gathering
slaves. The British government published Casement's
Congo Report in 1904, a year which also saw a crucial
stage in the development of his commitment to the
cause of Irish separatism. Six years later he investigated allegations of enslavement of rubber-gathering
natives in South America. By this time, after consular
postings in Santos and Pará, he had become Consul-
General in Rio. His report was published as a Blue
Book in 1912. Casement was knighted in 1911.

Retirement from the consular service meant that
undivided attention could now be given to Ireland.
After the outbreak of war in 1914 Casement went to
Germany, where he tried to recruit Irish prisoners-

of-war for a brigade to support a nationalist rebellion. His mission failed; Casement was returned to Ireland in a German U-boat, captured, taken to London, and sentenced to death and hanged for high treason.

During and after Casement's trial the so-called 'Black Diaries' – a collection of documents containing some descriptions of his homosexual activities – were shown to people in power who would otherwise have supported petitions for a reprieve. After Casement was hanged on 3 August 1916, efforts continued to be made by his enemies to use the diaries in order to poison his reputation in Ireland and America.

Roger Sawyer was educated at Wycliffe College, the University of Wales, and the University of Southampton. He was awarded the T. G. James Prize in Education and subsequently embarked on a schoolmastering career. After a housemastership at The Blue Coat School, Edgbaston, he became Deputy Head, then Headmaster, of Bembridge Preparatory School. He presented his doctoral thesis entitled 'Origins and career of Roger Casement with particular reference to the development of his interest in the rights of dependent ethnic groups' in 1979. He took early retirement in 1983 and has since concentrated on writing. His books include *Casement: The Flawed Hero* (1984), *Slavery in the Twentieth Century* (1986), *Children Enslaved* (1988) and *'We are but Women': Women in Ireland's History* (1993).

In 1985 he received the Airey Neave Award for Research into Freedom under National Laws. He is a member of the Council of Anti-Slavery International.

ROGER CASEMENT'S DIARIES

1910: The Black and the White

Edited by
ROGER SAWYER

PIMLICO

PIMLICO
An imprint of Random House
20 Vauxhall Bridge Road, London SW1V 2SA

Random House Australia (Pty) Ltd
20 Alfred Street, Milsons Point, Sydney
New South Wales 2061, Australia

Random House New Zealand Ltd
18 Poland Road, Glenfield
Auckland 10, New Zealand

Random House South Africa (Pty) Ltd
Endulini, 5A Jubilee Road, Parktown 2193, South Africa

Random House UK Ltd Reg. No. 954009

First published by Pimlico 1997

1 3 5 7 9 10 8 6 4 2

© Roger Sawyer 1997
Roger Casement's Diaries © Legatees of Mrs Sidney Parry

The right of Roger Sawyer to be identified as the author of this work has been asserted by
him in accordance with the Copyright, Designs and Patents Act, 1988

This book is sold subject to the condition that it shall
not, by way of trade or otherwise, be lent, resold, hired
out, or otherwise circulated without the publisher's prior
consent in any form of binding or cover other than that in which it is published and without a
similar condition including this condition being imposed on the subsequent purchaser

Papers used by Random House UK Limited are natural,
recyclable products made from wood grown in sustainable
forests. The manufacturing processes conform to the
environmental regulations of the country of origin

Printed and bound in Great Britain by
Mackays of Chatham PLC
ISBN 0-7126-7375-X

Contents

Preface

There have been times when the history of this book has seemed to be almost as tortuous as that of the diaries reproduced within it, and some explanation of its own origins may be necessary.

Initially, I was invited to edit Roger Casement's diaries because in 1984 I had published his biography, *Casement: The Flawed Hero.* Ten years after this, so I am told, a young historian was working in Rhodes House Library, Oxford with a copy of this biography open in front of him, when a friend working beside him pointed out that he knew me and was in fact due to meet me at the Anti-Slavery Society's office in a few hours time. A note was hastily scribbled, and there began an association, which sadly proved to be abortive.

When we were first commissioned by Pimlico to co-edit Casement's diaries, the young historian seemed to accept Casement as the author of the Black Diaries: they were not, as had been alleged, a forgery. More than 30 years previously, however, I had entered the controversy from the opposite position. Living in the Republic of Ireland, as I was at the time, all the signs were that the diaries had been forged, partly to make sure that powerful public figures would not support petitions for Casement's reprieve, but mainly to destroy his reputation as a national hero in Ireland and also in the United States.

Roger Casement had originally come into my life in his capacities as anti-slaver and frustrated poet; although his poetry was uninspiring, the way in which he had galvanized the British Consular Service into an effective force for the emancipation of slaves – principally in the Congo Free State – was an inspiration to anyone involved in the anti-slavery movement. When, in 1976, I decided to prepare a doctoral thesis, entitled 'Origins and career of Roger Casement with particular reference to the development of his interest in the rights of dependent ethnic groups', I was obliged to ascertain whether or not crucial primary sources relating to Casement – the diaries held in the Public Record Office – were in fact forged. After much research I found that they were entirely genuine.

My co-editor, on the other hand, made a journey in the reverse direction. After a period spent undertaking research in Ireland, he became convinced that the documents we were editing were forged. Not only that, but he was fairly confident that he could identify the forger. A meeting was convened by Pimlico, at which it was decided that the two editors should have equal space to examine the evidence and put forward their separate conclusions. This arrangement seemed at first to satisfy all parties. Eventually, though, my co-editor and initiator of the project withdrew from it.

There were, of course, areas in which we were in agreement. When the 1910 Black Diary was first published abroad,[1] the text contained many serious errors of transcription. It was riddled with misstatements and extraordinary mistakes: Coudenhove, an old friend of Casement had become 'Condenhor'; a Belgian, Thys, had become a non-existent Welshman, 'Rhys' – just two of the many absurdities. Clearly the Special Branch typists, working under great pressure to have their task of transcribing the diaries completed in time to achieve the aims of their masters, had experienced great difficulty in deciphering Casement's often illegible handwriting. In addition, they were not in a position to do much about Casement's occasional use of Irish lettering; nor had they the background knowledge to identify C.S.P. as Charles Stewart Parnell – information which would have undone another small confusion of transcription. Both editors felt that it was important to release into the public domain a copy of the text that was, so far as possible, error-free.

For myself, convinced as I am that the Black Diaries are genuine, it would have been better if the issue had not been forced by the publication of the Singleton-Gates garbled version in 1959. A good case could have been made for holding the documents back from public view, at least until the terms of the 100-year rule had been observed. The 'black' portions are personal and private and could reasonably have been ignored until well into the 21st century. As it is, with the revelations of Casement's homosexual activities having been made, a principal justification for re-publication today is to resolve the forgery issue once and for all.

The reader is advised to read the diaries in the order in which they are printed here. The same personalities are found in both diaries and, though there is cross-referencing, these individuals and other items are explained when they make their first appearance.

Inevitably much of the detail may be disillusioning to admirers of Casement's humanitarian work, but the subject matter of the diaries, both Black and White, has to be faced up to if an informed judgement, based on a comparison of the two documents, is to be made. While studying them, it is continually borne in upon one that these are the thoughts and actions of a man grappling with the realities of stamping out slavery in one of the most inhospitable parts of the world. Six years after writing them, and partly because of the content of the Black Diaries, Casement was to make the supreme sacrifice for his beliefs.

Roger Sawyer
Bembridge, Isle of Wight, 1997

---

[1] *The Black Diaries of Roger Casement*, edited by Peter Singleton-Gates and Maurice Girodias, The Olympia Press, Paris, 1959.

Acknowledgements

My first duty is to thank Elspeth Parry who, on behalf of the Parry family, gave permission for the diaries to be published. The Parrys, as residuary legatees of Mrs Sidney Parry (née Gertrude Bannister) are owners of the copyright in Roger Casement's writings.

Others must also be thanked for providing access to archives and facilitating publication of the papers in their care. Foremost among the repositories used are the Public Record Office[1] in London and the National Library of Ireland[2] in Dublin. Thanks are expressed to Anne Crawford, Bruno Derrick and Nick Forbes of the PRO, and to the Deputy Keeper of Manuscripts, Gerard Lyne, and the Council of Trustees of the NLI. Robert Kee kindly allowed me to use transcripts of his interview with the leading Counsel defending Casement at his trial, A. M. Sullivan, Second Serjeant of the Irish Bar.

Much help was also received from Dr Peter B. Boyden, of the National Army Museum, Andrew Brown, of the Metropolitan Police Archives Branch, Paul Buxton and Dr Charles Swaisland, of Anti-Slavery International, Nicholas S. Carlyle, of the Home Office Library, Andrew Davidson, of the Foreign and Commonwealth Library, Amanda Hill, archivist at Rhodes House Library, Oxford, Christopher Maitland, of the Royal Belfast Academical Institution, Dr S. G. Roberts, of the Royal Commission on Historical Manuscripts, Dr Séamas Ó Síocháin, of St Patrick's College, Maynooth, and Katharine Thomson, Modern Manuscripts Assistant at Balliol College, Oxford. Their assistance is greatly appreciated.

Occasionally, Casement's eccentric use of Spanish and Portuguese made it necessary for me to consult linguists, and my problems were solved by Arancha Hernando, Helen McCurdy and Alberto and Jenny Penalva. Similar confusing references, mainly geographical, were explained by Carmen Azurin, of the Peruvian Embassy (London), and by Anita Nueman, of the Swedish Embassy (London).

Librarians generally proved that the most obscure publications could be located, given determination and know-how. Those of my own village library – Rosemary Bell and Alison Healy – were second to none. And Joy Caisley and Nicholas Graffy, of Southampton University, never failed to deliver. Alan Phillips, of the British Humanities Index was a constant source of useful information, as was Lieutenant Commander David Webb RN.

Others whose advice is highly valued are best listed in alphabetical order: John Anthony, Monica Ayles, Frank Cakebread, Pamela Freeman, B. M. Hewitt, the

---

[1] Hereafter referred to as the PRO.
[2] Hereafter referred to as the NLI.

Lord Howard de Walden, George Mansur, Stuart Monard, Kurt E. Schmid, Robert Shanks, Richard Usborne, and Bill and Elizabeth Wall.

It was a privilege to be able at all times to rely on a member of the Casement family for inside knowledge. Hugh Casement was a volunteer, and his assistance was greatly welcomed. Subsequently, by what seemed to be an extraordinary and happy coincidence, it transpired that Colonel Patrick Montgomery, retired Secretary of the Anti-Slavery Society and my mentor and main supporter for everything I have written, is godfather to Hugh Casement's brother, Robert. My chief debt of gratitude is to Pat and his wife Moskie, who know best how to sustain a friend, especially when the going is not smooth.

Finally, I must express my appreciation for all the encouragement I have received from Will Sulkin, publishing director of Pimlico, who commissioned this book.

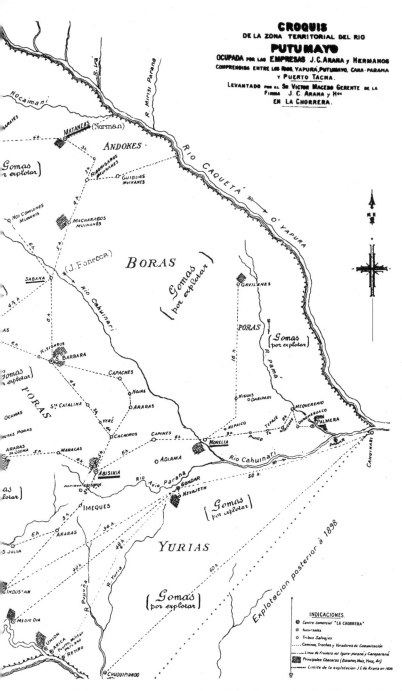

Map of the Putumayo River region of the Amazon Basin (Commissioned by Julio Arana's Amazon Rubber Company and reproduced by kind permission of Rhodes House Library, Oxford; ref. no. RHL MSS. Brit Emp. s 22 G 332).

Introduction

Compulsive diary writing was a fairly common phenomenon in Edwardian times, but Roger Casement's compulsion was exceptional. If his official reports are included, he was capable of writing no fewer than three versions of the same day's events, working at his largely self-imposed task long into the night, and into the early hours of the following day. And he did this after a strenuous day's work in a hostile environment, often when far from well. In addition to recording major and minor events in great detail, he wrote countless letters, both to officials and to friends. Some of the evidence of this is extant; some has disappeared.

Extant diaries are few. Four diaries[1] are held in the Public Record Office in London: the Congo diary for 1903, the Amazon diary for 1910, another Amazon diary for 1911, and a ledger or account book, also for 1911, which is near-enough a 'diary'. In Dublin, at the NLI, there are more extensive diaries: 'The Putumayo Diary', covering nearly eleven weeks of 1910, some diary MSS for parts of August and September 1910, and the MSS of diaries written in Germany at intervals during 1914, 1915 and 1916. All these documents are valuable for those interested in the life and times of a compassionate anti-slaver. However, it is by comparing the concurrent public and private accounts of Casement's thoughts and activities in 1910 that one can make an informed judgement, not only about the merits of the man's mission in life, but about the authenticity of diaries concealed for so long by the British authorities.

Ever since the 'Black Diaries', as they came to be known,[2] were used to poison the reputation of their author, it has frequently been alleged that an agency of the British government was guilty of forging them. Because of

[1] PRO HO [Home Office] 161: together with the Black Diaries was a fifth document, not a diary, which has by chance been lumped together with the four volumes which were used to discredit Casement. The fifth item is an Army notebook used in 1901 in the Congo to list place names, times, places, and ticket prices along the Matadi-Stanley Pool railway line, when Casement was a key figure in its construction. There is scarcely a complete sentence in the notebook – certainly nothing of a sexual nature.

[2] The four 'Black Diaries' comprise diaries for 1903, 1910, 1911 and a ledger for 1911.

these allegations the Black 1910 diary is reproduced here entirely unabridged, despite the presence within it of some details which appear insignificant, and others which some may find sordid. Buried within apparently trivial matter, as well as within more substantial entries, may be clues as to the truth or falsity of allegations about the diary's authenticity. But both the 'White' Amazon diary and the Black Diary for the same year (the latter being one of those seized by the Special Branch when Casement's treasonable activities were known) have other characteristics which could give valuable insights into the mind of an exceptional man. Roger Casement was probably the bravest, most selfless, practical humanitarian of his day, one whose acts of emancipation have seldom been surpassed before or since the Edwardian era, the period of his most effective activity. They deserve to be examined, if only because of who he was, and what he was.

The White Amazon diary is an altogether different type of record from the parallel document for 1910 which bears the words 'Private Diary', boldly written twice in Casement's hand on the front. Although it only covers the period from 23 September to 6 December 1910, it is by comparison with the other extant diaries, a vast tome – some 142,000 words. Luckily, from the point of view of anyone faced with the problems of editing it, it contains much repetition which, one imagines, Roger Casement would have been happy to see eliminated. Evidently it was written in the hope that it would eventually form the basis of a published work and, like its Black counterpart, it had the initial value of being a useful *aide-mémoire* for the official report which had to be produced by Casement on the atrocities committed in the Putumayo region of South America. Paradoxically, though, the White Diary's arrival in the National Library of Ireland was, for some time, almost as difficult to explain as is the provenance of the Black Diaries. The prevailing opinion today is that it was probably deposited there by Casement's cousin, Mrs Sidney Parry. Again, like the Black Diaries, it exists in manuscript form, and in a copy typed by someone who at times had difficulty with the author's handwriting.

As the forgery argument regains momentum, following the 1995 manuscript relaxations of the public record 100-year rule, much hinges on whether or not the Dublin-held Putumayo diary was used as a main source for the creation, by a forger, of the 1910 London diary, or whether Casement himself censored and expanded on his private record of events so that they could eventually become public? On the one hand, the spectacle is conjured up of a Machiavellian figure on the payroll of the Special Branch with a copy of the White 1910 diary in front of him. He is busy transcribing what suits him and inserting pornographic detail, in the hope that Casement's reputation will be forever blackened. On the other hand, and Casement's own comments support this interpretation of events, one must imagine Casement in his role as Consul-General occasionally checking a detail in his secret personal diary as he writes a fuller, official, version eventually intended to form the basis of a published work. Prior to this, though, the official version would be read by members of the House of Commons Select Committee investigating allegations of atrocities in the Putumayo. Great care had to be taken to ensure that details from the Black Diary were not inadvertently incorporated into the White. The author wanted posterity to know the truth of what it took to face up to, and to defeat almost single-handedly, a cruel system of slavery. In order to do this, he had to keep a meticulously detailed record of the facts that would form the basis of his report.

On three occasions in the Black Diary, the author seems to be alluding to the White Diary (4, 21, 29 October), and on the blotter facing 6–8 October he actually quotes from it. Moreover, various times have been added to the Black Diary as if to enable the author of the White Diary to refresh his memory about the exact sequence of events. It is also noticeable that the high-density entries of the Black Diary coincide with the weeks covered by the White Diary, while elsewhere entries are often comparatively thin. Either these links establish a certain interdependence of the two documents or they suggest that an astonishingly incompetent forger was employed.

As their traditional label suggests, all agree that none of the Black Diaries was written with an eye to subsequent publication. The obsessive quality of the erotic details has alienated many. Perhaps some of it is fantasy; but even that diagnosis can hardly excuse the man in the eyes of would-be admirers. All it does is confound those who argue that the scenes described could not possibly have gone undetected in such places as Iquitos; in addition, many of the physical achievements seem unlikely. It is frequently the case that the diaries of exceptional men (including those of Casement's Metropolitan Police inquisitor, Sir Basil Thomson), who are playing important roles in national or international affairs, betray evidence of their authors' conscious or unconscious conviction that their words might eventually appear in print; a good many are written specifically with publication in mind. So one has the – sometimes disillusioning – experience, when reading Casement's private diaries of seeing into a mind that is totally unprotected.

Although Casement had literary aspirations, and these were fulfilled to a limited extent by his published letters and political writings, the nature of his sexual orientation meant that he gradually learned to compartmentalize his life. This skill reached its peak when he was able to write, during possibly the most stressful period of his career, two contrasting diaries, while at the same time compiling consular reports in the uncomfortable and dangerous environment of the Amazon Basin. With the possible exception of the White Diary entry for 31 October, he succeeded in separating two very different sides of his character. Unfortunately for him, though, his urge to dwell on recent events or imaginings overcame his ability to exclude such details from the private record of his everyday behaviour. He was far too prolific a writer to be able to avoid temptations in this respect. However, believers in the forgery theory have long argued that the contrast between the sexual content of the Black Diaries found in London and the official record of events in the Putumayo diary[3] deposited in Dublin provides them with much support. Apart from the contrast in personal content, why did the only diaries known to the British Government during the First World War coincide with the periods of the Congo and Amazon investigations – that is to say the periods of Casement's career which had found their way by means of his most detailed reports[4] into the public domain?

One explanation of the disappearance of some of Casement's writings has been given, though it does not account for the survival of diaries matching the years of his Congo and Putumayo reports. Carelessness about his own safety was always a feature of his life. However, when in Germany, at a time when it seemed to him that the fate of Ireland depended not only on his physical survival, but also on the survival of his reputation, which could be endangered by the existence of certain documents, he decided that something had to be done about luggage which he had left with a friend in Ireland. Rather late in the day then, it came home to him that some of his private papers not only conflicted with the conventional morality of the day but also showed that he had long been a habitual lawbreaker. Unaware that British Naval Intelligence could read all Germany's coded messages, on 6 November 1914, Count Artur von Zimmermann, Secretary of State for Foreign Affairs in Berlin, transmitted several requests on behalf of Casement as Republican Ireland's emissary. These ended with the words: 'tell Bigger, solicitor, Belfast (?to) conceal everything belonging to me'.[5]

Francis J. Bigger, antiquarian, carried out his close friend's wishes. He had in his care a tin trunk which, because of the similarity between its

[3] NLI 13087 (25): Putumayo diary (handwritten by Roger Casement); NLI 1622–3 Typescripts of this diary, formerly in the custody of Roger Casement's solicitor, Gavan Duffy.
[4] *Correspondence and Report from His Majesty's Consul at Boma respecting the Administration of the Independent State of the Congo*, PP 1904 (Cd. 1933) LXII; *Correspondence respecting the treatment of British Colonial Subjects and Native Indians employed in the collection of Rubber in the Putumayo District*, PP 1912–13 (Cd. 6266) LXVIII.
[5] *Documents Relative to the Sinn Fein Movement*, 1921 (Cmd. 1108) XXIX, p. 4.

contents and those of the Black Diaries, inevitably became known as the 'Black Box'. After Casement's execution Bigger opened the trunk and found diaries, account books and letters from young men. Staggered by the explicit sexual contents of one of the diaries and the corroboration of its contents in the letters, he burned everything.

Bigger's reaction is reminiscent of the response of some of Casement's friends to news of his treason; they argued that Casement's alleged treachery must have been induced by insanity for him to conclude an exemplary humanitarian career in a betrayal of the very nation which had recognized his worth by knighting him. Sir Arthur Conan Doyle, for example, based his petition for a reprieve on the notion that the treasonable acts were brought on by his friend's sufferings in the tropics: 'it appears to us that some allowance may be made in his case for an abnormal physical and mental state'.[6]

F. E. Smith,[7] Casement's prosecutor, is not remembered as a friend of the defendant; nevertheless, as one completely familiar with the contents of the diaries, he felt that they could have been used to achieve a 'guilty but insane' verdict. When, at the age of 85, Alexander Martin Sullivan, Casement's counsel for the defence, was asked during a long interview whether or not it was true that the Crown had wanted him to plead insanity for his client, he replied: 'I'm sure that was the meaning of Freddie Smith sending me the diaries. But there were no grounds in law, from such a diary, to show that the man was insane.'[8] In his autobiography, published four years earlier, Sullivan had said that 'publishing this horrible document would have been a betrayal of the accused';[9] the man he was defending 'was not completely normal and one of the abnormalities of his type is addiction to lamentable practices... [and]... further affliction of the craving to record erotica'.[10] Given that the prosecutor, F. E. Smith, despite later alleged statements to the contrary,[11] seemed quite happy to allow the accused to

[6] Sir Arthur Conan Doyle to the Rt. Hon. H. H. Asquith, Prime Minister, on behalf of Roger Casement (n.d.). The text of the petition, with list of signatories, is reproduced in H. Montgomery Hyde (ed.), *The Trial of Roger Casement*, Edinburgh, William Hodge, 1960, pp. 298–9.

[7] Sir Frederick Edwin Smith, first Earl of Birkenhead (1872–1930), Attorney-General from 1915.

[8] Alfred Noyes Papers, Robert Kee, 'Interview with Serjeant A. M. Sullivan', 15 February 1956, photocopy of transcript from notes taken during the interview which took place at 25 Greenmount Road, Terenure, Dublin.

[9] A. M. Sullivan, *The Last Serjeant*, London, MacDonald, 1952, p. 272.

[10] Ibid, p. 271.

[11] Especially during an interview given in the United States: 'I threatened to resign from the Cabinet unless this traitor was executed'; *Boston Post*, 14 January 1918.

escape the gallows, provided that the treason was proved, Sullivan's decision that death was preferable to dishonour seems all the more high-handed (and cruel), especially as Casement had boasted to him that sodomy was inseparable from genius. Although Sullivan had had the best part of 40 years to rationalize his conclusion, in his own defence it should be said that there is no real reason to doubt the opinion he expressed in his interview. He had felt that the Bench might not smile upon the outcome of such a pact between prosecution and defence; in the eyes of the law, illegal sexual practice is not the same as insanity. But if the diaries were not to be used in the court-room to try to save a life, they were certainly used outside it to sacrifice one.

Once the text of the diaries has been read, it becomes clear that the author of them is sufficiently in possession of his faculties to be held to account for his actions. What is not so clear, and this is another level on which the documents deserve attention, is the extent to which his judgement is affected by the stresses and strains of his ambiguous past and his increasingly divided loyalties.

Casement's problems were complex and resulted from a combination of emotional deprivation, religious uncertainties, the duality of his political commitments and the gradual shift of his loyalty from one object of patriotic appeal to another. There is much here that could be of interest to a psychiatrist, and not merely the ambivalence of expression that is likely to be found in the writings of a man who crosses from one cultural tradition to another. On the whole, though, it is probably best to avoid taking too clinical an approach; the diagnosis of one doctor of the mind who analysed Casement's orientation during his lifetime was that the subject was 'a "woman" or pathic', and this was the gist of the report put before the Cabinet by its legal adviser, seventeen days before Casement's execution.[12] Another report, which emerged from Harley Street on 10 July 1916, spoke of 'sexual perversion of a very advanced type'.[13] A doctor of the body, rather than the mind, made much the same diagnosis as that put to the Cabinet. As people in high places were worried about the use to which the Black Diaries had been put, and wanted more substantial reassurance that the sexual events recorded had really happened, post-

---

[12] *Hansard*, vol. 552, columns 752–3, House of Commons, adjournment debate, 3 May 1956: H. Montgomery Hyde, 'A Copy of the Memorandum of 17th July, 1916 has come into my possession.' This had been prepared by Sir Ernley Blackwell, the Home Office's legal adviser to the Cabinet. He was officially designated 'Legal Assistant Under-Secretary of State, Home Department', a post which he held from 1913 until 1933.

[13] PRO HO 144/1636/311643/40: 'Casement Diary and Ledgers', Dr Robert Percy Smith and Dr Maurice Craig, 87, Harley Street, London, 10 July 1916.

mortem examination of the executed man seemed to offer corroboration of this fact. Dr Percy R. Mander, Medical Officer of Pentonville Prison, reported that he had 'found unmistakable evidence of the practices to which it was alleged, the prisoner in question had been addicted'.[14] Some of today's medical practitioners might not agree with such certainty. More convincing interpretations of the real man have come from outside the medical world, by writers such as David Rudkin and Alfred Noyes.

Whatever one's motive for examining them, the diaries are evidence of the emotional and mental state of an unusual man at the centre of great humanitarian events on the one hand, and of significant political intrigues on the other; and for these reasons alone it is important to have a reliable, authentic text to help one to interpret his life, and to substantiate or correct conclusions already reached about him. The flawed versions of the 1903 and 1910 diaries, and of the 1911 ledger, published in Paris in 1959, can mislead, if only because Scotland Yard's typists who originally transcribed the diaries, had an almost insurmountable task to accomplish in a short time. Moreover, Casement's handwriting can present difficulties to those without inside information, especially with regard to the correct identification of people and places.

The provenance of the Black Diaries has long been a matter of conjecture and controversy. Although Casement's sexuality had prompted much gossip when he was serving as Consul-General in Rio de Janeiro from 1908 to 1910, it did not interest British Intelligence until 29 October 1914, when he was betrayed in Norway by his manservant, Adler Christensen. That Casement's enemies knew of his special vulnerability some 21 months before his execution need not mean that they employed a Special Branch forger – although such men existed – to create the written evidence which they lacked. Men in influential places, such as Captain, later Admiral, Reginald Hall, Head of Naval Intelligence, and Sir Basil Thomson, Assistant Commissioner, Metropolitan Police, were already taking a very personal interest in the Irish knight's mission to Germany; moreover, thanks to decoders and others in Room 40 at the Admiralty Old Building, the Germans inadvertently kept them well-informed about the traitor's activities. They had everything that they needed to know for Casement eventually to be brought to justice and he himself knew, and had admitted his act of high treason; no extra evidence was needed. Only later, when the

[14] PRO HO 144/1637/311643/141: Dr Percy R. Mander to Sir Herbert Smalley (1851–1945), 3 August 1916 (the day on which Casement was hanged). Sir Herbert, knighted in 1913, was a Prison Commissioner 1914–17. Highly qualified in medicine, his career included being H.M. Prison Medical Officer at Dartmoor, Pentonville and Parkhurst.

political folly of the British government's execution of the leaders of the 1916 Easter Rising came to be appreciated, did it seem necessary to find some other means to prevent Casement from also achieving martyrdom.

Grounds for believing that the diaries were forged were made fertile by Sir Basil Thomson's several contradictory accounts of how they came to light – all made during the years when the Home Office consistently pursued a policy of refusing to confirm or to deny the existence of the documents. Perhaps the silliest of these appeared in an article in *The Times* during 1921; it purports to describe part of one of Casement's interviews which occurred over the Easter weekend of 1916, while other Irish separatists were committing treasonable offences in Ireland:[15]

> Towards the end of the interview a policeman who had been sent to search Casement's old lodgings in London, entered the room and said that he had brought away two or three trunks of clothing and wanted the key to unlock them...I asked Casement for the key and with a magnificent gesture he said: 'Break them open. There is nothing in them but clothing and I don't want the trunks again.' There was something in them besides clothing – a diary with occasional gaps from the year 1903.

The absurdity of this account does not depend on comparison with Thomson's other written testimony about the discovery of the diaries. The treasonable intentions of the retired Consul-General had been fully appreciated before he left the United States – which he visited in 1914 to gather support for the Irish cause – and an effort had been made to apprehend him whilst en route to Germany via Norway that same year. It is unthinkable that his luggage would have remained untouched while his every move was being monitored. His cousin, Mrs Sidney Parry, was not an impartial witness but there is no reason to doubt her word when she said that the trunks left in Casement's Ebury Street lodgings 'were handed over to the police by the landlady...as soon as Roger went to Germany in 1914'.[16] Clearly Thomson soon realized how foolish he had made himself, and when a year later his next version of this event appeared he attempted to make things more convincing by altering the timing of the discovery of the trunks. But, from his point of view, the correction only made matters worse as he failed to eliminate the extraordinary idea that they had not been opened:[17]

[15] *The Times*, London, 21 November 1921.
[16] NLI 11488: statement by Mrs Sidney Parry (née Gertrude Bannister), 10 January 1926.
[17] B. Thomson, *Queer People* [by which he meant forgers, traitors and spies], London, Hodder and Stoughton, 1922, p. 90.

Some months earlier, when we first had evidence of Casement's treachery, his London lodgings had been visited and his locked trunks removed to New Scotland Yard. Towards the end of the interview a policeman entered the room and whispered to me that Casement might have the key of the trunks. I asked him, and with a magnificent gesture he said, 'Break them open; there is nothing in them but clothing, and I shall not want them again.' But something besides clothing was found in one of the trunks – a diary and a cash-book from the year 1903 with considerable gaps.

It has been pointed out[18] that in the first account the policeman is supposed to have known that the trunks contained clothing before he opened them. This, though, was surely either a reasonable assumption on his part, or attributable to author's hindsight. There is no need to see anything significant in it. What *was* significant to advocates of the forgery theory was the addition of a second document. And they might have made more of Thomson's statement, made only two pages later in the same book, that he was certain that 'the obsessions...were of comparatively recent growth, probably not much before the year 1910'.[19]

In another version,[20] which appeared in 1925, there are only slight changes: Casement's landlord had brought two trunks to Scotland Yard, and 'key' had become 'keys'. Though these apparent discrepancies meant little on their own, put together with Thomson's other inconsistencies they became part of a dossier being assembled by Casement's Irish supporters to reclaim the reputation of a great Irish patriot. Thomson never alluded to seizure of other possessions of Casement's, which had been left in store at W. J. Allison's warehouse, 9 Farringdon Road, London. In an interview in 1972,[21] W. C. Allison (W. J.'s son), who had had dealings with Casement over a period of twelve years, made a tantalizing remark about this event. In response to a statement that the diaries 'were all seized at Allison's in 1916',[22] he said, 'Yes, of course, that wasn't... They seized everything that they were given but...' – the rest of the sentence was lost in knowing chuckles. When rumours arise about the existence of yet more diaries, if

[18] By Alfred Noyes, in his *The Accusing Ghost or Justice for Casement*, London, Gollancz, 1957, p. 99.

[19] Thomson, op. cit., 1922, p. 92.

[20] *English Life*, vol. 4, no. 4, March 1925, p. 250.

[21] Material in the possession of Roger Sawyer (hereafter RS): tape-recording of William Charles Allison being interviewed by R.S. at Allison's premises in Farringdon Road, London, 24 March 1972.

[22] The interviewer was quoting from H. Mackey, *Roger Casement: the Truth about the Forged Diaries*, Dublin, C. J. Fallon, 1966, p. 14.

any credibility can be attached to them, they are likely to have been found at Allison's. They could have been taken by Casement's sole heir, Gertrude Bannister (later Mrs Sidney Parry). Her devotion to her cousin would probably have meant that they would have been burned, unread. It is now known[23] that eventually Scotland Yard handed over to her some six trunks (plus one case containing a silk hat, and a canvas hold-all), information which further discredits Thomson's 'two or three trunks'.

Eleven years were to elapse before Thomson made his final contribution to the forgery debate by publishing extracts from his own diary:

Apr. 23 ... They were some time hunting up the Casement file ... Our interview was but half completed when Patrick Quinn, Superintendent of the Special Branch, peered round the door with the expression of Mephistopheles, tiptoed up to my table and deposited an MS. volume upon it. He then withdrew discreetly and left the interview to proceed ... Quinn had abstracted it from his luggage, which was lying in the Special Branch office. It was a diary, and when I came to examine it after the interview, I realised that it could not be printed in any language.[24]

Scotland Yard's Casement file[25] was transferred to the Home Office on 19 January 1925, where it remained until it was decided to move part of it to the Public Record Office nearly 40 years later. But, like the diaries themselves, much of its contents were leaked at an early date. The advance guard of the forgery school gained much of their credence from uncovering the indiscretions of public figures, especially those of Sir Basil Thomson, and consequent agitation for objective authentication of the documents proved embarrassing for successive Home Secretaries. One of them, J. R. Clynes, referring specifically to Thomson's writings in 1930, emphasized that 'any such statements were completely unauthorised'.[26]

---

[23] PRO HO 144/1637/311643/178: list of Casement's property at New Scotland Yard (released to Gavan Duffy, for Gertrude Bannister).

[24] Thomson, *The Scene Changes*, London, Collins, 1939, pp. 274 and 276.

[25] Its original reference number was 311,643/206a. In 1995 most of this archive was tranferred to the PRO from the Home Office (where it had been since 23 January 1925). The number 311643 is still an integral part of the reference used for many of the PRO's recent Casement accessions. The Prison Commission also released some documents in 1995; the Home Office retained a number of records, which will be considered for release in 2005.

[26] The Home Secretary to Professor Gwynn, 11 July 1930, quoted in full in D. Gwynn, *The Life and Death of Roger Casement*, London, Jonathan Cape, 1930, p. 19. John Robert Clynes (1869–1949) was Home Secretary 1929–31.

Long-standing Home Office policy was 'not to make any official statement as to the existence or non-existence of these diaries'.[27] This statement alone was quite enough for those whose prime motive was to establish that the diaries existed, regardless of the nature of their content.

The parties involved in the diary controversy at this time were united in one respect only: all found homosexual activity to be at least as damning as an act of high treason. And the trouble with their early debates – largely Irish versus British in complexion – was that there was no text over which to argue. Thomson said he had destroyed his copy: 'I committed it to the fire in case my executors should find it';[28] and even after the original MSS had been revealed public reaction, especially in Ireland, was slow to change. This can be illustrated by an exchange between a researcher and an employee of the National Library of Ireland, which took place in 1966. Discovering the nature of the research being undertaken the Irish librarian asked whether or not the researcher thought that the diaries were genuine. The reply given was that the librarian would only be disappointed if a truthful opinion were to be expressed. Disappointment surfaced immediately: 'Oh, no. They must be forgeries. You can tell by his countenance.'

Until 1959, several British authorities went to extraordinary lengths to prevent anyone from having sight of the diaries; that is, apart from a brief period during 1916, between Easter and the date on which Casement was hanged: 3 August. After the execution, although it was Cabinet policy 'by judicious means to use these diaries to prevent Casement attaining martyrdom',[29] not everyone in high places was happy with this. The day after the hanging, the editorial of *The Times* complained of 'inspired innuendoes which, whatever their substance, are now irrelevant, improper, and un-English'.[30] After the publication of this reaction by a respectable newspaper, official attitudes began to change. Whereas before and during the trial, and in the period of the circulation of petitions for reprieve, copies of the Black Diaries were seen by George V, The Reverend John Harris, on behalf of the Archbishop of Canterbury (Dr Davidson could not face reading them himself), John Redmond (leader of the Irish Parliamentary Party), Walter Hines Page (the American ambassador) and many other influential persons, few others were to see copies or originals for the next 43 years.

The exceptions which *were* made had the effect of leading the Irish Government into collusion with British policy in this matter. As soon as

[27] Ibid.

[28] Thomson, op. cit., 1939, p. 276.

[29] *Hansard*, Vol. 552, columns 752–3, House of Commons, adjournment debate, 3 May 1956. Montgomery Hyde, quoting from Sir Ernley Blackwell's Memorandum to the Cabinet, 17 July 1916.

[30] *The Times*, London, 4 August 1916.

certain nationalist Irishmen had become convinced of Casement's homosexuality, they put pressure on their own government to collude with the British in suppressing the release of the diaries, in order to protect his reputation in Ireland as patriot and martyr. In the early years after Casement's execution, two who knew, or thought they knew, that the diaries were in Casement's handwriting were Eamon Duggan and Michael Collins, who had been shown bound volumes by Lord Birkenhead (F. E. Smith) in 1921, when they were in London for the Irish Treaty negotiations. At that time, and until quite recently, it was considered some sort of heresy, and certainly political suicide in Ireland, even to entertain the thought that the national hero's private life was tainted in this way. Nevertheless, in the mid-thirties Eamon de Valera uncharacteristically let slip his fears in this respect, albeit obliquely in official correspondence, when Universal Studios in Hollywood were attempting to make a film of Casement's life. Although acceptable film coverage of the Easter Rising was greeted enthusiastically, de Valera wrote saying that 'a further period of time must elapse before the full extent of Casement's sacrifice can be understood'. He hoped that 'no attempt will be made to commercialize this great sacrifice ... through a film in which fiction will play any part'.[31]

Opposition did not come from Ireland alone. The film was abandoned when, in 1936, it failed to obtain a certificate from the British Board of Film Censors, thus preventing it from being shown anywhere in the British Empire. The previous year Lord Tyrrell, formerly Casement's superior at the Foreign Office and an old friend, had become President of the Board and he was not slow to declare that such a film would be 'extremely undesirable'.[32] In Ireland official policy mirrored that of the British Government; it was left to private individuals to agitate. Sometimes, though, agitation seemed to be in danger of getting somewhere. In 1966 the Irish Government tried to silence Dr Herbert Mackey, whose repeated demands for 'necessary and accepted scientific laboratory tests' were thought to be a potential source of embarrassment to the nation; and shortly afterwards he was silenced by his own death.

But the rule of secrecy, so far as the United Kingdom was concerned, was imposed for reasons which have received little publicity, possibly because they reflect only credit on the parties involved. If one bears them in mind, Lord Tyrrell's decision can be seen to have been an act of mercy for, as Bernard Shaw observed at the time, 'Casement's relatives view the threat of a film with consternation.'[33] When the first attempt was made to publish the

---

[31] RS: De Valera, President of the Executive Council, to Julius Klein, of the Universal Pictures Corporation, 11 February 1934.
[32] RS: Lord Tyrrell to Julius Klein, 23 January 1936.
[33] RS: Bernard Shaw to Julius Klein (photocopy), 19 December 1934.

diaries, Sidney Parry (the husband of Casement's cousin, Gertrude) sought and was granted an interview with the then Prime Minister, Stanley Baldwin. At that meeting it was agreed on purely compassionate grounds that Baldwin would 'assume personal control of the diaries': from that day onwards it would not be possible to inspect, let alone to publish, them, 'without permission in writing from the Prime Minister of the day'.[34] Although Parry might have preferred the documents to have been destroyed, for Baldwin to have sanctioned such a course, had it been within his powers to do so, would have amounted to surrendering to those who believed the diaries to have been forged. Given that Baldwin accepted that they were genuine, the diaries obviously had to be preserved as the only wholly acceptable evidence for refuting the charge of forgery – though, even today, despite their general accessibility since 1994, many observers remain unconvinced.

The threat of publication, which so worried the Parrys, had come from the journalist Peter Singleton-Gates, who was later to record on tape how he had been personally affected by the reactions of certain individuals to the prospect of his revelations:[35]

Q: How did you come by the diaries?

S-G: As a Fleet Street newspaperman, it is desirable that one knows a great many people. I did know a great many people, and, by virtue of friendships with some people, these diaries – copies of these diaries – and much correspondence appertaining to the Casement case, came into my possession.

Q: Who gave them to you?

S-G: I gave my bond of secrecy; I shall keep it till I die.

Q: Have you told anyone?

S-G: No one.

Q: Not even your wife?

S-G: No one.

Q: ... describe the efforts made to stop you publishing the diaries.

[34] D. Gwynn, 'The Diaries That Hanged Casement', *Catholic Herald*, London, 27 April 1956.
[35] RS: tape-recording of Peter Singleton-Gates being interviewed by R.S. at 38 Tregunter Road, London SW10, 20 April 1972.

S-G: ...having received copies in 1922, it took me till 1925 to produce a book, and in the *Evening Standard* on January 10th 1925 there appeared a preliminary article referring to this book, by the literary editor, as a result of which in two days' time I was ordered to see the Home Secretary at the Home Office, Sir William Joynson-Hicks. I saw Sir William and Mr Ernley Blackwell [Blackwell had, in fact, been knighted in 1916], then legal adviser to the Home Office. I refused to disclose to Sir William Joynson-Hicks from whom I had received the copies of the diaries and other material. He informed me that, 'Under subsection 6 of the Official Secrets Act, I can and,' he said, 'may well prosecute you for this refusal to disclose.' I was adamant and I said, 'Sir William, I am a newspaperman and apart from that I have given my bond of secrecy and I will not break it.' I pointed out to him that I was alone, whereas he, a solicitor, had also the advice of perhaps the most acute legal brain in England, that of Sir Ernley Blackwell, and I asked for a week to consider the situation...that I might consult legal advisers. A week later I was ordered back again to the Home Office, and the ban against the book was apparently still in force. Sir William Joynson-Hicks said, 'I am sorry for you, Mr Singleton-Gates. In ten years' time the situation in Ireland may be very different.' And I said, 'In ten years' time, Sir William, you may not be Home Secretary.' To which he answered, 'No; but the Act remains. Good day.'

...The curious thing is that within a few days a very high official at Scotland Yard, Sir Wyndham Childs [Basil Thomson's successor], head of the Criminal Investigation Department, sent for me. He said, 'You have been in trouble with the Home Secretary over the copies of the Casement diaries.' I said, 'Not in trouble. I refused to disclose how I received them, and I always shall.' Sir Wyndham Childs, who had been particularly considerate to me in my duties as a newspaperman, said, 'Would you like to see a couple of the diaries?' I said, 'I should, indeed.' The next day, with my copies of the diaries, he allowed me to see two of the diaries which showed that the copies I had were genuine.

...The next day, from a publisher friend of mine I learned that the Earl of Birkenhead, sometime F. E. Smith, whom I remembered interviewing in 1912 in the Hotel Alexandra in Winnipeg, had taken a drastic step which would prohibit the publication of this book. A private circular had gone to publishers warning them of the danger of publishing such material and that they were liable to prosecution under the Official Secrets Act. And that for me ended in 1925 the publication of the Roger Casement diaries...

Q: When you were called to the Home Office, were you not warned by a friend, who was in the Special Branch, that your interview was going to be secretly recorded?

S-G: I was warned, but I am not prepared to say that it was a member of the Special Branch... Yes, I had a warning before – an hour before – I went to see the Home Secretary, to be very careful in my answers, as he assured me that both questions and answers were being recorded. Though, when I asked Sir William Joynson-Hicks if that was so, he gave me his word as the Home Secretary of this country that that was not so. I know... the contrary.

[After a brief break, Singleton-Gates agreed to add a little more detail to his description of the scene at the Home Office]

S-G: The Home Secretary's room at that time was a very large room. I was ushered into it. The Home Secretary in a frock coat was sitting at his desk; upon a settee reclined Sir Ernley Blackwell. Sir William motioned me to sit in a low armchair. I declined. I said, 'May I sit in a high chair, Sir William?' 'By all means.' I picked a high chair from the side of the room and sat on it, for the obvious reason that I could look down, or at least eye to eye with Sir William, instead of him looking *down* at me. And it also gave me the opportunity to see what notes he was making. Most newspapermen can read upside down, being used to type. What notes he did make, I did not see. Sir Ernley Blackwell made no notes at all. He had neither paper nor pencil. And he asked no questions. It was a very amusing interview and I walked out into Whitehall and wondered what would happen next.

The next thing which happened was that Singleton-Gates's flat was searched, but he had taken the precaution of moving the evidence to another place, where it was concealed in his golf bag. The cloak-and-dagger features of the case, which Singleton-Gates evidently relished, were enhanced by his refusal to divulge his source; and he remained true to the journalist's code of honour to the end of his life. There now seems to be little doubt that his collaborator all along was Sir Basil Thomson, a man who, in 1925, fell from grace after being caught committing an act in violation of public decency.[36] Again, thanks to the 1995 declassification of files, one can be reasonably certain that Thomson gave Singleton-Gates copies of the diaries. An irate letter,[37] written in 1925, from the Commissioner of the Metropolitan Police, W. T. F. Horwood, to the Permanent Under-Secretary at the Home Office, the Rt. Hon. Sir John Anderson, intimates as much. After complaining about the way in which Thomson had 'filched' all documents likely to be 'productive of financial gain to him as a journalist', Horwood went on to give the opinion that 'knowing it would be a bit too hot to publish this book in his own name, he is in consequence utilising the services of Mr Gates, a newspaper man who calls here [Scotland Yard] daily for information from the Press Bureau'.

The book had to wait another 34 years until it was published in Paris in 1959. As soon as possible, 40 copies were sent to Members of Parliament, encouraging R. A. Butler, then Home Secretary, to announce to the House of Commons that the position with regard to Casement's diaries 'has been altered by the publication of the greater part of them abroad'.[38] In his introductory remarks R. A. Butler said that five volumes had been 'found in a trunk which the landlord of Casement's lodgings in London handed to the police at their request on 25 April 1916, two days after Casement had arrived in London under arrest'. This statement outdid even Sir Basil Thomson's best, or worst, efforts, to confuse the issue of the date on which they came into the hands of Scotland Yard. The Home Secretary went on

---

[36] Today some of Thomson's relatives steadfastly maintain that Sir Basil was emulating Gladstone in an act of charity and compassion with an underprivileged member of society (female); he was a victim of entrapment by enemies motivated by revenge. However, this does not tally with the line taken by the defence: that he had gone to Hyde Park, not to meet the prostitute Thelma de Lava but to find a Communist speaker who might provide material for a book he was writing. As for the Casement diaries, they believe that the circulation of them was entirely the responsibility of the Director of Naval Intelligence, Captain Reginald Hall – in the interests of bringing the United States into the war. Surely the granting of a reprieve would have been a better way of conciliating most Irish-Americans. But Hall did, in a different way, have great success in influencing the United States Government: by his skilful manipulation of the famous Zimmermann telegram of 1917.

[37] PRO HO 144/2345/311643/207: [Brigadier General Sir] William T. F. Horwood (1868–1943), Commissioner of the Metropolitan Police, to the Rt. Hon. Sir John Anderson [subsequently Viscount Waverley of Westdean] (1882–1958), Permanent Under-Secretary at the Home Office, 21 January 1925.

[38] *Hansard*, vol. 609, columns 1523–4, House of Commons, 23 July 1959. Statement by the Rt. Hon. R. A. Butler, Home Secretary.

to say that he had authorized their removal from the Home Office to the Public Record Office, where 'historians and other responsible persons who have made a study of Casement's life' would be allowed to see them, once they had obtained written authority from the Under-Secretary of State at the Home Office. Singleton-Gates had published the 1903 and 1910 diaries in his standard 1959 edition, and this version was also published in New York and London the same year; a limited edition from Paris also in 1959, contained Casement's cash ledger – not his diary, though described as such – for 1911. Interested parties were keen to see how closely extant copies matched the original manuscripts; they were even keener to see the additional volumes which the Home Secretary had mentioned.

Not all those who applied for passes authorizing access to the diaries at the PRO were granted them. Nevertheless, qualified historians found that no obstacles were placed in their way, except when it came to the manner in which they might examine them. Any sort of scientific examination was out of the question; even photocopying was forbidden. To make sure that there was strict adherence to the rules, the documents could only be examined in the presence of an invigilator. The task of authentication would not be an easy one.

  Those who belonged to the forgery school of thought had previously used five lines of argument to make their case, some of which overlapped with others. There were theories that a diary containing details of homo-sexual acts was being quoted; that the handwriting was (in whole or in part) not Roger Casement's; that the factual content could be disproved by internal analysis; that external allusions did not fit the facts; and that nobody had noticed the subject's alleged propensities before he fell foul of the British authorities. A popular belief was that the pornographic material was derived from a diary kept by perhaps the most evil of the villains Casement had exposed during his investigations in the Upper Amazon Basin. This man, Armando Normand, was certainly deeply corrupt, and, as he had been partly educated in England, he would conceivably have recorded his thoughts in English. It might have been feasible for Casement to have made private notes of sexual perversions which could be used in evidence, but would, perhaps, be difficult to express in normal consular despatches or reports. It was, though, conveniently forgotten that Normand's predilection was for the sadistic practices of a depraved heterosexual. Unfortunately for those who had based their con-viction on Normand being the author of 'the diary', or of scattered quotations within it, access to the MSS brought disillusionment. There were still, however, the alternative arguments. Was the handwriting all, or only partly, Casement's? Did the internal evidence tally with the known details of Casement's life? And finally, would ultra-violet tests ever be employed to solve the problem, once and for all?

From the start most arguments were about authentication of the handwriting. It was believed by many, including R. A. Butler, that an expert in this field would be able to pronounce a verdict acceptable to all. Before admitting the existence of the diaries, Butler had had them examined by the Director of the South Wales and Monmouthshire Forensic Science Laboratory, Dr Wilson Harrison, who had declared them to be genuine. Harrison had arrived at his decision by comparing the text of the 1910 diary, and both diary and ledger for 1911, with contemporary reports and dispatches in Home Office files. But the reliability of such methods was questionable and, by implication, doubt was cast on the degree of independence enjoyed by a British civil servant, singled out for this task by the Home Office. Why had the 1903 diary been ignored? More significantly, 'If Mr Harrison's usual practice is to carry out the necessary and accepted scientific and laboratory tests on suspect documents...why did he give such a positive and specific conclusion on a comparison study alone?'[39] This question was ignored again in 1994 when, to mark the lifting of the 100-year rule from the diaries, the BBC persuaded the Home Office to allow a repeat performance. This time, however, although the examination was solely devoted to comparing examples of handwriting, it was the BBC, not the Home Office, which chose the expert.

At least one of the traditional criteria was satisfied: without casting any aspersions on Dr Harrison's examination, the advantage of the BBC choosing the expert was that he could be seen to be independent of political pressure. Dr David Baxendale's verdict, although initially couched in cautious terms, amounted to the same as Dr Harrison's: 'I am satisfied that the bulk of the handwriting in there [the 1911 diary] is the work of Roger Casement.'[40] Asked about those diaries 'in which it was alleged that there had been interpolations', he replied, 'I found that the handwriting of all the entries which were of that nature corresponded closely with Mr Casement's writing, and there is nothing to suggest that anybody else has inserted anything.' He added 'a slight caveat' that when there was only a short entry the evidence could not be as conclusive as when he was dealing with a whole page of writing. Every now and again Xs appeared, and they could have been added by anyone. Particular attention was paid to the entry for 2 December 1910: a date on which the same events were recorded in the London diary and in the supposedly concurrent Dublin diary. In Dublin the entry is devoid of controversial matter; in London sexual details

---

[39] Mackey, op. cit., 1966, p. 76.

[40] 'Document: the Casement Diaries', BBC Radio 4, first transmitted 23 September 1993.

are to be found. Baxendale summed up his examination by saying that on the basis of the long entries, of which that for 2 December 1910 was one example, it all appeared to have been written by the one writer, namely Roger Casement.

Given that, unless laboratory techniques are employed, amateurs may be allowed to express opinions on the comparison of handwriting and personal impressions may be acceptable. On examining the diaries, one easily discerns three distinct handwriting styles; there are many gaps and, if the erotic entries were limited to one of them, there would be little difficulty in exposing the forger. Thomson once boasted[41] that he had employed an intelligence officer who had 'a gift for imitating handwriting' to extract money from a spy's employer for three months after the spy had been caught and shot. Perhaps the same officer's handiwork, if it was employed, has become less convincing as time has affected paper, pencil and ink. One's first impressions are then reinforced as one comes upon the occasional tell-tale smudge that is associated with the use of an old-fashioned ink eradicator. The best examples of conflicting handwriting styles are to be found in the unpublished 1911 diary. Reasonably enough they correspond with the use of three media: a fine-nibbed scratchy pen, a broad-nibbed pen and a pencil. The scratchy style has survived the years better than the broad-nibbed style and is much darker and clearer. Some of the fine-nibbed entries even resemble the style of Basil Thomson, himself an inveterate diary writer.

An investigator wishing to expose a forger would hope that erotic entries would be limited to one style and be confined to the interpolated passages. That is not the case here. However, the more dramatic entries are interpolations and constitute almost a fourth 'ecstatic' style of writing, though the details are often expressed in matter-of-fact language or are ruthlessly abbreviated for the sake of obvious expediency. It looks as though the writer was given to reliving erotic experiences; and some sections of text have led to the belief that the whole of this side of the author's nature belonged in the realms of his imagination. The notorious 1911 ledger entry of 13 May has four underlinings, using at least two different pens. The 1910 diary has a reminiscence on 11 August, where the last words of a pencilled addition have been gone over with a scratchy pen. As well as Xs, adjectives and exclamation marks are scribbled in the margins. Is one to believe that these details are the work of the world's most reckless forger? Regardless of the amount of imaginative detail contained here – the creation of the forger or the diarist – the dramatis personae were real enough, and they presented opportunities for authenticating the original documents.

[41] Thomson, op. cit., 1939, p. 329.

With enough internal evidence, appraisal of the handwriting could be shelved, at least until science is allowed to give its verdict. Many of the partners in the sexual acts, or hoped-for acts, were shadowy figures, anonymous in all other respects. But there are some identifiable real people. Noel Harris, son of a former missionary in the Congo, the Reverend (later Sir) John Harris (of the Anti-Slavery Society), has recalled[42] how it was the naming of a particular 'boy' in the 1903 diary which most upset his father. Nevertheless, despite having been named, this African remains effectively anonymous. Firm evidence involving individuals with proper documentation is limited to two Europeans: Adler Christensen, who figures in the German diaries, and Millar, the only partner whose social background had anything in common with Casement's. Others are named but either they have left no proof of their existence, apart from the diary entries, or allusions to them by Casement are ambiguous, possibly innocuous.

Herbert Mackey, though he always called for 'scientific' proof, was convinced that the forger stood revealed, to all who had eyes to see, on the basis of the internal evidence. He pinned his strongest argument[43] on the name Bulmer (Bulmer Hobson, the Irish separatist, a loyal friend of the diarist) having been cleverly altered to Miller (spelled '-er'), the point being that the 'l', the 'e' and the 'r' were in common. Had this argument had any validity, it would have shifted responsibility for this homosexual encounter to a conventionally heterosexual man who regarded such behaviour as depraved. But nothing was proved, if for no other reason than that the character's name was Millar (spelled '-ar'). Mackey was not to know, and very few knew until the relevant papers were released on 18 October 1995, that Millar had been found by a member of the War Office Intelligence Department.[44] Two days before the execution took place, he was identified as an Irish resident, Joseph Millar Gordon.

Stronger arguments can be built around evidence in the diaries which reveals Casement's attitude in 1903, and again in 1910, to what was alleged to be his own sexual orientation. How could he describe homosexuality as 'a

[42] When interviewed by RS at Old Vinesend, Worcestershire, in April 1974.

[43] Mackey, op. cit., 1966, pp. 52 and 61.

[44] PRO HO 144/1637/311643/139 (July-August 1916): unsigned minute refers to a letter 'dated 31.7.16 from Major Frank Hall of the War Office Intelligence Department reporting that the person referred to by Casement as "dear Millar", and to whom he says he gave a motor bicycle, has been identified as Joseph Millar Gordon: and that the transfer of a motor bicycle from Cyril Corbally to J. M. Gordon in 1911 has been traced'. This identification was inspired by R.C.'s 1911 cash ledger entries for 3 and 8 June 1911.

terrible disease',[45] or denounce the amusement of others at young boys' playing with each other intimately as 'a fine beastly morality for a Christian Co.' [46] if he was that way inclined himself? But such implicit contradictions may not worry those familiar with the ambivalence of the man's whole life. On the contrary, entries of this kind would surely have been deleted or altered by a forger. Production of the manuscript diaries did, of course, mean that one could see that the details tallied with Casement's movements. This did, though, fail to impress those who had noticed that the years 1903 and 1910–11, by some strange coincidence, were the very ones in which the famous humanitarian's movements were known to friend and foe alike. Why were there no diaries for the years of comparative obscurity? And why did the one diary which did not seem to have passed through the hands of the Special Branch contain no obvious sexual content?

External evidence both for and against the existence of the forger has had a disconcerting habit of falling apart at times when it has seemed as though the whole question has been resolved once and for all. Dr Herbert Mackey's strongest card was that there never was a Grand Central Hotel in Warrenpoint, where the most notorious sexual encounter had supposedly occurred. He stood his ground on this, and for many years those in the opposite camp were unable to contradict him. It was left to the playwright, David Rudkin, to point out that the encounter actually took place before the two men left Belfast for Warrenpoint.[47] In 1910, and until recently, there was a Grand Central Hotel in Belfast. On the other side of the barricades, one of Casement's seven biographers quotes from a letter to Mrs Alice Stopford Green, written on 17 September 1910. A draft of this letter is to be found on the blotter facing the 15–17 September spaces in the 1910 London diary, but the original letter was not to be found among the voluminous Green Papers in Dublin. The 1911 ledger has an unexpected mark of authenticity: a photograph of a small boy is stuck to the flyleaf, with the inscription, 'My godson *"Roger" Hicks'*. On 15 February 1910, the Consul-General had become godfather, necessarily by proxy (he was abroad at the time), to the son of Lieutenant Colonel F. R. Hicks, a member of the general's staff at Fermoy Garrison; the godson was to become Captain R. B. N. Hicks, DSO, RN. Again, though, impressions could be misleading; anyone could have stuck the photograph there. Lastly, in this list of blind alleys: as the best external means of authentication, the Black Box, is never going to be found, it can always be said that it never

[45] PRO HO 161: Letts's Pocket Diary, 17 April 1903.
[46] PRO HO 161: Dollard's Diary, 4 October 1910.
[47] D. Rudkin, 'Postface to "Casement"', *The Listener*, vol. 89, no. 2289, pp. 171–2.

existed. All this inconclusive evidence could make one sympathize with Mackey in his seemingly futile demands for the methods of the forensic scientist to be implemented.

From the beginnings of the Black Diaries' remarkable history, Peter Singleton-Gates has always been the key figure in their revelation, not least because it was he who eventually forced the hand of the British Government. It therefore seems to be only right and proper that he should have the penultimate if not the final word on the authenticity of these documents. He planned to publish the details of his most significant discovery in 1966, but again publication was prevented. His unpublished typescript has, however, survived, and it does not disappoint:

> I have inspected the diaries, all of them, many times...On one notable occasion, I was accompanied by that distinguished and able woman, Dr Letitia Fairfield, who has always shown and written of her deep interest in this particular case. As with all women of integrity, she had far more courage than I had, for she pleaded, and won her plea, that we might, as a special privilege, have the ultra-violet ray machine used on the documents.
>
> The paper of the worst diary, that of 1911, is very thin, and the viewing of the pages under the rays had to be limited to a few moments, then a period of cessation, and another viewing. The examination showed that no possible erasures had been made, and that there had been no interpolations. The ray revealed a consistency of handwriting, of the same ink, used on every page.
>
> It was clearly established in both our minds that this was the handwriting of one man, and compared with all the other documents of his official reports to the Foreign Office, it was the handwriting of Roger Casement.[48]

This was the test which Members of Parliament[49] felt was the only one which would satisfy all interested parties. It had only one disadvantage: apart from an anonymous official, there were only two witnesses. And now there is perceived to be another disadvantage: they are both dead. For present purposes, though, it may be taken to be the one act which guarantees the authenticity of at least one of the Black Diaries. It may be argued that there are still too many unexplained loose ends. Some say that, before copies of the diaries were clandestinely circulated, hardly anybody suspected that their alleged author was a homosexual. But that just does not square with the facts. Even if one discounts the Rio rumours

---

[48] P. Singleton-Gates, *Casement: A Summing-Up*, typescript, p. 240.
[49] Notably H. Montgomery Hyde, Member of Parliament for Belfast North.

which come from Casement's Vice-Consul, Ernest Hambloch[50] – who only knew him briefly – there are other sources, such as a letter from Sir Walter Raleigh, written on 30 May 1915 to H. C. Wyld:

> O, I must tell you – I made Kuno[51] blush. He was talking very magnificently of the patriot, Roger Casement, so I said 'That's all very well for the public, but you know as well as I do that Roger Casement is exactly like X.X.' It was a bow at a venture but it got Kuno right in the neck, and he blushed and changed the subject.[52]

Unfortunately Lady Raleigh, who edited her late husband's letters, thought that the other individual's identity had to be concealed; one can make little of the anecdote without the missing name.

Real evidence, apart from that seen in the ultra-violet test, was provided not only by Casement's Norwegian manservant, Adler Christensen, but by supporting testimony of other Norwegians. Christensen comes out of the whole sorry business more tarnished than anyone else. He was happy to betray his master solely for money. His visits to the British Legation in Christiania (the name for Oslo prior to 1925) are extensively documented, and his efforts to play both sides off against each other are revealed as much by Casement's own writings as by British sources. Nevertheless, British Intelligence took the precaution of finding additional sources[53] in

[50] E. Hambloch, *British Consul: Memories of Thirty Years' Service in Europe and Brazil*, London, Harrap, 1938, p. 74.

[51] Kuno Meyer (1858–1919), Celtic scholar and Professor of Teutonic Languages at University College, Liverpool, 1895–1915. He had founded the School of Irish Learning in Dublin in 1903, and subsequently became Professor of Celtic at the University of Berlin. While in the United States, Raleigh had seen Professor Meyer, whose methods of pro-German propaganda there had aroused some resentment among his old colleagues and friends in England.

[52] Sir Walter Raleigh (1861–1922) to H. C. Wyld (1870–1945), 30 May 1915; quoted by Lady Raleigh (ed.), *The Letters of Sir Walter Raleigh* (1879–1922), vol. 2 (of 2 vols), London, Methuen, 1926, pp. 425–6. Henry Cecil Kennedy Wyld had a distinguished academic career, some of it bringing him in contact with Kuno Meyer (see previous note); from 1904 until 1920 he was Baines Professor of English Language and Philology at Liverpool University.

[53] PRO HO 144/1637/311643/140/2026 Reports as to homosexual practices in Norway. Sworn testimony gathered from various members of staff of the Grand Hotel, Christiania, a guest there, a porter at the Victoria Hotel, Christiania, a 'gentleman' and an Inspector of Taxes. The other alleged 'sodomite' was 'from Bergen, the German teacher of languages named Bauermeister'. He was named, under oath, by the 'gentleman', H. Degerud. The British Vice-Consul at Christiania, Henry Charles Dick, witnessed the declaration which was made on 19 July 1916.

Christiania which provided details, not only of compromising master–servant conduct in hotels, but of an association with a 'sodomite' other than Christensen. Similar precautions were taken in London when, as the latest opening of archives has shown, the Foreign Office was asked to check the authenticity of the diaries by making sure that Casement's allusions to his dealings with its officials tallied with their own record of events.[54] It is as though the authorities themselves were fearful of being misled by a forgery.

The Norwegian evidence, when put alongside the ultra-violet examination of the diaries, eliminates a comparatively new line of argument: that although Casement was indeed a practising homosexual, as there was no proof, it was necessary to forge the Black Diaries. This approach could be partly motivated by the post-mortem report which was not available to previous researchers in this field. But, regardless of medical opinion, this new line of argument ignores too much. The authorities had quite enough in their arsenal to enable them to blacken the prisoner's reputation at home and abroad, and to prevent the granting of a reprieve without alluding to his homosexuality. Moreover, even if someone in authority had wished to make trebly sure that Casement's treachery should not be turned into a martyrdom, why go to such risky and complex lengths as to forge a whole diary when a few compromising notes or letters would do? And why, also, have the original manuscripts survived, against all the odds?

It may be argued that the strongest evidence for the genuineness of the Black Diaries lies in their continued survival. Once the forger's work had been done – the great humanitarian had been hanged, and his memory had been blackened – surely the obvious thing left to do was to destroy any damning evidence, the only evidence, of forgery. Nothing could have been easier than to burn the manuscripts during the 43 years when the rule of secrecy prevailed. Instead they have been most carefully preserved, and that they exist today must be attributed to the perpetuation of a continuing wish to rebut a diabolical charge. The shame and furtiveness attach not to the forger's activities, but to the malign use to which these genuine documents were put. Nothing can erase this malicious act; it remains, however, to clear the British nation's name of the secondary crime of forgery. To that end the diaries have been, and continue to be, carefully preserved.

[54] PRO HO 144/1637/311643/139/20261 Rex v. Casement. Copy of entries in Lett's [*sic*] Diary from 1st. January to 31st. December 1911, New Scotland Yard, June 1916. This file includes detailed checking of 21 diary references to the Foreign Office and its officials on 15 dates. On five days seven references (e.g. to dispatch of a telegram on 4 February 1911) could not be corroborated.

The sheer complexity of insider detail in the diaries, especially certain crossings-out, bears witness to the authenticity of the documents. One has only to cross-reference the footnotes which follow to see the pointlessness, and indeed folly, of undertaking the absurdly complicated task of fabricating such material. What then of Sir Basil Thomson's contradictory accounts of how he came by the diaries? Anyone familiar with the reminiscences of senior civil servants and politicians will not be surprised to find numerous errors in their utterances. Had Thomson had much to hide during this part of his life, he would have taken great care to be consistent in his recollections; as it was, he wrote too much and took too little care. Those who admire Casement for his humanitarian work, while deploring the promiscuity of his private life, might say the same of the restraints which he himself failed to exercise.

To arrive at a reliable conclusion it is best to take a multiple approach, putting together the newly released documents, the cross-referencing of internal evidence, the corresponding assessment of external evidence, comparative testing, and ultra-violet ray testing. It all points to the genuineness of the diaries. The British authorities are thus cleared of the charge of forgery; but they remain open to the far more serious charge of executing a man on the basis of irrelevant evidence. They sought to dishonour Casement, above all in the United States and in Ireland, to ensure that he was denied political martyrdom. The one redeeming feature of this tragic affair has been the embargo placed on the archive, to protect bereaved parties; at least those who most cherished Roger Casement's memory were spared further anguish. The truth has to come out in the end; it is now time that those who still admire Casement, the brave emancipator, come to terms with it.

A Brief Life of Roger Casement

Roger David Casement's father, another Roger, was described by his son as having 'an Irishman's innate sympathy with the oppressed and enmity towards the oppressor'.[1] Indeed, although Roger Senior's career was pursued within the parameters of the British Empire, he managed to combine service to the Crown with concern for the aspirations of Hungarians wishing to free themselves from Austrian rule. Moreover, he did this in a very practical way, riding through Europe in 1849 to deliver a message from Hungarian statesman Lajos Kossuth to British Foreign Secretary, Lord Palmerston; England intervened and the rebels were saved. The paternal family seat was Magherintemple in County Antrim, a Protestant House with a tradition of service to the Union, especially in the higher echelons of the Navy.

Roger David's mother was a Roman Catholic with a difference. At a time when most Irish Roman Catholics lacked democratic rights or social status, she was born into the Catholic branch of one of the most illustrious Protestant Houses in Irish history, the Jephsons of Mallow Castle. Anne Jephson met and married her husband in Paris, and the couple then started a nomadic pattern of married life by going back to Ireland. Anne was presented to her brother-in-law, John, at Magherintemple, after which travelling continued, the couple staying at various addresses in the British Isles and on the Continent, as the children began to arrive: Agnes, known as Nina (1856), Charles (1861), Thomas (1863), and Roger (1864). Anne was thirty when Roger was born. In 1873 she died in childbirth.

Loss of a mother when only nine was difficult enough for Roger to contend with, but other circumstances conspired to unsettle him. He went to live with his Uncle John at Magherintemple; his father chose to live 27 miles away, where, after a difficult period during which he dabbled in spiritualism, he died when his youngest son was nearly 13. By this time, Roger David was boarding at the Church of Ireland Diocesan School at Ballymena (now Ballymena Academy). Their father having died in reduced circumstances, the children found themselves wards in Chancery, dependent on the sympathy of Uncle John and that of other relations.

[1] R. D. Casement, 'Kossuth's Irish Courier', *United Irishman*, 25 February 1905, p. 3. (signed 'X').

As well as marking her youngest son for life by her early death, Anne left Roger another legacy. Although it happened when he was barely five years old, he was to remember his secret baptism as a Roman Catholic when he was in the condemned cell at Pentonville. This clandestine event occurred when Anne was holidaying without her husband in North Wales. The three boys were baptised by a Jesuit priest, Father Poole; the absence of Nina, the eldest sibling, may have accounted for Roger believing for most of his life that he was a conventional Protestant.

The children were passed around relatives from time to time, Nina and her youngest brother spending many holidays in Liverpool with their mother's sister, Grace. Roger was confirmed in the local Anglican church, St Anne's, Stanley, when almost seventeen years old; and he took up semi-permanent residence in his aunt's household when the time came for him to start employment. The domestic circumstances of his Liverpool years strangely echoed those of his infancy. Grace Jephson had married a Protestant, Edward Bannister, and nominally she became one herself, ostensibly rearing as Protestants the children for whom she was foster mother, as well as her own children: Gertrude, Elizabeth and Edward. Nevertheless there is an oral family tradition which suggests that in a quiet way Catholic influences were at work. Gertrude Bannister, Casement's favourite cousin, also embraced the Roman Catholic faith later in life.

John Casement of Magherintemple was a director of the Elder Dempster Shipping Company; the head of the firm, Alfred Jones, was a friend of the Bannisters. So both sides of Roger's family came together to get him his first post, a clerkship in the company. The drudgery of office work upset the young Casement, who was on the verge of dismissal for a trivial act of disobedience, when his Uncle John intervened, arranging for him to be sent overseas as purser on board one of the company's ships, the *SS Bonny*. This incident proved to be instrumental in setting Roger on the course that led to his becoming the celebrated emancipator of slaves.

Although Edward Bannister, Casement's unofficial stepfather, was employed by the Consular Service, in 1883 Roger had not seriously contemplated such a career. Doubtless his uncle encouraged him to move in that direction, but it was his short time with Elder Dempster which initiated his consuming love of Africa, which in turn led to his specific concerns for oppressed peoples and eventually led to a consular career. After three round trips to West Africa on the *SS Bonny*, the pursership came to an end, and in 1884 Casement went out to Africa once more, this time as an employee of the International Association. Originally known as the African International Association, this badly co-ordinated collection of national committees had an ill-defined aim to civilize the Congo; their chairman was the Belgian king, Leopold II. Impatient about his country's lack of competitiveness in the colonial field, Leopold intervened personally as key investor and the body, renamed the Congo International Association, became his direct responsibility. For several years, directly or indirectly, Casement's paymaster was the man he was to blame 20 years later for the brutal enslavement of natives. One of the members of the Association's executive committee was Henry Shelton Sanford, a rich American diplomat; the 22 year-old Irishman joined his expedition to survey the region, with a view to improving communications for the benefit of the native population.

Casement soon realized that the Sanford Expedition had commercial aims that had little to do with the welfare of Africans. He had been in charge of surveying the territory which the Congo Railway Company would soon develop and, once the survey was completed, he found himself temporarily unemployed. He was soon recruited as a lay missionary by the Reverend W. Holman Bentley, and worked for him throughout the rainy season. After that, in 1888, he 'left the Sanford Expedition to go elephant-shooting'.[2] But he soon returned, with a different contract, and successfully directed construction of the railway line from Matadi to Stanley Pool. Only then did he quit the service of the Belgian king and enter the service of Queen Victoria.

In 1892 Casement became an employee of the Consular Service, though not a member of it, in the Oil Rivers Protectorate, as Nigeria was then known. Later in the same year, while still only 28, he became assistant Director-General of Customs at Old Calabar. But he was more congenially employed when he became 'General Survey Officer'. During the next three years he distinguished himself by making three expeditions into territory unknown to white men, making maps and paving the way for subsequent British administrators of the country. He witnessed the terrible condition of slaves, and realized that they could only be freed by the Great Power which he served. Such was his record in the Civil Service that he was admitted to the Consular Service without examination and immediately despatched to a 'listening post', where he might take note of what the Boers were up to in the Transvaal. He arrived in Lorenzo Marques, Mozambique, in 1895.

After two years in Lorenzo Marques, during which Casement began to realize the nature of the gulf between consuls and ambassadors, both politically and socially, he was transferred from Portuguese East Africa to St Paul de Loanda, in Portuguese West Africa. The post had family associations for him: his uncle, Edward Bannister, had been Vice-Consul there only a few years before. Now, as he put it, he 'was really three

---

[2] British Library of Political and Economic Science (London School of Economics) – Morel F8, Casement to E. D. Morel, 27 June 1904.

consuls',[3] having additional responsibilities for British interests in the Congo and French Congo. Before long though he was back on 'special service'[4] in Lorenzo Marques, enthusiastically making sure that no arms were being smuggled through that port to President Kruger in the Transvaal. The Boer War saw Casement initiating and participating in a commando operation with the aim of severing rail communications between Lorenzo Marques and Pretoria. After he and his men had set off, they were recalled by Sir Alfred Milner (then High Commissioner for South Africa), who had had second thoughts about the effectiveness of Casement's scheme; all that came of the mission was the award of the Queen's South African medal to a somewhat disillusioned consul.

As if to placate their talented and keen employee, the Foreign Office implemented Casement's suggestion, made before his temporary return to Lorenzo Marques, that the consulate at St Paul de Loanda be split in two. Accordingly he was to go to Boma, seat of the Congo Free State administration, to set up a new consulate. But, before he did so, there occurred an unusual departure from accepted procedures: he was to meet the King of the Belgians both socially and officially. The king had so engineered things that from 1885 until 1908 the Congo Free State had become virtually his private property. In the lengthy one-sided conversation between king and consul, Leopold had done his best to discredit reports of enslavement and torture of rubber-gathering Congolese. Once at Boma, the consul lost no time in discovering the truth of the matter. Some of the background to his investigations can be seen in his 1903 diary, which is also the earliest extant document detailing his sexual activities. At first the allegations in the White Paper published as a result of Casement's dispatches seemed easy to refute, as names were not given, but in 1905 an official Belgian report gave what amounted to an admission that the rubber-collecting system had been much as Casement had described it. He was vindicated, and in 1905 he was awarded the CMG.

During the time which elapsed between the consul's investigations and general acceptance that he had been right all along, his relationship with his superiors at the Foreign Office had been under strain. They offered him promotion to the Lisbon consulate; he went to Ireland on leave and in the Glens of Antrim in 1904, influenced by several friends, realized that he had another loyalty which, in his case, did not sit easily with his professional loyalty to King Edward VII. One symbolic manifestation of this was his refusal, on a plea of sickness, to receive his award from the hands of his monarch. While in Ireland he came under the influence of his lifelong

[3] *Minutes of Evidence, Fifth Report of the Royal Commission on the Civil Service,* PP 1914–16 (Cd. 7749) XI Q 38,494.

[4] Ibid., Q 38,495.

mentor in separatism, Alice Stopford Green, though he was later to attribute his final conversion to a 'Scots Gael',[5] the Hon Louisa Farquharson, of the Gaelic Society of London. The months in which he felt the attractions of another patriotism coincided with periods of genuine ill-health and, when he went to Lisbon, he could only bring himself to stay there for two months. Back in Ireland, other loyalties proved increasingly attractive. Nevertheless, after well over two years without active consular employment (apart from Lisbon), and no pay for eighteen months, Casement was coaxed out of premature retirement. He was offered Bilbao, which with hindsight he wished he had taken; then he accepted instead another Portuguese post, Santos, in the Brazilian state of São Paulo. 1906 was his Santos year. Next he was offered and accepted the Consul-Generalship of Haiti and San Domingo, a much sought-after post, only to be asked to stand down in favour of a Boer War veteran. The alternative was a brief period as consul in Pará in Brazil, where his health deteriorated and he was soon in need of rest. It was while back home relaxing with friends in Ulster that he agreed to go to Rio de Janeiro as Consul-General.

1908 saw his arrival in Rio, and he carried out conventional consular duties there, albeit in ways which made clear his increasing sympathy towards Irish separatism, and in other ways which were only whispered about, until 1 March 1910. After that date, although he was still Consul-General, he never set foot in Rio again. Instead there occurred an extraordinary repetition in the Amazon Basin of the humanitarian investigation which he had carried out in the basin of the Congo. The atrocities in the Putumayo River region were even more horrifying than those which Casement had exposed in Africa. Tribal peoples had been enslaved by means of the local system of debt-bondage: peonage. To make matters seem worse still, the atrocities – far worse than the chopping off of hands, inflicted generally for failure to bring in the stipulated quota of rubber for the day, which had been a feature of Leopold's private kingdom – were committed in the name of a British-registered company. With his record, Casement was the obvious choice to head an investigation, his justification being the employment by the company of Barbadian British subjects. His terms of reference did not originally include exposing the plight of the Amerindians; in order that their interests might be served, the wording was discreetly altered by the Foreign Office, after the event.

As with 1903, the Congo year, the investigations of 1910–11 are recorded officially in government publications (the Putumayo Report appeared as a

<hr />

[5] NLI 13088: Casement's brief to Counsel. Louisa Farquharson's experiences in Ireland led to her being asked to address the Gaelic Society of London. This she did on 18 May 1905. Her lecture, entitled 'Ireland's ideal', was published as Gaelic League Pamphlet no. 31. In 1908 she became Chief of the Society.

Blue Book in 1912). It is therefore possible to make a detailed comparison of the private man and the public figure. The public figure became something of a British national hero: after accepting a knighthood, he was eulogized from the pulpit of Westminster Abbey; the private man however was becoming emotionally and intellectually sympathetic towards what he saw as another exploited race: the Irish. In 1913 he resigned from the Consular Service and soon entered wholeheartedly into a brand of Irish politics that was to stray a long way from the constitutional paths followed by the Irish Parliamentary Party.

Encouraged by illegal importation of arms by Unionists, as a valuable addition to the Nationalist fold Casement was keen to give strength to the newly formed Irish Volunteers. His idea of recruiting Germany to the cause was not exactly original; after the outbreak of the First World War its practicalities owed much to the example of the Irish Brigade, which John MacBride, a fellow Ulsterman whom he had met, had raised to fight against the British in South Africa. Before the war Casement had been party to Erskine Childers' gun-running enterprise, and when war broke out he was fund-raising in the United States. He lost no time in discussing with the German ambassador, Count Johann Heinrich von Bernstorff, the possibility of recruiting Irish prisoners-of-war to fight for the liberation of Ireland from the British.

The remainder of Casement's life was a series of disappointments and betrayals. Von Bernstorff had sent a telegraphic dispatch to Berlin and this had been routinely intercepted by Room 40 in London; from then on the Irishman's movements were monitored. En route to Berlin via neutral Norway, his Norwegian servant, Adler Christensen, was only too happy to tell Mansfeldt de Cardonnel Findlay, British Minister in Christiania, the true nature of his relationship with his master. Nor did he scruple at informing his master that the British were attempting to bribe him to deliver Casement into their hands, dead or alive. One side of this cloak-and-dagger affair is detailed in the German diaries, whose author became obsessed by the intrigue, and was completely taken in by Christensen. A price had been put on his head, in writing, but for capture, not assassination.

Although they signed a 'Treaty' with Nationalist Ireland's representative, the German authorities soon wearied of Casement's general behaviour, and of his failure to recruit more than 52 Irish prisoners for his brigade. He was jeered at in the camps. The Germans failed to give him troops of their own, and they only supplied inferior weaponry. They were relieved when he returned to Ireland in one of their U-Boats, now bent on preventing a rising that was doomed to failure. The Irish Volunteers were no better than the Germans. They failed to meet him at the appointed time; they failed even to try to rescue him, despite several extraordinary opportunities. Finally the British failed to give him justice. Of his treason, there was no doubt. But even F. E. Smith, the prosecutor at his trial, thought that the use to which the diaries were put was 'ghoulish'.[6] The last days of Casement's life were spent in the Tower of London, and two of London's prisons: Brixton and Pentonville. Meanwhile copies of the diaries were shown to people who might have had the influence and inclination to save the prisoner from the gallows, and who would have protected his reputation as a humanitarian. On 30 June 1916 the condemned man was degraded from his knighthood, a rare mark of disgrace. On 3 August he was hanged, his bravery throughout this grotesque ritual making a remarkable impression on the hangman, Ellis.

The German episode eclipsed practically everything else in the remarkable career of a man who had galvanized the Consular Service into an effective international human rights organization in two continents. Even in Ireland, few today are well-informed about Casement's brave, practical work on behalf of those who are least able to protect themselves. As soon as he was seen to be a traitor, and his homosexual activities were exposed, doubt was cast on the findings of his two courageous and thorough investigations. Casement's rehabilitation as an emancipator is long overdue; few have done so much to awaken their contemporaries to a problem which has yet to be solved: in his own words: 'These people have absolutely no human rights, much less civil rights'.[7]

[6] PRO FO 395.43 F. E. Smith to Sir Edward Grey, 29 June 1916.
[7] *Report and Special Report from the Select Committee on Putumayo, Proceedings, Minutes of Evidence.* 1913 (H. of C. Paper 148) XIV Q 2845 (part of Casement's answer to question put to him by Sir Thomas Esmonde).

Roger Casement: A Chronology

1864, 1 September	Roger David Casement born in Sandycove, County Dublin.
1865, 20 October	Anglican baptism.
1868, 5 August	Secret Roman Catholic baptism.
1877	Orphaned.
1880	Concluded education at Church of Ireland Diocesan School, Ballymena (now Ballymena Academy).
1881–3	Anglican confirmation (20 May 1881); clerkship at Elder Dempster Shipping Company's offices in Liverpool.
1883	Appointed purser, *S.S. Bonny*, trading with West Africa.
1884	In service of (African) International Association.
1886	Joined Sanford Expedition.
1887–9	Led Congo Railway Company's survey; assisted at Baptist mission station (for rainy season of 1887).
1890–1	Directed construction of the Congo Railway from Matadi to Stanley Pool.
1892–5	Employed by the Foreign Office in various capacities within the consular administration of the Oil Rivers Protectorate (Nigeria): 'assistant director of Customs at Old Calabar', 'General Survey Officer'. Made three map-making expeditions into the interior (maps published by War Office in 1894).
1895–7	H.M. Consul at Lorenzo Marques.
1898	H.M. Consul for Portuguese Possessions in West Africa, based at St Paul de Loanda.
1899–1900	On 'special service' during the Boer War; awarded Queen's South African Medal.
1900	Transferred to Boma, Congo State.
1901	Consular responsibilities extended to include French Congo.
1903	Investigated allegations of mistreatment of native rubber-gatherers.

1904	Congo Report published; spent crucial leave in Ireland; appointed H.M. Consul, Lisbon, but left after only two months, not having been properly installed.
1905	Made a C.M.G.
1906	H.M. Consul for São Paulo and Panama, based at Santos, Brazil.
1907	Transferred to Pará (Belém), Brazil.
1908	Promoted to Consul-General at Rio de Janeiro.
1910–12	Investigates Putumayo atrocity allegations; knighted in 1911; Putumayo Report (Blue Book) published in 1912; House of Commons Select Committee began its examination of witnesses: Casement examined on 13 November and 11 December, 1912.
1913	Retired on pension (which he drew until 7 October 1914).
1914	Mission to United States on behalf of Irish Volunteers; thence to Germany, via neutral Norway. Manservant Christensen conspires against Casement with British Minister in Christiania (Oslo).
1914–15	Attempts to persuade Irish prisoners-of-war to join an 'Irish Brigade' to participate in rebellion in Ireland.
1916, 21 April	Lands on Kerry coast; immediately arrested.
22 April	Taken to Tower of London.
22–4 April	Interrogated at Scotland Yard.
15 May	Magisterial Inquiry begun at Bow Street; diaries offered to defence (not accepted): transferred to Brixton Prison.
17 May	Inquiry concluded; committed for trial, charged with high treason.
26–9 June	Tried; found guilty; sentenced to death.
30 June	Degraded from knighthood.
17–18 July	Proceedings in the Court of Criminal Appeal dismissed.
21 July	Attorney-General, Sir F. E. Smith, refuses fiat for appeal to the House of Lords.
3 August	Received first Holy Communion as a Roman Catholic, having been accepted into the Church, *in articulo mortis*; executed.
1925	Attempted publication of Black Diaries prevented by Home Secretary, Sir William Joynson-Hicks.
1959	Flawed versions of two diaries and a cash ledger published in Paris; Home Secretary R. A. Butler

admits that the diaries exist and arranges for them to be transferred from the Home Office to the Public Record Office.

1965   Remains exhumed; state funeral in Dublin; reburied in Glasnevin.

1995   Home Office and Prison Commission release 'Files Relating to Roger Casement, 1916–69'. They are now accessible in the Public Record Office; some documents retained 'on the grounds of national security'. The possibility of their being released will be considered again in 2005.

Part One

THE BLACK DIARY FOR 1910

Note on the Black Diary for 1910

Although the 1910 Black Diary opens in the Brazilian state of São Paulo, and includes brief entries about visits to Argentina, the Canary Islands, Ireland, England and Madeira, the bulk of it is an account of Consul-General Casement's experiences in the Amazon Basin. Allegations of atrocities committed by employees of a London-registered firm, the Peruvian Amazon (Rubber) Company, had reached Casement's ears no later than 1907, when he was consul in Pará. Unfortunately, however, although he informed the British Legation in Petropolis at the time, his information went no further. This was a slip on his part, as well as a failure on the part of Milne Cheetham, chargé d'affaires at that time; contemporary *Consular Instructions* clearly stated that consuls must report matters of this nature directly to the Secretary of State, not just to the local diplomatic representative.

Walter Hardenburg, an American railway engineer, had discovered the horrors of the Putumayo while crossing the region in 1907. Eventually, when he was in London, *Truth* magazine published (September–November 1909) sworn depositions he had obtained from Benjamin Rocca, proprietor and printer of an Iquitos news-sheet. The nature of the testimony prompted the Foreign Office to make its own enquiries. Not only was a British company apparently enslaving and torturing Amerindians, but 196 of those apparently overseeing collection of rubber for the company were British subjects: Barbadians. Something had to be done, and obviously Roger Casement, famous for his investigation of comparable iniquities in the Congo was the man to do it. In order to avoid flouting the Monroe Doctrine on foreign intervention in the Americas, the British Government did not send its own commission of enquiry; instead the Peruvian Amazon Company was encouraged to appoint its own five-man commission. Casement, in his capacity as H.M. Consul-General would go as well, ostensibly independently, and make his own report. They all embarked on the *Edinburgh Castle* at Southampton on 23 July, 1910.

The entries for 1910 which follow are contained within a standard 2/6d. Dollard's Office Diary. The inside front cover lists sailing details of Casement's itinerary from Liverpool to South America, followed by a flyleaf on which he has itemized various expenses – travel, hotel bills, drinks, tips etc. – incurred both in London and Ireland. The final six pages of the diary also give similar detailed lists of Casement's expenditure on his South American journey.

As this is an office diary, there is no provision for Sunday entries. There are three days on each page and Casement did his best to cram in his Sunday thoughts at the head of alternate pages, above the space allowed for Monday. The pages were interleaved with sheets of blotting paper, which he often used for notes.

In the parallel 'White Diary', Casement sometimes made more than one entry for the same day under repeated date headings. These are differentiated in the relevant footnotes to the text by an (A) or a (B) following the date.

Because of allegations that the Black Diaries are wholly or partly forged, care has been taken that the text is reproduced as faithfully as possible. Ampersands, inconsistent spelling and use of accents, and poor punctuation have therefore been preserved. Spanish and Portuguese words and phrases have been translated in square brackets, wherever possible, though many of these appear in a corrupt or misspelt form – Casement's Spanish was unreliable, to say the least. Some Amerindian words have not been traced.

JANUARY, 1910

13, *Thursday*
Gabriel Ramos – X <u>Deep to hilt</u>.
Last time – 'palpito' [<u>palpite</u> = anticipation, fluttering] at Barca at 11.30.
To Icarsby 'precisa muito' [needs a lot] – 15$ or 20$.

Also on Barca [boat] the young caboclo[1] (thin) dark gentleman of Icarsby. Eyed constantly & wanted – would have gone but Gabriel querido [darling] waiting at Barca gate! Palpito – in <u>very</u> deep thrusts.

20, *Thursday*
Valdemiro – 20$

21, *Friday*
To Petropolis.[2] Sick.

[1] *caboclo*: of mixed race (Amerindian and Portuguese).
[2] Petropolis: 25 miles north of Rio de Janeiro; founded in 1845 by the Emperor of Brazil, Dom Pedro II, it was where, in R.C.'s day, the diplomatic corps was said to live in a world of its own.

22, *Saturday*
Sick in Petropolis.

24, *Monday*
Down to Rio to O'Sullivan Beare.[3]

FEBRUARY

24, *Thursday*
Valdemiro – Rua 20$

28, *Monday*
Deep Screw & to hilt. X 'poquino' [pouquinho = a little bit].
   Mario in Rio – 8 $\frac{1}{2}$ + 6" 40$.ooo. hospedaria [boarding house]. Rua do Hospicio, 3$ only fine room. Shut window. Lovely, young – 18 & glorious. Biggest since Lisbon July 1904 & as big. Perfectly huge. 'Nunca veio maior'! [Never see again]
Nunca.

MARCH

1, *Tuesday*
Left for São Paulo.[4]

2, *Wednesday*
Arr. São Paulo. Antonio 10$ooo Rua Direita. Dark followed & Hard. Teatro Municipal. Breathed & quick enormous push. Loved mightily. To Hilt Deep X.

3, *Thursday*
Saw Antonio at Cafe – watering plants.

4, *Friday*
To Santos [Crossed out: & Kee] Parminter.[5]

---

   [3] O'Sullivan-Beare, Daniel Robert [The O'Sullivan-Beare] (1865–1921): was to succeed R.C. as Consul-General at Rio de Janeiro.
   [4] São Paulo: capital of the Brazilian state of the same name. The consulate at Santos, São Paulo's main port, was where R.C. had begun, in 1906, the South American part of his consular career. He stayed there until June 1907.
   [5] Santos: see note 4. & Kee. [crossed out]: see note for 5 March (Guarujá). Parminter, Alfred: nephew of R.C.'s Congo friend and fellow pioneer, W. G.

5, *Saturday*
At Santos & to Guarujá.[6]

7, *Monday*
At Guarujá.

8, *Tuesday*
Left in 'Asturias' for B. Aires.

11, *Friday*
Arr B Aires & on shore to the Hotel of before. <u>Algerian.</u>

12, *Saturday*
Morning in Avenida de Mayo. Splendid erections. Ramón 7$ooo. <u>10" at least</u>.
X <u>In</u> [underlined twice] Sunday 13 To Hurlingham to Warden [*sic*][7] –

Parminter; they first met in 1885. R.C. asked the Foreign Office to allow Alfred to assume his duties when he moved on from the Lorenzo Marques consulate. The Foreign Office obliged reluctantly (Parminter having, like his predecessor, no qualifications for the job). He performed well enough at Lorenzo Marques until 1904, but was abruptly shifted to Panama for a year, before being told that the Foreign Office had no further need of his services. Casement felt that his protégé had been shabbily treated, and found him a post with a coffee firm in Santos. Reggie Parminter, Alfred's son, was one of R.C.'s godsons.

[6] Guarujá: on the seaward side of the island of Santo Amaro, which partly shelters the entrance to Santos harbour. R.C. had lived there, as a respected member of the English colony, during his time as the local protector of British interests. Guarujá was as far away from his place of work as his salary would allow.
It is reasonably clear from '& Kee..' (4 March) that R.C. was planning to spend time with another friend, John Keevil, manager of the London and River Plate Bank, a local resident of Guarujá with whom he used to stay whenever he could during 1906–7. The next two diary entries suggest that he stayed with Keevil for the weekend. For most commentators the presence of '& Kee..' rules out any involvement of a forger, at least with this part of the diary.

[7] To Hurlingham to Walden/Warden: Peter Singleton-Gates, working from a typescript, believed this reference to be to Lord Howard de Walden (1880–1946), the 8th Baron, who travelled far and wide. The 9th Baron says (letter to RS of 20 September 1995) that his family was living in Jamaica at this time. Hurlingham, now the Hurlingham Club, was their London house. Were it not for the mention of Hurlingham – Europeans having a habit of exporting European proper nouns – a more likely identification would have been Horace Walden. Casement was conscious of titles and usually recorded them. Horace Walden was an Irish friend of Lord and Lady ffrench, close friends of R.C. (see note 22) and the employer in Mozambique of Lord ffrench's brother Jack. To confuse matters still further, the 'Dollard's Office Diary' did not allow space for Sunday entries and R.C.'s efforts

Lunch. Saw Ramón get off tram at Zoo & sit down on seat & read – pencil under ear – watched long & then on to station. Back at 10 p.m. Met Ramón at Palace after sailor with request of fleet. Ramon 10$ooo to meet tomorrow.

14, *Monday*
Ramon. At Zoo entrance & Ramon to breakfast at Restaurant there – no it was in Chocolate House & name written on paper This pencil mine.. gave 20$ooo.
    Again at night.

15, *Tuesday*
Ramón. Breakfast at Restaurant arr at Plaza Hotel at 11 p.m.

16, *Wednesday*
Left for Mar del Plata.

17, *Thursday*
At Mar del Plata

18, *Friday*
At Mar del Plata

19, *Saturday*
At Mar del Plata. [Crossed out: Ramon 20$]

Sunday 20th Mar del Plata

21, *Monday*
Returned to Buenos Aires.

22, *Tuesday*
Ramon at Zoo again and in the Bosquet afterwards – By train to Belgrano & back.

23, *Wednesday*
Ramon X In To La Plata & lunch at Hotel there. Lay down after for an hour and then to Gardens & Tea & back at 5.30 train. At Club & arranged go San Marco tomorrow.

to squeeze them in meant that his handwriting is often unclear: in the original MS 'Walden' looks more like 'Warden'. But the matter is conveniently sorted out by reference to R.C.'s Cash Ledger for 1911: the entry for 25 March includes 'Wrote to Lord H. de Walden...about E.D.M. Testimonial'. For E.D.M. and the testimonial see notes 15 and 50.

24, *Thursday*
To San Marco by 6. Train with Eddy Duggan. Brothers there & played Bridge. San Marco interesting but very wet.

25, *Friday*
At San Marco

26, *Saturday*
At San Marco

Sun 27 Returned to Buenos Aires. At Station & sailors again.

28, *Monday*
Ramón. At Zoo & lunch & walk to Gardens of Palermo.

29, *Tuesday*
Ramón. Left for Mar del Plata but sick of night train – so stayed behind. Many types. Especially Martinez of Entre Rios.[8]

30, *Wednesday*
Left for Mar del Plata by Day train – seeing Hares & Birds – & Enjoying the journey.

31, *Thursday*
Mar del Plata

APRIL

1, *Friday*
Mar del Plata. Left Mar del Plata at 3 train & arrived B Aires at 11 p.m. To Hotel & bed.

2, *Saturday*
Wrote Ramon – Drew money £80 & got ticket for L'pool by Lamport & Holt 'Veronese'. Met Sailors of fleet & others.
At Club with 'Amethyst' officer.

Sunday 3rd Last time Ramon at Tigre. At Hurlingham & then to Tigre with Ramon from Belgrano. Saw last time at Belgrano. Never again.

---

[8] Martinez of Entre Rios. Not until October did R.C. visit Entre Rios in the Putumayo, where there was a Colombian called Gabriel Martinez. But this entry need not be proof of a forger's slip; both the surname and the place name (which means 'between rivers') are common throughout much of South America.

4, *Monday*
Left B. Aires in 'Veronese'. Wrote Ramón from Montevideo.

5, *Tuesday*
At Montevideo. Posted letter to Ramón. Sailed 4 p.m.

11, *Monday*
at Bahia.
    Type at night on board. Stevedore.

23, *Saturday*
At Las Palmas. Three types – one beautiful – Bathed with C.S.P. daughter
B. M. Moule.[9] Mason [*?*]
24 April At Tenerife all day – gardens & types. Left 2 a.m.

25, *Monday*
Left Tenerife at 2 a.m. On board about 11.30 after a pleasant day.

28, *Thursday*
At Vigo. Left early morning. Lovely – <u>but cold</u>. Left Finisterre at 12.50.

29, *Friday*
In Bay of Viscaya [Biscay]

30, *Saturday*
Approaching Lands End & in <u>Irish Sea</u>. Saw Ireland – & Lugnaquilla[10] &
pointed it out to Katherine Parnell.[11]

[9] C.S.P. [Charles Stewart Parnell] daughter and ['Bill'] Moule: Katie, the
younger surviving daughter of Charles Stewart Parnell and Katharine O'Shea,
had married in 1907 a friend from R.C.'s time in Africa, a Lieutenant of the East
Lancashire Regiment. Moule had been posted to West Africa. R.C. usually called
Mrs Moule 'Katie Parnell', emphasizing her paternity, though he gives her full
christian name in his entry for 30 April, below. In legal terms she never had been
a Parnell, as she was born during the marriage of her mother to Captain William
O'Shea. Two years after their brief time together in Las Palmas, Katie Moule was
to write to R.C. from the Ladies Army and Navy Club, Burlington Gardens:
'27th June 1912. Dear Sir Roger, I'm rather anxious about Bill as they've stopped
his increment...'. R.C. forwarded the letter to Mrs Green (see note 12), which is
why it is now to be found among the Green Papers of the National Library of
Ireland: NLI 10464.
[10] Lugnaquilla: Highest of the Wicklow Mountains (3,039 feet).
[11] Katharine Parnell [Mrs Moule, née O'Shea] (1884–1947): see note 9.

MAY

Sunday 1st May Arr L'pool & to London to Euston Hotel

2, *Monday*
At London. To Mrs Green & Col. Stopford[12] & to Earl's Court to 110
Philbeach Gardens. Miss Cox.[13]
Euston Hotel £1.18.6.

3, *Tuesday*
at London. At Miss Cox 110 Philbeach Gardens Earl's Court Greek
[underlined twice] [In margin £1.0.0.]

4, *Wednesday*
at London

5, *Thursday*
At London

6, *Friday*
At London. King Edward died. At F.O. & saw Tyrrell[14] who told me

[12] Mrs Green [Alice Sophia Amelia, née Stopford] (1847–1929): widow of the historian John Richard Green. A formidable Irish separatist, she was largely instrumental in seeing that Casement's views developed along lines which met with her approval. Among her influential writings was *The Making of Ireland and its Undoing*, London, Macmillan, 1908. The two exchanged many letters and worked practically together to promote their cause, though they did not always agree about methods. *Colonel Stopford*: Mrs Green's brother.

[13] Miss Cox: the diarist's landlady, at 110 Philbeach Gardens, Earl's Court, London.

[14] Tyrrell, William George, later 1st Baron of Avon (1866–1947): became one of the few Foreign Office officials with whom Casement was on good terms. There had been some social/intellectual contact between the two men in August 1900, when they spent time together at Francis 'Sligger' Urquhart's famously exclusive Alpine chalet. Tyrrell had married 'Sligger's' sister, Margaret Ann ('Maisie') Urquhart in 1890. A gathering that was predominantly a Balliol affair (Tyrrell was a Balliol man), was in 1900 attended by several individuals who were to have links with R.C.'s tragic history: contemporary 'Chaleyite' signatures in the visitors' book include four Tyrrells: William and Maisie and their two sons, Hugo and Frank. Another is 'G. Blücher': see note 50. (R.C. just missed overlapping with Maurice Bonham Carter, future prime minister Asquith's son-in-law; Gertrude Bell was there from 17 until 19 August; R.C. arrived on the same day as she did, but stayed until the 23rd.) Tyrrell was to have a long and distinguished diplomatic career. Private Secretary to Lord Sanderson, Under-Secretary of State

King was very ill in evg & prophesied it! At <u>E.D.M.'s</u>[15]

7, *Saturday*
Death of King announced in press. to Savoy & Dick[16] – poor old chap.

8th Sunday <u>at Selous</u> with Dick & <u>Mrs M. Selous.</u>[17]

9, *Monday*
Left Savoy for London again. <u>Nina</u>[18]

10, *Tuesday*
In London.

for Foreign Affairs, 1898–1903; Senior Clerk 1905–15; Private Secretary to Sir Edward Grey, 1907–15. From 1925 until 1928 he was Permanent Under-Secretary at the Foreign Office; then Ambassador to France, 1928–34. When Casement was brought to Scotland Yard for interrogation, his first request was to see Tyrrell, though the meeting was not permitted. After leaving the Foreign Office, Tyrrell became President of the British Board of Film Censors, and one of his early achievements in Wardour Street was to prevent Hollywood's Universal Pictures Corporation from making a film of Casement's life (see Introduction). Praised by R.C. as one of 'the Irishmen of the earth', he shared this distinction with others who feature in these diaries: Sir Edward Grey, the Reverend John Harris, W. E. Hardenburg and Captain T. W. Whiffen (see NLI 1622/3 5 October 1910).

[15] E.D.M.: Edmund Dene Morel [-de-Ville] (1873–1924), co-founder with Casement of the Congo Reform Association (23 March, 1904), though the consul, anxious not to appear partisan, allowed E.D.M. to have the credit as sole creator of the organization. Morel wrote many books and pamphlets attacking colonial misrule, especially by Belgium's King Leopold II, in Africa; a pacifist during the First World War he was then briefly a Labour M.P. from 1922 until his death.

[16] Morten, Richard (d. 1930): lived at 'The Savoy' – according to the headed paper used by Casement. In fact, this beautiful moated Elizabethan manor house, in Denham, was known by most of Morten's friends as 'The Savvy', and remained in the family for 189 years until Sir Oswald Mosley bought it in 1926. Dick Morten was as good a friend to Casement as he was a loyal subject of the king, and the Irish rebel often stayed with him and his wife, May. 'Roddie' invariably occupied 'The Moses Room', which bore on its walls frescoes, now papered over, of Moses in Tudor dress. From the condemned cell R.C. wrote to him: 'Dear, dear old Dick, you are, I think, the best friend I've got – in many ways you are nearer to me than those close to me by blood.' Pentonville Prison, 28 July 1916. Quoted by Montgomery Hyde, *Trial of Roger Casement*, London, William Hodge, 1960, Introduction, p. cxxx.

[17] Selous...Mrs M[arie] Selous: Frederick Courteney Selous (1851–1917) was a famous traveller and big game hunter.

[18] Nina [often just 'N']: Roger's name for his only sister, born in 1856 and christened Agnes. Later she became Mrs Newman.

11, *Wednesday*
In London. To 'Tales of Hoffmann'.

12, *Thursday*
At Caversham with Gee.[19] Milano Francesco

13, *Friday*
In London

14, *Saturday*
At Theatre with N, Gee & Miss Colles. At Robert Lynd's[20] till 8 p.m. At Exhibition & saw Formosans & Japs afternoon.

15th. At Kew with N & girls. Gardens. Fine day.

16, *Monday*
In London at Exhibition with Nina [underlined twice]. 519,000 people! Miserable.

17, *Tuesday*
In London. At Exhibition by self. Formosans & many others.

18, *Wednesday*
At Exhibition. Japs Exhibition good. Left Euston for Dublin. John Redmond on board.[21]

19, *Thursday*
In Dublin at Miss Ffrench's[22] & at Irish Opera 'Eithne'. Rotten. Stayed at Gresham. Very comfortable.

[19] Gee: Gertrude Bannister, Roger's favourite cousin. He spent much of his adolescence at her parents' house in Liverpool, with her sister Elizabeth ('Eily') and her brother Edward. Gertrude became Senior Mistress at Queen Anne's School, Caversham, but was summarily dismissed, without explanation, shortly after her cousin's execution.

[20] Robert Lynd (1879–1949): the essayist and journalist who stuck by his friend to the end and beyond; contributed to the defence, as did his literary wife Sylvia (1888–1952), née Dryhurst; active in efforts to obtain a reprieve, he revered Casement's memory for the rest of his days.

[21] John [Edward] Redmond (1851–1918): leader of the Irish Parliamentary Party. His efforts to achieve Home Rule fell short of Casement's more radical separatist beliefs. But, when the two men were alone together in the House of Commons after a meeting to discuss the constitution of the Volunteers, Redmond's parting remark was, 'Well, Sir Roger, I don't mind you getting an Irish Republic if you can.' NLI 13088 Notes to Counsel.

[22] Miss ffrench: R.C. was not alone in using a capital 'F', although he had known the family of Lord ffrench, 6th Baron (1868–1955), well since their days

20, *Friday*
Sent Ramon a post card of Zoo here. In Dublin at Zoo. King's Funeral
Service but did not go.

21, *Saturday*
In Dublin. In Phoenix Park, & lovely – at X where F. Cavendish killed.[23]

22 At <u>Tara</u> – with <u>Harris</u> & family.[24]

23, *Monday*
In Dublin. At 'Memory of the Dead'. Big party.
    Douglas Hyde & Mrs Hyde, Miss O'Farrelly & Arbuthnot & the
Wilkinsons.[25]

together in Lorenzo Marques. The Irish peer died childless; this Miss ffrench was
probably a niece.

[23] Cavendish [Lord Frederick]: Chief Secretary for Ireland, who was mur-
dered in Phoenix Park, Dublin, in May 1882. His assassins were members of the
'Invincibles', a secret organization composed of former members of the Irish
Republican Brotherhood.

[24] Harris [the Reverend, later Sir, John Harris] (1874–1940): former missionary in the Congo during Casement's time there; subsequently Secretary of the
Anti-Slavery and Aborigines Protection Society. When signatories were sought to
promote petitions for the traitor's reprieve, the Archbishop of Canterbury, Dr
Randall Davidson, asked him to examine the Black Diaries on his behalf. Harris
decided that the diaries were genuine. Although he continued to make discreet
attempts to help his old friend, things were never the same again: when he came
to write his own history of slavery, with chapters devoted to the Congo and the
Putumayo (*A Century of Emancipation*, London, J. M. Dent, 1933), he could not
bring himself to name 'the British Consul', whilst the names of lesser heroes were
there for all to see.

[25] Douglas Hyde (1860–1949): founder of the Gaelic League which, though
originally a movement to preserve the Irish language, had been infiltrated and
therefore politicized, by the Irish Republican Brotherhood. Though a Protestant,
Hyde was to become the Irish Free State's first president.

    Miss [Agnes] O'Farrelly: despite being one of the more conservative members
of the Gaelic League, Miss O'Farrelly later found herself the first chairman of the
women's arm of the republican movement, Cumann na mBan (Irishwomen's
Council). Co-author (and signatory) of one of the petitions for R.C.'s reprieve.
Donated £50 to the cost of the defence.

    Arbuthnot and the Wilkinsons: part of 'a generally Anglo-Irish crowd' (B. L. Reid,
The Lives of Roger Casement, New Haven and London, 1976, p. 95). The likeliest
Wilkinsons at this 'Big party' at this date were the family of Captain (later Major Sir)
Nevile Rodwell Wilkinson (1869–1940), who had been Ulster King of Arms and
Registrar of the Order of St Patrick since 1908. In an entry in the Cash Ledger for 11

24, *Tuesday*
In Dublin.

25, *Wednesday*
In Dublin.

26, *Thursday*
'See it coming'! In Dublin. To Belfast, John McGonegal X 4/6. Huge &
curved. Up by Cregagh Road met by chance near clock tower & off on
tram – it was huge & curved & he awfully keen.

27, *Friday*
Gresham Hotel bill £7.7.5. [Crossed out: Left by train for Belfast at Royal
Hotel. Ormeau Park & Gordon. Met J. McG 4/6 Huge & curved.] To
Richhill Castle To Mrs Berry. Gordon & Art.[26] Last time. [4/6 recorded
again in margin.]

28, *Saturday*
Left for Warrenpoint with Millar.[27] Boated & Huge Enjoyment. Both

February 1911, R.C. was to record that he and Eddie Wilkinson had dined together.
R.C. was in Dublin again, and the cost to him of this meal was 9/2d.

[26] Mrs Berry, wife of Major, later Colonel Robert G. J. J. Berry, of Richhill
Castle. A 20-year friendship with Major Berry dated from happy days spent
pursuing common interests, largely botanical, in South America. Casement often
stayed at Richhill Castle but, as his separatism developed, arguments became
heated. Eventually, in 1913, the nationalist convert went too far: he tried to
persuade Berry to resign his commission with the British Army and prepare to
take command of a nationalist one. There was a serious row and, at 3.00 a.m.
Casement left the castle and walked the six miles to Portadown Station. Although
he wrote a letter of apology a few days later, the incident marked the end of the
friendship. [Desmond Berry, Colonel R.G.J.J. Berry's son, to RS, 1972, 1973, 1978
and 1979; interview with Desmond Berry, June, 1973. Desmond Berry hoped to
write his own book about Casement, *A Knight in Tarnished Armour*. RS therefore
agreed that he would not say anything about 'the serious row', until after the
Berry book had appeared or until Berry had died.]
    Gordon [W.R.], a member of staff of the Royal Belfast Academical Institution
(appointed in 1901) His surname, his interest in art (confirmed by the School:
Christopher Maitland, of RBAI, to RS, 27 November 1995) and the closeness of
this entry to that of 28 May 1910 – all suggest that he and 'Millar' were related to
each other (cf. note 27).
[27] [Joseph] Millar [Gordon]: the only one of R.C.'s Irish homosexual partners,
featured in the diaries, whose existence is corroborated in the Dublin archives
(NLI 15138). The diary entries relating to Millar – for this date – for 29 May and

Enjoyed. He came to lunch at G Central Hotel.[28] [In margin: Turned in together at 10.30 to 11 after watching billiards. Not a word said till – 'Wait – I'll untie it' & then 'Grand' X Told many tales & pulled it off on top grandly. First time – after so many years & so deep mutual longing.] Rode gloriously – splendid steed. Huge – told of many – '<u>Grand</u>'.

29 At Warrenpoint and Rostrevor. Enormous over 7 $\frac{1}{2}$" I think. Asked after <u>friend</u> – repeatedly. Millar again! Back – Back <u>voluntarily</u>. <u>First time he turned his back</u>. 'Grand' [underlined twice].

30, *Monday*
Left Warrenpoint to Belfast together. 'Aye! if she's running to time like'. Saw F.J.B.[29] Ned Dickey. Bulmer.[30] '<u>It's Grand</u>'. Green jersey at 11 – at Hotel. Did <u>not</u>.

for 20 June – have more than any others interested those anxious to prove or to disprove allegations of forgery (see Introduction). One of the files released in 1995 from the restrictions of the 100-year rule is prefaced by the following unsigned minute: '*See* also letter within dated 31.7.16 from Major Frank Hall of the War Office Intelligence Department reporting that the person referred to by Casement as "dear Millar", and to whom he says he gave a motor bicycle, has been identified as Joseph Millar Gordon: and that the transfer of a motor bicycle from Cyril Corbally to J.M. Gordon in 1911 has been traced.' PRO HO [Public Record Office: Home Office] 144/1637/311643/139 REF 20261. The transaction in question is recorded in R.C.'s Ledger entry for 3 June 1911, the cost of the motor bicycle being £25; the item appears again in R.C.'s summary of his June expenditure, where it is listed with presents to six other individuals. This was one of British Intelligence's checks on the authenticity of the diaries; for the most part investigators concentrated on seeing that R.C.'s references to his dealings with the Foreign Office actually tallied with the details of correspondence received.

[28] Confirmation of this event is found among the sundry items listed on the diary's flyleaf: 'Lunch Grand Central, Millar & J 7/6'.

[29] F.J.B.: Francis Joseph Bigger, a Belfast solicitor and antiquarian; author of many books and articles on historical subjects, mainly to do with County Antrim. Casement often stayed with him.

[30] Bulmer [Hobson]: born a member of the Society of Friends, but resigned in 1914 when he realized that his commitment to the Irish Volunteers was incompatible with Quaker pacifism. After leaving the Friends School, Lisburn, he joined various organizations dedicated to the promotion of aspects of 'Irishness'. In 1904 he joined the Irish Republican Brotherhood, and by 1912 the senior IRB posts which he held included membership of its Supreme Council (as Leinster's representative). With Denis McCullough he had started the Dungannon Clubs in 1905, dedicated among other things to 'Regaining the Political Independence of Ireland.' In 1905 he founded the separatist newspaper, *The Republic*, which he also edited; in 1907 he spoke for Sinn Fein in the United States; in 1909 he helped Countess Constance Markievicz to start Na Fianna Eireann (nationalist Ireland's answer to the Boy Scout movement),

31, *Tuesday*
At Belfast. To Giants' Ring with Millar.[31] Wrote '<u>Northern Whig</u>' 'Irish in Ulster'

JUNE

1, *Wednesday*
Wrote many letters. Sent £100 Rio for Brian B.[32] Wrote Rio & others.

2, *Thursday*
At Belfast

3, *Friday*
At Belfast. Left for B'mena – Lunched Travie & Bertie Orr & Mrs King – on to Ballycastle by 4.29 train. At Brannigan's.

4, *Saturday*
At Ballycastle. Dined Roger & Susie.[33]

[Sunday] At Ballycastle & Hurling Match & to Woodsides.

and became its president. At this time he was also working on the separatist newspaper, *The Irish Peasant*. From 1912 until 1914 he edited *Irish Freedom*; in 1914 he organized the Howth arms-landing. When it became known to senior members of the IRB that he was convinced, as was Casement, that the Rising would fail, he was entrapped by several of their gunmen and held incommunicado from Good Friday until Easter Monday. A loyal friend of Casement, he always believed that the indecent diary entries were interpolated by a forger.

[31] Giant's Ring: a prehistoric earthwork four miles to the south of Belfast; it surrounds a cromlech known as the Druid's Altar.

[32] Brian B[arry]: an old boy of R.C.'s school, Ballymena Academy (which had originally been known as Ballymena's Church of Ireland Diocesan School). Casement had been instrumental in getting Barry a vice-consulship at Victoria (Brazil) and, despite a fracas about Barry decorating his table (at his own house) with orange lilies, the loyalist and the separatist got on well together. Barry was 'a native born subject of his Majesty, having been born at Castle Blaney in Monaghan, Ireland, in 1854.' (PRO FO 369/196 Casement to Lord Dufferin.)

[33] Roger and Susie: Roger Casement (1850–1928) and his wife Susanna, née Beatty. This Roger, head of the family at this time, was living at the family seat, Magherintemple, Ballycastle, County Antrim. Roger was a favourite Casement name, a fact that made it comparatively easy to omit the traitor from successive editions of Burke's *Irish Landed Gentry* and *Landed Gentry* – he disappeared into that handy genealogical phrase 'with other issue'. He reappeared in *Irish Family Records*, London, Burke's Peerage, 1976.

6, *Monday*
At Ballycastle. Hugh Duffy [written in Irish] called on way to Glenshesk [in Irish].

7, *Tuesday*
At Ballycastle.

8, *Wednesday*
At Ballycastle – & to C'dall [Cushendall] to [Glen]shesk, but heard of Jack's[34] sudden death at C'dall & up to Glenville – & Home at 8.30.

9, *Thursday*
At Ballycastle – Lunched with Roger & Susie & walked down with Mrs Robertson.

10, *Friday*
At Ballycastle all day. Wrote M & others. Drew £10 from Bank. (First since £20 on 20 May)

11, *Saturday*
Over to C'dall with Roger & Reggie[35] to Jack's funeral. Then to Cushendun & up with Miss MacNeill[36] to Shane O'Neill's[37] [Crossed out: for] Cairn. Ethel Johnston came. Sunday 12 June At Cushendun all day.

Sunday 12, June. At Cushendun all day.

[34] Jack: Rear-Admiral John Casement (1854–1910); 'C'dall' is Cushendall on the coast of one of the Glens of Antrim.

[35] Reggie: Edgar Reginald Casement (1886–1962), fifth son of 'Roger and Susie' (see note 33).

[36] Miss MacNeill: Ada ('Ide') McNeill (no 'a') was one of the McNeills of Cushendun, an Ascendancy family. The only child of an eldest son, she owned the whole of the Cushendun estate (south of Cushendall) in her youth. Despite her origins, she moved steadily towards acceptance of current Sinn Fein ideals, whilst managing to remain on good terms with her cousin Ronald, first Baron Cushendun, the prominent unionist. Ada had the misfortune to fall in love with R.C. She was something of an artist and Millar (see note 27) was commissioned by the object of her affections to buy two of her paintings at an exhibition of her work.

[37] Shane O'Neill: sixteenth-century claimant to the O'Neill earldom; a legitimate younger son who challenged the succession of an illegitimate elder son. He was the people's choice in Tyrone. 'Shane O'Neill was a barbarian, cruel and tyrannous...But he was an efficient barbarian.' (Stephen Gwynn, *The History of Ireland*, London and Dublin, Macmillan, 1923, p. 210.)

13, *Monday*
Left Cushendun with young C'dall car boy driving. He is 19 on 29 August next. Tiny wee Jack MacCormack talked Irish on road – To Dobbs[38] to Lunch & then up by Parcmoft [?] car to Ballymena & to tea with Kings[39] and on to Coleraine by 6.51 train & to Clothworkers Arms. Lovely room.
Millar and Argentine sailors <u>X.X.</u>

14, *Tuesday*
To Portrush during day – Nina came over & called on Eddie Pottinger & to Miss Reynolds where Mrs Dobbs of Castle Dobbs was with others. Back by 4.25 train & at home at 6.10. & found letter from Millar.

15, *Wednesday*
No letters of any interest. At Ballycastle all day.

16, *Thursday*
At Ballycastle – Up Glenshesk to Glenbank & then Dunlops with Hoppy & Nina.

17, *Friday*
At Ballycastle – up to Magheranteampul [*sic*][40] by myself. Got letter from Anti-Slavery people[41] about Putumayo River & the Amazon Rubber Coy. Answered by wire at once and wrote also. Called on Father Eardley & gave £1.

18, *Saturday*
Lovely weather. Gave £10 to Rathlin School Fund to Miss Gough of Coleraine and at meeting with her & Miss MacNeill. Further letter from Putumayo people – also from E.D.M.
Very seedy all day – lay down. Drew £10 at Bank.
Going to London on Wednesday morning.

Sunday 19th June – Rathlin Island. Lovely day.

[38] Dobbs': the family seat was Castle Dobbs; Margaret Dobbs was a keen participant in the Irish cultural revival.
[39] Kings: Mrs King, who lived in Ballymena, was the widow of Dr Robert King who had been responsible for R.C.'s education at the diocesan school which became Ballymena Academy. She had, in effect, been matron.
[40] Magheranteampul: a playful rendering of Magherintemple, the Casement family seat.
[41] Anti-Slavery people: the letter was from the Reverend John Harris, saying that he had told Sir Edward Grey that R.C. was the man best qualified to investigate allegations of atrocities committed in the Putumayo by the Peruvian Amazon Rubber Company.

20, *Monday*
Gave £2 for Irish prize on Rathlin to Father MacKinley. Left Ballycastle at 4 train. Millar to dinner at N. Counties Hotel. Splendid. Gave Millar <u>pin</u> for <u>tie</u>. Stayed till 9.30 & in Room. XX Then to his Mother's, on foot & by tram. <u>In deep & warm.</u>

21, *Tuesday*
At Belfast. To Castle Dobbs in afternoon & lunch there. Coming back with medical student in train – Charming view – & nice face. Medical student – smiling face. Left for L'pool – Bulmer to see me off. Charming day. [In margin: With A. Dobbs at Castle Dobbs. Eden S.O. Carrickfergus.]

22, *Wednesday*
<u>In England</u>. Arrived L'pool & to London at noon. To Exhibition – Takayaki <u>Morohoshi</u>. [Morohoshi spelled out twice]

23, *Thursday*
In London. To Anti-Slavery & H. of C. Dilke, Wedgwood[42] & other M.P.s – Splendid talk – Noel Buxton.[43]

24, *Friday*
To dine with Conan Doyle.[44] Morel there & to 'Speckled Band' after.
  1. a.m. <u>H.B.</u> 10/- & 1.45 a.m. <u>Jamaica!</u> 6/6 [In margin: 16/6]

---

[42] [Sir Charles] Dilke [M.P., 2nd Bt.] (1843–1911): Under-Secretary for Foreign Affairs, 1880–2; divorce caused his temporary retirement from politics. In 1892 he re-entered the House of Commons where he pressed for municipal enfranchisement of women; he had spoken effectively against slavery in Zanzibar and in Leopold's Congo.
  [Josiah Clement] Wedgwood, later 1st Baron of Barlaston (1872–1943): of the family long associated with the anti-slavery movement (the family ceramics firm designed and manufactured products to promote the cause).
[43] Noel [Edward Noel-] Buxton, [later, 1st Baron Noel-Buxton] (1869–1948): of the family who, with the Wilberforces, ensured that abolition by law of the slave trade and slavery would be followed by emancipation. Both families have continued their efforts in this field throughout the twentieth century, through the same society, now known as Anti-Slavery International. Noel Edward became a president of the Anti-Slavery Society. Not all Buxtons have been happy to accept a hyphenated version of their name.
[44] [Sir Arthur] Conan Doyle (1859–1930): a firm friend of R.C., despite differences of attitude to Germany as war approached; in his *The Lost World*, Lord John Roxton, 'the spare, handsome, exquisitely dressed battler for the underprivileged' (Charles Higham, *The Adventures of Conan Doyle*, London,

25, *Saturday*
To Carlton Park at 4.55 train. Lady S. Lady Caledon[45] & Lady Morgan.

[Sunday] At Carlton

27, *Monday*
Left Carlton & to London. To Exhibition. <u>Greek</u> [underlined twice] Fled

28, *Tuesday*
In London. Lunched at Prince's with Lady Caledon & sisters – Lady Caledon Lady Margaret Lady Charlotte. Last time of seeing Sheelagh.[46]

29, *Wednesday*
In London

30, *Thursday*
In London.

JULY

1, *Friday*
In London. Welsh Will. Splendid <u>6' 3½"</u> [underlined twice] 10/- & <u>Japan</u>. [underlined twice]

Hamish Hamilton, 1976, p. 235) was modelled on R.C. Conan Doyle was author of the principal (best-supported) petition for a reprieve. One of his arguments was that the prisoner's lack of judgement could be attributed to exposure to tropical diseases. R.C.'s experiences could have led to 'an abnormal physical and mental state'. (H. Montgomery Hyde, *Trial of Roger Casement*, Edinburgh, William Hodge, 1960, pp. 298–9.) Doyle donated more than any other individual (£700) to the cost of his friend's defence.

[45] Lady Caledon: widow of the 4th Earl of Caledon (see note 46).
[46] Lady Caledon and sisters: were the daughters of Hector John Graham-Toler, 3rd Earl of Norbury (1810–73); Lady Elizabeth, his second daughter, married the 4th Earl of Caledon (1846–98); Lady Margaret, 3rd daughter, married Edward Boycott Jenkins, a barrister; Lady Charlotte, 4th daughter, was a spinster. Sheelagh appears to have been Sheelagh Jane, 2nd daughter of the Hon Charles Alexander, 3rd son of the 3rd Earl of Caledon. The Caledons had two family seats in County Tyrone; the Norburys had extensive estates in various Irish counties. On 8 July 1915 Lady Margaret was to give to the police a map showing various places in Ireland visited by her former friend; it 'had been pointed out to her by Mrs Pope Hennessy [Una, later Dame Una, Pope-Hennessy (d. 1949)]' that 'This particular part of Ireland . . . would make an ideal spot for the landing of rifles, or for use as a submarine base . . .' PRO HO 144/1636/311,643/3a.

2, *Saturday*
To Savoy to Dick. Very pleasant.

[Sunday] At Savoy.

4, *Monday*
At Savoy

5, *Tuesday*
At Savoy

6, *Wednesday*
Left Savoy for London. To Gloucester Road and lovely type X to Bolton Gardens & home. Marylebone at 1 p.m. Lizzie.[47]

7, *Thursday*
At London. With Lizzie to Hampstead. Lunched at Metropole with Doyles. Called Lord Listowel.[48]

8, *Friday*
[Crossed out: Lunched at Metropole] Dined with Mr Hicks & Mrs Hicks[49] at Les Lauriers. Home & out Carlo Zioni [In margin: 12/6]

9, *Saturday*
Lunched with Mrs Green at 1 o'clock. To Louie & together to Savoy.

[Sunday] At Savoy.

11, *Monday*
At Savoy. Left at 3 p.m. to London. Lay down awfully tired. Dined

---

[47] Lizzie: R.C.'s cousin, Elizabeth Bannister (Gertrude's sister).

[48] Lord Listowel [3rd Earl] (1833–1924): recruited by his son, Lord Ennismore, at the request of R.C., to give social and financial support to the Congo Reform Association. The young Irish viscount had formed a lasting friendship with his fellow countryman. The Listowel family is still closely associated with the anti-slavery movement. At this time, like many of his English contemporaries, R.C. dearly loved a lord – or (equally platonically) a titled lady.

[49] Hicks: On 15 February 1910 R.C. had become godfather, by proxy, to Roger, son of Lieutenant Colonel F. R. Hicks, a member of the general's staff at the Fermoy Garrison and brother-in-law of Dick Morten. A photograph of the new Roger, subsequently Captain R. B. N. Hicks, DSO, RN, is attached to the fly-leaf of the 1911 Cash Ledger, where, with the inscription 'My godson *"Roger"* *Hicks'*, it continues to suggest the volume is genuine.

Blüchers.[50] Morel Testimonial Lord Cromer's[51] letter appears in 'Times', 'Morning Post' & other papers. [In margin: Wrote to Tyrrell saying had heard I was to go to Putumayo & was ready if Sir E. Grey[52] wished it.]

12, *Tuesday*
At London. To Lunacy Commission for Mrs Beere – & to E.D.M. To Louie at 4 p.m. Morel Test'ial. Splendid leader in 'M. Post'. Packed up to go to Ireland but got a wire from Tyrrell asking me to call noon tomorrow F.O. To Welsh Will – but too late 9 p.m. On & many types. Wire from Tyrrell.

13, *Wednesday*
To F.O. & Mrs Green. Carlo but did not go. To F.O. at 12 & then at lunch Mrs G. & then at 3. Sir E. Grey & others at F.O. Putumayo. To F.O. & saw Tyrrell who told me Sir E. Grey was decided to send me to Putumayo

[50] Blüchers: The Count Blücher (1865–1931) and Countess Blücher, an Englishwoman, née Evelyn Stapleton-Bretherton. He was Gebhard Lebrecht, and became the 4th Prince Blücher of Wahstatt in 1916. Casement had got to know them well in Africa, and the friendship was to enjoy its final flowering – and withering – in Berlin. The Count was a joint treasurer, with Conan Doyle, of the Congo Reform Association, and much of their conversation over dinner will have been about the 'Morel Testimonial': the efforts being made to raise funds to enable E. D. Morel to continue his work as emancipator, free of financial constraints (see note 15).

[51] Lord Cromer [1st Earl] (1841–1917): consented to launch the Morel Testimonial appeal; the fund was, at R.C.'s suggestion, to be in trust for Morel's wife and children. When the British Government's Agent and Consul-General in Egypt, Lord Cromer had visited the Upper Nile and drawn his own conclusions about the contrast between life on Leopold's side of the river and life on the British side.

[52] Sir E[dward] Grey [Bt.] (1868–1933): Secretary of State for Foreign Affairs, 1905–16. In a year's time Grey was to recommend R.C. for a knighthood, in recognition of his services in the Putumayo. It was Grey who ensured that R.C.'s brief was widened retrospectively so that the scope of the Putumayo investigation was not limited to enquiring after the welfare of the very few British subjects in the region. The sentence empowering him to make enquiries about the treatment of Amerindian labourers 'was interpolated just before the Blue Book was issued': Rhodes House Library, MS B.Emp. S22. G344, Casement to Charles Roberts, 4 January 1913. Although, on the eve of his expedition to Germany, R.C. was to denounce Grey as a 'wicked, stupid, obstinate fool' (NLI 10464 Casement to Mrs Green, 11 October 1914), and the Foreign Secretary was to be the object of much wrath when attempts were made to apprehend R.C. during the German adventure, Grey continued to treat the traitor with remarkable sympathy and respect. Grey was appalled by the use to which the diaries were put.

& wished to see me at 3 today. Lunched Mrs G. & then back to F.O. Saw Sir E. Grey & long talk with him.

14, *Thursday*

At F.O. from 12.30 looking at Putumayo papers. Lunched Spicer[53] & to Booth Line for passage to Pará.[54] Lizzie to dinner.

15, *Friday*

At F.O. from 11.30 looking over papers till 5. Home to Lizzie & Louie[55] & after dinner to Brompton Rd & Albert (10/-) X in Park. Then M. Arch & fine type in Park but fled & home at 12.50. [In margin: Albert 10.0] 15 $\frac{1}{2}$ years Albert. Morel Testimonial Letter of Committee Splendid.

16, *Saturday*

At Alisons'[56] to get things. Lunch Holborn & then home & Lizzie & Louie. Dinner at Holborn restaurant & at 8.45 to Dublin by Euston. Lizzie to see me off. Very tired of London.

Sunday 17 July. Arr Dublin 6 a.m. In Phoenix Park after dinner at zoo. Fine type. Stiff. [underlined twice]

18, *Monday*
In Ireland.

19, *Tuesday*
In Ireland.

[53] [Charles Sydney] Spicer (1874–1942): Assistant Clerk in the Foreign Office. After his promotion to Senior Clerk in 1912, on behalf of the Foreign Office's American Department he was to inform the House of Commons Select Committee investigating the Putumayo allegations that no information about ill-treatment of labourers had been received before September 1909. He had to correct this error when it was shown that the first complaints had arrived in May 1905.

[54] Pará [Brazilian name Belém]: the scene of R.C.'s consulship for 1908; by his account a squalid, unhealthy port. It was, though, the gateway to the Amazon and the main exporting centre for the Amazon rubber industry, particularly during the boom years of 1910–12.

[55] Louie [Heath]: a friend of Elizabeth Bannister who lived in Chelsea. Her sympathy was much in evidence during R.C.'s final days.

[56] Allisons: W. J. Allison and Company, Farringdon Road, London: the firm which equipped missionaries and the like for their ventures into inhospitable regions. They also acted as shipping agents and provided storage facilities in their warehouse (see Introduction).

20, *Wednesday*
Return to SASANA [England][57] – beastly Hole. At F.O.

21, *Thursday*
<u>Morel Testimonial</u>
Lunched with Doyles. He reports £350 only in.

Add to this: A. Emott [sic][58]£	50		217
R.C.	50		567
Dick	10		
F. Ware[59]	5		
Mrs Green	30		
Collected by her	70		
Lizzie	2		
Will Reid?[60]			

Stationery for my Journey 1.0.0.
At H. of C. & Emmott

22, *Friday*
Busy all day. at 'M. Post' 3 times, at H. of C. Lunch with Emmott. Met Hugh Law & Boland[61] & others. To Lizzie & to Gilmours'[62] at Fagan of

---

[57] *Sasana*: Irish for England. This word flummoxed those whose job it was to type out the diaries so that copies could be used by the Special Branch and by Naval Intelligence. The 1910 diary's typist put 'London', a reasonable guess, as that is where R.C. was to be found the following day. The 1911 typist, lacking such evidence, made an artist's impression of what he saw and inserted a single holograph word on the page in question.

[58] A[lfred] Emmott, M.P. (1858–1926): Under-Secretary of State for the Colonies, 1899–1911; active supporter of the Congo Reform Association; he became 1st Baron of Oldham in 1911. 'Dick' was Richard Morten (see note 16).

[59] F[abian] Ware [later, Major-General Sir] (1869–1949): editor, *The Morning Post*, 1905–11.

[60] Will[iam] Reid: co-owner, with his brother Alfred, of the famous Reid's Hotel, which still flourishes on the island of Madeira. R.C. stayed there on his way to Africa in 1903, and became a friend of 'Willie' (as he was known to most people), son of the hotel's founder, William Reid, Senior.

[61] Hugh [Alexander] Law (d. 1943): Nationalist M.P. for West Donegal, 1902–18; member of Irish Free State Parliament, 1927–32.

[John Pius] Boland (1870–1958): Nationalist M.P. for South Kerry, 1900–18; a junior whip of the Irish Party, 1906–18.

[62] [Thomas Lennox] Gilmour (1859–1936): Barrister; Assistant Private Secretary at the Foreign Office; London managing director of the Mozambique Company; supporter of reform in the Congo. When R.C. seemed determined to retire from the consular service, he offered him a post in Mozambique looking after the finances of a new cotton growing venture.

British Museum. Wrote E.D.M. letters till 2 a.m. – Wrote to '<u>L'pool</u> <u>Courier</u>' & '<u>L'pool Daily Post</u>'. Wrote many letters.

23, *Saturday*
Expect to sail by '<u>Edinburgh Castle</u>'??? Cabs 5/- Luggage 7/- Ticket to S'hamp/ 11/- [In margin: 1. 3. 0.] Typed copy of Anti-Slavery matter [In margin, in £ column: 5.] To Southampton. Mrs G., E.D.M., Harris, W. Reid.

Sunday 24 July 3/6. At Sea on 'Edinburgh Castle' Ran 261 miles. No meals because 'Commission' at my table. [In margin, total of previous two days' expenses: 7. 3.0.]

25, *Monday* 3/6 At Sea. Rather rough. Writing many letters about E.D.M. testimonial. Ran [blank space] miles. No meals all day!

26, *Tuesday* 3/6
[Crossed out: <u>Madeira?</u>] No meal till dinner time.
Wine 10.6

27, *Wednesday*
Madeira? Tips to Stewards. Luggage on shore –   1. 5.0.
                                 Hotel   1. 0.
        <u>17</u> Carlos Augusto Costa   12. 6
          189 Rua dos Ferreiros,
               Funchal,
               Madeira.

28, *Thursday*
10.12. 6
Hotel   1. 0. 0.
    Splendid testemunhos – soft as silk & big & full of life – no bush to speak of. Good wine needs no bush.[63] Carlos Augusto Costa – 189 Rua dos Ferreiros, Funchal 7/6 Very fine one – big, long thick. Wants awfully & likes very much. João – Big £1.12. 6. Internacional Hotel. Bella Vista.

29, *Friday*
Hotel 1.0.0. Carlos Augusto Costa 1.10.0. Total £2.10/- Last time Carlos. 9 to 11. Huge Extension.

[63] In describing this particular encounter, R.C. employs a double sexual pun. *Testemunhos* – Portuguese for 'testimonies' plays on the English slang usage of 'testimonials' – 'testicles'. Similarly, the sexual connotation of 'bush' leads him to an apposite quotation from the Epilogue to Shakespeare's *As You Like It*, which extends the double enterdre.

30, *Saturday*

Hotel	1. 0. 0.
João	£10. 0. 0
Hotel	11.12. 6
C.A. Costa	2.10. 0
	£14.2.6 in <u>Madeira</u>

Sunday 31 July. Sailed from Madeira
in '<u>Hilary</u>'

Hotel	13.12. 6
	1. 0. 0.

AUGUST

1, *Monday*
At sea – not well at all. Feel very low. Lay down all day – & Read a bit.
Ran 333 miles in 23 $\frac{1}{2}$ H.

Sweep	2/0	
Bridge	2/6	4/6

2, *Tuesday*

Ran 343 miles.	Bridge 3/0	Sweep 2/-	5/-

3, *Wednesday*

Ran 348 miles.	Bridge 12/6	Sweep 2/6	<u>14/6</u>
			1. 4. 0

4, *Thursday*
Losings on board 1.4.0 Ran 351 miles, only 1376 miles from Pará – 19/-
Lost at Bridge 4/6. Sweep 2/- 6/6

5, *Friday*
Hot morning. 344 miles.

6, *Saturday*
337 miles. Current against us.

Sunday 7 August [no entry]

8, *Monday*
Should arrive in Pará and get on shore by 6 p.m. Will go Valda Peso – &
Cafés <u>first</u> – then to Theatre & then on to Cafe in Independencia – & back

to Theatre about 10.30 & Valda Peso at 11. Camerinos' [dressing rooms] first.

Arr Para at 2. Alongside 3.30. – Tea & at 5 with Pogson[64] to Vaz Cafe. Lovely moço [young boy] – then after dinner to Vero Peso. Two types – Also to gardens of Praca Republica. 2 types – Baptista Campos <u>one type</u> – then Senate Square & Caboclo (boy 16–17). Seized hard. Young stiff, thin. Others offered later. On board at 12 midnight.

9, *Tuesday*

Called Pickerell.[65] Shall I see João – dear old soul? I'll get up early & go to Ruy Barbora by 6.51 & wait till 7.30 – & on all morning till 9.

No sleep hardly – Up at 5. on shore at 6. a.m. Lovely moco in tram – to Cemetery & lo! <u>João</u> coming along. Blushed to roots of hair with joy – handfast & talked. Gave 10$ – Said he thought it was me. [In margin: João Anselmode Lima – 251, Baptista Campos.] To [insert: Consul U.S.A.] & Then to Marco. Lunch Pogson. Dined Barry. Left 11.10 Barry. One <u>type</u> 11.30. too late. Rain & on board midnight.

10, *Wednesday*

On Shore at 6.35. Met João again at Cemetery. He gave Roses. Promised to call on him later & he said roses. To stream in forest. Two caboclo boys there at hut – Bathed & back 'Hilary' at 10.30 very tired. Letters from Home – Kate Parnell & others. Afternoon on shore a minute – too hot. Then after dinner to big square & all over place – including Baptista Campos – but none – altho' several possible types.

[On blotter, facing 7–10 August:] Errin Eren <u>Dublin London</u> Era Erie <u>Eire Eire</u> [By the end of his doodling R.C. had arrived at the Irish version of 'Ireland' that was to be adopted by the Free State.]

11, *Thursday*

Out to Ornstein's & on to Forest Stream & bathed – <u>Huge</u> caboclo – thin, 40 years. Antonio & Francisco out at Charcoal. Policeman at Station. At Zoo & Museum & breakfasted with Jimmy Hall & Mrs Hall at 143 Ruy Barbora. very good breakfast indeed. Back on board.

---

[64] [George] Pogson (1853–1914): R.C.'s successor at the Pará consulate. It was Pogson's despatch (PRO FO [Foreign Office] 369/198), on the subject of a recent expedition to the Putumayo made by Captain Thomas William Whiffen (1878–1922), which gave the Foreign Office access to its first independent witness – one who might testify as to the authenticity of atrocity allegations made in *Truth* magazine.

[65] [George Henry] Pickerell (b. 1858): United States consul at Pará, preferred by R.C. to the United Kingdom's Pogson; retired from consular service in 1924.

Barry, H, Pogson & Davis dined on board with me. Left at 10 with them to Square & all over. No type – but at 12.30 Darkie policeman 'en paisana' [in plain clothes] – enormous = 5$.

12, *Friday*

Very hot day. To call on Governor, but owing to Pogson's folly failed to find him high or low. Pogson is an ass! Back after luncheon with Barry & H (Bertie there)[66] and on board. Left Wharf at 4 sharp. Pogson arrived 5 minutes too late! He is an ass! Out to Bay & anchored till 12 midnight & then up anchor & off up River!

Nice pilots on board – one Paraense [from Pará] boy of 18 or so.

13, *Saturday*

Steaming up to Entrance of Creek. Due to arrive at Manaos on early morning of 16th. Pilot boy is Augusto de Maranhos – 18 of Pará. Steaming all day. The praticante [pilot's apprentice] Augusto is the son of Rubim of Port Works, and very like him.

Sunday 14th August Lovely weather – Lovely All day steam. Talked Pilot Augusto 7.50–8. Passed Obidos 8.30 p.m. Lights.

15, *Monday*

Passed Beautiful cliffs at 7. Augusto said were named – forget name. Lovely Banks. Col. Bertie advised by Dr. to go home at Manaos. I agree.

Stayed at Itacoatiara at 5. But Brazilian Customs refused to allow the cargo to be landed for the M-M. Railway. What utter Rotters. They had telegraphed from Para to Manaos on 11th for the permission! As 'no cargo, no mails,' said Skipper Collin[g]s & on to Manaos! A beautiful instance of Brazilian competency.

16, *Tuesday*
At Manaos

[66] Bertie, Colonel the Hon. Reginald Henry (1856–1950), formerly of the Royal Welsh Fusiliers: leader of the Peruvian Amazon Company's five-man commission of enquiry into the Putumayo atrocity allegations. But (see diary entries for 15 and 16 August) became ill and had to return to England. Louis H. Barnes, a tropical agriculturalist, assumed the leadership. The other members of the commission were Walter Fox, a botanist with a special knowledge of rubber, Seymour Bell, commercial expert, and Henry Lex Gielgud, formerly a clerk with Deloittes, who had kept the books for the Peruvian Amazon Co., but had changed employers and accepted the post of company secretary and manager.

Arrd. Manaos at 6 a.m. Lovely view over broad bay of Rio Negro. On shore at 10 to Booth's[67] & Chambers to Breakfast – after b'fast out by Flores tram. Joao [Good] Pensadors shut up but to further stream. Filthy Portuguese vendors – Back to J. Flores & on board at 4. Wrote F.O. of Col Bertie's return & on shore at 6. To Gardens by Lyceo & Barracks. Several policemen wanting, I think. One lovely schoolboy. Back & forward several times & at 8.15 to Chambers & stayed all night there in good bed & room.

17, *Wednesday*
Left Manaos for Iquitos.

Up at 6.30. Down to Theatre & town. Wire from F.O. John Brown[68] can't come he is sick in Montserrat. Called Aranas & got card of Colombian Consul in Manaos – Dr Rozo. Refused to meet him. Lunched at Derings[69] out by Igagarape Grande. Beautiful water. Manaos a horrid town! Very hot. No Barbadians came. At 4 on board, cleared out baggage

[67] Booth's: office of the Booth Steamship Company. R.C. had been impressed by Margaret and George Booth's account of their 1908 journey from London to Lima, via Pará. They had used the Amazon as their main transcontinental thoroughfare and, as far as possible, the steamships of the family firm as their means of transport. On their return, their experiences had been privately published, mainly in the form of Margaret Booth's diary: Margaret Booth, *An Amazon Andes Tour*, London, 'for private circulation', Edward Arnold, 1910.

[68] John Brown, was supposed to be R.C.'s interpreter, having recently performed the same service for Captain Whiffen (see note 64), as part of his wider responsibilities as personal servant. But he arrived at Pará too late to be of much use during 1910. Whiffen had acquired John Brown in the Putumayo, where Brown had been one of the 196 indentured Barbadians whose presence as British subjects justified consular inspection of the region in which the Peruvian Amazon Company (registered in London) operated. At this time Whiffen leased an estate on the British island of Montserrat, to which he had taken Brown, despite the Barbadian's confession to complicity in atrocities. Casement regarded Brown as a 'useless brute' (see this diary's entry for 9 November.)

[69] [Herbert Guy, later Sir Herbert] Dering (1867–1933): had been appointed Counsellor of Embassy in the Diplomatic Service, 1909; served in a series of diplomatic posts from 1892 until 1926. Dering was identified by the Foreign Office Enquiry Centre. The entry for 22 November 1910 in NLI 1622/3 has 'I wrote orders...and to Mr Derring, the Vice Consul in Manaos, to look after the men on arrival', while that diary's entry for 29 November has 'I am writing to Mr Dening or the Vice Consul [in Manaos] rather...' – two of many examples of difficulties encountered when deciphering some patches of R.C.'s handwriting. From 1909 until 1916 the United Kingdom's vice-consul in Manaos was Wyndham Robilliard; he had been acting vice-consul in 1908.

& to 'Huayna'. Beastly ship. Left anchorage at 5. Israel[70] & other passengers on board, including Javari family with boy Luiz. 17 on 15 July last, returning from Lisbon after 6 years. Entered Solimoes before 6 p.m. Dark Brown water again. Steamed all night. [In margin: Luiz de Veiga son of Pio D'Azeredo Veiga.]

18, *Thursday*

Steaming along South Bank. Passed Purús main entrance about 10.a.m. Very hot morning. Only one Bath & W.C. for all <u>Men</u> passengers – 27 of us. Food bad. Ship old & smelling. Great tornado in afternoon cooled air greatly. Talked Luiz & others especially after dinner. Steaming slower. Solimoes current is stronger than that of Amazonas. Turned in at 10.15 after chat with Luiz. Cool night.

Anchored from about midnight as pilot was sick. Last clear <u>6 Hours</u>.

19, *Friday*

Not well. Headache. Air in cabin very confined. Food abominable & ship dirty. No bath today!

Passed beautiful banks – often high red clay today. River often 3–4 miles broad. 7 fathoms & no bottom at a point 4 miles broad at 4 p.m.! Passed Camara in morning – Coary in [crossed out: evening] afternoon. Cool day & night. Slept on deck till 10 and then turned in at 10.15 in cabin. Cool night. Passed 'Athaulpa' [*sic*] at 3. She reports only 18 feet of water. We draw <u>21</u>. [*Encircled by R.C. and linked with another margin entry of following day*: Passed Ega or Teffe of Bates[71] at 5.30 a.m. 20th.]

20, *Saturday*

Warm & brighter morning. Near mouth of Japura – [*In margin*: 380 miles from Manaos at <u>5.30 a.m.</u> Doing about 150 miles per day] No bath again! Feel seedy & bored. We shall be stuck very soon now – after Jurua. Did not see Japura at all. Steaming well. Banks often high 50 or 60 feet. Splendid trees. Birds often – eagles & gulls. Saw turtle at 5.30 swimming. An Indian boy on board 3rd class. River still splendid stream. Expect reach Jurua in night about 3 a.m. Slept till 1.30 on Deck. Passed Fonte Boa at 5.40 Sunday morning.

Sunday <u>21</u> Steaming well. At Jutahy R. will be halfway to Iquitos. Anchored at <u>11.40 a.m.</u> to take soundings about 25 miles below Jutahy.

---

[70] [Victor] Israel: had his own rubber concession on the Ucayali River – the Pacaya Company.

[71] [Henry Walter] Bates: author of *Naturalist on the River Amazona*, London, John Murray, 1883.

Launch returned at 3 – with a hatfull of turtle eggs in Antonio's hat. Anchor up – plenty water – and at 3.10 off = 3½ hrs. Steamed past Favorima – high red banks & anchored at 6.30 p.m. close to Jutahy River.

22, *Monday*
Up anchor 5.45 & off at 6 a.m. in lovely cool morning. River like silver. Don't suppose will do 80 miles today – probably 60. Passed Jutahy R 6.35 a.m. [In margin: ½ way to Iquitos] 5–7 fathoms. 2 p.m. anchored in 60 feet – sending out Steam Launch at 2.26 only for soundings – below Timbatemba Island. We have steamed about 46 miles I reckon since this morning's start. A loss of ½ hour from anchoring & nearly 40 mts. from time we slowed (1.53) down. Stayed at anchor all night – Launch returned at 6 from sounding, reporting plenty of water all the time. Wasted 16 Hours! Slept on deck, fearful flies & mosquitoes. Heavy rain – but my bed good & I got none.

Off Timbataba Island.

23, *Tuesday*
Up anchor at 5.45 & on. Off Putumayo River mouth at 1 p.m. High land on left bank since this morning – with many very pretty places & clearings like Missions perched on the hills. Read over all papers of the Enquiry, 3.45. Passed on right bank, south one mile & half, high red cliff & fine houses – Colonia Rio Jajo. [In margin: Colonia Riojano] On across River to Maturas Island & then steep banks both sides – river (whole of it) some ¾ mile wide or less. Very deep, swift current. Maturas town – very pretty. South bank with Church – the first seen from Manaos – & after about 6 miles more we anchored at 6.10. about 12 miles below Larangol. Miserable!

24, *Wednesday*
Plenty mosquitoes.

Up anchor & off at 5.50 in misty morning. At 7.10 ran on a bank but getting off quickly – 'deep six' – cool and rainy. Expect 'Urumaguas' [*sic*] tonight possibly – but more likely not before Tabatinga on Friday. Passed Recreio at 10.45. Passed São Paulo de Olivença at 1.10. Steaming badly – about 44–46 miles since we started at 5.50. At 2.5 passed N. bank. Plantation with English flag called Tupenduba (9 miles above Sao P.) Half speed at 2.20. On again. Passed 'Bom Future' at 3.50. Many Siphonia Elastica trees – some tapped. Steamed on splendidly till 6.30 in sight almost of Boa Vista. Have done about 82 miles today. The chief Pilot, Noronha, has bet C/S Champagne will be in Tabatinga tomorrow night. It is about 92 miles away.

Actual run about 85 miles.

[On blotter, facing entries for 21–24 August:
3 $\frac{1}{2}$ Hours anchored from 11.40 to 3.10. 6 Hours – on night of 18th. At anchor 11 $\frac{1}{2}$ Hours. Total to date <u>21 Hours</u> 33 minutes lost from time we slowed ship to departure of Steam Launch. Should be <u>770</u> miles instead of only <u>620 about!</u> 22–23rd At anchor _____ $\quad$ 15 $\frac{1}{4}$

$$\overline{\quad 36 \ \tfrac{1}{4}}$$

124

<u>84</u>

213 miles from Putumayo to Tabatinga

<u>289</u>

502 miles from Iquitos to Putumayo

Another all night sitting <u>12</u>

$$48 \ \tfrac{3}{4} \text{ Hours}$$

At 10 o' clock we are 129 miles from Tabatinga. $\frac{418}{807}$

With good luck we should reach it on Friday afternoon some time. Then left 289 miles to Iquitos.]

[On other side of same blotter, facing entries for 25–27 August:

Carrier Forward $\quad$ 48 $\frac{3}{4}$ Hours

24th–25th Anchored $\quad$ <u>7</u> $\qquad$ "

$$55 \ \tfrac{3}{4}$$

24)161(Hours

$\frac{144}{17}$ 8_ 17.0

Lost at Gate [?] & Esperanza (Javari) $\qquad$ <u>2</u>

$$57 \quad \tfrac{3}{4}$$

25th–26th At anchor

<u>off Javari all night till 9. a.m.</u> $\qquad$ $\frac{15 \ \frac{1}{2}}{72 \ \frac{1}{4}}$

26th at Tabatinga - noon $\hfill$ 1 $\frac{1}{4}$

$$\overline{73 \tfrac{1}{2}}$$

26th 27th " Leticia (say 18) $\hfill$ 17 $\frac{1}{4}$

$$\overline{88 \tfrac{1}{4}}$$

If "Uramaguas [sic] left night of Friday 19th she will be 8 days out tonight – Say she makes average 100-110 miles per day, she will be tonight from 800–880 miles from Manaos. By distance chart Tabatinga is 861 miles. So she cannnot well be there before tonight or tomorrow morning.

After Juana Island & Parana the water of the river is much clearer. Why–because Current very slow.

27th. At anchor Loreto Channel 6 $\frac{1}{4}$

$$94 \ \tfrac{1}{2}$$

Night of 27th – 28th anchor $\quad$ 11 $\frac{3}{4}$

$$\overline{106 \ \tfrac{3}{4}}$$

25, *Thursday*
Up anchor at 1.27 a.m. Full speed 1.33. Passed Boa Vista at 2.10. steaming
well. At 6.10 Belem and on full speed. Noronha has done the trick! Should
be in Tabatinga <u>at 4. p.m.</u> Bath in Dr's bath. Very seedy feeling. Slept from
8.30 to 3 when out on deck. Orique – 9.40 a.m. (45 miles from our starting
point 4 miles below B. Vista). Only 44 miles to do now at 9.40 to
Tabatinga = <u>4 p.m.</u> At 2 at Guanabara, close to S.E. mouth of Javari –
a Brazilian flag at a good house & party on verandah. They fired three
shots, we stopped – I presume a half caste pic-nic wants a passage!
Detained 40 minutes. On at 2.40, Esperanza at 3.35. Mouth of Javary
[sic]. Landed Luiz & father. [crossed out: On at] On again at 4.53. Lost 1.
17 Suddenly struck ground just past Javari 2nd mouth & anchored all night
<u>in 23 feet.</u> [Notes in margin: 'Liberal' Launch reported at Guanabara as
having cleared there at 7. a.m. for Iquitos from Ica, with 45 tons Rubber &
a 'lot of sick people' on board.
10 $\frac{1}{2}$ fathoms = 63
add rise   27
              90ft]

26, *Friday*
Steam Launch out at 5.45, sounding. Return reporting only 24 feet. At
anchor at 9.a.m. & on to Tabatinga in less than 6 ft. At 10 a.m. getting
near Tabatinga & arrived at 11.15. Brazilian military post – 2 small field
[crossed out: guns] pieces on earth platform & a House of Commandant.
Anchored within 15 yards of shore in 12 $\frac{1}{2}$ fathoms. River dead low, breadth
1000 yards, depth say <u>100 feet.</u> Current very slow, less than 1$\frac{1}{2}$ miles an
hour. Below at Javari current about 5 miles per hour but depth only 21–24
feet. Group $\frac{1}{2}$ dozen soldiers by guns. The Commandant came on board,
but we had to send a boat for him. What is the use of this post? They do
nothing. It will cost us some £30 to pay this absurd visit, as well as the
delay! The soldiers all visibly niggers, the 1st Liberian Army Corps all
over again! Left Tabatinga 12 noon for Leticia just up stream. Arr. Leticia
at 12.15 and anchored near 'Esperanza'. She high and dry on the bank in
midstream. 5 Peruvian soldiers off – Cholos – fine chaps. One splendid
fellow, gave cigarettes. Also Brazilians from 'Esperanza' & at 5 all bathing
on sand bank & summersaulting. [Note in margin: See from Tabatinga the
'Esperanza' aground at Leticia.]

27, *Saturday*
<u>All night at Leticia.</u> Expect 'Uramaguas' hourly! Wasted 6–7 hours at
Leticia. Proceeded at 5.45 a.m. after 18 hours wasted deliberately at Leticia
– pretext steering gear needed attention. Pilots all went for a spree to
'Esperanza'. Bright sun this morning. Soundings across river from Xinari

to Ronda gave least water $6\frac{1}{4}$ fths $= 37\frac{1}{2}$ feet. River about $\frac{1}{2}$ mile wide or less, current slow. Islands few & small. Similar to Lulanga at junction of Lopori, but rise here very marked on bank – fully 35 to 40 ft I should think. Steaming very well. Near Loreto (39 miles) at 9.50. Captain timid, however, & stopped on N. bank in 'no bottom at 10' (60 feet). Launch for soundings ready. We could easily go on to S. P de Loreto, another 40 miles. Anchored 9.53 in 'no bottom at 10'. Launch did not leave until 11.10 = 1 [h] 17 deliberately wasted. She takes 6 hours coal. Launch returned 3.45, reports 22 feet. Captain I can see will stay all night! He is talking of whirlpools in this calm, lake like river. He fears everything – not the man for the job. 4, under way again till 6. (2 hours lost over & above the time needed!) 6. 10, slowed for anchor. Very shallow in Loreto Channel. Only 22 ft & we heeled over twice.

Launch 'Inca' came up from Javari & anchored.

Sunday 28 Up & off 5.45. 'Inca' left at 5. At Caballo Cocha at 7 stopped. Launch left 7.32. River dirty again & evidently rising. Huge logs, trees & grass & scum floating past. Launch returned 10.45 a.m. We started 11.10. SS 'Javari' passed down 12.15. Reports 'plenty water' in channel right up to Iquitos. She was ashore at Tigre – 3 days anchored. 4.17 – Launch not off till 4.55. (38 minutes lost). Launch returned 7.30 – 22 feet. 'Inca' passed up. Turned in at 10. 'Urimaguas' reported. Came alongside 11.30. Anchored.

29, *Monday*
No sleep. Getting ready to tranship to 'Urimaguas' at 5 a.m. Did so, along with four others – Israel & Kouriat & two more. left 'Huayna' about 6.30. Passed steam launch sounding up above. Waved farewells. All party on board. Steaming well, but not so fast as 'Huayna'. Passed San Juan and later on San Pablo de Loreto (187 miles from Iquitos). 'Urimaguas' is a Launch of 110 tons built at Glasgow to order of E. da Costa & Co of Liverpool. She burns coal or wood. Our supply of former running short they say – we must stop to buy wood. Will not reach Iquitos until Wednesday morning. Day delightfully cool. Many Indian houses on the right, or South bank, which we are skirting most of the time. Better built house than those one sees in the Brazilian woods, & some plantations around each. Cassava, mealies & so forth. Many more people too, & they look happy – and <u>are</u> certainly Indians, not mulattos – altho' <u>clothed</u>. Even the children are clothed. Played Bridge with Barnes, Gielgud & Fox till 11 or later.[72]
[On blotter, facing 28–29 August:
$\frac{1}{2}$ hour lost in sending <u>launch</u>

[72] Barnes, Gielgud and Fox: three members of the four-man commission of enquiry sent by the Peruvian Amazon Company (see note 66).

Carried forward	102	15
Launch about 3.15		
28th Hard off Caballo Cosha	4.	<u>10</u>
10 $\frac{1}{2}$ Hrs anchored 4.10 = 6.20		
steaming = <u>38 miles at outside</u>		
At 6 a.m. 29th 'Huayna' at anchor		
all previous night <u>from 7 p.m.</u>	<u>13.</u>	<u>43</u>
	120 Hours.	8]

30, *Tuesday*

Going well. Stopped for an hour owing to fog from 4. to 5. 15 a.m. Passed Pebas in the night – 114 miles from Iquitos. Urimaguas does not do more than 5 knots over the ground I think. We should be at Iquitos early morning. There are many more Indians & inhabitants along the Peruvian than the Brazilian Amazon. Stopped at La Colonia Braziliana for firewood. Saw two Boras Indians.[73] Caught young – Dark, fierce, brutal faces. Other Indians. Wood is sold at 30 Soles the 1000 billets = £3. On again & passed mouth of Napo about 5 p.m. Will anchor in night so as to reach Iquitos early morning.

31, *Wednesday*

Arrd. Iquitos at 8. All on shore. To Booth's office & then to Consul Cazes.[74] Lunched his wife & he. Took room 'Le Cosmopolite'. Hotel dreadful. Called on Prefect Dr Paz Soldan at 4 to 5.45. Talked fully. He declared the stories 'fables' – but much that he said confirmed to my mind their truth.

Very hot at Iquitos, & lots of mosquitoes. The town is very well situated, but horribly neglected & dirty. The 'streets' atrocious, the houses poor. Hundreds of soldiers in blue dungaree – splendid looking Indians &

---

[73] Boras Indians: one of the four principal tribes of what was then – in fact, if not in law – the Peruvian Amazon region. The other tribes were the Huitoto (who accounted for about three-quarters of the labour force), the Andoke, and the Ocaina. Andokes, otherwise known as Matanzas, was the name of the rubber trading station which exploited traditional Andoke territory: 'Andokes', writ large on the Company's map.

[74] Consul Cazes (d. 1915): David Cazes, a Gibraltarian, was the classic embodiment of one of Casement's most deeply held aversions: 'honorary' consul-ship. Swift MacNeill M.P., member of the Select Committee on the Putumayo, shared the Consul-General's distaste for this easily-compromised arm of the Consular Service: 'a Consul with a foreign name, 1,200 miles from the scene of operations, was the only person with whom these people could communicate if they could escape from the hands of these company exploiters.' (*Minutes of Evidence, Report from Select Committee on Putumayo*, 1913 (H. of C. Paper 148) XIV Q 211). Moreover, in many ways Cazes was beholden to the most powerful exploiter of the Amerindian rubber-gatherers, Julio César Arana (see note 76).

Cholos.[75] Nearly all are Indians – a conquered race held by 'blancos'. They are finer men than the 'blancos' & with gentle faces, soft black eyes with a far off look of the Incas.

SEPTEMBER

1, *Thursday*

On board 'Urimaguas' for bag. Met Lizardo Arana[76] & to his house for Barnes. He spoke of the great prospects of the Putumayo. Its many Indian tribes, its fertility etc & hoped the result of the visit of myself & the others wd be the introduction of 'fresh capital'. The late acting French Consular Agent Vatan[77] called on me & told me that the condition of things in the Putumayo had been disgraceful – that the existing method was slavery pure & simple – but that it was the 'only way' in Peru as she exists. The evil inheritance of an evil past – a conquered race outside the constitution & the law with 'no rights' – the Indians had to be 'civilized' & this is the way it is done. Interviewed two Barbadians just from Putumayo. One confirms well nigh everything. Engaged him to return with me – the other saw only good & gave a clean bill.

[On blotter, facing 1 September: Interview with Vatan. Interviewed Bishop & Nellis Walker][78]

[75] *Cholo*: alternative Spanish word for 'Mestizo' – an Amerindian of mixed race.
[76] Lizardo Arana: brother of Julio César Arana, whose Peruvian firm, J. C. Arana y Hermanos, was based in Iquitos. Other senior officials of the company were the Arana brothers' two brothers-in-law Pablo Zumaeta and Abel Alarco. In 1907 the Aranas had registered their firm in London, where it became the Peruvian Amazon Rubber Company, Ltd., acquired four British directors, and raised £135,000 by sale of shares. Later the word 'Rubber' was dropped from the company's stationery. Allegations of atrocities committed by servants of the company had first come to Casement when he was consul in Pará, and he had notified the British Legation in Petropolis of his concern. But ill-treatment of the labour force did not become a government issue until the national conscience was aroused by a series of articles in *Truth* magazine. From the pen of an American explorer and engineer, Walter Ernest Hardenburg (1886–1942), they spared the reader few details of rape, murder and mutilation carried out in the course of enslaving rubber-gatherers.
[77] The late Acting French Consular Agent Vatan: had traded in the Putumayo for fourteen years.
[78] [Frederick] Bishop and Nellis [or Nellice] Walker: the two Barbadian employees of the Peruvian Amazon Company interviewed on this day. Bishop admitted that, under orders, he had often flogged Indians, and he corroborated the reports of those who had first revealed the inhuman practices of the company. R.C. was soon placing considerable trust in Bishop, the only Barbadian on whom he felt he could depend.

2, Friday

The Iquitos 'El Oriente' of last night has long account of the 'Commission' declaring it is solely to get fresh capital for the Putumayo – in fact the article is clearly dictated by Lizardo Arana – acting on the lines of Julio's letter to Cazes. Interviewed Dr Pizarro – Federico M. Pizarro –[79] who 'knew nothing'. Also A. Guichard who equally knew nothing about any of the 'Truth' deponents.

Spoke again to the Barbadian, Frederick Bishop, who seems a little bit afraid now & hopes there is 'nothing political' to get him into trouble. Cazes says the Prefect thinks me prejudiced and taking a partisan view – another Arana insinuation I presume.

In evening 'El Oriente' a telegram from Lima saying the Govt are going to enquire into the Putumayo charges – a letter from Barcelona to the 'Comercio' having excited great sensation from Deschamps, a French geographer.

[On blotter, facing 2 September: Pizarro & Guichard. X]

3, Saturday

Called on Barnes & others suggesting to take the statement of Bishop when I can get him – all of them to come. In house all day getting things unpacked & writing to F.O. Bishop came at 5 – & told me further horrible things recently done on Putumayo by Moung or Montt.[80] Macedo[81] is supreme he says & the Peruvian soldiers at La Chorrera a farce – & the Indians all slaves. He flogged them for not bringing rubber.

Cazes wrote also to say an important witness from Putumayo had come down & in evening told me it is a Spaniard who declares that all in 'La Felpa' and 'La Sanccion' [*sic*][82] was true! & he will prove it. After dinner Cazes and I talked till 11.30 on this Putumayo Horror. He explaining his reasons for not having taken action.

[79] Dr. F[r]ederico M. Pizarro: an Iquitos lawyer, who had taken statements from the earliest witnesses willing to complain about atrocities in the Putumayo. The statements had been published in a local news-sheet, *La Sanción*, in July 1907.

[80] [Alfredo] Montt ('Moung' in John Brown's statement to Commissioner of Montserrat): one of 'seven monsters' (q.v. Normand, Aguero, Fonseca, Jimenez, and two Rodriguez brothers: Aurelio and Aristides) responsible for the deaths of some 5,000 Indians by 'shooting, flogging, beheading, burning... and starvation.' NLI 13085–86 19 November 1910. Montt was section chief at La Chorrera's Atenas section.

[81] [Victor] Macedo: chief agent at the trading post La Chorrera, the Aranas' main agency. Presumably Macedo was not one of R.C.'s 'seven monsters' because, for the most part, he commanded others to do the actual bloodletting. He was in a class of his own.

[82] *La Felpa* and *La Sanción*: mastheads for the same news-sheet, published in Iquitos by Benjamin Saldana Rocca. Rocca, who was printer as well as proprietor,

[On blotter, facing 3 September: Saw Bishop <u>again</u>]

Sunday 4 Sep. Interviewed F. Bishop & Juan Guerrido on Putumayo. Dreadful story – all Commission present. Went tram ride with Mr & Mrs Cazes – & then Gielgud & Barnes to dinner, played Bridge.

[On blotter, facing entry for 4 September: Interviewed Juan Guerrido[83] Ditto Bishop–By all Commission.]

5, *Monday*
Heavy tornado last night & rain & another this morning at 6.30 a.m. Very heavy rain often all day – & again at night heavy rain & apparently throughout the night.

Cazes told me of Burga, the Comisario of Govt in the Putumayo – also of the Peruvian Captain & the two Indians in guns at Nazareth on Javari – for 'running away' – also of young Borda, son in law of Morey, the leading merchant of Iquitos, who is now trying to filibuster & seize by force an 'Estate' down at Caballo Cocha which he Cazes, is agent for. Threats of force are being used, on both sides. Young Borda says he is a 'brave', a 'valiente' & no one shall stop him – the owner threatens his rifle.

Played Bridge with Commission at their House.

6, *Tuesday*
Heavy rain still, River risen 18" last two days. Another statement by Bishop, dreadful! – perfectly awful. Told Commission of it [crossed out: – who are now as convinced as I am of the horror of it all] Have invited them & Zumaeta & Arana to dinner tomorrow with Com. & Consul. River risen over 1 foot last night = 2.6" in three days.

Wrote F.O. & wrote out Bishop's Statements telling Commission all the added facts. Bishop's statement today incriminates Macedo & Ocaña of Savana [La Sabana] & worst of all Martine[n]gui who went to Lima by last 'Liberal' with the plunder of <u>Atenas</u>, leaving the Indians starving.

[On blotter, facing 6 September: Bishop again]

launched a series of attacks on Arana's activities in July 1907, in his news-sheet, *La Sanción* ('sanction' or 'penalty'). They consisted largely of depositions, mostly anonymous. In December 1907 the paper's name was changed to *La Felpa* ('A Drubbing'), and the last issue appeared on 5 January 1908, not long before the police expelled Rocca from Iquitos. Crude productions which appeared irregularly, their sensational content was picked up by other publications and relayed throughout South America. Hardenburg obtained the original depositions from Rocca's son, and they formed the core of his *Truth* articles.

[83] Juan Guerrido (Garrido): said to have shot two Indian boys to put them out of their misery. They were being fried over a stove by Normand.

7, Wednesday

River risen a lot in night. A Govt. Launch left early down river. I wonder where for? I am terribly suspicious of the Local Authorities! – more so of them than of the Coy. Warm day again. Three Peruvian gunboats came, led by 'America' bringing back 123 soldiers 'Volunteers'! from the Napo.[84] Splendid men – all Indians nearly – sturdy & fine, gentle-faced, handsome chaps. Poor Indian people. In house all day nearly, save for once to Booths' to get Time Table. Reading 'Forest Lovers',[85] after many years. Today 88th anniversary of the Independence of Brazil. Dinner at 7.30 – Lizardo Arana & Pablo Zumaeta,[86] Cazes & the four men of the commission. Drank health & prosperity to Peru.

8, Thursday

Lovely day at 7 a.m. River risen again fully one foot or more. Sandbank getting covered. Huayna's passengers all came up yesterday. Met some of them. Out by tram to forest pool – Morona Cocha. Fine types, one with shotgun lovely & strong. Indian Cholo in Brick Works. Stayed at Britos' house (£1500) & saw nice children & then back at 11 & a fearfully hot day. Did little or nothing – it was too hot. At 5 out to Shooting range but did not find it with Fox & Bell & then stupid dinner & out again to Commission & played Bridge till 11.30 winning two Rubbers. Home at 12 & young Cholo policeman on Malecon – splendid young Indian. Turned in 1 a.m. very hot still. Shall be glad to get off from Iquitos – hope on Monday. Hear that the Interpreter at Copal Urcu[Urco] is not to be found. Nous verrons when Argentina comes.

9, Friday

River risen steadily since Monday. The big sandbank nearly covered this morning & various channels through it. 'Argentina' returned 11 a.m. No Interpreter! Alack. I walked Punchana 9–10.30 a.m. Wretched. No plantation or life at all. Women bathing in stream. 2–4 Cholo soldiers discharging 'America' in blazing sun. Almost all Indians & a few half-castes, all fine, splendid youths. One half-white muchacho[87] magnificent display & a young Cholo with erection as he carried heavy box. Down left leg about

---

[84] Napo: tributary of Amazon River, running south-east, parallel to the Putumayo River.

[85] *Forest Lovers [The]*: a novel by the prolific English author, Maurice Henry Hewlett (1861–1923). It was first published in 1898 and, after a number of reprints, Macmillan brought out a new edition in 1909.

[86] [Pablo] Zumaeta: see note 76.

[87] *muchacho*: a member of the lowest level bar one of the rubber-gathering hierarchy. At the top were the chiefs of sections, mainly Peruvian (although Normand was Bolivian). Next came the remaining whites, the 'blancos'; then the

6–8". They are far too good for their fate. It was not the 'Argentina' after all, so there may still be a chance. Called at Vatan's store and asked him to call. At 4.45 began taking statements of 4 Barbadians & one of them amply confirmed Bishop's story. The others had seen nothing, but had been on the Launches all the time. Turned in early not feeling well at all. Took 16 grs Quinine in night – no sleep at all. Terrible storm. Rain, thunder & thunder Bolt! <u>2 a.m.</u>

[On blotter, facing 9 September:

Walcott
Ford
Jones
Labadie][88]

10, *Saturday*
River still rising. Heavy rain last night – torrents. 'Liberal' returned, reports 'Huayna' may arrive today. My wine a/c £4.3.9 on Huaynas – & 6 bots of Whisky for voyage £1.10/-. Also £5 given to Stewards on board, poor souls. Informed that Stanley J. Lewis[89] a Barbadian referred to in Declarations is on board '<u>Liberal</u>'. Sent for him twice. He came to Cazes' first in forenoon, but as soon as Cazes told him that I wished to see him he bolted C says. Said he had to go to Prefectura with a paper & that he wd. come back. At 3 I sent Bishop for him & he returned saying Lewis would not come! He did not know why. I said nothing, only that 'I'd see him later on' and it did not matter. The Brazilian Consul General called – 'A. Aranjo Silva, Consul Général des E. U. du Brésil, Iquitos (Peru)' – Why the French? I was out. My washing back today 16.80 + 7.80 + 7.50 = 32.10 = <u>£3.4.2</u>. Cheaper than I expected. The dinner to Arana & Zumaeta was 120.00 = £12. Turned in early on my own bed and slept <u>all</u> night – God be praised. Cool & nice. Heavy rain and tornado of wind at 8

Barbadian indentured labourers, who held sway over the 'racionales' ('rational staff' in R.C.'s words), usually half-breeds who could read and write and who were paid a salary (see White Diary entry for 15 October. The *muchachos* came next. They were selected Indians, whose job it was to discipline the 'wild' Indians. In various places in both diaries, R.C. uses the term *muchacho de confianza* ('trusted boy') a name for those hand picked *muchachos* or 'trusties' who were armed with rifles in order to enforce the system.

[88] Ford [Preston] and Jones [Joseph]: Barbadians employed on the Peruvian Amazon Company's river launches. The men were not involved in rubber collection. Labadie [Joseph]: another Barbadian; he was seemingly innocently employed in Iquitos.

[89] Stanley J. Lewis: Barbadian steward of *Liberal* (steamship). Gave testimony on five occasions, including one to the Peruvian prefect of Loreto, the large administrative area which included the Putumayo.

p.m. Sunday 11. Sept. Lovely morning after rain. River rising. Sandbank shows big heads only. River still more all day. Called on Mrs Prefect, Ernestina G. de Alayza, a nice woman. The Alcalde, Dr Lucas Rodriguez called to return my visit, but I was out. Barnes & Co examined the Peruvian I sent them who speaks Huitoto & Boras[90] & was in Arana's service. His evidence incriminates Miguel Flores & he will prove it.

12, *Monday*

'Urimaguas' leaves for Manaos at 2 p.m. with mails. I am not writing officially by her, as Arana goes on her & all letters might easily be opened. The two Barbadians, Gibbs & Lewis asked to come to see me refused to come. 'Argentina' returned from Copal Urco without the Interpreter, who was in the bush. A great pity in every way – but will get the Peruvian now.

Very seedy all day, altogether quite unable to do anything. Running blood last night and left me weak & faint & my head aching dreadfully. 'Huayna' came up ydy and got alongside only at 5.30. p.m. this evening – on account of 'Urimaguas'. They can waste time on this Iquitos route & no mistake! A Dr Jemuro Herrera, Editor of 'El Loreto Comercial' called twice to see me and try to interview me – but I escaped, the last time by going to bed straight on his arrival & refusing to get up! This at 8 p.m. I spent a truly awful night. Mosquitoes like drops of fiery poison all over me – pale yellow beasts & horrors. Bishop says Gibbs[91] tells him of Norman[d]'s doings – burning people alive often & killing them. Gibbs is on the 'Liberal'. 'Argentina' returned from Copal Urco. No Interpreter.

13, *Tuesday*

A fine morning indeed, but going to be stifling. Adolphus Gibbs came at 9.30 & told us his story of service at Abisinia & Morelia.[92] At latter saw Jimenez[93] chop off the head of a Boras cacique [tribal chief] who had been in chains for 2 weeks & tried to escape. Saw heaps of floggings but had not flogged himself. Looks a rascal. Busy writing out depositions of the Barbadians with Mr Osborn as copyist. He is willing but slow. Dr of

[90] Huitoto and Boras: The languages of the two main tribes whose exploitation R.C. was investigating.

[91] [Adolphus] Gibbs: Barbadian who testified the following day.

[92] Abisinia and Morelia: Abisinia was one of La Chorrera's ten 'sections'; Morelia was one of Abisinia's two 'sub-sections'. R.C. was amused by the inappropriate names which had been attached to some of these vast tracts of jungle.

[93] [Augusto] Jiménez: chief of Ultimo Retiro, one of La Chorrera's sections; in 1904 he had shared a bottle of cognac with Abelardo Aguero, Abisinia's chief, before they killed eight trussed-up Indians.

'Huayna' to breakfast with me at Bella Vista – it cost 17 soles = 1.14/- for 2 of us! <u>Carlton Morris</u> did not come.[94] Went to Booths at 5 & sent letter to F.O. to Spicer with depositions of Barbadians to go down by 'Huayna'. Met Jensen who told me much about the Indians & <u>about Arana getting</u> hold of the Putumayo & killing Serrano etc.[95] & starving the others out.

[On blotter, facing 13 September:
<u>Adolphus Gibbs</u>
Carlton Morris – The 'Barbadian Consul' did not come – will await my return – he said to say He is a carpenter in Iquitos.]

14, *Wednesday*

Packed up & down to 'Huayna' to breakfast and then at about 1.30 p.m. left in 'Liberal' for Putumayo. Gibbs & another Barbadian deserted! after getting advance too. The swine. Captain Carmino Regado furious & no wonder. Cook drunk. A Peruvian Engineering Officer on board going a trip to the Putumayo from Lima. Our Interpreter looks a decent muchacho. About 23, wild hair, dark eyes, <u>splendid teeth</u> & a bright smile. He is half caste & looks good sort. Indian pilot young man – fine chap & Cholo steersman too. Ship is comfortable & quiet & better than 'Urimaguas'.

Played Bridge after dinner until 8.30 & then turned in in a Hammock on deck. Cold & not nice.

[On blotter, facing 14 September: Left Iquitos]

15, *Thursday*

'Slept' or rather lay in hammock on deck last night – Beastly – will not do it again. Got sore <u>throat</u> badly from it – no blanket. Anchored in night from Storm 10.30–12 midnight. Carmino told me of Burga & his Cia [compañia = company] Cohero de Alto Maranon at Morona & Santiago. Wiped out by <u>Huambisas</u> who killed 2 sons, 2 priests & all party. Burga about. These Indians big strong fellows – got guns & use them & shoot well. They are now going to be conquered. 'Cosmopolita' passed Pongo de Manseriche 4 months ago with Lores as Captain & the American prospecting party. At 2.30 near 'Santa Sophia' tremendous hurricane – fearful storm, nearly swamped. Captain said the worst he had ever experienced in his 14 years of Amazon life. Lasted $\frac{1}{2}$ hour & rain another $\frac{1}{2}$ hour. Near

[94] Carlton Morris: a Barbadian resident in Iquitos who, at Cazes's request, told other Barbadians that they should go to the consulate to see R.C.

[95] [David] Serrano: a Colombian who had employed 45 Huitoto families in La Reserva, an area coveted by Arana, and, as with much of the larger region, claimed by Peru. Although Serrano lost his battle – he was murdered with other Colombians in 1908 – Colombia eventually won the war: 24 million acres of Putumayo territory were ceded to Colombia during the second term of office of Peruvian President Augusto Leguia. This included all the land claimed by Arana.

Leticia saw 'Perseveranza' steaming splendidly up stream full speed for Iquitos. Alack, our mails on board & so near & yet we shall not get them until end of October. At Leticia. 'Esperanza' has 3 feet of water. River risen some $5\frac{1}{2}$ or 6 feet since I passed up on 26 Augt. Practicantes on board. Gave cigarettes nice Paraense moco [young boy from Pará]. On to Tabatinga & Javari. Many mosquitoes. Left Javari at 9.30 & on to Putumayo.

16, *Friday*

Out on bosomy <u>Solimoes</u> ('only Lemons'. River's Eng Portuguese navigation!) Hot enough, but night was cool. I have a very bad sore throat from sleeping in Hammock. Passed São Paulo de Olivença at about noon. Beautiful situation. It has clearly deserted the high steep cliff Herndon & Bates[96] speak of for this cliff now lies about $1\frac{1}{2}$ miles up stream & the town, with its Church, is on high sloping green pasture. At 2.30 coming to Maturas which passed on 23 [August], coming up at about 5 p.m. then. Heavy tornado from down stream. Turned nose up River to avoid it and lost fully $\frac{1}{2}$ hour. Coming to Colonia Rio Jano at 3.30 p.m. for mules. Cooler after rain. On shore Colonia Rio Jano. Got 12 mules with great trouble, but a tremendous storm first below Maturas. Left Colonia at 10.30 after long delay & mosquitoes & got to Putumayo Mouth at 11.30 but I in bed. A few <u>miserable</u> Indians at Colonia Rio Jano. We started up Putumayo – white mist at 4 a.m.

17, *Saturday*

Delayed in Putumayo early morning 2.30 a.m. to 4 a.m. by white mist. Up only at 9 a.m. ill with fever & saw little of River at all. The Banks seem of clay – hard caked clay – Stone <u>sand</u> shown & a few sandflies.

Steaming <u>all</u> day. At 5 p.m. passed mouth of a biggish tributary on S.W. bank – sandflies not so bad as I expected. Mosquitoes none at all. At dinner heard of the attack on La Union in Jan 1908. The Engineer now on board was here then & our Indian pilot was shot in ear & head. River is deep & connects with Amazon by side channel but the phenomenon of this depth is that of the Amazon itself – not the great quantity of fresh water <u>delivered</u> by this region, but the great quantity held up & restrained by the influence of the Ocean. 'Liberal' steams $7\frac{1}{2}$ knots; current say $2-2\frac{1}{2}$.

It is 42 Hours steaming from mouth of Igaraparana to Caraparana, says Captain.

[On blotter, facing entries for 15–17 September, and alongside the beginnings of a diagram estimating 'Ocean level': The young Quichua

[96] [William Lewis] Herndon: and Lardner Gibbon, authors of *Exploration of the Valley of the Amazon made under Direction of the Navy Department*, 2 vols (one by each author), Washington, 1854. Bates: see note 71.

pilot on Liberal is named Simon Pisango – a pure Indian name – but calls himself Simon ['de la' crossed out] Pizarro, because he wants to be civilized! Just like the Irish Os & Macs dropping first their names or prefixes to shew their 'respectability' & then their ancient tongue itself, to be completely Anglicised.

Simon Pisango still talks Quichua – but another generation of Pizarros will speak only Spanish! Men are conquered not by invasion but by themselves & their own turpitude.

The man who <u>gives</u> up his family, his nation, his language is worse than the woman who abandons her virtue. What chastity is to her, these essentials to self respect & self knowledge are to his manhood.][97]

Sunday 18 Sept. Mist in night & anchored. Cold – pleasant. No mosquitoes at all. Many sandflies this morning, but not so many as I expected. <u>Lots</u> of small green parrots in bushes – tiny chattering things. No araras [macaws]. Many assai palms & bactois. Herons too. Stopped twice today at Brazilian stations. Military post and Customs station. Latter had 3 white Brazilians – dreadful hole. Then at 5 at Cotuhi River. 2° 53'. 12 S. – 69°. 41.10" West Greenwich.

19, *Monday*

Lovely morning – passing a new palm, the Punchana pilot calls 'Pona' – a lovely thing indeed. Fox raving about it & well he may. Beside the assai it shoots up its graceful stem with from 6–12 magnificent fronds like those of a harts-tongue fern on top – & then a green bulging head to its long stem. Five lovely and quite differing palms growing here close together & in enormous numbers. The young pilot calls the ground – an 'island' probably – '<u>achawa</u>'. 8.30 a.m. a <u>deer</u> swimming down midstream at tremendous rate. Lowered canoe & after long chase, deer often turning up stream & beating canoe, one man jumping over, but being beaten <u>hollow</u> by the deer, the poor little chap was caught by the hind leg, after many failures & dragged into canoe, tied by legs & hoisted on board. I <u>should</u> like to save him & take him home to Ireland. He richly deserves his life. I do not want to eat him! Captain Carmino, decent man, won't kill him, but has put him in a fine cage to keep & tame him. The Quichua name is 'Juíchu'. On thro' desolation of desolations – at 9.30 passed 'Pupima' river) – misnamed so as they are not puprima palms at all, but pona.

[97] This text is said to be the draft of a letter to Mrs Green (René MacColl, *Roger Casement, A New Judgment*, London, Hamish Hamilton, 1956, p. 85); unfortunately it is not to be found in the NLI 10464 Green Papers. If it were to turn up it could play a significant part in the forgery debate.

20, *Tuesday*

Hot morning. Interviewed Stanley S. Lewis at 8.30 to 9.30 & got revolting particulars from him which I could check by Marcial G's & from Juan Castano's statements[98] – all true!

Stopped at Pescaria a fishing station of Coy's, 10 hours below Arica & mouth of Igaraparana. Several women of Huitotos there in sexual servitude. A 'whiteman' from Lima with certainly two Huitoto concubines, mothers of two, separate, boy children. Two dead monkeys smoking on fire on verandah. Bought a pirarucu [South American fish] lance of hard wood. On at 11 a.m., the river broader than ever. Magnificent palms, & innumerable too, a real forest of them. Splendid sunset over broad reach of river, often $\frac{3}{4}$ to 1 mile broad. Clear beautiful night. Arrd Mouth Igaraparana at 9.30 p.m. About 150 yards broad or less. Putumayo sweeping from a South reach some 500 yds broad. We are about 400 miles from mouth of Putumayo.

[On blotter, facing 19 and 20 September, beside sketch of tropical tree: Immense numbers of 'Pona' (Quichua) Ariartea orbigniana. Also of Javari (Astryocaryum) the spring palm & of Assai (Enterpe precatora). Bates lovingly calls the Assai palm the Enterpe oleracea. Urucuri attalea Excelsa were Splendid leaves & fronds, at 3–4 p.m. only a few of them. of D'Orbigny Ariartea. Orbigniana]

21, *Wednesday*

Steaming very fast up Igaraparana – it is less than 100 yards broad, but looks deep & current not nearly so strong as Putumayo. Rise of 6 feet – 8 feet apparent in mud of overhanging bush. Water clearer than than it looks – In general more like pea soup or lentil broth. In night steaming round a sharp curve vessel listed & my Winchester fell on filter, smashed basin & I cut my finger. We must be doing $5\frac{1}{2}$–6 miles an hour now in this weak current, so that at 9.30 we shall be some 70 miles up this Canal in the Woods. At 8. a.m. a good sized & lazy tributary from South bank. Name not given. 9 a.m. arriving at Indostan, some 65–70 miles up from mouth. Found prisoner heavy chain ('Bolivar', a Boras boy) crime trying to escape. The 'hands' absolutely miserable – starving. 2 girls in dreadful state & high fever. Gave Quinine. 2 lads also ill. Woman sleek & fat – the concubine. Others loading wood – 2 girls & 6 lads (one a half caste) all starving. Gave Biscuits & bread to them. Indostan has about 50 acres

[98] The names referred to are probably Marcial [Sifuertes] and Juan Cardanas: the former is the only Marcial on R.C.'s list of those supposedly on the payroll at La Chorrera; the latter, a 'table steward' is the nearest approximation to what, in R.C.'s handwriting, looks like Juan Castantos. Marcial was at a fishing station. R.C. did not always record events in the order in which they happened; Marcial could have been questioned at Pescaria.

cleared with casava [*sic*], rice, sugarcane, coca, lentils, pine, etc., etc. Passed (ruin) Santa Julia at 12 noon. Fine clearing.

[On blotter, facing 21 September:

Told that there are about 15 'hands' all told. The Chief poor white (with revolver on hip) named Sumaran. Says he needs 50 hands – he explained the chained Bolivar by saying he had tried to escape to Brazil (Escape to Brazil!) by stealing his only canoe with 'four others' & had taken a 'cup of wine'. He explained with great emphasis on it that 'he had not flogged' Bolivar. Bolivar said that he had been 'castigated'. We released Bolivar & took him on board (in new pants & cap) for La Chorrera. Left at 11.40 or 12 say.]

22, *Thursday*

At 7 a.m. in sight of high forest land in West. About 450–500 feet the beginning of La Chorrera cutting. First high land since Santarem. River swifter – Banks steep, clay, rock & soundings 38 feet, breadth 60 yds – 80 – 100. Steamed all night without stopping. Dreamed & planned a great Irish romance of the future. Interviewed James Clark of Barbados. Interviewed Stanley S. Lewis again this morning & got the most disgraceful statements about Ultimo Retiro & J. I. Fonseca[99] from him – murders of girls beheadings of Indians and shooting of them after they had rotted from flogging. Asked he wd. come with me he said yes only Fonseca had threatened to shoot him if he ever saw him again! Arrd. at La Chorrera at 12.30 & Macedo, Tizon, Dr Rodrigues and Ponce[100] and others came on board to welcome us. Also 7 Boras Indians, nude save for their bark covering, to carry our Baggage. 5 Barbadians there also to drive them. Three of the Boras show broad scars on their bare buttocks – some of them $1\frac{1}{2}"$ or 2" broad. Weals for life. This is their wealfare, their daily wealfare. All slaves. Walked to cataract with Cipriani.[101]

Played Bridge with Tizon. Macedo looks a scoundrel. The whole place is a Penitentiary.

23, *Friday*

Heavy rain in night. A young Englishman Parr[102] in Store here. Talked to him. Got in the five Barbadians in the Station this afternoon before Sr. Tizon & Mr Barnes & interrogated them. Three had 'seen nothing', two,

[99] J[osé] I[nocente] Fonseca: chief of the section of La Chorrera known as Sabana.

[100] [Juan Manuel] Tizon: Manager, or chief overseer, for the Peruvian Amazon Company. Dr [José S.] Rodrigues: attached to the staff at La Chorrera. [Francisco] Ponce: accountant at La Chorrera.

[101] [César A.] Cipriani: this fellow passenger on the *Liberal* was a civil engineer from Lima.

[102] [H.S.] Parr: storekeeper at La Chorrera.

Stanley Sealey and James Chase,[103] spoke out like men and told of dreadful things. They had flogged men and seen them flogged & killed too – often, & said so & maintained it. Tizon did not like it at all, but bore it and in evening began flattering me after dinner & saying nice things about me and how glad he was my Govt. had sent a man like me. Is it sincere or is it part of the game?

24, *Saturday*
Interviewed Dyall[104] who accused himself of <u>five murders</u> in presence <u>Barnes</u> – atrocious crimes. Bell seemed to think that everything was right, so I asked him to come with all Commission this afternoon to my room & Tizon, where we had his Statement read over and confirmed & I then called Bishop & S. Lewis to confirm and they did and we thrashed the matter out. Tizon practically chucked up the sponge and admitted that things were very bad & must be changed. In evening he complimented me – said he was very glad I had come, that the F.O. had chosen the right man. We decided to take Sealy, Chase, Dyall up with us & to confirm on the spot their charges – but late at night Tizon asked me to try & stop this & promised to carry out <u>sweeping reforms</u> & to dismiss all the incriminated men. This up to midnight & later.

[On blotter, facing 22 and 23 September:

2. Matanzas
1. U Retiro   9
4. Santa Catalina
3. [Crossed out: Abisinia] Savana
1. Oriente   S. Lewis &
3. Abisinia   Ultimo Retiro
2. Steam Launches
<u>16</u>)
3 Another man [totals + 'Another man' crossed out] Cho 19)

Headman	Donal Francis
The Baker	Greenwich [Greenidge]
Cook	Lawrence
Commission	= James Chase)
Do	= <u>Stanley Sealy (Sily)</u>)]

---

[103] Stanley Sealey and James Chase: Barbadians; Sealey was engaged by R.C. as a guide; Chase became a personal attendant to the Company's commission of enquiry throughout their journey, and Sealey joined him in this capacity once R.C. had left the Putumayo.
[104] [Joshua] Dyall: It is clear from repetitions in the Dublin Putumayo diary that R.C. was haunted by the manner in which this Barbadian had committed the crimes to which he confessed.

24th Sept 1st <u>Dyall</u> = to myself

Barnes present
After   Dyall)   before
           Bishop)   all
           Lewis)   <u>Commission</u>
                            Tizon
Tizon gives in & accepts Statements.]

Sunday 25th. Another general meeting of Commission & Tizon & myself. I insisted on acceptance of Barbadian testimony if the men did not accompany us to press their statements & <u>he made his promise in face of Commission</u>.

26, *Monday*

After yesterday's dreadful 'field day' I feel tired out – but I have practically done all I <u>can</u> do now. There are only 9 more [interpolation, extending on to adjacent blotter: + 2 slaves... actually 11] Barbadians in the Company's service – 4 at Savana – 2 Matanzas – 1 at Ultimo Retiro and 1 at Abisinia, & then King[105] at El Encanto,[106] the Arch-Murderer. 'Liberal' left for El Encanto at 9 a.m. & I bid Cipriani goodbye. His name is César A. Cipriani – Ingeniero Civil Lima (Peru). Goodbye. Sick Boras Indian (no medicines) the eighth man. Also the 'Muchacho de Confianza' [trusted boy] – I gave him a magnificent pyjama suit, for his three <u>photos</u>. Flores[107] & his woman & the 8 Boras & other '<u>muchachos</u>' (<u>Machetes</u>) went on board, with a stack of Winchesters. 7 of the Boras in Singlets & trousers – the sick man in none & no medicine either. Decided to take Sealy, at his request, up country with us. Rain & packing up. Very tired – <u>very</u> tired, very sick of everything. God help all.

27, *Tuesday*

Left La Chorrera in 'Veloz' launch[108] – Commission, Tizon & myself. Also the Mayor Domo and Bruce[109] & Garrido = 9 whites. 3 Barb – Bishop,

---

[105] [Armando] King: a Barbadian infamous for his ability to flog Indians to death.

[106] El Encanto: a Peruvian Amazon Company trading station second only to La Chorrera.

[107] [Miguel] Flores: attached to Abisinia, one of La Chorrera's sections.

[108] 'Veloz' launch: operated on the Igaraparaná river, above the cataract at La Chorrera.

[109] [Guillermo] Bruce: member of the crew (engineer) of the launch *Huitoto*, which operated on the Lower Igaraparaná, below La Chorrera. Here he is a passenger on the *Veloz*. About six weeks later he was to be used by Jiménez as interpreter in an attempt to get R.C. to 'whitewash' the notorious section chief in

Sealey & Chase – arrd. Victoria & discharged some of our grub – the lighter we are towing is too heavy. Current very strong, river deep, a deep forest river between silent walls of trees. Generally 80–100 yards broad, sometimes broader. Arr Naimenes Sucursulo at about 4 p.m. the chief Rodriguez (Colombian) & a second man Acosta[110] in charge. Found here the <u>very</u> girl Bishop had flogged at orders of Elias Martinengui & on whom that wretch had inflicted the nameless crime. She had a Baby by a whiteman, Jose Maria Twesta, who died of fever in the Caqueta, last year, so Acosta said. I told Tizon & Barnes. Former refused to investigate, threw up sponge again & said 'he accepted, he accepted'. I gave the woman tins & things thro' Bishop & we steamed on again at 6 p.m. All night in great discomfort on launch. Stopped for hours. On at 3 a.m.

28, Wednesday
Arrd. at Ocidente [Spelled with one 'c' until entry for 4 October] at about 9 a.m. Very tired, no sleep. Found <u>Velarde</u>. Torrico in charge & Rodriguez also,[111] came overland to greet us, arriving long before we did. A fine station – big house, clearing & a huge Indian <u>Maloca</u>[112] behind. Cheery boys, '<u>muchachos</u>' to clear our luggage. All of us tired, & slept most of day until nearly 5 p.m. Commission deciding on rest of route. Andokes for cigarettes at 4 & asked me to give them, looking so gently and fingering anxiously his pierced ears. He said several things to me in a soft low voice, asking questions, I thought & looking longingly. I gave him a packet of cigarettes but he did not want to go. Played Bridge this evg until 11.25 with Tizon as partner. He & I won 2 out of 3 Rubbers. The Commission talked over their plans with Tizon & Velarde asking latter many questions as to rubber production & natives of his District. He expects 500 'men' to a Dance tomorrow.
    [On blotter, facing 26–28 September:

the presence of witnesses. That, at any rate, was R.C.'s interpretation of the strange interview which occurred. NLI 1622/3 14 November 1910 (B).

[110] [Eugenio] Acosta: was in charge because Elias Martinengui had left the company, having driven the Indians especially hard to ensure that he took a high commission with him. His 'nameless crime' committed against the young Indian girl was described by Bishop in his 'Further Statement', Enclosure 1, Consul-General Casement to Sir Edward Grey, 21 March 1911, p. 4: he made an Indian boy 'insert firebrands into her body'.
[111] [Fidel] Velarde: normally in charge of La Chorrera's Occidente section. [Manuel] Torrico was standing in for him to greet R.C. [Juan B.] Rodriguez was 'Sub-Chief' of the neighbouring Entre Rios section, but there were five men with this surname on the company's books at this time.
[112] A large, circular communal house with a conical roof made with rough wood and covered with palm leaves or grass.

Saw James Chase again about flogging & killing <u>at Abisinia</u>. <u>John Brown's credit</u> 301 − 85 + £ <u>30</u>) = [blank space] Captain Whiffen[113] to F.O. claims that he had taken over this & paid John Brown the £30 − & that the money was his. To write to Chief of [crossed out: Station] Putumayo Sr. Macedo & suggest that this money be remitted to the Governor of Barbados.[114] R.C. 26 Sept 1910

'Andokes' huge erection <u>at 3 p.m.</u> − in stern asleep. Small boy on Launch.

[After arrow pointing from entry for 27 September]: Tizon assured me at dinner that since his promise before he had issued a Circular to all Sections & Chiefs saying that if any more cases of flogging came to his knowledge he would at once dismiss the employe & hand him over to the Peruvian authorities. He had issued the Circular with Gielgud he said. I said good, but that the Coy must go further & <u>prosecute</u>, not sit by with closed hands but give the evidence & <u>press</u> the charge.]

29, Thursday

Up till 3 a.m. hunting out the record of Velarde in my documents − it is a bad one. He is one of the chief criminals. I slept from 2.30–3 a.m. only after finding out about <u>Velarde</u>. Then wrote it out & put a few questions to Bishop about Ultimo Retiro & Aquileo Torres.[115] Velarde was his jailor for a long time at Port Tarma. Poor Tizon. I <u>am</u> sorry for him! but I am far, far sorrier for those wretched Indians. God help them. Tonight's dance promises to be a big thing. Lots of Indians arriving from 11 a.m. onwards − the women mostly stark naked, the men (all undersized) some in dirty pants & shirts, but mostly in 'fonos' [bark loincloths]. Many of them whose limbs are bare show clear marks of flogging − one small boy, a child, quite recent <u>red weals</u> unhealed & many other small boys show marks of flogging. There will be near 1000 people here tonight, all the population of this District. I see many faces I saw Naimenes. The dance a Success − these poor gentle creatures have few occasions like this. I photo'd a lot of them. I never saw anything more pathetic than these people. They move one to profound pity.

[On blotter, facing 29 September:
At Ocidente. <u>Fidel Velarde</u>. Dance.]

30, Friday

Another long talk with Tizon. He admits practically <u>everything</u>? The Dance stopped only at <u>5 a.m.</u> I was up in night from 2.30 till a glorious sunrise. Bishop told me that 'Francisco' the capitan [tribal headman] of one

[113] Whiffen: see notes 64 and 68.
[114] It was the Governor of Barbados who had sent Brown to join R.C. Although a Montserratian, Brown had been recruited in Barbados.
[115] Aquileo Torres: normally employed at La Chorrera's Ultimo Retiro section.

of the 'Nations' & another had come to him in the night complaining of recent grave illtreatment here – one of them even having been drowned by Acosta in the river[116] – the new method of torture being to hold them under water while they wash the rubber – to terrify them! Also floggings & 'putting in guns' – & flogging with machetes across the back. Told Barnes & Bell & they interrogated Francisco & then I told Tizon at 1.30 when he came to talk to me. He went – I sent him – to B & B & they sent for Francisco & will interrogate later tonight. I bathed in river – delightful & Andokes came down & caught butterflies for Barnes & I. Then a Capitan embraced us, laying his head against our breasts. I never saw so touching a thing! Poor soul – he felt we were their friends. Gielgud must be told to drop calling me 'Casement'. It is infernal cheek. Not well. No dinner.

[On blotter, facing 30 September:
At Ocidente [*sic*]. The Capitan Francisco tells his story to Bishop who comes to me. I send Barnes & Bell after him, Bishop having stopped him. They took his Statements & then I told Tizon who spoke nicely to me after lunch & sent him in to them. He said he would question. Tizon told me of his intention at Abisinia & Matanzas.]

OCTOBER

1, *Saturday*
October 1st. The Commission & Tizon off to see the actual method of tapping Rubber trees by the 'Labourers' of the Coy. They took Rodriguez, Torrico, Acosta to guide them, as they 'know the labourers'. They found two Indians, rubber tappers, the only 'labourers', & seemed surprised! I asked Barnes if he had not yet grasped the system – that I was surprised he was surprised. We were simply in a Pirate Camp, nothing more. The Indians the absolute slaves of the pirates who [illegible] is Velarde, then Fonseca, & so on. I stayed at home and interviewed Stanley Sealy, both on his own acts & then on the Commission. On one of the latter with Jimenez to Caquetá in May or June 1908 he was eye witness of three awful & hellish acts committed by that monster. I took down his statement almost word for word, and shall never forget the effect it produced on me. It was told with a simple truthfulness and even grace of simplicity that would have convinced anyone in the English-speaking world of the man's absolute good faith and scrupulous exactitude & controll [sic], with appropriate gesture and restraint of gesture too. Wrote out Memorandum on the stations & their personnel. Very hot day. The others returned at 1. p.m. & all did nothing till dinner, & then Bridge. Another talk with Tizon & Bell this time.

[On blotter, facing 1 October:

[116] [Eugenio] Acosta: at Occidente.

At Ocidente. At dinner time Bell assuring Tizon all must go & complete change of system.]

Sunday 2

All off some 4 miles through forest to Indian House of rubber workers. 6 there, but 2 away. Saw 4 of them loading rubber – all bore evidence of flogging, one man dreadfully scarred & further around in Hut there were 11 Indians. All had been flogged they said. Back on foot, beating launch with Gielgud. In bed early, very tired. In night Bishop brought letter from Herman Gusman.[117]

3, *Monday*

Asked Tizon & Commission to come together. Could not discuss anything in the House, as all is open & the pirates can overhear. Suggested Indian House. We went out, all pretending to catch butterflies & when there I asked Sealy & Chase to stand & deliver the appalling story of Jiménez. They did so & again a veritable tussle – this time chiefly with Gielgud who opposed much. Tizon bewildered – after another battle Royal carrying Barnes & Bell absolutely with me (& Fox, of course) we agreed to accept Sealy & Chase & that Tizon should of course dismiss Jiménez. He is in despair – so am I. Garrido called, went back on everything he said at Iquitos. A cur! I gave Tizon Gusman's note implicating Alfredo Montt, explaining its coming by Bishop last night. I told Tizon coming back from Indian House of the murder of the 4 muchachos in January last at Ultimo Retiro, by Rodriguez, Lopez[118] & the others. Played Bridge & to bed.

[On blotter, facing 3 October:

Dreadful nightmare. I yelled for help in night Waking all house! Sent Bishop down to Chorrera by launch.

I protested against feeding with Jiménez – the thrice accused murderer.

My clothes brought by Sealy at 3. When I went to pay find they have been washed by one of Velarde's 'four or five wives'! Measured stocks in 'Cellar'. 21 Holes. In 5th, holes 33" apart.]

4, *Tuesday*

Heavy rain last night, & afternoon. River rising again. At 9 to bath & found Andokes, the light boy & a little boy in their hammock outside Bathroom, all doing what Coudenhove[119] once said of the boys of Rome &

---

[117] letter from Herman Gusman: [Jeremias] Gusman (R.C. later realized that he had used the wrong christian name) was responsible to Montt at Atenas. His message is quoted in the White Diary. NLI 1622/3,3 October 1910.

[118] [Suen] Lopez: was responsible to Jiménez at Ultimo Retiro.

[119] Coudenhove [-Kalergi]: ('Condenhor' in the Special Branch's version, according to Singleton-Gates). Two Austrian brothers Coudenhove, Count

Johnston[120] of the Nyasaland Boys – without concealment! The boat servants looking on practically while these three boys played with each other with laughter & jokes! A fine beastly morality for a Christian Coy at 9 a.m. with three of the domestic servants.[121] Wrote till late last night. Aquileo Torres from U Retiro Talked to Barnes & Bell. Wrote out a lot of

Richard and Count Johann, became friends of R.C. during his time as consul in Lorenzo Marques. They were also friends of the family of the 6th Lord ffrench and the Blüchers (see notes 22 and 50). The reference here must be to Johann – known as Hans – Coudenhove (1863–1925). He had been in the Austrian Diplomatic Service in Rome and elsewhere, after which he turned his back on Europe and from 1897 spent the rest of his days in Africa – mainly in German East, South Africa and Nyasaland. In 1913 he was to write to R.C., about the 'jolly book of yours with the blue cover'; he was worried about the difficulty of ensuring that the villains, especially Normand, received 'an adequate reward.' NLI 13073, Hans Coudenhove to Roger Casement, 25 May 1913.

[120] [Sir Harry (Hamilton)] Johnston (1858–1927): later to testify at the proceedings of the House of Commons Select Committee which investigated the Putumayo atrocity allegations. He was, and still is, famed for his career as explorer, colonial administrator and author. R.C. had with him the 'first copy' (complimentary) of his latest book, *The Negro in the New World* (1910). See also the White Diary, 23 November 1910, NLI 1622/3

[121] This is one of the Black Diary entries that has provided ammunition for both sides of the forgery controversy. Casement was appalled because servants, looking on while two young boys 'played with each other', found the spectacle amusing. His reaction is distinctly puritanical; surely these lines expressing his disgust would have been erased/written over/modified by a forger wishing to give the impression that the diarist was himself addicted to similar practices. Could it not be argued therefore, that if the diary *is* a forgery then this is an example of the forger making a serious mistake?

The answer is to be found in a comparable 'mistake' made in another Black Diary on 17 April 1903, and compounded on 19 and 30 April. There R.C. recorded his distress on hearing of 'Sir Hector Macdonald's suicide in Paris'. After a singularly distinguished military career, Macdonald had become embroiled in a homosexual scandal in Ceylon (Sri Lanka) and was on his way to face court-martial charges when he shot himself in a Paris hotel. Casement was shaken by the news: 'The reasons given are pitiably sad! The most distressing case this surely of its kind and one that may awake the national mind to saner methods of curing a terrible disease than by criminal legislation.' Two days later the matter was still worrying him: 'Very sorry at Hector Macdonald's terrible end.' And again at the end of the month: 'Hector MacDonald's [*sic*] death very sad.'

It is not impossible to believe in Casement's case, that whilst addicted to homosexual practices, he did little to resist them; like a drug, they seemed to bring their own particular consolations. Moreover, in the climate of opinion of the day, it was easy – unless one were caught in the act – to divorce one's principles from one's practices; or simply to rationalize one's actions by stating, as R.C. did my Diary[122] since Friday. Several Capitans came in to be instructed by Fox in better methods of preparing latex. Called Sealy to explain to Bell & Barnes the method of collecting the Indians every 10 days or 15 days, as he had done it at Sabana, Abisinia & Ultimo Retiro. Bell thinks it is quite differently done. He got explanation from Torrico of the mode per at Occidente & Torrico says it is the 'Same at all the stations'. Bell is a queer character. He is frequently taking the explanations of these people as final. I don't!

[On blotter, facing 4 October: Aquileo Torres arrd on foot from Ultimo Retiro on way to Chorrera.]

5, Wednesday
Charlie's 49th Birthday[123] – I will write to him.
Did not write to dear old Charlie – will do so by this mail (28 Oct). Spent a lazy day, writing my notes of things, discussing with Fox & G. who are still of opinion it is a trading Coy. G's naivete delicious. It is commercial if you please 'because it buys things' (His very words to my objection but I could see no element of Commerce in the whole structure). I retorted 'so do I buy things' – 'But it sells them'. When I said, not here. ['] Yes, it sells bottles of Scott's Emulsion at Chorrera to its own staff – the Baker – at £1 per bottle.' He shut up. Aquileo Torres contd his journey to Chorrera I am told today, early morn. One less to encounter at U Retiro, thank God. Gusman arr on foot from Naimenes & reported 'Veloz' left there at noon. He arrd about 4 p.m. She came only at 8 p.m. Bishop reports Mings[124] from Sabana was there with sore feet but working. No incidents at Chorrera. I turned in without bridge tonight, tired. We are to leave in morning. Did not write much tonight. Too tired altogether. Slept till 1 a.m. or 2 & then very badly later.

to his defending Counsel, that such inclinations were inseparable from genius. Just as, in his political philosophy, R.C. moved from one extreme to another, so one can trace a change – certainly an acceleration – in his commitment to homosexual activity. As his views evolved, he passed quite near to the more thoughtful and acceptable viewpoint of those who are opposed to penetrative physical contact between those of the same sex: that a homosexual is 'handicapped', but with a difference. The difference is that, unlike the blind and the deaf, he may not recognize that he is handicapped. Casement might have had difficulty, though, in recognizing that condemning the act might make it even more necessary to respect those of that inclination who divert their energies into higher things – thereby perhaps releasing their genius. Those who accept the genuineness of the Black Diaries should have no difficulty with the apparent contradictions in their author's views. Sexuality was just one area of ambivalence in R.C.'s many-sided life.

[122] my Diary: first specific reference to a diary; see note 129.
[123] Charlie: the eldest of the three Casement brothers.
[124] [Joseph] Minggs: a Barbadian attached to La Sabana section.

[On blotter, facing 5 October: Aquileo Torres on to Chorrera.]

6, Thursday

Always <u>cold</u> Coffee at these abominable stations. <u>Cold</u> & <u>late</u> rarely before 7 & often nearer 8.

Left Occidente at 9.20 a.m. The Staff standing to see us. The Cholo man-servant Pena shook hands with me gratefully – this for a bottle of Jameson I gave him. Shook hands all round but no farewells. Many Blue Emperor butterflies – splendid things, lots of others. Measured the 'stocks' before leaving by myself, see page 13 small green book & up to p. 19. Same for notes on this day written in the Launch. We had one fine passage of what Tizon said was a Chorrera at low water – took us all our time to get past. Passed Emeraes Rion about 4 p.m. Nothing of interest all day beyond the butterflies and my reflections, if these could be called interesting which I doubt. I am wondering how to convert Fox & G to a healthier frame of mind. Arr. Puerto Peruano at close on 7 & up to the Shelter house with Tizon. Dined on board & then on shore to sleep at 8.30 in this House. F & G one room, Tizon & I the other. I like Tizon.

7, Friday

Heavy rain in night & on to this morning. Up at 6 a.m. but did not leave till 8.10. How these Peruvians mismanage things. This tiny launch could have been easily off by 6.30. On the Congo we should have left at 5.30, firewood & all. Nobody of the crew gets regular meals, or rations. Scraps are hoarded. I had to give my private stores both today & yday to the 3 Barbados men, altho' one of them is the Coy's servant (Chase) & Sealy is supposed also to be chiefly theirs – only Bishop wholly mine. So, with the Steersman, table boys, wood boys, etc, all are hungry & <u>always</u> hungry & get no regular meals but 'bits' over that Garrisi the Steward chooses to spare them. Again today <u>magnificent</u> display of Butterflies – beats anything I've seen yet. For most of today see Note Book (green) 20–27 & my following notes. Arr Ultimo Retiro at 4 p.m. Jiménez & his staff the greatest set of villians yet. Concubines everywhere. The stocks in place of honour amidships – the house built like a ship – a Pirate Ship. Each room named after the Captain, '1st Officer' etc. I am in [blank space]. The bows front river – the thick stockade of basement walls (16') rises 2' above Verandah & makes the bulwarks. A sentry at night. Warned Bishop & B's to sleep together & no girls!

8, Saturday

A sentry, I think, pacing all night – someone certainly shaking the ship. Please God I'll shake this ship of state to its bilge. We are going to have a demonstration of the 'cepo' [stocks] today.[125] The black hole, too, with its trapdoor. The vile, squalid place is filled with women & concubines of all ages & is a den of vice and degradation. 18 women making steps to privy under direction of a 'whiteman'. 3 Naked as born, rest dressed – but all women. How paid? Nothing in Store. Examined Edward Crichlow[126] – another tale of shame. Also of brutal ill-treatment of himself by Aurelio Rodrigues[127] and F. Velarde.[128] Had Barnes & Fox to it. It took all afternoon – also raid to Japura & invasion of Colombia, a truly fine proceeding for an English Company, in <u>May 1910.</u>

I wrote all day nearly – very tired indeed. Macedo ordered the raid to Colombia. This alone warrants his dismissal from the Coy's service.

[On blotter, facing 6–8 October:

On 8th Oct at Ultimo Retiro. Measurements of one man & a woman. The man's name <u>Waiteka</u>, 'the fearless skeleton' of my Diary,[129] who denounced the '<u>cepo</u>'. <u>Age about 35–40</u>. Weight, say 120 lbs. Height 5'6". Chest 35". Thigh 17". Calf 11 $\frac{1}{4}$" – (his ankle in cepo just fitted.) Biceps 9$\frac{1}{2}$" Forearm 8" Stomach 32.

<u>Woman</u> Theorana by name. Age say 22 yrs. Weight 104. Height 4'7". Chest below breasts 31". Stomach 33". Thigh 19 $\frac{3}{4}$. Calf 12$\frac{1}{4}$. Biceps 9$\frac{1}{2}$". Forearm 8".

<u>Edward Crichlow</u> Very damaging Statement. Capture of 21 Indians in Colombia and 3 Colombians.]

---

[125] For a fuller description, see White Diary entry for this day.

[126] Edward Crichlow: attached to Ultimo Retiro under Jimenez. The frankness of this Barbadian's testimony, despite attempted bribery, led to his accompanying R.C. when the Consul-General left the Putumayo.

[127] Aurelio Rodriguez: one of R.C.'s 'seven monsters'. When R.C. returned to Iquitos in 1911, he was disappointed to discover that this man was the only one of the named accused awaiting trial.

[128] F. Velarde: (see note 111). Scotland Yard's typescript (as published by Singleton-Gates) has Fidel Velarde, while R.C.'s original (PRO HO 161) has F. Velarde. Is this just a question of a typist getting a bit too familiar with the substance of his text? By the same, or similar, token, the number of inconsistencies in the printed version of R.C.'s report circulated by H.M.G. makes one wonder about the standard of civil service copy-editing at the time.

[129] my Diary: one of four precise references to a diary, and the most important because it quotes accurately from the White Diary. NLI 1622/3 8 October 1910 – 'I was smiling with pleasure that this fearless skeleton had found tongue...' The three other references to his diary appear on 4, 21 and 29 October; what is probably another reference occurs on 14 November. It has to be said, though, that R.C. also writes of 'my Diary' in his 1903 Congo diary, and no parallel 1903 document has come to light. And in the White Diary he writes, 'No time for diary today'. NLI 1622/3 1 November 1910.

<u>Sunday 9 Oct</u> All of us off to Meritos Indians. One family makes this Nation. I photo'd all of them at once. Road made by slave labour, no pay, food supplies. Monkeys, etc. Butterflies & all. (<u>Gave food to Indians</u>). Swam river & returned to Ultimo Retiro.

10, *Monday*
Took name of one Indian boy Riaquéro – flogged by Velarde whom I think of taking home if possible. The Commission, all except Bell, out to forest. I stayed with him. Gusman arrived from Occidente with 3 more loads of ours – 18 hours behind the Indians he came with. They had already started from home this morning. No pay at all. Commission returned. Fox & Barnes thoroughly disgusted at the floggings they had seen traces of – one on a tiny boy of 10 or 11 – 'Cut to ribbons', Barnes says. They photo'd him. My eye is very bad indeed, left eye and I have it bandaged with [crossed out: Carbolic] Boracic lotion & the Dr. of Hilary's stuff. Turned in early with wet bandage over eyes. Took details of Crichlow's raid across Caquetá to Colombia. Twesta died up there he says – the husband of the unfortunate girl at Naimenes, I think. Heavy rain in night.
    [On blotter, facing 10 October:
<u>Riaquéio</u> X Riaqueyo – <u>Naimenes</u> below <u>Occidente</u>.
                    the boy in red jersey is a boy of <u>Francisco</u>.
    Told Tizon & Gielgud that the Barbadians intended to claim compensation and that I should support their claim. I called <u>Crichlow</u> & Bishop.]

11, *Tuesday*
Heavy rain delayed our leaving Ultimo Retiro for <u>Entre Rios</u>. We are to start now after lunch – & stop at Puerto Peruano tonight instead of going on today to the Indians' house in the forest. Rain stopped at 10 a.m. I am far from well, my left eye very bad. Pig Kille[d] 'Bridget'. Stern morality of the place that she was at once taken out & shot! – Playing with Fox! Jiménez saw us off toward his camp. Pity we cannot wave his head, the scoundrelly murderer. Steamed down river to Puerto Peruano. Left Ultimo Retiro 1.21. Arr. P. Peruano at 4.34 = 3H & 13M @ say 6 miles p.h. = 20 miles – it may be more. Found about 40 Indians from Entre Rios waiting for us. Camped the night there. Fires etc below house. Indians sleeping there, sent down to Chorrera for more food. All these Indians flogged too, but not so badly as the Occidente or Retiro ones. Heavy rain in night. An Indian recently flogged, within 30 days, by Barbolini – the white executioner at O'Donnell's.[130] Shows himself to Bishop who showed him to Fox.

[130] [Andres A.] O'Donnell: in charge of Entre Rios section. This man was as cruel as most of his fellow exploiters of the Indians. However, his Irish surname which has a prominent place in Ireland's history and mythology – led R.C. to be somewhat inconsistent in his attitude to him.

12, *Wednesday*

Left P. Peruano at 7. a.m. Bruce on launch to Chorrera. Indians the most dreadfully willing carriers in the world. The 'road' atrocious & such as it is all due to the Indians' slavery. Trees down, bridges made, saplings made, steps often 100 feet high up & down inclines, all by these poor patient beings. I will pay my carriers anyway. Got to Monones – deserted Indian house – on road & lunched. A 'blanco' there named Barbolini with mule & horse. Fox & Bell on them. On to Entre Rios arr about 3.15 – total distance from Puerto I should say 12–14 miles. Soon after Peruano steep hills & streams all to Igaraparaná – then space & then the river to Cahuniari. So the steep hills & heights about 100 feet above Igaraparaná are the divortium aquarium [watershed] between Japura & Putumayo. Entre Rios in midst of fine plantations, a circular clearing about $1\frac{1}{4}$ miles diameter, largely cleared & planted. O'Donnell far the best looking agent of the Coy we've met yet, honest even & certainly healthy. Has been shot at often – even here on river bank bathing. Turned in early without dinner. Martin Arana here, said to be a brother of Julio Arana.[131]

[On blotter, facing 12 October: Barbolini]

13, *Thursday*

Bell already again gone astray. Thinks Jiménez 'all right' in spite of the evidence of his crimes. This not to be regarded now, because the Indians at R 'seem to like him'. I am disgusted with the lack of character & humanity of these shifting, vacillating men. It is not a Commission at all.

Bad night. Liver deranged badly. Took medicine. Bishop spent one year here – flogged and flogging he says – once ordered by Barbolini to shoot an Indian & refused & even the muchacho refused to do so. Bishop says the Colombians did treat the Indians much better than the Peruvians. He saw it. Armando King murdered Justino Hernandez at Loayza's direction,[132] so he says. Visited Rubber Store – a great deal of Rubber & very big lumps & loads. The cepo here has 24 holes & one head hole in centre. Must weigh their loads. All furniture in my room made by Bishop including the door to 'sitting room' – he got nothing for it, but had to go on Commissions too. Then got Chase up & took his Statement of all his term of service at Abisinia, the most awful things happening right up to three or four months ago. Perfectly atrocious. Took all morning at this. Heard O'Donnell lying to Commission. Afternoon Bishop & to Cahuniari with him to write down further Statements. Evening Bridge & bed.

[131] Martin Arana: "a brother of Julio Arana" – I think it means a half-brother (by an unwedded woman); possibly only a cousin.' NLI 1622/3 12 October 1910.

[132] Justino Hernandez: a Colombian. According to Armando/Alphonzo King's Statement of 10 November 1910, King shot Hernandez in self-defence, having been told to do so by [Miguel] Loayza, chief at El Encanto.

14, *Friday*
Busy writing all day. There is to be an Indian 'ball' tonight – but it is
raining & I don't think they will come. The Manguari is beating its
summons. Got Sealy in to confirm Whiffen & Celestine Lopez & others
in H documents.[133] He does so in some cases but not in all & he & Chase
show that some of Broga's[134] statements are lies.

The Dance afterwards – about 500 Indians, O'D says. I should say 350
at outside in to it. Bathed in Cahuinari.

15, *Saturday*
'You buy these with the rubber we produce'. Indian Chief looked thro'
glasses [field-glasses] like the entrancement by Una.[135] Weighed rubber in
store and photo'd a lot of carriers of rubber. Interviewed Pinedo[136] (with
Bell) to confirm his statements to Sealy of the recent brutal murders by
Aquileo Torres on march & at Ultimo Retiro. Told Pinedo to tell Tizon.
Busy writing and talking to Indians all day. Took measurements of one &
gave away small things. Bathed twice in Cahuniari – only 3 feet deep now
or less – it rises another 3–4 feet in flood. A narrow ditch about 8–10 feet
deep (at highest bank) and about 20 feet broad. Played Bridge with Fox &
won Rubber.

Turned in early.

[On blotter, facing 13–15 October:
Barbolini then cut the Indian's head off himself. Chase second Statement. Sealy in to confirm Whiffen. Pinedo]

Sunday 16 Left Entre Rios for Andokes. Many streams. Some bigger than
Cahuniari, & lovely water. Slept at Muinanes house, deserted & a nightmare in night. Rain too. We have about 40 Indians. Picked up crumbs.

17, *Monday*
On from Muinanes House by atrocious 'road' thro' forest at 8 a.m. A
lovely river named [blank space] the clearest water yet, and then a big,
deep river. Bathed in both. Indians got a little beans at starting & at 11.30 a

[133] Celestino Lopez: an overseer who would, it had been hoped, confirm (with
others) the truth of the depositions collected by H[ardenburg].

[134] [Joao Baptisto] Braga: a Brazilian who, when joining the company as an
overseer, had witnessed his section chiefs, Aguero and Jiménez, kill eight bound
Indians. See note 93.

[135] Hallucinogens were frequently used by the Amerindians of the Amazon–
Orinoco area in Shamanic rituals. One such potion, derived from the *Banister-
iopsis* (liana tree) produced visions, such as those described in the parallel entry
for 15 October (B) in the White Diary. It is possible that *una* here is linked to the
Quichua verb *umuna*, meaning to practise witchcraft.

[136] [Eusebio] Pinedo: of Entre Rios.

pot of rice. Enough to give each man about 3–4 ounces of it. They scoffed it in a brace of shakes. They picked up the crumbs from the table again – tiny scraps of biscuit – like birds. All beg & beg for <u>food</u>. On & passed a Muinanes house that Normand burnt & killed its people – so Andokes says. Heavy rain in afternoon, a deluge came on: Indians made umbrellas of palm fronds. Trees much bigger, at last, about Andokes.[137] Arr. there in deluge 3.30 or 4. Normand absent on a 'correria' [round-up of runaway Indians]. Did not expect us. Had sent for. Bustamante rec'd us.[138] Cannot go down stream, save with 4 guns guarding. Normand arr. 5 or 5.30. A rifle shot & he came! A <u>loathsome monster</u> – absolutely filthy. Played Bridge & turned in at 9 p.m.

18, *Tuesday*

7 <u>Harems arrived</u>. Normand's Harem arrived <u>2.30 a.m.</u> & tried to get into his room where Barnes & Bell were! I up & saw it all. They had his tula[139] & other things. He had 'run' on the road. Up at 6.30. Levine[140] is still out at Normand's house – only James Lane[141] here now. Will see him today & sent for Levine. Told Tizon I would leave tomorrow for Entre Rios. James Lane again at 9.30–11. Again disgraceful things revealed & brutal murders. An Andokes man flogged to death last month at La China.[142] Later on Westerman Levine who arrived – He is a blackguard, but I made him speak. He lied first & then admitted all. I told Tizon & brought him in to the confrontation of the two, when Lane forced Levine to admit his lying. A disgusting day. Found 'cepo' covered with palm thatch. Two prisoners sent off previous day by Bustamante. Down to stream. A dance in evg of the Boras Indians who brought in <u>enormous</u> loads of Rubber – some of them 140 lbs weight I fancy. Women & children. Several women & <u>tiny</u> children flogged.

---

[137] In his Black Diary it may not always be easy to distinguish clearly between Casement's four different uses of 'Andokes': as a place/section, as a language, as a tribe, or as an individual member of the tribe (see also note 73). Any confusion can be eliminated by consulting the Dublin diary, NLI 1622/3 (e.g. 30 September, 14 October, 15 October (a), 21 October).

[138] [César] Bustamante: deputized for Normand at Andokes (Matanzas) section of La Chorrera agency.

[139] *tula*: a canvas bag, worn like a rucksack, in which rubber was transported manually.

[140] [Westerman] Leavine: a Barbadian under the command of Armando Normand. His testimony against his section chief was among the most damning – imaginative torture, beheadings, burials whilst alive, burnings, multiple shootings.

[141] James Lane: had to testify on three occasions, partly in order that differing versions of events could be cross-checked.

[142] La China: The station where Normand lived, about 30 miles from Matanzas.

19, *Wednesday*

The Boras Indians despatched with Normand's rubber at 6.30. I followed at 7 with Bishop, Sealy & James Lane (Lane & Levine both discharged at my request). On road found a 'boy' of Matanzas with rifle lying on road in dying condition. Has been 12 days out without food to look for the 'wife' of Negretti[143] who had 'run away'. I tried to help him on & fed him, but he could not walk over 50 yards without falling. So I left him at last under shelter with my umbrella to keep off the rain & sent Sealy on to get 3 carriers to go back & help him on to Muinanes where I decided to sleep. Then an Andoke woman with heavy load of rubber absolutely incapable of walking, so I laid her load down & helped her on to Muinanes. My 3 Indians came in at 5.30, turned back by Negretti, who refused to allow the sick 'boy' their way. Had sent him to Matanzas. But he cannot walk half a mile! Negretti is expected & B says will insult me! – purposely.

[On blotter, facing 16–19 October:

5 Hours march – took us 6¾) Total distance
5 Hours march = about 6 Hours) 28–30 miles

Very heavy rain storm at 2.30 – 3 p.m. Poured a deluge on us in the forest.

James Lane & Westerman Levine at <u>Matanzas</u> 18 October 1910.

From Matanzas to Entre Rios 19 Oct but slept at Muinanes owing to the sick boy & Andokes woman ill on road]

20, *Thursday*

Normand came to Entre Rios (without Levine) who passed on road to Puerto, & stayed the night. Tried to talk to me to convince me of his gentle treatment of the Indians & to make me change my 'assertions'. I said, 'I make no assertions.' Left Muinanes House at 8 a.m. or 7.45 a.m. The beast Negretti arrived at 7, bringing up the rear of the fabrico caravan.[144] 42 people, all except 3 women & <u>tiny</u> boys with small girls too. All carrying heavy loads. Four women left sick, including my poor old woman unable to proceed. The Boras left at 5.15. I followed at 8, leaving Lane to guard the sick women & inform Barnes (by letter) of the state of things. Passed Negretti & the Boras rubber carriers, & on to nice stream near the Savana where bathed & breakfasted. On at 11 – fearful road. Ten [?] sent out by O'Donnell just past Indian house & in at 1 a.m. to Entre

[143] Negretti: listed in the company records as Adan Negreto; one of Normand's chosen lieutenants: 'vicious-looking, thin half-caste from Moyamba, I should say'. NLI 1622/3, 21 October (after a – deleted – second heading 'ENTRE RIOS. FRIDAY, 21st October, 1910').

[144] fabrico caravan: R.C. used the term *fabrico* for the consignment of rubber being brought in by a group (cf. 'This was Normand's fabrico, the first part of it' NLI 1622/3 18 October 1910 (B)).

Rios. Met by Fox & O'Donnell. Very glad to see both. Latter quite an angel after Normand.

The poor Rubber caravan arrived at 5.15. Exactly twelve hours, the beast Negretti bringing up the rear. He drove them on. <u>Hiti</u>, <u>hiti</u>, ['Go on, go on'] without pause – & Fox got only two photos of them. He stayed to sleep & eat. They to be all night in open.

21, *Friday*

Negretti did not turn till 8 a.m. on road to Peurto [*sic*]. God help these poor people. I am writing up my Diary[145] since Monday. He slept & got food here. They lay in the open. Then some stragglers came at 10.30 or 11. One tiny kid of a boy & others. I photo'd several but they were in fear. One boy had 37 kilogs on his head. I photo'd him & weighed it. Then just before breakfast a poor being staggered in & fell, in a faint almost. He lay groaning & saying he was dying. I sent whiskey & food & got him into the store on a rug, & weighed his rubber – 50 kilogs! Not a scrap of food with it. The man lay like a log. Then another while we were at breakfast, bent double & feet dragging, but he passed on. No one to help him! Then Normand himself. Wonderful flight across 'Chacara' [ranch/rubber plantation]. Then he came. 2 shots & then the Commission, with news of the boy & the 'old lady'. Both better. Thank God. Normand tried to talk to me. I left him to Fox. Stayed in room, writing till nightfall. Played Bridge till 9.30 & turned in.

22, *Saturday*

No water hardly in Cahuniari. Up at 5.20 decided to stop Levine going down with Normand to Chorrera. Asked G. tell Tizon to give the order. (N. green with rage). He had decided, I am sure, to bribe Levine to retract & then he, Macedo & Levine would be free to corrupt all the 8 Barbados men who are waiting my arrival. 8 of them to be there by end of month. I further determined send Bishop to Chorrera to spike their guns. Got B. off ostensibly to send me up things I need & with letter for Macedo. Normand off at 9 a.m. & Bishop too. Will Levine return? I fancy not, altho' G. says T. gave positive orders. Tizon must find me an abominable nuisance, but I cannot help it. I will take no risks, & playing with the Devil I'll not go Spades & leave him to double. <u>Heavy</u> rain at 1 o'clock & got heavier & heavier. Down to stream at 4.30 – risen only about 10". Rain cont'd in night. Huascar & Lincoln[146] <u>playing</u> by kitchen. Played 3 Rubbers Bridge

---

[145] my Diary: third specific reference to a diary.

[146] Huascar: '"Huascar", O'Donnell's favourite boy...' NLI 1622/3, after deleted second date heading for 21 October 1910. Lincoln: Spanish-speaking 'trusted boy' (*muchacho de confianza* – see note 87) to Manuel Torrico. Ibid.

– Lost 2. Turned in 11 p.m.
[On blotter, facing 20–22 October:
<u>Heavy rain</u>.
He was a thin fellow with [crossed out: legs] arms like a child's.
Heavier Rain. Break up of recent dry weather, Fox thinks. Glad of it.
Sandflies dreadful – the rain will clear them out.]
Sunday 23. Rain all night. Levine <u>should</u> return today. <u>Nous verrons</u>. Some
of the men came up. No Levine. At 2.30 a letter from Bishop saying he
refused to come as I fully expected & that Normand & he were plotting.
Tizon sent imperative order for his return at once.

24, *Monday*

Heavy rain all afternoon & y'day & night & some of today. Cahuniari
nearly full again. Some of the Boras & Andokes – some 60 passed back
today. Two very <u>sick</u> old men. No scrap of food! I gave tins of meat to
several. I want to get Doi a Boras boy home with me.[147] A large wood ibis
at lunch sailed round & alit close to House. Fox & I saved it from being
shot. It was like a stork, a big white bill, white body & broad black ends to
the wings.

Extraordinarily tame, it was within 20 yards of the house & wheeled off
twice & returned. I tried to photo, but failed. It then soared off higher &
higher. The Indians said a bad sign! Tizon got letter from Normand
refusing send back Levine, alleged a bad leg! A lie. Tizon knows now
the trouble begins. We had long talk till 7. I told him all my fears. He sees
their force & agreed to go to Iquitos with me if necessary. Played 33 hands
& 2 Rubbers Bridge.

25, *Tuesday*

The Commission & Tizon left for Atenas. Atenas, the city of Montt. I
stayed with O'Donnell. Wrote Gordon, John Gordon,[148] of the 33 bridge
hands last night. Think I'll go over to Atenas tomorrow to lunch & return
in evg. Hot today after the mountains. Read thro' last night & today E. P.
Oppenheim's 'The Yellow Crayon'.[149] 4 Boras (a young man, splendid
type, a boy of 12, & 2 women) came down, guarded by 1 armed footpad
from Matanzas, with 2 loads of rubber. I photo'd them & gave a tin of
meat. The boy terribly <u>flogged</u>, all over his backside & thighs. Enormous
weals. A beautiful boy. The young man fine fellow – <u>very</u> light skin.

[147] See footnote 154.
[148] John Gordon: NLI 1622/3 diary of same date (b) has 'I wrote a note to
John Gordon with the Bridge record of last night.'
[149] E[dward] P[hillips] Oppenheim (1866–1946): prolific, best-selling novelist
of thrillers and espionage stories.

Heavy rain in afternoon, a deluge. Rode with O'Donnell round his chacara – it is some 300 acres of felled forest, about 50–60 acres planted with yuca, maize, sugar cane. Old Indian house in midst. Sick (skeleton) brother of [crossed out: Muinane] Muitudifos chief in maize. Splendid deer brought in. Weight (cleaned) 36½ kilogs. Also squirrel. Fine Muchacho carried deer, beautiful limbs, thighs & chest – light coffee colour. Rain much in night.

26, *Wednesday*
Left E.R. 8.5) 2.45. Left Atenas 3.) 2.54.
arr Atenas 10.50)   arr E.R.[150] 5.54)
  I off to Atenas with O'D. It is reckoned 3 Hours. We went very quick & got there 2H. 45M. I reckon it 12 miles. Past 2 fair-sized tributaries of Cahuniari. Bathed Atenas in Cahuniari – splendid stream there 8 feet deep. Strong current. Old Bridge 10–12 ft above river which rises to great volume very quickly O'Donnell says. Montt is insignificant looking little wretch. The one-legged man here. Rubber is very thin – Putumayo sausages – M says 24 tons. Had 790 men. Now about 250. Says Indians 'very bad' – cannot coerce them. Not enough empleados [workers], only 4 all told. About 12 muchachos. Station in ruins. Enormous clearing, but <u>no</u> planting to speak of. Very badly flogged specimen – old thin man – called by Sealy. Left Atenas 3. Terrible rain, all way nearly. Tried Banana leaf – caught blue & brown butterfly, magnificent specimen. Walked very fast back & arr. just before 6. Dinner & turned in. Reckon it 24 miles today – O'D says fully or some more. Many <u>sandflies in night</u> – awful biting. Could not sleep. Commission leave for P.P. [Puerto Peruano] tomorrow direct. I go down with O'D on horseback.
  [On blotter, facing 24–26 October:
  Punia shot by <u>muchacho</u>. O'Donnell said my letter to Bishop had been <u>delivered</u> & then Tizon showed me <u>Normand's</u>. Bathed at 2–3 in Cahuniari with a boy dreadfully flogged. Was a carrier to Andokes. I noticed then, but now <u>worse</u>. Awful scars. A nice lad of 17 about & six tiny boys – gave all soap – they revelled in it.
  <u>2 p.m.</u> [facing 26 October: On their way to [crossed out: Mata. .] P. Peruano, the footpad carried only his gun, one woman a basket & tula, the others food I presume of sorts. The footpad gave them a small bowl of cassava & bean broth – cold water!]

27, *Thursday*
Leaving E.R. today to return to P.P. & get Veloz tomorrow mg for Chorrera where the <u>big</u> row begins. Normand, Macedo & Co there with

[150] E.R.: Entre Rios section.

their beautiful Levine. Tizon & I to fight. I go down today with O'D, I on Horse, he on mule. I made him run y'day sometimes but he could beat me on the hill. I am going down Hill! 47th year & he is only 27. Rather weary, but more from bad night. Read 'Yellow Crayon' again in night. Left Entre Rios about 8.30, I on horse, O'D on mule & to Monanes house where we lunched, Barborini cooking it. Luggage by 'muchachos' – one very fine lad, fair skin & nice face, about 19. Met 'Muchacho' of Occidente at ¾ hour from E Rios with letter for O'D. On & met Commission at Lunch & then on together to P.P. over Nimue, a fine stream. Heavy rain. Atenas carriers of Commission absolute skeletons – photo'd four [crossed out: boys] skins of bones. Gave meat to them, all the tins I had left, after Sealy kept for himself & Chase. Played one Rubber of bridge & turned in at 9 p.m. in same room of house. Arevalo in charge of Launch. Hear that Normand etc went by land. A batalon [= *batelón*, literally 'canoe'] with rubber is lying in port. Caught three splendid butterflies on road. O'D & Sealy in fingers. Beauties.

28, *Friday*

Left P.P. at 7.18. Before going, the beautiful muchacho showed it, a big stiff one & another muchacho grasped it like a truncheon. Black & thick & stiff as poker. On Boat Lincoln & Occidente muchacho doing same.

		H	M	Miles
Left P.P. 7.18. Arr. Occidente 11.10 ½ =		3	52 ½	25
Passed Naimenes	3.11 – slower current	4.	00	20
" Victoria Beach	5.28 ½	2.	17 ½,	11
Arr. Chorrera "	5.37		8 ½	1

Fr om P. Peruano to La Ch: Roughly   57 miles
River about 7 feet lower at Port Victoria, but below rapid at La Chorrera it is fully 16 feet down. Bishop brought a written statement of all that has transpired since he left me. Amusing in its way. Told Tizon & talked with him till near midnight after one rubber of Bridge.

29, *Saturday*

Boy of Launch also stiff, y'day & again this morning, pretending to do it to small boy with huge thrust. Swam in river which is fully 16–17 feet lower – big sand islands showing in mid-pool & the fall sunk to very narrow confines. It has gone down 16 feet [*sic*] I found. Bought things from Store and wrote up my Diary[151] since Entre Rios and got various papers in order. Normand is here but goes back to Andokes & will not sail in this 'Liberal' so Tizon says.

[151] my Diary: fourth specific reference to a diary.

All goes well. N. wanted to go to Iquitos by her, but Tizon stopped it. <u>Very</u> hot day. I bathed in river in morning. The Indian boys are swimming all afternoon. Lovely bodies out in the stream & the girls too, paddling logs across to the islands & lying there awash by the hour. After dinner talked two Risigaros – muchachos – one a fine chap. He pulled stiff and fingered it laughing. Would have gone on & other too (keys on chain in left pocket) looking for <u>cigarettes</u>. Awfully exciting & stiff stiff work. Thought of Joao & Flores.

[On blotter, facing 28 October:

This day last year 'Vaseline' at dear old Icarsby – <u>To think of it!</u> – opposite 29 October: This...]

[Sunday, 30 October] Lovely day. River dropped a foot today. 'Liberal' will not be able to get in here. <u>N</u> returned to Andokes early <u>at 2 p.m.</u> by launch. <u>Doi</u> to come down. Sabana Barbados men arrived. Got Greenidge's[152] contract & papers from <u>Fox</u> & wrote a good deal.

31, *Monday*

Saw 'Andokes' bathing. Big <u>thick one</u>, as I thought. Called Batson[153] & took his Statement, a dreadful one. Then Sur Rubber arrived. Huge loads – lots of Indians, fine, handsome types of Naimenes Indians of Sur. Chose one small boy, a dear wee thing named <u>Omaríno</u>. His weight 24 Kos in <u>fono</u> & his load of rubber 29 Kos. Weighed a load 63 $\frac{1}{2}$ Kgs.[154] & another 50. A fine muchacho named Arédomi wants to come. Very fine lad –

[152] [Siefert] Greenidge: the Barbadian in charge of the bakery at La Chorrera.

[153] [Evelyn] Batson: a Barbadian, he made a statement which did much to incriminate others, whilst (unlike the testimony of many other Barbadians) to some extent he failed to incriminate himself. He had been allowed to give up the task of flogging Indians 'as he had rheumatism in his right hand and wrist, and could not wield the lash.'

[154] Arédomi and Omarino: the two Indians acquired by R.C. and taken by him to London. Omarino (later 'Hamurummy') was bought for a shirt and a pair of trousers; Arédomi (elsewhere 'Pedro' or 'Ricudo'), a married man, then proved a greater attraction than Doi, an Indian whom R.C. had, for some days, hoped to take away with him (see diary entries for 24 and 30 October). The corresponding entry for 31 October (B) in the NLI 1622/3 White Diary is the only one in Dublin which has been thought by some to suggest that R.C. had the proclivities attributed to him by his enemies; most, though, would say that, if the Black Diaries did not exist, the thought would probably not occur to the reader.

Fresh from the jungle, the two Indians were not particularly at ease in London at the close of the Edwardian era, and they created the odd problem for R.C.'s landlady, Miss Cox. Soon they were sitting for their portraits before leading portrait painter of the day, William Rothenstein (1872–1945), and they were entertained between sessions, by the artist's son, future Director of the Tate, Sir John Rothenstein (1901–92). But the time soon came when, partly because of

Would like to take him. He followed like a dog all afternoon. Gave breeches to him. His beautiful coffee limbs were lovely. Promised to take him home if I could manage it. Spoke Tizon. Bought Omaríno. More Rubber in evg from Sur, 9 or 10 tons of it. Miranda[155] at head. All slept under House – his Indians. I looked & saw several & one boy caressed hand & shoulder. River falling enormously, down a foot today. Equal Bridge. Won 2, lost 2. Stiff asleep ones.

NOVEMBER

1, *Tuesday*

River still falling in morning. Arédomi I saw for a moment and then no more. Fear he has been sent off. Very heavy rain in afternoon <u>pouring</u> & River began to rise almost within $1\frac{1}{2}$ hours of it. Took Statements of Sidney Morris, Preston Johnson & Augustus Walcott.[156] All from Sabana. All wish to go away with me. Dreadful deeds by Normand. 'Huitota' arr up River from S. Julia with Aguero & his Rubber & Alcosta of Oriente & his Rubber & Ocainas Indians. I was too busy right up to 6 p.m. with the Barbados men to see any of it. Met Aguero & Alcosta at dinner. Velarde also down from Occidente – going home with me! Told Tizon of Batson's Statements and of Morris on Normand & of Aurelio Rodriguez. Saw big ones on Indians at dinner & before.

2, *Wednesday*

Up early. Ocainas & others about, & some of the Sur Indians & Miranda's. One boy with erection, fingering it long & pulling it stiff. Could see all from verandah. <u>No fono</u> – only grey twills. The River has risen fully 3 feet in night & is a good deal bigger now than when we came on Friday. Sent

---

R.C.'s constant need to travel, a choice had to be made between committing them to a boarding institution and taking them back to more familiar surroundings in South America. The Irish poet and nationalist schoolmaster, Patrick Pearse, had offered to board them at St Enda's, the school he had founded in Rathfarnham, near Dublin. R.C., though, decided to take them with him on his return to Iquitos in 1911. He never got round to settling his account with the painter Rothenstein. It was eventually settled by R.S., when the double-portrait was rediscovered.

[155] [Carlos] Miranda: chief of La Chorrera's section Sur. R.C. learned of his 'cutting off "the old women's [*sic*] head and holding it up as an example" to the rest.' NLI 1622/3 15 October (A).

[156] Sidney [Sydney] Morris, Preston Johnson and Augustus Walcott: all three Barbadians had been under the command of Fonseca. Walcott had been born in Antigua of Barbadian parentage.

Bishop at 6.30 to look for Arédomi. Fear the poor boy was sent off with the Naimenes men y'day with one Bowl for his Rubber! Bishop reports he is over on the Chacara cutting firewood for the launch – & soon I saw him turn up smiling. I interviewed Five Barbados men today. It took me all the day. Their Statements cover a lot of ground and in some cases show grave illtreatment of themselves, particularly by Normand. Further infamous acts of cruelty against Normand and Aguero & the rest of these monsters & infamous treatment of Clifford Quintin,[157] by Normand. Wrote till 5 p.m. or later. Mapp & others back to S. Catalina to get their things down. Acosta, Rodriguez & others from Occidente. A holy gathering. Very little rain today, but still it passed St Swithun's without rain. Walked after dinner & turned in early.

[On blotter, facing 31 October–1 November:
Evelyn Batson's Statement 4
  Hallow Eve
Walked till 12 with Arédomi X & Others.
Sidney Morris X Preston Johnson X Augustus Walcott X]
[On same blotter, facing 2 November:
James Mapp 3 Alfred Hoyte 2 Reuben Phillips Clifford
Quintin X Allan Davis 1][158]

3, *Thursday*
Lovely morning. River risen some 7 or 9 feet since 1st instant. Cataract Huge now. Davis too. Chase told Bishop he saw it. Rajina – her name.[159] Huitota woman. Arranged with Macedo to take Arédomi. He has no

[157] Clifford Quintin ['Quintyne', according to the signature at the foot of his statement]: had suffered punishment floggings, in one case of fifty lashes. He confessed, after having been challenged, to the murder of several Indians.

[158] James Mapp, Alfred[o] Hoyte, Reuben Phillips, Allan Davis: the 'X' against a name in the Black Diaries has been taken to signify a sexual encounter, which it lacks here. It might have signified that the Barbadians indicated were illiterate, were it not that only Walcott is shown as having made 'his x mark', and there is an unexplained X against Arédomi's name. Was R.C. simply checking that relevant details in this comparatively short diary had been dealt with in the much longer one which he was writing with much more care and attention? Another explanation could be the checking of company accounts against the Barbadians' names (see entry for 7 November and 6 November in NLI 1622/3). Given R.C.'s known working habits, more than one reason could make up the X explanation. The numbers are probably to do with dependants likely to accompany the men, should they leave the Putumayo with R.C. at the end of his investigation – or with their order of priority, when it came to departure.

[159] Rajina: Huitoto woman given by Macedo to Aguero 'to swell his harem' NLI 1622/3 3 November 1910 (A).

objection. Gave Garece £5 for the recent journey & all his trouble. Arranged Sealy to stay with Barnes & go on with Commission at £7 per month & be repatriated by them. Bishop says the Atenas carriers of rubber not allowed over this side. They came in during evg & even long after nightfall. These were the lights we saw on the opposite hillsides last night. They did not want us to see their starved condition. So after a march of 13 hours (two days with rubber) these poor boys are hunted back without food. We saw the skeletons at [crossed out: E.R.] P. Peruano. Last night Aguero took away the sweeping woman from this to add to his Harem. A shame & disgrace. Told Fox & Commission at breakfast. Busy all day over A/cs of the Barbados men & with Tizon on the subject. He offers to take away 25% as their back a/cs on ground of overcharge. They accept gladly. Also the 50 cts. per £ for the men with sterling contracts & the <u>medicines</u> altogether wiped out. Then to pay compensation to the men grossly injured by the Servts. of the Coy – Crichlow, Quintin, Dyall & Augustus Walcott. Very busy all day at this & wondering what is the best course to take. I think the interests of the men should be the first & that seems to demand acceptance.

4, *Friday*

A poor sick man at Sur called me '<u>Mare Capitan</u>' [a good chief] & patted me. Commission went to Sur at 7.30. I followed at 8 with Sealy carrying coat etc & Arédomi small tula. Took names of the buried at Cemetery. Found an orchid on Road. Arr Sur 9.30 & bathed Arédomi carrying clothes showed huge. Told him bathe too, and he stripped. <u>No fono</u> on – Carbolic soap – glorious limbs, a big one. Back & pineapples. A decayed Station. Big cepo in the stockade is under post. Miranda alone. The road $\frac{1}{2}$ trees, some 20,000 at least. Counted nine to the yard & 2 miles of this = 30000 saplings. Returned with Sealy & Arédomi at 4. Heavy rain on way & thunder. Arédomi's wife & brother came. Gave Salmon to the family. She wants much to go with him. It is a problem. I can't take her & fancy it is scarcely fair to take him, altho' he is most anxious to go & says she will be well cared for by her mother.

River still rising – the ledge of rocks across the fall nearly covered now. Velarde & Juanito Rodriguez at dinner & talked of walking. Bishop says Juanito threatened to flog an Occidente Capitan I dared to give a knife to!

The reference to compensation in this entry tends to jar, when one considers the crimes that these men had committed. R.C. was inclined to forgive atrocities, when the agent complained that he was only obeying orders. There is an irony here, in that R.C.'s own defence at his trial was to be assisted by John Hartman Morgan, who later became adviser to the American War Crimes Commission at Nuremberg, where the same arguments for mitigation were rejected.

Told him he was to say nothing to us that 'The Englishman' had nothing to do with the Indians & they were not to speak to us. <u>The brute.</u>

5, *Saturday*

Bishop says some of the Indians have broken into the Stores & stolen – dug a hole & took rice & food & fled in Greenidge's boat. They think it is the decent Boras Indian with the child's face who wanted to return to his wee son at Abisinia. Commission to return from Sur today. Expect 'Liberal' today. Barnes, Bell & Fox arr. before lunch, G & Tizon stopping for an Indian Dance at Sur till tomorrow. River rising fast now. Again rain today – but not so much. Many of O'Donnell's Indians are down from Entre Rios – sent beforehand to help carry the rubber over from P. Victoria. Such a waste of their lives after all they have suffered. Read over several of the B'bados men's statements to them & got them signed by them today. Find Allan Davis was sent to Encanto y'day just to guard an Indian boy sent there for a case of Soap! A nice use to put civilized beings to at £7 per month. They are hunting for the runaway Boras Indian & those who are supposed to have stolen the things. They may be some of Velarde's Occidente Indians of whom many are down also waiting for that fabrico. River rising all day & night. Bathed with Arédomi in hill stream. Second time.

<u>Sunday 6</u> Did more of the Barbados men's statements this morning & got their signatures. Rain came today again, fairly heavy. No sign of Liberal. Arédomi and his wife together all the time now. Bishop wants me to take them. River rising – well – cataract a line of snow. Barbados men from S. Catalina with Fonseca himself came down by the road & crossed over. Bathed.

7, *Monday*

[Boldly over-written: This is <u>Sunday. One day out</u>] Took further Barbados signatures this morning – S. Morris, Preston Johnson & Augustus Walcott. Then looked more & more into their accounts and compared the prices charged them with those charged to me at Iquitos by The Iquitos Trading Coy & I find in some cases nearly 400% on top! Rice is 200% on top and Butter some 350% Nothing less than 150% to 200%, and a great many over, & then the Iquitos price represents itself fully 150% on European price. It is monstrous & I fear I cannot agree to the men accepting 25% reduction, for their sake as well as for other reasons. It is a pity, but I think I have no right to compromise or accept anything <u>without</u> permission of F.O. At night a lunar Rainbow, 7.30 to 7.50 in the East & then rain. River rose since last night 5–6 feet & is now almost to the steps where it was on our arrival on Liberal. It had fallen 20 feet below that. Rain came 7.45 & dissipated the lunar rainbow. Played Bridge at 9.30. Won 1st Rubber with Tizon. Lost 2nd thro' Fox's bad play. I went once No trumps. Barnes doubled (24) I redoubled (48) & he redoubled (96). I got 4 tricks = 384 below. Aces easy! Wild ducks on diminishing edge of the sandbank at 5 p.m. B'bados went to shoot them & killed one with a Winchester but did not get it.

8, *Tuesday*
[First version crossed out: Lovely morning at 8 a.m. Reading Lt Maw again about the Indians & Putumayo in 1827.[160] Hope 'Liberal' comes today. They are trying to put the 'Alvaringa' on barge 'Putumayo' into the river today – the high waves are awash of her.]

<u>8 Tuesday – made a mistake of a day since Saturday!</u>
    River dropped since y'day evening, best part of a foot up to noon today. O'Donnell arrived from E. Rios by Veloz, bringing letter from Crichlow asking me to recall him. 'Huascar' arrd with O'D – & smiled on me with big left erection. Butterfly. Very hot afternoon. Fonseca going away for Sabana. Saw his head muchacho & tulas paddle across at 12 noon & then Huascar with butterfly. Expect 'Huitota' surely today, and hope Liberal also today. O Spent a lazy day. Walked to hills in evg. by stream & at 6 Arédomi came with a plume head-dress quite well arranged, for me as a present.[161] Poor boy. He had been home for it – far off all day to show his gratitude. A little rain, but not enough to influence river – it is still falling steadily. It rose 16 ft from Tuesday to Sunday – 5 days.

9, *Wednesday*
Did nothing all morning. No sign of 'Huitota' or 'Liberal'. What has become of both. Such a waste of time as they manage to get thro' here! I am heartily sick of this place. Rain at 1.15. River fallen a lot – fully 2 feet in night – and still falling. The Entre Rios rubber coming over all y'day & today from P. Victoria – about 10 of these poor Indians are down here at the miserable job. Velarde has disappeared! Gone back to Occidente I presume. 'Veloz' left early today for Ultimo Retiro & to bring Crichlow

---

[160] Lt [Henry Lister] Maw [R.N.] (b. 1804): descended the Amazon from Peru in 1828. R.C. was reading his *Journal of a passage from the Pacific to the Atlantic*, J. Murray, London, 1829.
    [161] A plume head-dress: which Arédomi was later to wear when sitting (standing, actually) for his portrait by William Rothenstein. They wore 'feathers... and not much else': comment by the artist's son. Tape recorded interview of Sir John Rothenstein by R.S., Beauforest House, Oxfordshire, 27 January 1984. The artist had expressed a similar recollection: 'he arrived at my studio with two young savages... Their bodies were a rich golden colour, and their dress simple – but a few brilliant feathers strung together. Such models were rare.' W. Rothenstein, *Men and Memories: Recollections of William Rothenstein* 1900–1922, London, Faber and Faber, 1932, p. 170.

down. He wrote me he was not safe there & wished to return. Looked at mules – they made 10 journeys today to the port. Misused dreadfully. Called Tizon, Barnes to see. 'Liberal' arr. at 5.45. John Brown arrd. – useless brute. A big mail from home, nothing interesting in these surroundings. Mrs G.[162] as usual good beyond measure. All well. Davis, King & Dyall from [entry concluded on adjacent blotter: Encanto. John Brown from Barbados]

[On blotter, facing 6–9 November:

Sunday 6th Nov. New moon on 2nd Nov. 4 days old.

Lunar Rainbow at Chorrera. 7.30–7.45 p.m. seen first by me who called Fox, Bell, Barnes, 8. Tizon, Macedo & F. Velarde all saw.

9th October [sic] 'Liberal' arrived. Mail from Home, but really no news of any interest and nothing in papers about Putumayo.]

10, *Thursday*

'Liberal' brought some Peruvian soldiers under a Captain Delgado, to go to Encanto. Their passages not paid! As I fully expected all along. Very busy day. Went over remaining Barbados Statements & got them signed. Took King & J. Minggs two Statements. Both liars! Told Tizon feared could not accept his offer without first reference to F.O. & begged him to refer to Coy. He has read full P/A from Iquitos house. What right have they to grant it? He says Columbia [sic] is going to invade the Putumayo & is making a road from Pasto. Peru getting ready, Prefect writes him. Also Lima 'Commercio' has article about forthcoming enquiry into the crimes here. Attorney General has moved for it in consequence of Deschamps[163] letter to Barcelona. Why not have done this when all the facts were stated in Iquitos. Went on board Liberal & saw C. Reigado[164] & two new men from Coy – 'agricultural experts'!!! Burke there.[165] The three Barbados men, J. Mapp, R. Phillips & A. Hoyte returned by the 'Huitota' without going to S. Catalina, owing to conspiracy to murder them on way

[162] Mrs G: see note 12 ('G' in the Putumayo is Gielgud).

[163] [Emil] Deschamps had made similar allegations to those which had been made by the Anti-Slavery Society. R.C. is plainly irritated that it took the publication of his letter in the *Comercio* (Lima, 7 August 1910), and a related article of 10 October 1910 (quoting Deschamps), to make the Peruvian Attorney-General order a judicial enquiry into atrocity allegations which had long been ignored.

[164] C[aptain] Carmino Reigada: For much, but not all, of the time R.C. placed considerable trust in the captain of *Liberal*.

[165] ['Guillermo'] Burke: Australian, said by R.C. to be engineer of the steamship *Huitota*, but shown in the company pay list as being solely in charge of the launch *Audaz*, on the Cahuinari. In fact, company employees, including section chiefs, were often shifted from one post to another.

by Blondel[166] & Aguero, so they say. I told Tizon & he heard Mapp's Statement. The men say there was a plot to kill them, Batson says to frighten the Commission from going to Abisinia. I was busy all day with the Barbados men's accounts until 5, when on 'Liberal'. The men very anxious for my accepting the offer of 25% reduction, I can see. Gielgud agrees with me, before the Coy, that matter ought to be referred home to his Board. Learn of the Revolution in Portugal & flight of King Manoel & his mother to Gibraltar by Brazilian Dreadnought, S. Pello. The Peruvian soldiers under Delgado left for Iquitos. They do <u>not</u> pay their passages. Gielgud admitted it & Bell said they appeared as debtors.

11, *Friday*
Another long day – The rectified a/cs of the Barbados men brought to me by Tizon. They show, when gone thro' a gain of some £650 to the men, who accept gratefully, again going thro' them, checking & finding errors, and the men putting forward further claims that will bring the amount up to over £800. Incidentally I find that while much of their indebtedness arises from gambling debts with Chiefs of Sections & other employés, the notes they gave for their debts are sometimes forgeries by the Peruvian who presents them. Specific charge of this made by Levine against F. Borbor[167] now at Andokes, also against Bustamante. Tizon present asked him to take Levine to Macedo to repeat the charge. This he did. Tizon brought two signatures of Levine's – the 'forged' one & an admitted one. They resemble each other, an expert could decide. I think personally it is <u>not</u> Levine's signature – so did Batson who was present when Tizon brought it. Davis thought it was Levine's. The whole thing is disgraceful, another illustration of Macedo's principles of management – the booking of gambling debts & carrying them to debit and credit through the Coy's books. The cheating of the men has been colossal and the deliberate neglect of any attempt at decent control or protection of their interests. <u>All</u> the men now say they will go home, save Francis, Greenidge & Lawrence the Cook[168] – also King, of course, who returns to El Encanto. He is a cut-throat scoundrel. I shall leave the men complete liberty of choice. There will be another & I hope the final row. It cannot be helped, for I cannot act as arbitrator, or bind the hands of my government. I have no authority to do it.

[166] [Armando] Blondel: third in line at Abisinia section, where Abelardo Aguero was chief.

[167] F[rancisco] Borber: 'Barbolini' mistakenly given by Singleton-Gates, whose source evidently had in mind Maximo Borbolini (usually spelled Borbolini by R.C.), O'Donnell's bloodthirsty lieutenant at Entre Rios.

[168] [Philip] Lawrence: cook at La Chorrera; a Jamaican, aged only nineteen.

12, *Saturday*

Again a lazy day. I am awaiting developments. The a/cs of the men will, when completed, be brought to me to hand out to them. I shall refuse & tell Tizon it must be done by the Coy, that I am not paying the men but he. Had a long talk with him after lunch. He was very frank and said he was going to do his duty & polish off Zumaeta, Arana & all, that he was now 'a member of the Commission'. He begged me to go to see the Prefect and talk to him 'frankly' and urge him to come round to this. I said I should do so. Velarde is not going by this steamer, but by next. Torrico is in charge since 1st. Got all the a/cs back from Tizon of the 19 Barbados men. They show a gain to them of some £850. Not bad. Told Bishop I should advise none – that they were to choose for themselves.

Up the hill & bathed with Arédomi in upper river.

[On blotter, facing 10 November: <u>Liberal's mail</u> Joseph Minggs, A. King recalled Dyall and <u>Allan Davis</u> who returned from Encanto y'day & got all remaining Statements signed except Greenidge & P. Lawrence.]

Sunday, 13 Nov. Sealy came to report that Borborini [*sic*] (O'Donnell's man) had cut a Sur Indian's head open last night with a fillet of firewood. Found the man & sent him to Tizon all bleeding – via G. Tizon dismissed Borborini on the spot to go home by this steamer! Good. Very hot day. Looked at papers & decided <u>not</u> to take Mrs <u>Arédomi</u> home & told Miranda about her who pledged to see her safe.

14, *Monday*

A busy day. Gielgud & Tizon with the a/cs of the Barbados men all morning. The men accepted the gift of 25% back and the matter is settled thus. There were incidents I did not like but they must pass. Crichlow came down from U.R.[169] with Jiménez who came to me after lunch to protest against the 'Truth' charges with Bruce interpreting. A queer scene indeed! – recorded more fully elsewhere.[170] A very hot day – river falling fast. Some Entre Rios Indians also down here now – altogether then there must be 70 of these beings here. I am thinking all evening of possible trouble in Iquitos on arrival there with all these Barbados men. Their evidence constitutes the case against Peru, more really than against the P.A. Coy, & I fear Tizon & the Prefect acting on T's advice will try to nobble these witnesses. I told Barnes of my fears at night, talking to him till near midnight. Told him I should put matters to a test tomorrow by saying I wanted the passage tickets made out to Javari in Brazil – & if they object I shall know the plot that is in view.

[169] U.R: Ultimo Retiro section.
[170] recorded more fully elsewhere: probably a reference to the White Diary entry for the same day, 14 November, 1910 (B) – (NLI 1622/3). See also this diary, note 109.

15, *Tuesday*

A very anxious day. My last in Chorrera. I told Gielgud after lunch that I should like the passenger tickets for the men <u>all</u> to be optional either for Iquitos or 'intermediate ports'. He went to see & came back from Macedo to say this wd. be done provided the Brazilian authts. allowed it. I visited the Brazilian Customs officer on 'Liberal' (Mathias) & he said there was no objection at all. I then again saw G. & made sure the tickets were as required. I had told Bishop in the morning of my fears & that I thought it might be very well to land him & all the men at the Javari to await my coming down river on 'Athualpa'. I could go on to Iquitos & collect their money & pick them up on my return in a few days. I spent a very anxious day, meditating all sorts of ways of getting away, but there seems no way except by 'Liberal'. I finally decided to go by her with all the men, & with this option of landing at Javari all may be well, & I can leave all or most of the men there if necessary. Heavy rain all afternoon, & got cooler. River began to rise again, the sandbank showing. Talked to Burke after dinner & he like Bruce gave the show away completely. Played Bridge for E.D.M. testimonial & got £1. 18/- (G. £1. Fox 10/- & Bruce 8/-). Called on Mrs Macedo & bade her goodbye.

16, *Wednesday*

River has Risen 6" inches in night. My last hour in Chorrera. Poor Donald Francis[171] came & cried & cried in my room, wanting to go home with me to his old mother in Barbados. Poor boy. I <u>was</u> sorry for him. A scene with Dyall & his 9th or 10th wife, she refusing to be parted from him & trying even to get on board the 'Liberal' but turned back on gangway. All settled & all on board at 9.30 a.m. & off at 9.45. Last I saw of Chorrera was the group of Tizon, G, Barnes, Bell & Fox with Sealy, Chase, Francis & Greenidge waving adieux. Sealy & Chase came to bid me goodbye after drinking. Four of the Boras 'wives' with them. The skipper C Reigado gave me assurances in front of Tizon, Gielgud, Barnes that the men could land where they pleased. So off on my last fight! Passed Port Tarma at 11.30 – naked Indian women, the last I shall ever see probably. Came to the great highland forested ridge at 12.15. – it is over 500 feet high, fully 600–700 I think, a curving sweep, three or four parallel ranges of forested upland. Jeremias Gusman on board, and Garrido the

---

[171] Donald Francis: this Barbadian, who worked at La Chorrera, was listed in the company's pay list as a 'peon'. Although 'servant' was the intended meaning, it will not have been lost on R.C. that what he was investigating was the traditional form of Peruvian slavery: peonage, or debt-bondage.

traitor, sent back by the Commission. Eclipse of the moon, just as it rose at 6 – half covered. Became total eclipse at 8.[172] Lovely night.

17, *Thursday*

Very handsome Cholo sailors on board. One is a young half Indian moço of 18 or 19 – <u>beautiful</u> face & figure – a perfect dusky Antinous,[173] would make a fine type for H.W.'s[174] statues of the Upper Amazon.

Steaming down [crossed out: Putumayo] Igaraparana & at 10.45 saw Putumayo & entered it about 10.50. It is <u>very</u> low & a huge sandbank blocks mouth of it. Called Arédomi to see it & explain thro' Bishop – He calls it Haumia – & Igaraparana is Cottué. He came to my room & I showed him many pictures of Bates' book[175] & others to his great delight. It got up I think – was thick anyhow. Passed <u>Puerto</u> Parena at 12.12 on left bank. High ground, cleared but house gone as at <u>Arica</u> at mouth of Igaraparaná. On to Puerto Parena, another abandoned site on left bank & then at 4.30 to Pescaria, where the <u>beast</u> Cerra[176] came on board. Sandflies & other horrors. At 5.30 off again down the Putumayo of the Palms. Wondrous palms on left and right. The river often $\frac{1}{2}$ to $\frac{3}{4}$ mile or more broad, nearer 1 mile I think. Captain says about 20–25 feet deep. Current slow, not over 1 mile I should say. Splendid moonrise. Turned in at 9 p.m. & slept well.

[172] Eclipse of the moon: In support of the argument that the Black Diary is a forgery, Hugh Casement has provided RS with a detailed analysis of this event. He concludes that the important thing would seem to be a comparison between moonrise and the times of the eclipse as recorded in the diary. 'I can't reconcile them unless the boat was in a different part of South America! Or did Casement see the moon disappear at 18.55 and assume the show was over? The other possibility is that my computer is more accurate than the forger's...'(letter, 7 October 1996).

[173] Antinous [*c.* AD 110–30]: The Roman Emperor Hadrian's favourite male companion. After his early death by drowning, Antinoüs was deified by Hadrian and many statues were made of him.

[174] H[erbert] W[ard] (d. 1919): The traveller and sculptor was a close friend of R.C. for many years, though Ward refused to sign Conan Doyle's petition, believing the Black Diaries to be authentic. One of Ward's sons had been christened Roger Casement Ward. The family was so appalled by R.C.'s conduct that they petitioned parliament for his Christian names to be changed to Rodney Sanford. Then they could still call him 'Roddie'.

[175] Bates' book: see note 71 for 20 August.

[176] Cerra [Cerron]: R.C.'s handwriting misled both typists, the one employed by Scotland Yard, and the one acting on R.C.'s behalf. The former gave 'Curran'; the latter gave 'Cerra'. The 'beast' in question was Jose Cerron, who was at a fishing station down river from La Chorrera. Careful examination of the manuscripts removes any doubts.

18, *Friday*

In Yaguas River 9′27 = 3′45° to Recreio. Steaming fast down Putumayo to get to Yaguas River today. 10.8. entered Yaguas – a fine river about 250 yards broad at mouth. Called up all Barbados men to see what they wish to do. 1.53. arrd at small palm House on right bank. This is <u>Recreio</u>. River evidently rises 12 ft. No current to speak of at all, just a deep ditch where level depends for miles on that of the Putumayo.

. On to Trunifo an hour later & left it at 4.15 & got to Putumayo 7.35. Many palms along Yaguas banks, especially this beautiful <u>Assai</u> & the queer looking popunha [palm tree] – but not popunha. No moon to speak of. Arédomi at 7.30 nude <u>torso</u> beautiful bronze for medicine against sand flies. Gave it to him & rubbed it on his lovely body, poor boy. Young pilot prentice again on Deck. Arranged (I think) to leave the men at Javari.

19, *Saturday*

We arrived at the 1st Brazilian post at 2 a.m. & anchored alongside & got papers & then on to the second. 1st the Custom House at 2. & then the Military post till 5. 3 hours lost – We bought wood at the post. £3 per 1000 billets – 1½ tons. Coal in Iquitos is 38/- per ton of 1500 cwt, only. It is called a ton of measurement but works out at 15 cwt.

10.50 a fine tributary on right bank, 150–200 yards broad – 'Urute' river – & then at 11.20 a Brazilian trading house, served by two launches from Manaos at the mouth of this fine deep river – its own river, no one else allowed up. This house has Ticuna Indians as its slaves Reigado says. Then a Columbian [*sic*] main hut & clearing on a parana [tributary] and we went down it six miles. An old negro, his wife & baby in a canoe going down stream waved to us. More huts & we bought firewood at one & saw several other houses on left bank of Putumayo – also a biggish canoe going up with a sail, and then another with four Indian or cafuzo [mixed-race] paddlers, a woman & a boy steering. A dark night & we got to Amazon about 1 or 2 a.m. = 76 hours down from Chorrera – or about 620 miles I should say.

Sunday 20 Nov. A bad night with skin eruption like heat lumps. In Amazon & stopped off Colonia Rio Jano till daylight. Then on to Amatura (Matural) where we bought firewood. I on shore & visited church – no padre for 3 years, many children to baptise. Left Matural 8.15 a.m. Hear 'Javari' & 'Athualpa'[177] have both gone up, one of them on 14th. Captain's steward an Indian boy of 19, broad face, thin. Huge <u>soft</u> long one. Also Engineer's steward, big too. Steaming up Amazon all day. Very slow & tired. 4.30., 6 Ronsocos on bank, quite close. They stood watching us 40 yds off.

[177] Javari and Athualpa: Booth-line steamers.

21, *Monday*

A big sea-going steamer with green & red lights passed down last night at 9 p.m. Fear it is the Javari gone down. We stayed a long time at Boa Vista getting firewood from about 3 a.m. to near 6 a.m. this morning. On in drizzle. Deck hands washing decks – then lovely Cholo types, three big ones. Cholo Steward too, (young 18) enormous in new bags. To decide now if the men for Javari or Iquitos. 10. a.m. Stopped Palmeras. Beautiful soil, forest etc. 1 Hour stop. On at 11 – & at 11.45. passed Belem with church & many buildings. River Calderon – & Launch. On to Cacaus river, 80 yds, & alvarenga [a lighter] & canoe two Indians 12.15. Same owner. River for 6 Hours in big Steamer. Mafra (Peruvian of Italian descent) the owner.[178] Our pilot Manoel Lomas has been up Cacaus 6 hours in big launch. Says Ticuna Indians work the rubber. On slowly, the firewood very bad, the Captain says. Steaming very slowly indeed. The river deeper than I thought – it has risen a great deal since end of August. Shall not get to Javari till 10 p.m. the Captain says, but at 11 we are not there. Turned in. Made all arrangements for landing 14 men, 4 women & 4 children at Javari. Bought a lot of food for the men from Reigada.

22, *Tuesday*

We got to Javari at 1 a.m. Reigado told me the 'Javari' S/S had gone down four days ago, and the 'Athualpa' had passed up on 13th! Landed all men & women etc. Young Brazilian Customs officer very kind & pleasant face too. He embraced me! It is very good of him to take the men so willingly. Got off at 3 a.m. Dyal [*sic*] tried to sell his son, or rather the Chief Engineer tried to bag him! I stopped it. One of these Peruvian beasts, the 2nd Cook Bishop thinks, threw his puppy dog over in the night. Bishop is very sick about it. Took 3 hours from Javari to Tabatinga!!! Only 6 miles. River rushing down. Brazilian troops & young striped sergeant on board, off at once. At Leticia delayed for 2 hours by the lazy Peruvian brutes there. River risen about 8 feet since Augt. Captain says he must get to Iquitos on Thursday. I doubt it. The Peruvian Comisario & Lt here wanted seize Liberal to go back to Brazil to catch 4 soldiers who ran away last night. Good soldiers. On at 11.15 after 4 hours delay over this folly. Got wood & popuncha peaches at a clearing at ancient Loretto. All on shore & then on at dinner time steaming badly. Turned in early, seedy.

---

[178] Mafra...the owner: the Peruvian-Italian, like other 'Solimoes magnates', as R.C. termed them, owned quite a lot. With stores and huts for the workers, 'A fine-tiled house...every proprietor here his own river, with a steam launch snugly stowed away.' NLI 1622/3, entry for same date.

23, *Wednesday*

A hot day. Steaming past Peruvian chacaras all day. Some good ones like San Tomás. Saw mills. River rising. Read Johnston's 'Negro in the New World'.[179] Very good.

After dinner spoke to Steward Indian Cholo about frejol [= *frijol* literally 'food'], & he got some for me & then another thing. It was huge & he wanted awfully. He stood for hours until bedtime & turned in under table – also small party Engineer's youth & pilot's apprentice too – all up – till midnight & then at Yaguas & saw two Yaguas Indians in their strange garb of Chambira [= *Chambera*, prickly pear] fibre died [*sic*] red. On at 1 a.m. after wood & palm at Yaguas. Three Yaguas Indians on board, I think. Steward's Cholo very nice. Smiled & fingered & hitched up to show.

24, *Thursday*

Due at Iquitos today. Will it be peace or war? Gave small boy Victor Tizon 2S/P. Very rainy morning. Cleaning brass work. Cholo steward did mine & Captain's & showed it again huge & stiff & laughed. Smiled lovingly. Got cheques ready for Iquitos. All hands cleaning up. Engineer says we shall be in Iquitos by nightfall. I doubt it greatly. At earliest 9 p.m. & probably midnight. Slept better last night but fear attack of gastritis is coming on as in Pará. Stopped for wood at Murupa, opposite the mouth of the Napo & at 3 on again – very hot. Nice Indians at Murupa. Many small chacras [chacaras]. Passed mouth of Napo at 3.30 & slowed down as cannot get to Iquitos tonight in time for landing. It is 8 hours steaming from Napo. Will be there this morning. Steward showed enormous exposure after dinner, stiff down left thigh. Then he went below & came up at St Thereza where 'Elisa' Launch was & leant on gunwhale with huge erection about 8" – 'Que, [illegible], Senor?' Garrido watching. I wanted awfully.

25, *Friday*

Gave Engineer's small boy 2s/1 & Steward [name?] £1.0. Asked my Steward his name. Ignacio Torres[180] he said & I asked him come to Cazes' house. Arr. Iquitos at 7 a.m. On shore to Cazes & then to Barber with Aredomi & Omarino. Met Sub-Prefect there who gave me warm

[179] Sir Harry Hamilton Johnston: see note 120.

[180] Ignacio Torres: is mentioned in the Dublin Putumayo diary as performing the duties of a 'guide'. NLI 1622/3, 4 December 1910. A different sort of relationship, somewhat one-sided, is indicated in PRO HO 161. Other allusions to it occur occasionally until R.C. leaves Iquitos on 6 December. It is known that R.C. tried to get in touch with Torres later, as a letter from D. Brown (see note 187), partly about photographs, states that 'up to the present I have been unable to find the boy Ignacio Torres' and adds that he is said to be in the town [Iquitos] and 'we should be able to find him'. NLI 13073, 29 April 1911.

welcome & then told me an 'Auto' had been opened & all was to be investigated! Cazes says the Judge from Lima[181] is a fraud: that all is a sham! Visited Booth & down to 'Athualpa'. Dr. of her an Italian gave me a medicine. Saw Reigado & his Cholo sailors – all had been drunk & he put them in the hold, the brute, 'to sweat it out'. Saw Ignacio Torres on the deck looking at me. Visit from Prefect A.D.C. & also from Pablo Zumaeta but I was out. Spent pleasant day & was very tired at nightfall. Lots of mosquitoes again & I could not sleep well. Talked to Cazes till fairly late. I am very tired of the C's & Iquitos. 'Athualpa' does not sail until 2nd or 3rd. I hope will catch Clement at Manaos.

26, *Saturday*

Called on Prefect with Cazes. Long interview from 10.15 to 11.40 a.m. Told him much & promised to send Bishop to him on Monday at 10. He says the Commission of Justice will sail next week. A Doctor goes too – and officers & soldiers. In Govt. Launch. Doubtless 'America' which is being fitted up already I see. He says they will <u>punish</u> as well as reform. Asked me for help to see that the Commission went straight when there. Heavy rain at 6.30. Went to dinner at Booth's house & played bridge. Rain all time. On board Athualpa again & saw young Customs officer from Manaos – great. I will indeed, only a boy almost – <u>pure</u> Indian too. Also fair-haired pilot boy, tall & nice, from Pará. Took my room No 1. 'Athualpa' leaves only on 4 Nov., Sunday next.

Will miss 'Clement' at Manaos. She sails on 7th.

<u>Sunday</u>. 27. Off in '<u>Manati</u>' pic-nic to <u>Tamshiako</u> 25–30 miles up river. Prefect brother & Lt. Bravo[182] & all, etc., etc. Pleasant day. Again told Prefect many things of Putumayo. Saw Indian cook boy on '<u>Inca</u>' – enormous, lying down & pulled it often. Huge, thick, big lad 17. Also <u>Ignacio Torres</u> & told him come 8 a.m. tomorrow. Saw him twice. Told Pinheiro come too. Told Bishop get Lewis.

[181] the Judge from Lima: initially Judge Valcarcel was appointed to lead the Peruvian Government's commission of enquiry into the Putumayo allegations. He was, however, replaced by Dr Romulo Paredes, another judge. R.C. sometimes had more difficulty with foreign names than he had with Iberian languages. When he first attempted to write down Valcarcel's name (28 November), he thought it was 'Belcarce' (interestingly altered by the Special Branch's typist, or by Singleton-Gates, to 'Valcarel' – almost correct). R.C.'s second attempt (1 December) is a considerable improvement: 'Valcarce'. It too became 'Valcarel' when it made its way into typed copies. (Cp. R.C.'s versions of the name Laurens/Laurenson/Lorentzsen: 20/24/25/31 December.)

[182] Lt. Bravo: Peruvian Naval Lieutenant; one of the 'foreign guests' on the picnic. Cp. NLI 1622/3, for same date.

28, *Monday*

Heavy rain all night nearly & this morning pouring. 9.30 No Bishop, no Ignacio, no Pinheiro & no Lewis! What is up? Ignacio Torres came at 10 a.m. Clean & nice. Gave him £1 & a portfolio for Captain Reigado – asked him to return with the cover. He has not been to Brazil. Running [?] from Iquitos – in bare feet. Gets £3 per month. Bishop late. Sent to Prefect at 10.30. only. He returned 11.15. had told him <u>everything</u> – (in 30 minutes!) & I saw John Brown & S. Lewis & will send them tomorrow. Saw Ignacio Torres below at 2.30. looking for me with my portfolio, J. Clark with him. Door shut, so he went on to the office, poor boy. I should like to take him too. Saw him later when with Cazes & he said he was coming at 8. a.m. tomorrow & then saw him at band. Also saw <u>Viacarra</u> who shouted at me again & again & looked very nice. He was talking to Bishop. Manuel Lomas the Pilot stood me a drink of ginger ale & begged me to visit Punchana & see him. Regretted church not here in Iquitos. Played Bridge with Cazes & Harrison[183] & walked with latter till 11.30. Fireworks. Cazes says the Judge Belcarce[184] is very well spoken of locally as honest.

29, *Tuesday*

Expect Ignacio this morning – am on look out for him. He came at 8.10. with my portfolio & I sent him for cigarettes. He brought wrong kind & I gave him 2/- [2S/-] & patted him on back & said all [?] to go & be 'Hasta luego' [See you later] & he left at 8.20. Last time of meeting probably. Will go to Manoel Lomas[185] today. Expect Jeremias Gusman this morning to send to Prefect. He came at 10 & I sent him along with Brown & Lewis. Prefect not in. Told by orderlies to come in 3 Hours. They went, all three at 1–3 & waited but Prefect could not see them & told them to come tomorrow at 10. I walked to Booths & on to <u>Punchana</u> & to Manoel Lomas house & then talked to Vatan about things. He said my coming was a blessing to <u>all</u> (not only to Putumayo, but to the whole Department [ )]. That the Prefect had acted in a very bad way over the Dutch Expedition & that if it were not for my official position I'd have been shot in the bush & now they were afraid of me & my evidence & wd. do something. Walked after dinner to Booth's House & then with Harrison to Square. Walked round it. Many beautiful types Indian & Cholo. Saw <u>Ignacio</u> at Merry go Round & pulled. He rushed & approached. Another Cholo with him. Waited longer hoping till 10 p.m. & home to bed.

---

[183] Harrison: on the staff of the Booth Steamship Company.
[184] Judge Belcarce: Judge Valcarcel. See note 181.
[185] Manoel Lomas: 'Our pilot' – see entry for 21 November, above.

30, *Wednesday*

Saw 'Liberal' Cholo sailors going home at 5.30. All smiled. Wrote to Vice Consul at Manaos to send by 'Clement' the 7 Barbados men who wish to be repatriated. Sent for John Brown to go to Prefect & Lewis & Guzman. They all went as far as I know at 10 a.m. but have not seen one of them since. They are lazy swine. Lent J. Clark £3. Saw Vatan again & asked him for Memo: on the Dutch Expedition. Went on 'Athualpa' to lunch. Afterwards back to the house in atrocious heat. Called on Mrs Prefect and told her a good deal of Putumayo. Heavy rain at 6.30 all night. Spoiled all attempt at going to the Cinematograph at Alhambra. Walked round Square with Mr & Mrs Cazes. Atrocious dinner! Played Dummy bridge – a very stupid party. I am as sick of the Cazes as a man can be! & of Iquitos. No sign of Bishop since this morning. I will pay him off tomorrow and finish with him. The 'Rio Mar' left for Manaos with Philip & J. Clark. I wrote down twice to Manaos about the men there.

[On blotter, facing 29–30 November:

Ignacio at Merry go Round 10 p.m. Last seen.

John Brown & S. Lewis to Prefect. He took their Statements in writing.]

[On other side of same blotter, facing 1 December:

'Rio Mar' left.

Guzman to Prefect but told come today.]

DECEMBER

1, *Thursday*

[Inserted at top of page: I fear the 'Athualpa' will not sail until Monday 5th, certainly not till Sunday 4th. Huge erection Indian boy at C Hernandez corner at 3–4 a whole Hour [underlined twice]. Up at 5.30 & out for coffee. All closed at 7. Fingered & pulled. Back to tea & out to Booths at 7.35. a.m. again.]

River risen 7' feet since Athualpa arrd. on 13th. It is now 62' – was 48' when we were here, a rise of 14 feet since Sept. 6th or 10th. Its highest is about 80, but no one seems to keep any record! A lazy shiftless lot. Went to Booths to meet all the Barbados men. Only two came & I sent them to Booths' office to get work. Walked to Morona Cocha with 'Wags'. Very muddy indeed. Letter from Simon Pisango[186] against Captain in 'Loreto Comercial' of 30th. With Brown[187] in afternoon & he dined with me at

---

[186] Simon Pisango: pilot of the *Liberal*, and husband of Manoel Lomas's sister. He was the subject of the supposed letter-draft to be found on the blotter opposite the entries for 15–17 September; see note, above.

[187] [David/Dan – NLI 1622/3 is inconsistent] Brown[e]: on the staff of the Booth Steamship Company.

Bella Vista & then to Alhambra to Cinematograph & Pablo Moronez came in – & <u>lots</u> of Indians & peons. Splendid chaps & Cholo soldiers. Back at 11.30 p.m. in rain. Brown told me of Lt Bravo's estimate of the Judge Valcarce[188] – as a man <u>who could be bribed</u>. Brown says the Indians are <u>all</u> treated badly & tells me of the killing of Valdemiro Rodriguez[189] on Madre de Dios by 8 Indians only a month ago. The news came first by the Indians themselves who talked of it on the Plaza.

No sign of Ignacio Torres since Tuesday night. Not a glimpse. Fear he has gone in Launch. Saw 'Julio'[190] in white pants & shirt at Alhambra. <u>Splendid stern.</u>

2, *Friday*

Heavy rain in night & all y'day afternoon & it will quite spoil the discharge of '<u>Athualpa</u>'. Saw 'Julio' at Pinto Hess. Gave cigarettes. He said 'Muchas gracias'. Enormous limbs & it stiff on right side, he feeling it & holding it down in pocket. Saw <u>Huge</u> on Malecon. Looked everywhere for Ignacio. No sign anywhere. Very sad. Guzman [did] <u>not get</u> [to] see Prefect. Saw Guzman at 10 a.m. Waiting for Prefect with elderly Indian woman. Prefect 'too busy' again! – Bishop tells me. At 5 p.m. Guzman was told to come at 3 p.m. This is Friday & he was first sent on Tuesday! To Booths & with Brown – saw 'Julio' again at Store & asked him come to Punchana. He said 'Vamos' [Let's go] but did not follow far. He asked when I was going to Manaos. Saw some really stiff ones today on Cholos. Two Huge erections & then four boys at 5 on seat in front – & then <u>lovely</u> type in pink shirt & blue trousers & green hat & later in Square with 'Wags' the same who looked & <u>longed</u> & got Huge on left. To Alhambra with Cazes at 9.30 seeing many types & 'Julio' in white again in a box. Met outside & asked him come Punchana tomorrow. He said 'Vamos' & asked when to meet. I said at 10 a.m. but he probably did not understand.

3, *Saturday*

Went out at 9.30–10 to look for Julio but no sign of him. Took John Brown's Statement up to 9.30. Bishop says Guzman saw the Governor only

---

[188] Valcarce: Judge Valcarcel. See note for 25 November, above.

[189] Valdemiro Rodriguez: 'the biggest Cauchero in Iquitos'. NLI 1622/3, 1 December 1910.

[190] Julio: like Torres, was considered by R.C. to be a potential sexual partner, and was sufficiently highly regarded to find his way into the apparently innocent White Diary. There he is ' "Julio" of the Portmertu', observed at the Alhambra Cinema, Iquitos, with 'another big fine chap and many young ones.' NLI 1622/3, 1 December 1910.

a short time y'day and that he told him to go back at 6.30 today & wd. probably send him back to Putumayo as Interpreter Viacarra is going down to Manaos on a Launch. Good riddance! altho' I like the Rascal's bright face & Indian skin & splendid teeth. Went on 'Athualpa' at 10. & talked Skipper & Brown & then lo! Ignacio on the Mole shovelling potatoes into a sack! So I asked him to come & see me today at 6 p.m. He said 'Where', & I told him at C's [Cazes'] house. Reygada [*sic*] called on me at 3 & told me he leaves for Putumayo on 7 Decr. Waited till 6.40. No Ignacio, or sign of him! Alack! To Booth's to dinner after turn round Square. Saw Beauty last night first in work clothes & then again in pink shirt at 5.30 in front of Cazes. After dinner round Square very many times till near midnight & saw some types especially Cazes' office or shop. 'Passeando.' ['strolling'] & feeling left pocket.

Took photo of young Booth Customs' Clerk, <u>Antonio Cruz Perez</u>.

Sunday <u>4 Decr. Very hot morning</u>. Looking out window saw <u>Ignacio</u> waiting. Joy. Off with him to Tirotero and Camera. Bathed & photod & talked & back at 11. To meet tomorrow. Gave 4s/. At 5.30 Cajamarca policeman till 7 at Bella Vista & again at 10.30 passeando & at 8. long talk. Shook hands and offered. Tall, Inca type & brown. Cards & Bridge & stupid party till near midnight. Saw Cajamarca several times from window.

5, *Monday*

Ignacio at 6.30 & off together to Tirotero & bathed. On to Indian chacra & mule boys (brown legs, etc) with lína passed in to town. Gave £1. '<u>tanto ufano</u>' (so much contented) but no more! On to Hospital & to Itaia River by Telegraph – pretty & sat down by 'Azul'. He comes from Tarapoto, is $19\frac{1}{2}$ & left the soldiers in Aug. When with 72 Tarapotanos he had volunteered for 8 months. Poor lad! 'Some day will go to Brazil for caucho [rubber]'. What a fate! To Store & ginger ale & gin & on slowly, painfully dragging back towards House. At length the parting – & at Factoria Calle said Adios, for ever! He nearly cried I think. I gave him 2s/ more – & I think he was wretched. He said 'Hasta luego' [see you later]. I turned back & found him still standing at corner, looking straight in front. I to Fotografia & he crossed street. Last time I saw him was there standing and looking. Poor Ignacio! Never to see again. Wrote a little and out to Booths to get tickets (£37. 10/-) an awful fraud. After dinner out to Square & saw several types, one young & lovely & a soldier from Lima – also the huge Cholo policeman with his sweetheart. Drank Beer. Looked for Ignacio, but no sign anywhere. Turned in at 11.45. Very hot.

Pablo Zumaeta called on me at 2.30 for a list of the criminals!

6, Tuesday

Packed up early & called on Prefect. He has properly been fooled. Told me Dublé[191] was going round to Putumayo! Dublé. I wrote Barnes & all. At stage Zumaeta & Raygada [*sic*] & others to bid me goodbye, including the Prefect's ass of an A.D.C. – a young ruffian that. Zumaeta going also to Putumayo! A nice beginning to the 'Judge's' mission! 'Athualpa' off at 11 – a crowd on pier – but no sign of Ignacio. I thought he wd. have come, but he has not. Poor boy. Said farewell to Iquitos with every joy, but regrets for Ignacio & the Indians all. God bless them. Steamed down river. Lots of people on board & had to shift cabin. The Franco Dutch people (2) on board. Some fine Cholos going to Manaos to go up to Acre for caucho. One tall 6' foot lad told me for 3 years. Poor boy. Gave many cigarettes & sat up till 10 on lower deck. Some of them willing & soft.

[On blotter, facing 6 December:
Left Iquitos. Goodbye <u>Ignacio</u>! [underlined twice]
<u>Never to see again!</u>]

7, Wednesday

Rain in night & I out at 3 a.m. & moved chair. At Leticia at 6.30 a.m. & on to Tabatinga & then to Esperanza at about 10.30 a.m. The Customs officer of 'Liberal' came off & I learned from him that the Barbados men had gone down to Manaos in the 'Andresson' two days after I left them at Javari. 15 days ago I left there, so they have about 13 days start & must be in Manaos about 5 days already. We soon left Javari and on full speed, and at 8 p.m. passed São Paulo de Olivença on its cliff, its lights showing. I talked to tall seringueiro [rubber-tapper] lad from Iquitos, José Gonzalez born there 1885 & going up Acre for 3 years[192] – a fine young chap. Turned in at 9.30 or 10 p.m. after talk with Engineer.

8, Thursday

Passed Jutahy at 8 a.m. Great firing of guns to us as 'Athualpa' was once 4 months aground there, & on full speed. Made out accounts of Bishop & of

[191] Dublé: senior official of the Peruvian Amazon Company. Like Pablo Zumaeta, had ingratiated himself with the Iquitos prefect Dr Paz Soldan, so that the two men were actually encouraged by the Iquitos authorities to go into the Putumayo to pave the way for the Peruvian commission. R.C. was disgusted by the '<u>cleansing arrangements</u>' ... 'to precede the Commission by a fortnight and to practically get <u>their</u> witnesses ready.' NLI 1622/3, 6 December 1910 (A) and (B).

[192] Acré: westernmost, forest zone of the Brazilian Amazon River basin; its chief natural resource was rubber.

the B. men at Manaos to be ready for arrival there on Saturday morning. The day passed quietly, and rain in night. We passed many seringals [rubber plantations] and pretty places on the river bank.

Heavy rain in night.

9, *Friday*
Heavy rain all morning & most of day.

Passed a lot of places – lakes & rivers without end. We are steaming very well and shall be in Manaos soon after midnight.

Passed Purus River at 5 p.m. a fine broad opening. A lot of the poor Iquitos folk who came down by 'Rio Mar' are camped there on both banks, waiting the launch that will take them up – Their 'patrons' on to Manaos.

At midnight saw the glare of the electric lights of Manaos (12 miles N.E. across the intervening peninsula) & we got there at 3 a.m.

10, *Saturday*
On shore at Manaos at 9 a.m., & arranged with Dering for paying off the Barbados men. Most of them are going to Madeira Mamoré Railway, only 5 to Barbados. At Booths' office & then to Chambers[193] to lunch & met Laughlin & at 1 back to Booths & paid off the men, losing some £40, at least, by the transaction. On board at 5 p.m. & off in 'Athualpa' to Pará. Poor wee Ricudo is sick – temperature 104° in Hospital. In Manaos saw the results of the bombardment of 2 months ago. Quite disgraceful the whole thing. All our Iquitos Cholos left at Manaos – poor boys – they go to that Hell the Acré.[194] We hope to reach Pará on Tuesday afternoon in time to land. I hope so. I shall go to the Hotel & have a good time of it – at last!

<u>Sunday 11 Dec.</u> Steaming well down river. Splendid breeze. Ricudo sick & in Hospital – poor wee chap. New Pilot from Manaos, a fine chap indeed & huge Pará caboclo. Passed Parintins. Villa Bella first and on all day till Obidos at 7.30 steaming fast. Santarem at 12.20 midnight. Long talk with Dr. (an Italian)

12, *Monday*
Very cool strong breeze. Passed Monte Alegre at 6.30 or 7 a.m. in haze. To reach the Narrows this evening, and it is very doubtful if we shall get to

---

[193] Chambers: with whom he had eaten and stayed on his way up the Amazon (see entries for 16 and 17 August).

[194] see note 192.

Pará tomorrow in time for the visit. I hope so, as I want much to go on shore & find João. Have a lot to do in Pará – & will certainly see him this time – poor old José is dead & gone. I think of Ignacio all the time. Steamed down past mouth of Xingu at 5 & to Gurupa island & town at 6. Saw the great flood of the Amazon going N.E. as we turned into Gurupa entrance. <u>Adios</u>. Talked to the pilot who told me lots of stories of Xingu Indians & others & at 9 entered the Narrows – a fine night. Turned in at 9 & read till 11 & slept all night.

13, *Tuesday*
Out of Narrows about 4.30 & steaming across the beauty [?] expanses of clear water by Marajo, a wondrous inland sea, but fresh water & delicious water. Passed between Murumuru Island & Javaeita, & many houses & canoes & they put off to avoid swamping. Mouth of Tocantins at 12.30. & on full speed on falling tide to round the lower island & sighted Mosquerio at 3 p.m. a steamer going up. Turned up stream at 4 p.m. opposite Mosquerio & arr. off Para – 5.15. 'Trader' behind us. Customs & Dr. visited 6.30 & on shore with Atahualpa [*sic*] Purcell at 7.30 to Hotel de Commercio, where got room & out to Marco by tram for a cool ride. O[lympio] 14$000 A[lves] 10$000 & Beer etc. 5000 = O. 29$000 A 10[$]000. 'Olympio' first at big Square, then Polvora & followed & pulled it out & to <u>Marco</u> when in <u>deep</u>.

14, *Wednesday*
Lib[eral]   191
La[bour]   35
Irish   <u>63</u>
              289

   Nice day – out for a walk & at Cemetery after going around Baptista Campos etc. met <u>João</u> at 8 a.m. & he gave me a big bunch of flowers – very nice indeed. To meet at B. Campos. Pogson called. To lunch with Southgate in S. Jeronymo 111 – & then got things out of Customs & all bags on shore & at Hotel. Letters from home & by telegr. see that General Election is nearly over = 518 seats filled with a Liberal-Labour-Irish majority so far of only 60. Conservatives 229 & the others all told only 289. After light dinner out to B. Campos till 8.10 & then to Valparaiso & back home at 10.30. Theatre & grounds lit up finely. Sorry I did not meet João this evg., as I wanted to give him something.
[On blotter, facing 14 December:
Last time of seeing João Anselmo de Lima at Cemetery corner at <u>8 a.m.</u>]

15, *Thursday*

Not feeling well. In Hotel all day nearly writing & getting ready to go home by 'Ambrose'. She arrived at 6 p.m. or so. Saw Kup[195] at lunch & arranged for Lewis to work here at Port Works. Bishop & the Indian Boys to go to Barbados & wrote to Father Smythe[196] at St Patrick's about them. Also had Kup out to dinner in evg & talked to him & a Frenchman till 8.30. Then out for a stroll. To Big Square by Palace & then to B. Campos – none & on to Nazareth & Valparaiso, where soldiers wanted to enter the Show. Back to B. Campos & down to Palace Square. Two – one same as Nov. 1908. Grown bigger & well-dressed. This is at 10.35 or so p.m. Back to Nazareth at 11.20 & down to Paz for Beer & thro' gardens home on foot to Hotel at 12. 'Sereno' in Hammock at door. Enormous, only 18. Huge.

16, *Friday*

In House all day. Got £60 from Bank. Bill No. 4. They gave me only 882$800 = I have lost about £6, I think, between them & Booth's over the tickets in this exchange business. Boyd[197] of the Amazon S.S. Coy to lunch & complained bitterly of the Minister & F.O. not backing them up more. They got £50,000 from Port of Pará. Boyd says that <u>all</u> the Brazilian Rivers for Rubber are worked by slavery pure & simple. The men <u>don't</u> get down. It is the 'Cuenta' ['settling of accounts'] business & the 'rule of the rifle' begins right here at Pará, so he says. Sent most of my baggage on the lighter to go off to 'Ambrose'. A <u>very</u> little rain at 3 p.m., the first since I landed on Tuesday night at 8 p.m. & yet this is the 'rainy' season! It is hot daily, and I am ill & glad to be going. Gave Bishop letter for Governor of Barbados & £2 for the Boys & a cheque for £20 – also some milreis [Brazilian currency]: Lewis 15$000. Dined & Pickerell called & at 9 to Anderson till 10.30 & then to Theatre & met Alves after another type & to Independencia. 'Soldads' [soldiers], he said. 10$000 & back at midnight. <u>Into</u> Alves back door.

[195] Kup: one of the more socially acceptable residents of Manaos, he had accompanied George and Margaret Booth on a picnic up the River Negro on 15 March, 1908. He distinguished himself by shooting a monkey (killing it with his fourth shot): Margaret Booth, *An Amazon Andes Tour*, privately printed, London, Edward Arnold, 1910, p. 26.

[196] Father [Frederick] Smythe: Jesuit priest in Barbados, given the duty of preparing R.C.'s two Indians for the impact of London life. Barbados was considered to be some sort of halfway house, between the jungle and the metropolis.

[197] Boyd: a Brazilian, whose views are valued by R.C. because of the need for 'Brazilian testimony support' (see entry for, below 26 December).

17, *Saturday*
Left Pará in 'Bullrush'. Bishop & Ricudo on board 'Ambrose' with Kup & others & off at 10.30 or so. Few passengers. Fine breeze blowing up the splendid estuary of Pará. Pinheiro & Mosgueiro passed & blue sails flying before the wind. Far distant line of Marajo island. Off Brogança & Dalinas & out to sea with splendid trade wind blowing right in our teeth. Ship has about 400 tons rubber. Captain Jones in command. A Heavy head sea & very strong Trade wind as soon as we got to the open. Ship pitching a lot.

Sunday 18 Very rough. Everyone nearly seasick. At noon 337 miles from Pará.

19, *Monday*
Heavy head seas & Trade wind very strong against us.
    At noon 330 miles.
    A poor elderly Portuguese died of Beri-beri – our second 1st Class passenger dead since 'Ambrose' arrived in Pará.

20, *Tuesday*
Sea slightly better.
    M. Julien Fabre[198] gave me the Quito paper 'El Ecuador' of Wednesday 2 March, 1910 with a long translation from a 'Truth' article on the Putumayo & 3 Declarations I have never seen as to the infamies of that hellish Peruvian region. How can it be ended for good? How?
    Ran 329 miles.
    Very heavy head sea & wind. Played Bridge – Captain Jones, Nurse Thomson, Norwegian Laurens [en] & I.

21, *Wednesday*
Ran 309 miles only. Sea worse & wind stronger. Such trades.
    Played Bridge again – impossible to write or do anything. Ship like a girl on a skipping rope, jumping & kicking.
Half passengers still seasick.

22, *Thursday*
Ran 281 miles.
    Very heavy head sea & wind. Quite a gale. Never saw Trades like these.
    Mon. Fabre told me today that Pablo Zumaeta came to him 3 or 4 days before he left Iquitos at the Hotel (introduced by the Hotel proprietor) &

[198] M. Julien Fabre: R.C. had learned from Vatan of the failure of Fabre's 'Dutch-French Colonizing Company', for which Vatan was 'Agent of the Syndicate'. 'Everyone had been threatened'; 'disgraceful measures undertaken against them by the Prefect'. NLI 1662/3 29 November 1910. See also PRO HO 161 22 December 1910.

told him Julio Arana was trying to sell his shares in P.A. Coy & wd. give them for a very good bargain. He pointed out that J.A. held the bulk of shares & if Fabre's Franco-Dutch Syndic. bought them they wd. possess the Putumayo. He gave Fabre J.A. address in London. The affair had not been going well lately owing to 'various causes', partly the boundary conflict with Colombia. He said it would be a 'coup de fusil' (!) – for whom? <u>What</u> [underlined twice] d-d scoundrels. Fabre evidently wanted my opinion. I said only '<u>Prenez garde</u>' [take care]. This confirms Cazes' opinion that J.A. wishes to clear out & had been rushing the rubber in order to raise [?] his share. What a murderous ruffian! By God's help I'll unmask him.

23, *Friday*

Sea a little quieter today & wind too gone down – & we seem at 8 a.m. to be making better way. Skipper said yesterday that to reach Lisbon by noon on Tuesday we had from noon y'day to make 13 knots = 312 per day. This we can easily do if the weather doesn't get infernal, but it may be touch & go. I do want to get to Lisbon by daylight on Tuesday in time to land if one <u>can</u> land – after our two deaths on board – one of yellow fever, poor young Boyd at Pará & the poor old Portuguese at sea three days ago. I fear we shall be quarantined at Lisbon, but if not I hope to go on shore & see Agostinho & Antonio too!

Ran only 291 miles. Sea fell slightly, but got up again in night. Wind shifted to N.N.W.

24, *Saturday*

Wind N.N.W. or more N. Ran <u>319 miles</u>.

Are now 1070 miles from Lisbon. To get in by say 5 p.m. we must do 330 miles or 13.7 $\frac{1}{2}$ miles per hour. This tub cannot do that except in quite smooth water – as soon as there is any swell she skips & loses way. We are now well out of tropics & getting colder too. Very tired of this voyage I must say. This is Christmas Eve.

Play Bridge every night with Captain Jones, Nurse Thomas & Mr Laurenson, a young Norwegian from Carnolim [County Wexford] & Christiania.

<u>Sunday 25th Decr</u>. Ran 342 miles. Lisbon 728 miles.
Stupid day. Played Bridge & lost 4 Rubbers after dinner.

26, *Monday*

We pass Madeira about <u>1.30 a.m.</u> Lost 15/- at Sweep y'day & today 5/- to Dr. on bet that we should do nearer <u>350</u> than <u>346</u> miles. The '<u>Ambrose</u>' an old tub.

Ran 339 miles – Lisbon distant 389 miles. A wretched performance. Everything favourable, wind, sea & all & yet this is all the so-called 15 knot 'Ambrose' can do. We <u>may</u> arrive about 4 p.m. at Lisbon, in good time for the visit. Lost my 5/- bet with the Doctor, or rather this miserable tub lost it! Stone of Serpa told Luarens[on] of the killing of the Cearenses [people from Ceará] up the Acre[199] [or?]. when they have a credit. Boy was to 'come tomorrow' & get his Saldo [balance of money owing]. Warned in night to scoot. Had 3 ½ centos due & fled rather than be shot 'by others'.[200] So got down river & Stone engaged him. Is there now on Stone's farm. Many similar cases occur & this is further Brazilian testimony supporting Boyd of Amazon Coy who is also a Brazilian.

[In margin: 10/- to Band – an awful fraud.]

27, *Tuesday*

Read y'day splendid speech of Thys[201] on Congo govt. & future of the natives. A very fine statesmanlike pronouncement. I will write & congratulate him. This morning we have head sea & wind again & ship pitching & rolling heavily once more.

Ran [figure not entered]

Arrived in Lisbon 4.30. but the idiots wd. not give [previously entered at this point: 5 P.M. <u>Should</u> be in Lisbon roads off Carcavalhos. (Sat. 24 Dec)] us pratique [licence to enter port] & quarantined us all night. I never knew such rubbish.

[199] See note 192.

[200] This kind of intimidation was typical of the *cuenta* or peonage known as debt-bondage system. See White Diary entry NLI 1662/3 28 September, 1910 for a fuller account.

[201] [General Albert] Thys (1849–1915): Belgian founder of the Compagnie du Congo pour le Commerce et l'Industrie (1886); he participated in the planning and supervision of the African International Association's expeditions to the Congo (1887); on behalf of the Compagnie du Chemin de Fer du Congo he was responsible for building the railway line from Matadi to Leopoldville, 1890–8, having scuppered British plans to provide the capital for this enterprise. R.C. played a considerable role in the construction of the line, and will have made Thys's acquaintance during this part of his career. An ardent nationalist, Thys did his best to keep the Congo a wholly Belgian sphere of influence, and eventually pressed for annexation. He was worried about the way Europeans treated black peoples and did what he could to bring about a hierarchical administrative system which would make government clearly responsible for protection of human rights. In 1904 Thysville (the station of Sona Qongo) was named after him. (In Singleton-Gates's version of this diary, 'Thys' was given as 'Rhys').

28, *Wednesday*

On shore at Lisbon at 10 a.m. & to Avenida where long-legged boy types & sailor. Then to Largo Cauroens & to Taurus to lunch & then Largo again & young soldier lad (18 or so) in grey twill – Splendid – followed to O'Neills house & down to Largo near Consulate where arranged things & on to Arsenal & Necessidades Palace & several types & back to Avenida & then by Banco di Portugal an <u>enormous</u> offer, about 9", lying on one like Agostinho, but too late & so to Consul Somers Cocks[202] & off at 4 on board & 'Ambrose' sailed for Oporto.

29, *Thursday*
Oporto & Vigo

Lovely day, sea like pond & bright sun, altho' very cold. At Leixoes at 7 a.m. Glorious sunrise & everything beautiful. Left at 10 a.m. for Vigo by Spanish coastline. Exquisite – winter's day. Very cold but delicious sunshine.

Arr. Vigo at 3 p.m. <u>Wrote to Ramón</u>. Poor Snra. Villalaz, her daughter, & other passengers from Iquitos were quarantined for 5 days at Vigo – had to go in a barge to Lazaretto with 27 Deck passengers – poor souls. The wee girl cried. 'Avon' off at 4 & we at 5, following her. Glorious day & sunset. Cool & clear & delicious air.

30, *Friday*

[Crossed out: Cherbourg in evg.] Overhauled 'Avon' at 3 a.m. but then we slowed down, Captain says, and she went away. Lovely day over Bay of Biscay, we <u>should</u> do 360 miles easily. Wrote to Tyrrell at F.O. saying I was going to Paris from Cherbourg & sent Life Certificate to Chief Clerk. Cannot get to Cherbourg till 8 or 9 a.m. tomorrow morning & hope to get to Paris by 6 or 7 p.m. Sending most baggage to Liverpool.

31, *Saturday*

Fishguard tonight & probably London. Arr Cherbourg – early on shore & to Station & at 12.56 after rotten lunch to Paris. We were Lorentzsen [*sic* = Laurenson], Van der Est, Fabre & the train very slow. Due 6.58 but arrived only at 8.25 Gare St Lazare. To Hotel Terminus & got vile room. Out to Place de l'Etoile after dinner & 32 Artillery. Denis Hilaire there & to Grand Armée. Later in Champs Elysée soldiers & then in B. des Capucines green hat & small. Two last no copper – but Denis 10/-. Mild evening, great crowds. Boulevards & Capucines & everywhere silly songs being sung & pretended gaiety without heart in it. Wrote F.O. Life Certificate & so to bed at end of year – already in <u>1911</u>.

[202] Consul [Philip Alphonso] Somers Cocks (1862–1940): served at Lisbon from 1907 until 1911.

Part Two

THE WHITE DIARY
FOR 1910

Note on the *White Diary*

The provenance of the one 'White' diary is, to some, almost as obscure as that of the Black Diaries. Although it only covers the period 23 September until 6 December 1910, it is more extensive than all the Black Diaries put together (including the 1901 War Office Army Book and the 1911 Cash Ledger). It also exists in two forms: as 512 foolscap original, handwritten pages, and as 408 typewritten pages in two folio volumes, each signed in Irish script by George Gavan Duffy, Casement's last solicitor. Like his Special Branch counterparts, the typist sometimes had difficulty in deciphering the author's handwriting. But it has to be said that errors are rare.

It is now reasonably certain that Sir Basil Thomson's men found the Black Diaries in Casement's trunks, and that Thomson passed copies to Peter Singleton-Gates. The circumstances of the White Diary's arrival in the National Library of Ireland was for many years confused by those who, understandably, wished to believe that it had at some time been in the hands of the forger. In the early days of the controversy, friends of Casement, such as Bulmer Hobson, thought that a document held in London would turn out to be a harmless diary with obscene interpolations taken from the writings of a known Peruvian deviant. When production of the MSS undermined this belief, some fell back on the theory which is still current: that the White Diary – with consular reports – provided the forger's main source of information for a much more ambitious project, the forging of documents in their entirety.

The truth is much more straightforward, and documentation to support it is in the National Library of Ireland (NLI 13073), and in Rhodes House Library, Oxford (MS B.Emp. S22 G 344). To assist the House of Commons Select Committee in its investigation of the affairs of the Peruvian Amazon Company, Casement offered its chairman, Charles Roberts, the use of his diary, which he was to describe as 'an *aide-memoire*, and mental justification, and safety valve'. Students of Casement, familiar with his literary aspirations and attitude to money, may be amused by the hesitation which occurred before Roberts felt able to have the document typed out at public expense. Few were more generous than Casement when it came to largesse to friends or causes; few were more penny-pinching in other respects (as is demonstrated in the diaries and, especially, in the Cash Ledger). The White Diary was 'typed by an expert'. Then, on 5 June 1913, Roberts wrote, asking what he should do with 'your diary, & the typewritten copy I have for you'. Subsequent correspondence indicates that these items '& a good deal besides!' were returned to their owner when Casement was guest for lunch at Roberts's house in Palace Green.

Understandably, Gertrude Bannister, sole beneficiary of her cousin's estate, did not recognize a 'diary' amongst the extensive collection of effects – the contents of six trunks, one case, and one canvas hold-all – delivered to her by Gavan Duffy after the post-execution formalities had been completed. She said she received 'the Putumayo things, but no diary'. As anyone who has examined it knows, the manuscript of the White Diary looks nothing like a diary. And, of course, typed volumes, had they not been previously entrusted to George Gavan Duffy, would not have been relevant to her quest for evidence with which to expose the forger. She was to deposit in the National Library of Ireland everything that historians could hope to find, including much seemingly trivial matter. Later, an enquiry about the manuscript's provenance, addressed to the NLI's Department of Manuscripts, elicited the reply: 'the indications are that it . . . came to us through Mrs Parry' [née Bannister].

What follows is an abridged version of the White Diary which, as far as possible, limits omissions to repetitions. Many of the individuals mentioned have been footnoted in the 1910 Black Diary. It begins the day after Casement and the Commission had arrived at the Peruvian Amazon Company's main agency. Hitherto they had heard much; now they were to see as well as hear.

Sir Roger Casement's Diary, September to December, 1910 [Abridged]

AT LA CHORRERA, FRIDAY, 23RD SEPTEMBER, 1910, 2.15 P.M.

I asked Captain Carmino Regardo to-day if he could spare the man Stanley S. Lewis to accompany the Commission and myself as a servant. He at once demurred, (and I thought with alarm and suspicion) saying that he was bound by the Port regulations of Iquitos to bring back every member of his crew, under a penalty. I asked what the fine might be, and he said he would look up his book of regulations. I said that, of course, my request depended solely on his ability to release the man, and also on his willingness to let him go – that if he needed his services on board very much there could be no question of my taking him – and, equally, that if the Port regulations of Iquitos were as he stated, then the matter ended.

On telling Bishop this (and Messrs Barnes and Fox) Bishop said that already Sr. Macedo was acting behind our backs. That this morning when I was speaking to a crowd of Indians through a Barbadian workman, who all were standing at the door of a Store to get their rations, Sr. Macedo had sent Laurence, the Cook, to stand behind and hear what I said. My questions had been of the most innocent kind and made quite aloud and generally, such as any traveller would put as to the Customs and habits of a strange people.

Incidentally the Barbadian to whom I was speaking pointed out one young Indian lad, a Muchac[h]o De Confianza presumably[1] – who, he said, had 'already killed plenty of men', but that he was 'not yet civilized'!

Mr. Fox was standing by all the time we were talking and Sr. Macedo himself came along too, and stood by grinning – but not following the remarks – hence the Cook!

Bishop went on to say that after he had come down from Ultimo Retiro, as he had related to me in Iquitos, a Mr. Rutter, a young English clerk of the Company had asked him, Bishop, for details as to the ill-treatment of Dyall by Montt long ago. He had written down for this Mr. Rutter the facts, as he related them to me – and then had left La Chorrera for Iquitos.

[1] See Black Diary, note 87.

He now finds from the Barbadians who are here, that after the 'Liberal' had left Sr. Macedo had somehow or other found out about the writing concerning Dyall and had questioned them all – threatening them.* They had all denied any knowledge of the Document, whereupon he said: 'Then, there was only Bishop, and he has gone away' – and that Macedo had then threatened all of them with being shot if they said anything against him. He had said to them: 'I won't shoot you myself, but I can easily get you killed' – and he had also threatened them with the 'cepo' or stocks. This was August last – some five weeks ago.

Bishop says the men would all like to go away with me, that they don't think they will be safe after I leave. I have told Srs. Tizon and Macedo that I wished to speak to all the Barbadians on the Station to-day if convenient, and they have agreed and will send the men to me at 3. o'clock. Immediately after this I saw Macedo on board the 'Liberal' talking in earnest talk with the Captain, who, of course, has told him of my interviewing Lewis and Clarke.

Bishop says one of the Barbadians – the man I happened by chance to be talking to at the Store door – Donal Francis – would like very much to get away, and come with us. That he has been employed on the usual dreadful tasks and is sick of them and also that he has an Indian 'wife' about to give birth to a child and he is very anxious to get her out too. I said that I intended asking for the loan of this young man, in any case, as I had already been asked by Mr. Barnes and Fox to get a Barbadian for them, as the Interpreter is sick and Garrido is also complaining and may not go on, and that I thought this young man would make a good servant.** Bishop says all would like to go away now – they are frightened – and he adds that Sr. Macedo is still more frightened! What a situation! Here, at the very outset, we are face to face with grave difficulties, and there seems no way out. Any sincere interrogation of these five Barbadians here at La Chorrera, must bring to light a state of things that cannot openly be tolerated, and both Tizon and Macedo will, at once, pretend that this is such serious evidence of wrongdoing, (of which they had no knowledge) that a Peruvian Court must enquire into the charges. If on the other hand, I intimate to the Barbadians that I am only going to make a perfunctory enquiry, as to whether they are happy, well treated, or in distress &c., they could truthfully reply, so that nothing real comes out, and that is an end of

* Note in margin: Mr. Rutter has gone home – he had intended coming up with the Liberal this time, but Barnes told me that he thought he had got alarmed and was clearing out.
** Note in margin: I said to Bishop that I might be able to take the man & the other Barbadian away when I went, but that I was not at all sure I could do anything about the Indian 'wife' – that the Agents here might keep her as she was a Peruvian and I could do nothing in the matter.

their evidence for any purposes of useful reform. If, however, I induce the men to speak out, under a promise of protection, it is clear their accusations would involve Macedo, and doubtless many others in the Sections at this moment, and I could not very well pretend that my enquiry had been an entirely pleasing one. Besides Tizon or Macedo may wish to be present, and I have thought from the first that one or other <u>should</u> be present, and then the fat would be in the fire at once and these Barbadians will practically be under arrest — or secret threats — or worse — unless I take all away with me, and even then there is the very real danger of Tizon or Macedo writing down to Iquitos to have 'an enquiry' held there and take the depositions of all these men on their arrival.

Indeed, that is certain — and what sort of 'Enquiry' would that be at all? Obviously one solely directed to screening Macedo & Co., and therefore inculpating the Barbadians. They would be made the scape-goats, both to justify Macedo and clear the Peruvian authorities too, and also to destroy any real evidence of the wholesale crimes that have been allowed for years in this unhappy region.

One is surrounded by criminals on all sides. The host at the head of the table a cowardly murderer, the boys who wait on you, and the whole bag of tricks. To go on through this District <u>pretending</u> one is hoodwinked and accepting at their face value all the things we see, will defeat the end in view — for we cannot, later on, bring forward as trustworthy evidence, tales and stories told to us in secret with men posted to see there are no eavesdroppers and acting as if we were the criminals afraid of being found out. And yet, if we don't act like this, I see that almost at once we shall be up against a dead wall, for it is obvious that these men, guilty and evil as they know themselves to be, are not going to sit down idly and see us steadily piling up a dreadful case against them. They will act to protect themselves, and that action clearly will take only one shape, namely, to 'accuse' the Barbadians, or to say that, as such very grave charges are now being made to the Commission, <u>and to me</u>, it is the imperative duty of a Peruvian Court of Enquiry to investigate these charges, and all this comes back to the same thing.

The Barbadians will be nobbled and terrorised into denying everything — indeed, it would be only sufficient to lock them up in Iquitos, thus demonstrating my entire inability to protect them to get them to say anything the investigating Court desired.

And so here I am with the clock on the verge of 3 p.m., waiting to interrogate the Barbadian hands of this Stronghold of wrongdoing. What shall it be? a real interrogating covering the ground of their relations to the Company and the duties they have been put to perform, or a merely sham one to allow me to 'save my face' and assure Tizon that the men 'seem happy, and all say they are well treated and properly paid' &c.

This last thing, or anything like it, once said, becomes irrevocable. On the other hand I cannot keep entire silence, neither will the men themselves, at least not all of them. One or other, perhaps the Cook ('with £200 to his credit') will tell Macedo just what sort of questions the Consul put to them, and there is always, too, the question of whether it may not be the right thing, from the broad point of view, for me to invite either Macedo or Tizon to be present, just as I shall invite Barnes.

JASPER DYALL.
AT LA CHORRERA, SEPTEMBER 23RD, 1910.

6. p.m. after my interview with the Five Barbadians with Barnes and Tizon present.

7.p.m. – I decided to invite Mr. Tizon to be present when I interviewed the Barbadians – it was the lesser of two evils. I also asked Mr. Barnes and, thus constituted, I had them brought in one by one. The room with open door on the main verandah of house. Sr. Macedo came and planted himself at door for a time, but, as I made no sign to invite him inside he had to go away, and walked up and down the verandah during most of the time.

The Barbadians presented were the following:-

No. 1. a Liar – Donal Francis, Engaged 1905. He lied throughout.

No. 2. Said Nothing – Philip Bertie Lawrence – (Jamaican) Engaged by Juan B. Vega as Servant Cook at Chorrera. In Chorrera all the time.

No. 3. Saw little – Seaford Greenwich. Baker at Chorrera. Engaged in 1904. Well-treated and is a man of confidence. Has saved over £100. Was once only out of Chorrera, and that was end 1904, and beginning of 1905, when he was in Matanzas. Saw Cyril Atkins there shoot the Indian woman. Since then has been always in Chorrera.

No. 4. Saw much and said so – James Chase. Engaged 1904. In Sections often on Commissions. Witnessed floggings and killings – up to quite recently.

No. 5. Saw much and said so – Stanley Sealy (or Sily) Engaged in 1905. On Commissions often and has flogged frequently himself for not bringing in Rubber.

Had Sr. Tizon not been present I am confident a great deal more would have been said – especially by Francis, the first witness.

This man, I am assured by Bishop, knows a lot and it is evident he could not have been at Matanzas, one of the very worst Stations, for 1 year and 9 months merely 'planting yuca' and 'guarding himself against the bad wild Indians'. Is leaving in December.

Bertie Lawrence, the Cook, seemed a decent lad – and as he has been here all the time in Chorrera it is possible he was seen very little altho' even here Indians have been flogged often enough it is clear, and the 'cepo' have been in evidence until not long ago. Is leaving in December.

The Baker, it was evident, did not speak all the truth. He tried to answer questions within the narrowest limit of reply. He is evidently well-treated, has made money over his job and wants to get away in December with all his earnings, and without being troubled or delayed by possible enquiries in Iquitos or elsewhere.

The two last witnesses, Chase and Sealy, both spoke out and the former asserted in the most painfully timid manner that was all the more convincing that he had seen Indians, shot and flogged to death – not dying actually under the lash, but dying very soon after from the flogging – and shot, both after flogging, and shot also without having been flogged. Although Sr. Tizon several times interrupted at this stage, the man adhered quite firmly to his statements and when asked if there was flogging now in Abisinia said yes, and then to please Sr. Tizon who intervened said it was 'not so bad' as formerly, but still he had seen Indians flogged up to quite recently, and always for the same crime – not bringing in Rubber, or not enough.

His evidence to my mind was very convincing – Barnes, too, felt as I did, although he thinks this man when he said that he himself had never flogged any one was not speaking the truth. I think so too. I think it highly probable he must have flogged Indians but is ashamed to own up to it. That will come. It should be remembered that this man is in a very embarrassed position. He has no money, may even owe money to the Company, he is sick now, his feet wrapped up in bandages, and he has just come from a Section whose moral atmosphere is one of the worst in the whole of this land of crime.

The fifth and last witness, Sealy, spoke like a man throughout and my heart warmed to the ugly black face, shifting from side to side, his fingers clasping and unclasping, but the grim truth coming out of his lips. Yes, he has flogged Indians himself – many times – very many times – at Abisinia; at Savana always because he was ordered to by the Chief – who decided which Indian was to be flogged. It was always for not bringing in rubber – some getting 25 lashes, some 12, some 6; and some only 2 even – according as the rubber was 'short'. The Indians would 'lie down of themselves' and take the flogging 'like a dog, eh?' I threw in. Their backs, or buttocks rather, would be cut – often badly cut – and so the ghastly tale came out. The Indians were not happy and brought the rubber because they were afraid. They got food 'in the Sections' – but not when collecting the rubber in the bush. He had seen women flogged just like men, and a boy flogged in Savana.

I told Sr. Tizon pretty well just what I thought of it when this last witness had gone, and he had to admit that it was rotten and infamous and <u>must be swept away</u> – but that all stations were not like Savana and Abisinia.

AT LA CHORRERA – SEPTEMBER 24TH 1910. 8 A.M.

The man Dyall, referred to in John Brown's Statement to Governor of Barbados, arrived down country last night Bishop tells me. I have asked Bishop to bring him to my room this morning – so that I may speak to him, if possible, before Macedo has been at him. I expect, however, that Macedo has long since seen him or has had him prepared by the Baker, so that it will be a well-worked up witness I shall see. One moves here in an atmosphere of crime, suspicion, lying and mistrust in the open, and in the background these revolting and dastardly murders of the helpless Indians. If ever there was a helpless people on the face of this earth it is these naked forest savages, mere grown up children. Their very arms show the blood-lessness of their timid minds and gentle characters.

Dyall came at 8 or 8.30 a.m., and I had Barnes in to hear his statement – one of the most revolting character. The man is a brute but has been employed by greater brutes.

As his statements are so grave, he owning up to five murders of Indians by his own hands, two he shot, two he beat to death by 'smashing their testicles' with a stick under Normand's orders and with Norman[d] help-ing, and one he flogged to death. I thought it wise to have his evidence stated in full before the Commission and Sr. Tizon. I therefore asked Tizon to meet them all in my room at noon where I had a very grave statement to read to him. Dyall came and I read his evidence, a statement rather, and he confirmed it, and then I had F. Bishop and Stanley & ['S.' mistaken by typist for one of R.C.'s ampersands] Lewis up and all three testified as to the deeds they had witnessed, the illegal acts they had themselves per-formed under orders of their Chiefs of Sections, and the character of the system of 'trade' they were put to enforce over the Indians.

Their statements, particularly Bishop's, were convincing enough for any fair man I should think, that what he had been employed on could not rightly be termed 'commerce' or 'trade' in any civilized or accepted sense of the term.

One of the punishments described by Dyall for Indians who failed to bring in the rubber required of them by Normand had been to haul them up by a chain round the neck high off the ground, and then let them drop suddenly, so that they were insensible and had to be brought to by pulling their arms about – in a way he demonstrated before us.

(Bishop has previously told me exactly the same thing of Sections where he has been employed, and described one case of an Indian so hoisted, who when he fell, fell back insensible and bit his tongue through. He has volunteered to assert and 'prove' this statement anywhere and before anyone).

Sr. Tizon in vain sought to weaken these three men's statements, but they did not vary them nor withdraw, and I asked both him and the Commission to put any questions they pleased to them. I said that, for my part, unless these Statements were refuted I was bound to accept them: not perhaps in every detail, but in the main as constituting a very grave indictment of the whole system and revealing a state of things that was wholly wrong and could not be allowed to continue. I refused to admit that flogging Indians for failure to bring in rubber required of them, even when they had 'accepted advances' of goods, was to be tolerated for one moment, and that to my mind the state of dealing with the Indians that had been described was slavery.

It was immaterial who had originated it, Columbians [*sic*] or Peruvians – the Company was a civilized institution, it had inherited the claims of the founders of this method and it <u>must</u> sweep away this system and establish a lawful and civilized and humane method of dealing.

With regard to the Barbadians they accused themselves, which, in great part, went to prove the truth of their statements. I could not see what motive should induce any man to charge himself with grave and dastardly crimes, as Dyall had done, unless it were that he was confessing.

If these men were guilty, as I believed they were, of criminal acts, it was not they so much as the men who had ordered them to do these things who were the real criminals, and if there was a question of punishing anyone, I should seek to defend these men and should ask for legal advice and help.

Tizon was in great embarrassment and later on confessed that he was prepared to accept the men's charges 'in the main' and did not wish to confront them with the men they accused.

He said that no good could come of accusing Fonseca, Montt, &c., to their faces, that we were not a judicial body, and that there is no one in the Putumayo empowered to investigate criminal acts, and that there has been no effective administration in the past, owing to the boundary dispute with Colombia, by Peru, and these lamentable deeds have been committed with impunity.

Later in the evening, in the course of a long conversation with me he practically threw up the sponge, said that the system was slavery, that it would have to go, and that these criminals, who were dangerous men, capable of anything, with their arms, their 'muchachos' and their local power might arm the wild Indians and do anything. ...

BEGINS 28TH SEPTEMBER, 1910. NOTES AT OCCIDENTE.

We arrived here at about 9 a.m., being greeted on landing by Fidel Velarde, the Chief of the Section, Manuel Torrico, his second, and Rodriguez and Acosta, whom we left at 6 last evening down at Namienes. They had walked over this morning, and it is evidently not far by land, as Chorrera itself is only 7 hours, or possibly 8 hours by land.

Velarde looks a perfectly awful type – worse, if possible, than Miguel Flores, who left so evil an impression on me at Chorrera. I must look up Velarde's 'criminal record'. As I had been lying on a plank all night, and not a very level one, and it had rained too, I got very little sleep last night, so soon after landing I turned in in the best guest room on a fine big iron bed, very kindly placed at my disposal by Tizon. I slept most of the day. The Commission decided on the route they propose taking from this, and also on what they shall do while staying here. I did not join these deliberations, as they were purely concerning the business of the Company, but I saw Velarde sitting there, and looking like a convicted criminal. I subsequently am told by members of the Commission that his examination by them had produced the worst impression. They believed he was lying, and had so told Tizon. He had been unable to give them any help in their 'economic and mercantile' mission. He had told them that he had 530 rubber collectors or 'labourers' on the list of his employés, this not including 'muchachos' and 'domestic servants'. The former are the armed Indian boys kept at each stronghold, the latter are for sexual intercourse chiefly, and carrying water from the river. I expressed no opinion on the statement that this Station of Occidente has 530 'labourers', simply because I have 'no opinion' of the statement. It is a lie. There are doubtless 530 Indians inscribed, whose duty is to bring in every three months some 30 kilogs of rubber against battle, murder, and sudden death if they don't, but I must prove this for the satisfaction of the Commission before I openly question the 'facts' they think they are eliciting. Velarde, I understand, told them, and Gielgud did, that this station produces 50 tons of rubber per annum. Let us see how that works out. Say 30 kilogs per man per quarter gives 120 kilogs per annum plus 530 'labourers', gives 63,600 kilogs. The actual quantity collected per man must, therefore, be less than 30 kilogs per quarter. Yet in the Store today I weighed one of the one-man loads lying there, and it came to $33\frac{1}{2}$ kilogs, and I was told it did not represent the full amount for a 'fabrico', or rubber term. The 'cepo', or stocks, are also in this rubber store. There is nothing else. It is the whole of the ground floor of the big house, and is lined round the two long sides with shelves on which the rubber lies, according as each Indian 'labourer' brings it in every ten days or fifteen days. To be accurate, he does not bring it in, I am told. Although a collector, he is himself collected when the rubber is 'due'. The 530 labourers are scattered all over Sr. Velarde's Section, and they are collected fortnightly, we will say, by armed bands of muchachos under his, or Rodriguez' or Acosta's leadership. They are marched down to the Station here, each man (or family) with his or their load of rubber, which is here weighed. If correct, the man escapes back to his forest home to begin almost immediately collecting afresh. If not up to weight he gets flogged or put in 'cepo'. Such is, mildly, the system. At the end of the fabrico, which is five of these collections, he receives not payment on the 30 kilogs, or whatever the exact amount may be he has gathered, but an 'advance' against the next fabrico, that is to say, he is kept on 'the books' of this commercial establishment as a debtor to the firm. He is not asked if he wants an advance, or what he would like, he is only too happy to escape with a whole skin, or with his wife and daughter.

I did not gather any of this from the Commission. They merely told me they were convinced Velarde was lying. I am writing down what I believe to be the system, as I have both read it and had it described by the various Barbados men I have interrogated (See some of their statements). I hope to convince the Commission of the full working of the system before we part, but it will be very difficult, for I cannot question anyone save the Barbados men, and they cannot question anyone save the Agents of the Company, who have an obvious interest in lying. No one is to question Indians, the best witnesses of how the system works, because that would upset every-thing. Moreover, the Commission's only interpreter is the Barbados man, Chase, who joined them solely because I asked him to.

Velarde has issued invitations for a big Indian dance to greet us. Our coming had been known for long. The manguaré, or Indian drum, in the 'Muchachos' house was beating almost all the time – <u>exactly</u> like the native drums on the Upper Congo. The identical system I should say. These tappings and boomings were to say, 'Come to the ball', 'Come to the ball', and in the night the beating went on often for lengthy periods.

I sat up late at night hunting up the 'record' of this man Velarde in my police news. Did not get to sleep till after 3 a.m., as I had to go all through the 240 pages of typed document. I find he is one of the 'principal criminals' of the Putumayo of that extraordinary record. There are not many incidents given against him, but several of the witnesses put his name down in their lists of the chief wrongdoers they had met in the region....

THURSDAY, 29TH SEPTEMBER.

From 11 a.m. the Indians began to arrive for the dance. Men, women, boys, girls and children 'on back', not children in arms, the women mostly stark naked and generally painted, sometimes quite artistically in yellow and red, and feather fluff on their legs. The men are all under-sized, some half skeletons, at least very underfed, and with wretched arms and legs, some of them only 'fono' [loincloth], their native work dress, but others came in 'gala dress', that is to say, a soiled flannelette shirt and a pair of check pants, the two worth about 3/6d.

The naked men in fono are better off, to my mind, than the poor specimens in shirt and trousers. The dance begun irregularly in parties and processions, and gradually enlarged and developed. We photographed many – Gielgud and I. We visited the Indians' house (the Muchachos' house) where the Indians were dancing both in afternoon and evening. I saw many men, and boys too, covered with scars, and often drew the attention of the others to this, but they were looking for themselves. Some of the men were deeply graved with the trade marks of Arana Bros across their bare buttocks, and the upper thighs, and one little boy of ten was marked. I called Bishop and we both verified it, and I tried to photo him. One boy had red weals across his backside quite recent. The Commission was more than ever convinced by Velarde's lying to them yesterday. He had declared that no one had been flogged at Occidente since he took charge in January last, and that only one 'labourer' (that is to say, only one forest Indian) had run away. The Indians danced all night till 5 a.m. One could hear their chants. No food was given to them, that is to say, presents of sardines and salmon occasionally. Many of the Indians brought in presents, birds, game birds they had killed, fruit, and even a little 'paca'[2] alive. They presented these so courteously to Velarde or another of these gentlemen as they arrived. There were no fine feather head-dresses, these are all gone, if the Huitotos ever possessed them. Tizon assured me he intended to close down Abisinia and Matanzas, the two worst stations, and open simply trading stores there, with rubber for the currency. I warmly approved. The stores would have to be guarded, of course. He said he had decided on this already before I came, but his decisions were being hastened, the need for change and immediate change was so apparent. I told him I thought his plan was excellent. At these two Sections, where possibly the worst crimes against the Indians have been committed in the long period of lawlessness and anarchy, he will abolish compulsion altogether, and leave the Indians perfectly free to come or not to the Stations. If, as he hopes, they now want things, they will try to procure them by bringing in rubber, and the deal will be a proper commercial transaction. The goods will have a fixed price and rubber a fixed local value. I said 'good agents' would be needed, and he should see

[2] A tailless rodent, also known as the spotted cavy, found in the forests of Brazil.

that more useful and civilizing articles were selected for this barter than any I had yet seen. The silly 'caps' with a gilt anchor, worth 6d. I should think at outside, the worthless pants and shirts, no healthy covering at all in themselves, might be replaced by more useful and enduring articles. The present system is not merely slavery but extermination. A slave was well cared for and well fed, so as to be strong for his master's work. These poor Indian serfs had no master who fed them or cared for them, they were simply here to be driven by lash and gun fire to collect rubber.

Our great height excited comment at the Dance. We were often surrounded by gazing and smiling bands of boys and men. Barnes, who is 6'4" (almost) was actually measured by one elderly Indian man with a thin rod he had carried in (as a wand for the Dance) from the forest. He broke off the tip at Barnes' height, and carried off his measure of the tallest white man, or any other man, who has ever been in the Putumayo probably. He measured Gielgud and myself too – we who are both less than Barnes – and then returned to Barnes and took his stature definitely as I have described.

I think the Indians already perceive that something is up. ...Everyone is kind to them, even Velarde and 'the others', surely an unusual experience. They came round us again and again and stared and smiled. Fox is highly popular, dancing with them, keeping step, and playing with the children. Hilarity increases. Bishop assures me this is not an ordinary dance. He says he has seen Indians at these dances, which are only permitted once at each fabrico – that is to say rather less than 4 times a year – who were cuffed and kicked, and at night he has known the 'blancos' [whites] go out, excited with drink, and commit abominable orgies with the women and girls by force – even raping prisoners in the 'cepo'. He blushed I think – he certainly cried the other day when telling me one of these filthy stories of crime. So, I must say, did I when listening to Dyall's relation of his own atrocious acts. He tells me that he has been roused from bed by the chief of his Section more than once late at night and sent off to some Indian house near the Station where a Dance was going on, to stop it. I thought this was because the Chief was disturbed and could not sleep. 'No, sir,' he said, 'I was sent to stop the dance, because, he said, they would not be able to work caucho [rubber] tomorrow if they danced.' Poor Indians! Everything they like, everything that to them means life, and such joy as this dim forest at the end of the world can furnish to a lost people, is not their's [*sic*], but belongs to this gang of cut-throat half castes. Their wives, their children are the sport and playthings of these ruffians. They, fathers of families, are marched in, guarded by armed ruffians, to be flogged on their naked bodies, before the terrified eyes of their wives and children. Here we see all before us, men and husbands and fathers, bearing the indelible marks of the lash over their buttocks and thighs, and administered for what and by whom? For not bringing in a wholly lawless and infamous toll of rubber, imposed upon them, not by a Government, as in the case of the Congo pillage, but by an association of vagabonds, the scum of Peru and Colombia, who have been assembled here by Arana Bros. and then formed into an English Company with a body of stultified English gentlemen – or fools – or worse – at their head.

And the charming Lizardo Arana tells me in Iquitos I shall find 'such splendid Indians' here, and that he feels sure the result of my journey to the Putumayo will be more capital for the Company! Yes, more capital punishment if I had my way. I swear to God, I'd hang every one of the band of wretches with my own hands if I had the power, and do it with the greatest pleasure. I have never shot game with any pleasure, have, indeed, abandoned all shooting for that reason, that I dislike the thought of taking life. I have never given life to anyone myself, and my celibacy makes me frugal of human life, but I'd shoot or exterminate these infamous scoundrels more gladly than I should shoot a crocodile or kill a snake. ...

NOTES AT OCCIDENTE, 30TH SEPTEMBER, 1910

After the Ball.

... In the afternoon an Indian capitan came and embraced me, laying his head against my chest, and putting his arm round my wai[s]t. He did the same to Barnes, who was standing by. Both of us were touched. I knew quite well what it meant.

I bathed in the river, and 'Andokes'[3] and Barnes caught butterflies. I was not well today, and turned in without dinner. ...

MONDAY, 3RD OCTOBER, 1910

... the matter of Francisco, the local capitan of one of the Indian tribes came up. I think it was Barnes brought it up as proof that, within the last few weeks, here at this very station an Indian had been drowned by Acosta, one of the 'rationales',[4] and Velarde the Chief had not thought it worth while to report it. This, apart from the fact whether the man had been purposely drowned or not. Barnes put forward the very argument I had first raised. When there was doubt expressed by Tizon as to the deliberate drowning of this Indian by Acosta, the story, as told to him, being that Acosta had merely given the man a shove, while the Indians

[3] See Black Diary, note 137.
[4] See Black Diary, note 87.

were washing rubber at the river bank, I had said that all these Indians, it was admitted (and obvious) could swim from childhood, and an Indian thrown into the river (here very narrow) if not previously greatly exhausted, would be very unlikely to drown. The story, as first related by Francisco, had been that the Indians were now being 'held under water', when washing rubber as a new punishment to take the place of flogging (prohibited by Tizon under apparently honest circulars), and that this particular Indian, struggling to escape from Acosta, who had him under, had got away and been drowned. My comment had been that inherent probability was with this argument, since, if the man had not been exhausted and dazed from immersion, I saw no reason why he should be drowned from being pushed into water he was accustomed to play in and swim in from early boyhood.

Barnes on bringing forward this story of Francesca, however, was at once greeted by Gielgud (and Fox) with the remark 'Why were we not told of this? This is the first of this we have heard.' The reasons for their not having been informed earlier were given by Barnes and Bell, and then on their understanding of these, Gielgud said 'I regard this as much more important than anything brought forward by the Barbados men. Here we have first-hand information.' I said quietly 'Pardon me, the other is first-hand information too – the statements of [an] eye witness. The only difference is one of date.' He shut up like a trap.

They agree. The thing admits of only one explanation, the reign of terror that exists, and the absolute ignorance in which Tizon has been kept. I begged him to be very careful in his enquiry, as the man Gusmán had begged Bishop, when giving me the pencilled note[5] to explain that on no account was I to let 'the others' here know that he had spoken. 'The others' mean Fidel Velarde, Rodriguez, Acosta, and, possibly, the other 'racionales' of the Station. According to the 'Planillas de Sueldos' (Pay Sheets) for September, I saw the other day the 'rational' staff of Occidente consists of Velarde (paid by results – 2 soles (4/-) per arroba [15 kilog.] gross weight rubber and 7%) Manuel Torrico, Eugenie Acosta, Apolinar Atravea, and Augustin Pena – the latter is the Cholo man-servant from the Andes, who waits at table. He is almost a pure Indian, like the soldiers in Iquitos, and is a fine, sturdy, well-built young man of 27 or so, capable in the hands of a decent master and mentor of being a faithful and devoted

[5] Alfredo Montt: – Tiene indios en cadena y les esta pegando por que elevan muy poco caucho, los indios estan con el culo roto todo rajados lo mismo las mujeres de los muchachos estan todas flageladas. ['Has Indians in chains and has them flogged for bringing very little rubber. The Indians have wounds on their backsides, all lacerated. The same (goes for) the wives of the muchachos who have all been flogged.] See Black Diary, note 117.

servant, I should say. Here, in such an atmosphere as this, he has no doubt fallen with the rest. Acosta is now gone away again, I suppose back to Naimenes. Gusmán's name does not figure, but a Jerminos [Jeremias] Gusmán appears on Atena's list.

The discussion in the Indians' house today after the evidence against Jimenez had been admitted more or less took for a time a sharp enough aspect. Gielgud constitutes himself a sort of advocatus diaboli [devil's advocate]. First, too, in the story of the Barbados men he intervened in the same direction. When Sealy came to Jimenez crossing the Caquetá (into the Republic of Colombia) with armed men in quest of 'Indians', Gielgud interrupted to ask him 'whose' Indians these were? Whether they were men who dwelt across the river or fugitives who had run away from the 'Section'? Sealy said: 'He say they was Indians from dis side. I don't know. I think so.' The habitat of the Indians was quite immaterial from any civilized point of view. The clear point established was that Jiménez, a servant of this English Company, was conducting an armed raid of the Company's servants in pursuit of human beings into the territory of a neighbouring South American State. Mr. Gielgud's thought seemed to be, to more or less justify it, on the ground that the Indians might be fugitives from the Company's territory, as if an English Company who indignantly deny the existence of forced labour, who speak to our Government of their purely 'commercial' relations with these Peruvian Indians, 'who are protected by an effective administration, &c.' could claim to own Indians just like rubber trees. I let Gielgud's interruption pass in silence, but Barnes very justly struck in at once. 'That's immaterial, the Company doesn't own the Indians, we are told they are free.'

Not wanting to 'rub it in', I did not add that 'this much more convincing' statement originated, like every scrap of evidence so far submitted to the Commission in the same quarter, viz: myself. Francisco's complaint had been made not to Sr. Tizon on the Commission but to me through the Barbadian, Bishop. It was I who had told Mr. Barnes and Bell, it was I who had sent Bishop to stop Francisco, and it was even I who had the same day told Sr. Tizon, and asked him to enquire from Barnes and Bell. Again, during our discussion, I said that, apart from all question of murder and illtreatment of Indians, it was convincingly clear to me that, instead of the Putumayo being policed and administered by a civilized power, as the Company asserted to the F.O., there was here a rule and reign of lawlessness, of an entire absence of law. The members of the Commission (save Gielgud) agreed, and so did Mr. Tizon. Gielgud's interjection was that, in the absence of local authorities the local agents of the Company had to devise and apply law!

I again pointed out that this was the very objection raised from the first by H.M. Government in their correspondence with the Company, which had been so indignantly met by the absolutely warrantless statement that the Peruvian Government maintained efficient and complete civil and military control. Gielgud shut up again, and poor Tizon said 'The military were only for political purposes as connected with the disputed boundary with Colombia.'[6]

...That I am, after all, the guest not of Tizon but of the local Chief of Station is apparent, despite Tizon's attempt to assure me otherwise. Here at Occidente I sleep in Velarde's bed, the sheets, pillow-cases, &c. marked with his initials. An amusing demonstration occurred soon after our meeting.

My washing came back, brought in by Sealy. I asked him how I could pay for it, which woman of the numerous domestic staff one sees here I could pay by giving a present to. He said simply 'The Manager's wife, Sir, wash de clothes.' I said 'Oh! Do you mean Mrs. Velarde. I can hardly give her a tin of meat. Did she wash them herself?' Then the grim Barbadian features expanded into a pleasant grin. 'He got four or five wives, Sir', and we both laughed. I did so openly, and so did Sealy, who had been forced, blushingly, two days ago to inform me of his various marital establishments on the Putumayo. Sealy, however, had had only one wife at a time. It is reserved for Chiefs of Sections and the higher agents of this commercial establishment to take their matrimony like their rubber, by a toll on the 'gross product' of the district. Here is this Fidel Velarde who gets only '2 soles per arroba' with a mere bagatelle of 'four or five wives', one of whom kindly does my washing, while Normand in far-off Matanzas, with his 20% on the 'peso bruto' should have a Harem of at least a hundred handy maids. I told Barnes and Bell – they roared with laughter – but their laundry, too, goes through just the same intermediary. We cannot escape from our surroundings, and I said that it was all very well for Tizon to say I was his guest, or the Company's guest, I was really the wretched Indian's [*sic*] guest. They paid for all. The food we eat, and the wine we drank, the houses we dwelt in, and the launch that conveys us up river – all came from their emaciated and half-starved, and well flagellated bodies. There is no getting away from it, we are simply the guests of a pirate stronghold, where Winchesters and stocks and whipping thongs, to say nothing of the appalling crimes in the background, take the place of trade goods, and a slavery without limit the place of commercial dealings.

...I am getting positively ill. My nightmare last night was a composite creature of all these criminals, a sort of Velarde–Jiménez–Aguero–Flores– indescribable and blear-eyed, sitting at the door of my room waiting for me. That was all. Just waiting. No wonder I yelled in my horrid sleep, and roused the whole house!

[6] See Black Diary, note 95.

In the afternoon, while the rest slept, all of us fatigued and worried and upset, I visited the 'stocks' with Sealy, and took some measurements of them, while he explained their mechanism and method of work. ...

TUESDAY, 4TH OCTOBER.

... So it goes on, on every side. Wherever they turn for information they say – they who are sent out by the Company to aid and advise – are met by concealment or untruthful statements or an entire absence of any documentary evidence they may call for, and which should be forthcoming instantly. Here are no books at all, they say, nothing but 'blancos' lolling in hammocks, idle (often absent) muchachos, who go and come into the forest armed, but never a stroke of work of any kind done on this so-called factory. No one works. Even the table boys go to their hammocks at 9 a.m. and lie down three deep playing with each other. ...

When Bridge was over and the party going to bed, I was walking up and down outside, and Barnes and Bell came and joined me. It was then 11.30 p.m., and we were quiet, and removed from eavesdropping, and I told them of the fear that these last incidents of today had wakened in my mind. My argument was this.

Here we are, all groping in the dark. So far the only 'evidence' of any direct and open kind has come from Barbados men, made to me, their Consul, under belief in my power and ability to protect them. I was responsible for the safety of these men. They had relied on my obvious right to ask them to state the truth, as far as they knew how. They had, more than once, shown and expressed great fear of the consequences to themselves, and it was their trust in and belief in me that led them first to speak, to offer to confront their Chiefs of Section, even face to face, and, finally, to accompany us up country. But I had no power to protect them, there was no law or authority of any kind in this country; the Prefect's letter to the 'authorities' they saw themselves was a farce. Bell said its only value now was a 'curiosity'. ...

WEDNESDAY, OCTOBER 5TH. AT OCCIDENTE.

Having pledged them on their honour and good faith to adhere to their present attitude towards this execrable regime of man hunting, we went to bed after midnight. I did not sleep much. Here I am, at 5.30 a.m., up again and writing out an 'agreement'.

The Launch has not yet returned from Chorrera. This, too, gives me a little uneasiness. There may have been some devilment down there, and with Bishop alone, surrounded by those scoundrels, who knows what they might attempt? Make him drunk and pump him, and take down his 'evidence' against us all, or me rather, and try to make trouble in Iquitos with it. It is obvious these ruffians will stick at nothing. If they are now assured, as is likely enough, that Tizon is an honest man and adopting our views and going hand in hand with us, they must all know their tenure of their lucrative posts depends on getting up a conspiracy, and a successful one, against him. To do that they must damage in some way the chief object of their fears – myself. It is solely through me and the loyalty and trust of these three or four ignorant blackmen to their Consul that the truth has come out. We three, late last night, agreed that the situation was really incredible – that no one could believe it. Bell (the sceptic at first) laughs and laughs at this aspect of it – that they, a Commission of Experts sent out by a powerful English Company to advance its interests, should be forced to act like guilty men, to hide their minds, to refrain from asking the most necessary questions, and to be forced to declare that of every agent of the Company they have met up to this only one man, Tizon, seems an honest man. (Torrico doesn't count. We <u>think</u> him better than the others here, but we really know nothing about him.

It is now 9 a.m. and no sign of the Launch – over two days away, and she should have been back yesterday. Tizon says he gave positive orders for her immediate despatch. Either she has met with an accident (highly possible), or she is delayed at Chorrera through some devilment of Macedo.

Garrido, I am told, will be left here. His 'resignation' relieves the Commission of the difficulty of discharging him, and giving their reasons. He will return to Iquitos by the 'Liberal', and Barnes is going to write to Cazes. Both Barnes and Bell say they need no further evidence as to the true state of things. I have entirely convinced them, and can leave them in the assurance that nothing will induce them to modify this view. As I am myself convinced, I see only possible grave trouble to everyone in continuing to take evidence under such conditions of peril as surround us here. To go to Matanzas would be madness – to the arch-murderer Normand. Torrico, Bell says, told him that the out Stations towards the Boras country, Sabana, Matanzas, &c. were all really 'forts'. Nothing open below – all fenced in up to the ten or 12 foot verandah, and armed guard kept day and night! No one goes in to the forest there save in numbers and well armed.

I should dearly love to see these things with my own eyes – to be able to record the methods used there in this 'commercial' and 'industrial reclamation' of the Indians, but how can I? The Commission will hardly go to Matanzas, they say, or to Abisinia, the roads are long and full of water. To me, personally, it would be a real pleasure, but I am gravely alarmed for the results – the possible results. It might mean the murder of the Barbados men, under our eyes almost. Of course, it would be the 'cannibals' or the 'savages' who had done it, or it would be the 'injured husband' or something of that kind. No evidence possible of a crime. Besides, these men have never been punished for the most awful offences against humanity. Not one. They have been here for years committing the most hellish crimes, as we all now believe, and they were openly denounced in Iquitos three years ago, with many witnesses walking the streets of that Capital city asking to be brought before a Court. And what followed? Nothing, absolutely nothing. They have either retired with a small fortune like Mr. Rodriguez of Iquitos, or are still active agents of the Company, drawing very handsome incomes from their sections. Barnes says this man, Velarde, who is not worth £5 a year to any house of business, gets, he believes, fully £600 a year, and he has 4 or 5 'wives' free, a house built by the Indians, servants and washing by the Indians, a garden and plantation by the Indians, everything save European supplies, levied by crime from the surrounding defenceless population.

The others are out shooting at a target of an Austrian soldier as I write. It is well to keep up appearances, and this we do pretty well, although my constant writing in my bedroom is suspicious. I cannot help it. I try to do as much as I can at night, but one gets very tired in this climate, and often I give in and go asleep. Poor Barnes is ill. He takes 40 grains of quinine daily, and is really looking painfully thin and haggard. Gielgud, who is still under 30, looks very well. For any serious purpose, however, I fear he is useless. The whole question doesn't strike him as serious, I fancy.

(Charlie's Birthday).

I was up at 5.15 a.m. Saw first a girl come out of Torrico's bedroom close to mine, on same verandah. Seeing me at my door she bolted. I stayed on verandah, and saw four girls or women come out of Velarde's house (where he and Rodriguez, and I conclude Agriléo Torres, are sleeping), and, at same time, four of the water carriers appeared on our verandah to get empty tins and go down to the river. At same time I saw women at the doors of the Servants' rooms round the other side of this side.

Here we have a pretty big female entourage, all unaccounted for by any useful work, save these poor water girls who begin at 5.30, and are often carrying water up to 8 p.m. They, or some of these female slaves, wash our clothes. Last evening Sealy brought Gielgud's laundry and Tizon's, and I asked G. (on purpose) how he paid for washing here? 'Oh!' he said, 'I don't pay. I regard it as one of the things the Company provides.' I nodded, and asked innocently, how were these women who did it paid by the Company. 'Oh,' he said, 'they get good food. They are not paid. They get presents and tins of sardines, and things.' 'I see,' I said, 'but if they are servants of the Company and engaged as such, surely there is some rule or scale of payment.' He gave no answer. This was before Tizon, and all of them. Just before dinner, and this is what he finds 'so good'!

Just now (10 a.m.) Sealy in my room cleaning up. I told him that when we left this for Ultimo Retiro I desired all three men to sleep near our rooms, and explained that there must be no tampering with the morals of the Indian girls, that it was dangerous and also wrong to me, that if charges were brought against them on this account, or even worse things, not only could I not protest, but then all their testimonies might be aside, and it would be said indeed that they had 'told me lies'. So that everything required them to be chaste, their honour and loyalty to me, and their Government. It is a pleasure in these abominable surroundings to feel that these simple, ignorant Africans have still enough <u>manhood</u> to understand when their honour and their hearts are appealed to. God bless their black faces! Sealy swung his head from side to side as he does when moved, and said 'All right, Sir. I know. I know.' He then again assured me that Chase had not tried anything wrong with the girl yesterday, that he had only spoken to her about Gielgud's watercan, and Rodriguez had made that the pretext for the accusation. He said that Rodriguez, when recently in Chorrera had actually tried to steal his own 'wife' from him, the one who is there now waiting his return – that 'de woman' tell him so. Rodriguez had asked her to 'run away'. He then went on to say that 'they was drowning Indians here.' I said I had heard of one such case, but that it was denied. He said at once 'Two, Sir – James Mapp was here then, and saw it, and told me when he came down to Chorrera quite lately. He is in Santa Catalina now. You will hear when we gets there. These two Indians was tied. Its the way they punishes them now – they holds them under the water till they's half drowned to frighten them, and these two men was dead.' I said again that I had heard of one, but that it was stated that Acosta had only 'shoved' him into the water. Sealy said 'He lie, sir. They ties their hands and holds them under. Wait till we get to Santa Catalina.' And there I left it. And so the fearful tale goes on, quite unsought and unsuspected out comes this, when I was merely talking of the dangers of sleeping <u>en garcon</u> [all men together] in these halls of Circe![7] Shall I tell Barnes and Bell? What use. They said last night they believed <u>all</u>, that they needed no more testimony as to the atrocious regime, and would not henceforth for their parts attempt to make any enquiries as they were convinced, that I had amply fulfilled my part, and there was no shadow of doubt in their minds.

[7] Circe: Greek enchantress, who, in Homer's *Odyssey* turned Ulysses' men into swine.

I am becoming the bête noir of the Show. Every-time I approach these poor gentlemen it is with a New Crime on my lips, or in my eyes. And I cannot help it. If I say nothing to anyone, and later on these matters have to be made public (who knows) the Commission might well say 'But we were with Mr. C. all that time, sleeping next door, meeting every hour, dining and lunching and playing Bridge together, and he never opened his lips, and yet he was receiving this dreadful evidence, and now states he believed it.' However, this cannot arise now. They say they are convinced that I have done my duty by them in fully exposing and offering to any test they choose to apply the statements of these men.

The most impossible person of the Commission is Gielgud. He is to a great extent committed to this evil state of things, and seeks many occasions to defend it. He would say, doubtless, to defend the Company, but his defence really is of a system that to any discerning eye is indefensible. Of course, there are lots of people in this world who will defend anything that exists – merely because it exists, and they are so mentally constructed that they cannot imagine another state of things. Their thought is applicable to those circumstances, forgetting that circumstances are very largely of human contrivance. What is, and what has been going on for years may be, perhaps, not right, or the best, but the best under the circumstances, and, therefore, why not profit from it? This is very much the point of view of Gielgud, so far as I can gather, that he has any fixed point of view at all. His powers of observation are certainly not acute, and he cannot, so far as I can see, think very clearly. His heart may be allright, but his mental powers are distinctly deficient when it comes to a human problem of this kind, for his heart and head must balance each other. Thus today he and Fox, before luncheon, have been seeking to find good points in this system of slavery. They say in one breath it is slavery, and then that it is a 'commercial transaction', that the Indian 'owes' money to the Company. And this in face of all the lashes and scars, to say nothing of the murders, we have witnessed the last few days, or have been directly informed of. Gielgud passed through this district a year ago, slept in the very room I am now in, and found everything 'allright' – rudimentary, perhaps, but quite suited to the surroundings. He will revert to this attitude of mind tomorrow, if the constant presence of wellnigh daily exposure that I have to make is relaxed, and who will keep it up when I am gone? That is why I told Barnes last night at midnight I should never forgive him if he went back on his promise to condemn the thing lock, stock and barrel on getting home. He had said that I could count on him, if on no one else, that his mind was as fixed as mine. Fox is out of his depth completely in these surroundings, a man of most kindly heart and human sympathy, but of inadequate grasp of a complex situation like this. He can see a little way, but not far enough. Thus while he is horrified at the stories of Jimenez and the burning of the 'old lady' of Sealy, or the beheading of the little boy, he thinks these are 'individual outrages' – this is what I gather – and that because he can find Indians who dance, who sing, who smile like children, that this is evidence they are happy and not 'all illtreated'.

It is the Congo question over again, with the same type of careless-minded or not logical minded defenders. A thing cannot be slavery, and, at the same time, be a voluntary contract. When I contested to-day, for instance, in this talk with Gielgud and Fox, that the arrangement as to 'paying' the Indians in advance after each fabrico was legitimate trading, or that it afforded any pretext in law or out of law for flogging an Indian subsequently who had taken these goods for not delivering the 'price' put upon them, he demurred. He did not defend the flogging, but he did uphold the 'contract'. I said there was no contract, no proof that the Indians voluntarily accepted the goods or willingly contracted the obligation to pay for them with 30 kilogs of rubber or with anything else. Both he and Gielgud at once said 'I was assuming' this, arguing on an assumption. I said my argument admitted of simple truth, but when even this or any other form of proof was called for we had been told that to question the Indians, to try to <u>prove</u> well nigh any statement affecting them would upset the whole show, and create 'chaos'. Thus flogging was not to be tested by direct questioning of the men whose scarified backs we could see, because that meant 'accusing' the local whiteman and also exposing the Indian to his vengeance after we had left, and so wherever one turned the same diffidence to bring it to the only test available was apparent. One saw a thing that one's reason and one's principles, no less than one's common sense, question, and you were debarred from putting that question. Nothing would be easier than to <u>test</u> this matter of the 'payment' of the Indians, for instance were they prepared, was Mr. Gielgud prepared, to put it to this test? At the next 'fabrico', for instance, would he let me ask, or would he ask, the Indians whether they wanted the 'advance' or payment, or would rather not have it, and be released from the obligation to bring rubber. (This advance is indifferently called by both names, according to the line of argument advanced in its defence; sometimes it is a payment for rubber delivered, or even for rubber 'sold'. Then when the evidence of the lash or the 'cepo', or even the killing is pointed to it becomes an advance that has not been made good, and the whipping, a bit barbarous and so forth, is merely the rough and ready way of dealing with a defaulting creditor. These were not their words, but this is the theory of defence they distinctly put forward. In one breath they agree that the system is a bad one, that the people are slaves, and, in the next, that it is not <u>all</u> bad. And that to condemn it sweepingly, as I do, savours of 'exaggeration', because I do so without 'proof', and on 'assumption'. I say 'Allright, then, I am prepared any time you like to <u>prove</u> my assumption, but you demur, on two grounds – one that this is "Peru", and the other that it is not Peru, and there are no authorities at all, it is impossible to investigate anything of this kind, because as your investigation will end in criminal charges – must, indeed, necessarily end in criminal charges – you must abstain from making it, since there is no one to arrest the criminal or punish the crime you may bring to light. What delightful reasoning, if reasoning it can be called! It is really a waste of time and breath to try and convince this 'Commission', apart from Barnes already convinced, and Bell. The latter still clings to some extent to some of the 'commercial' side of the argument, and the duty to 'make the Indian work' (for his own good, of course – it is always for his own good a man is enslaved. This is not Bell, but me). But he is convinced, I think, that this system is 'one of slavery' pure and simple, and I hope he will not denounce it as such.

I don't object at all to Gielgud trying to defend his Company, that is loyal and right, but an Englishman educated at an English University should be able to <u>smell</u> right and wrong in a case of this kind. This thing we find here is carrion – a pestilence – a crime against humanity, and the man who defends it, is consciously or unconsciously, putting himself on the side of the lowest scale of humanity, and propagating a moral disease that religion and conscience and all that is upright in us should uncompromisingly denounce. I find Tizon, the Peruvian ex-official, who was ignorant of much until we arrived at Chorrera far more sympathetic, far more humane, far more lofty-minded than this product of an English University.

Every day the battle has to be renewed, and when I think I have won and established once for all the <u>principle</u> that should guide their investigations, I find one or other of the Commission (not Barnes, he is now, and since Iquitos with me) breaking away and harking back to the Leopoldian arguments – expediency 'the only way', 'the beginning of things', &c. Yesterday it was Bell with Torrico's explanation of how the rubber is brought in, and the rubber conveyed to Chorrera (and the houses built) another <u>chacra</u> or so-called plantation here made by the Indian women, a description that is the very definition of slavery, and which he yet found 'allright'. This was how he described it to Barnes and myself, as he came fresh from Torrico's version, and I give Torrico's version in Bell's words. Then I get today Fox and Gielgud assuming that my condemnation is based on 'assumption', is even 'exaggerated', and that, putting aside individual outrages, the thing is not 'so very bad'. It has its bad features (these to be suppressed), but also its good. To say, as Fox does, that it is not altogether bad, that there are some good features about it, is about the same as to say that human nature is not altogether bad. Of course not. But one does not spare a criminal, or seek to maintain a crime, or any part of a crime, because the criminal was a human being and had a human heart.

This thing that we see here is either good or bad; either decent or indecent, either defensible or indefensible. We are dealing here with first principles of right and wrong, and all the argument in favour of this damnable thing is, originally, inspired by greed, and only maintainable by concealment of fact.

Here we are confronted on every hand with concealment. When I said that the Indians were slaves, then Gielgud (as I shall call him now) and Fox demurred and wanted my 'proofs'. I said to Gielgud 'I'll prove it very soon if you, that is to say the Company, permit the test.' He said the demand should be addressed to the Government of Peru! Harking back at once to the old yarn, the lying yarn told to the F.O. I said, but you admit there is no Government here – of Peru or any other State – that has been put forward more than once as reason for <u>not</u> taking any action, or submitting any of these charges of the Barbados men to investigation. Therefore, they don't appear on the scene. Our proof lies with the Indians, your Company's 'creditors', as you assert. Let me, the next fabrico, ask (I'll find the interpreters) whether they wish, man by man, to take the cap and pants, or whatever the things are you give them, for a further supply of rubber, or whether they would prefer to be free of this obligation? It's a very simple test. If they are 'free' they have an absolute right to refuse your 3/- or 4/- worth of stuff, or whatever the goods may be. But do you ask them? You know you don't. You compel them without question asked or put, to take these things. It is immaterial whether they <u>select</u> them or you bestow them. And then, when they have gone off to their houses, – poor scarified devils – you follow them up and intrude upon all their home life, and force them to bring you in rubber at a rate of exchange <u>you</u> prescribe mind, and if they don't satisfy you you flog them, as well nigh every male stern in the district can testify, and you challenge my condemnation of this thing, and say I argue from assumption. Why, the test is the simplest in the world, and you won't apply it! Line the Indians up here before me, or before any of us, and let them be told that they need not bring in any more rubber unless they like, that you won't 'ask' them to kindly take a pair of cheap pantaloons, a 6d. cap, and a flannelette shirt for the ensuing term, and let us see who then is reasoning from assumption?

There is an even simpler test. I may wish to <u>walk</u> back to Iquitos. This is a free country, so we are told. The natives are citizens of Peru, so we are told. Well and good. There is nothing to prevent me sending out to engage as many Indian carriers as I wish to carry my things to Iquitos. May I do it? You know perfectly well I cannot, and may not. It would not be allowed by your Company. These Indians then become their 'labourers' on the list of your local agency, and they have received 'advances of goods' from your Company, and so are not able to go away, and so forth. All right. I'll admit even this. Produce your account with your contract with these labourers. I'll pay their debt, I'll even pay it with 100% added. Will you consent? No, you won't, and you know it. You want not your 'debt', not your trumpery trash of a few shillings' worth of cheap and useless goods, but the 30 kilograms of Indian Rubber, that at 5/- per lb., or maybe 4/- per lb. is worth £15 or so to you, and your contract is null and void in all equity, since it is made, not between man and man, for value proferred and accepted, but is violated every day of its existence by the application of force, on one side, of punishment with law (where there are no magistrates), of stripes by the lash, of invasions of domicile, and forcible capture, and detention in stocks and cells, and all the damnable expedients we have been hearing of since the beginning of last month. It is the system that is the crime, not the criminals who administer it, and you, when it becomes demonstrably indefensible, adopt the argument that this English Company is not responsible, because the Government of Peru is callous, indifferent, absent, or non-existent. I did not say all this to Fox and Gielgud, but a good deal of it, and a good deal more that it is impossible to recall or write down, for man's speech is sometimes fluent, and I said a good deal, and they too. To write all would mean a shorthandwriter everytime and all the time, and even then much irrelevance on both sides slides in. I put this forward only as a part of my argument that they say rests on 'assumption' – the main and unchallengable argument being that they dare not allow me to put any assertions at all to the test, and that they – I mean the Company – while denying much, demonstrate nothing. So far as my eyes can convict them, all that any man of sanity and decent thinking sees here must convict this system they have sought to defend.

I don't wish to be unjust to Gielgud in thought even, and so I sometimes try to provoke argument in order to allow him to recover lost ground, but it is hard work and dispiriting. Perhaps I am too belligerent. I try to be cautious and even enquiring.

As regards the 'goods' they advance or pay to the Indians at each fabrico, there should be the very simplest proof here on the spot of their actual value of their worth to the Indians and of their relative value to the goods the Indian is forced to supply in so-called exchange for them. This Station gets 50 tons of rubber per annum (more or less) worth, say, £10,000. Where is the Goods Store, and let me see the goods you have in depôt to meet the forthcoming fabrico, of, say $\frac{1}{4}$th of this total, or delivery of £2,500 worth of rubber? (As a matter of fact there is no Goods Store. There is a small room where Gurusi [Garece] the Steward, and Garrido sleep in hammocks, with the smallest assortment of trash I've ever seen anywhere. It knocks any Congo Store, of Bula Matadi or Domaine de la Couroun into a cocked hat. There is not at the present moment in this Store anything that a Congo native would give a goat for. It is a thing 'dispense', [dispensary] where table food, butter and things for the household use are mixed up with a few, and a very few articles, such as hammocks or pieces of cotton. From what I have seen of it, the total European value is certainly not £5 for everything – food included – now in this Store.

I asked yesterday Barnes and Bell, as Chiefs of the Commission, to take an inventory of it. They refused, from laziness I think. Bell said they could always find out what goods came to Occidente by consulting 'the books' at Chorrera. The task of taking this inventory would not be half an hour's. I've looked in the Store more than once, but *I* cannot go and do this. It would give great offence, and would at once provoke the question 'What are you doing here?' The Commission can, if they will and ought, to do this. One inspection of this kind, along with one visible 'payment' of these '530 Labourers' for a 75 days' supply of rubber would remove many doubts, and prove who was exaggerating, or reasoning from 'assumption'. But here, again, all demonstration is denied or withheld. I cannot wrangle with the Commission. My wish, and earnest and constant wish is to convince them, but it is very hard to be alone, to be the only one with a constant and absorbing wish to get to the bottom of the whole thing. To find Englishmen of the type of Gielgud, more keen, I fear, to defend than to reform, more swift to find the good than the evil, in a thing that is evil, is a very great disappointment. Here a man who defends becomes, to my mind to some extent particeps criminis [a partner in the crime]. ... There is no Chief to the Commission as it is, each one goes his own road, no collective enquiry beyond a certain point, and up to this that has been very much due to my dinning and insistence on one line of investigation.

This Putumayo Slavery is, indeed, as Hardenberg [*sic*] said, and as I laughed at when I read it a year ago in 'Truth', a bigger crime than that of the Congo, although committed on a far smaller stage and affecting only a few thousands of human beings, whereas the other affected millions.

The other was Slavery under Law, with Judges, Army, Police and Officers, often men of birth and breeding even, carrying out an iniquitous system invested with monarchical authority, and in some sense directed to public, or so-called public ends. It was bad, exceedingly bad, and, with all its so-called safeguards, it has been condemned and is in process, thank God, of passing or being swept away.

But this thing I find here is slavery without law, where the slavers are personally cowardly ruffians, jail-birds, and there is no Authority within 1200 miles, and no means of punishing any offence, however vile. Sometimes Congolese 'justice' intervened, and an extra red-handed ruffian was sentenced, but here there is no jail, no judge, no Law. Every Chief of Section is judge and law in one, and every Section itself is only a big jail with the Indians on the treadmill, and the criminals as the jailors. As Barnes and Bell said last night, it is 'incredible'. And, yet, here are two kindly Englishmen not defending it – that I will not say – but seeking to excuse it to some extent, and actually unable to see its full enormity or to understand its atrocious meaning.... The world I am beginning to think – that is the white man's world – is made up of two categories of men – compromisers and – Irishmen. I might add and Blackmen. Thank God that I am an Irishman, that I am not afraid to 'assume', that I won't shirk the charge of 'exaggeration'. Let that be. I shall drive home this nail, and if these unhappy, these enormously outraged Indians of the Putumayo, find relief at last from their cruel burden, it shall be through the Irishmen of the earth – the Edward Greys, the Harris', the Tyrrells,[8] and even the Hardenbergs [*sic*] and the Whiffens. The 'Blackmailers' are far better men than the Company promoters. Tizon spoke from his heart last night, when he said 'I, too, if I acted from my heart, would sweep the Company away and chase the Aranas and those men from the public and social life of my country.'

The explanation of the poverty of the Store here in anything resembling trade goods is now given me by Bell. I returned to the charge today with Barnes, Bell present, as to taking an inventory of the 'trade goods' in this trading agency. Bell said nothing at the time and Barnes did not move. I had just told them, privately, of the unsought confirmation of Francisco's statement of the drowning here that had come from Sealy, reporting James Mapp's statement to him as to the two Indians drowned here. I had told them this assertion, but said I did not propose doing more, that they had told me the previous night that they needed no more of this evidence of crime, and that they were convinced. Moreover, we had now ample demonstration of the futility of discussing further these aspects of the situation – since nothing could follow. No action could be taken by anyone to verify the statement; there could be no 'accused' and no prosecution, any more than any defence. All was swallowed up in Tizon's reiterated assurances that he accepted all, without going into details, and would act as if the charge were proven.

With that they were content, and I was not a prosecuting counsel. As they were satisfied, no more need be said. Barnes remarked that when they got to Santa Catalina they could interrogate James Mapp. I said no more, because it is obvious that interrogation would end when it began. In the extraordinary state of things around us it is quite farcical to call this a Commission of Anything, just as it is equally farcical to call this Company a trading Company. Here at one of its chief trading stations it has not in store sufficient trade goods to meet the demand on a tenth-rate Banyan Store outside, say Delagoa Bay. Its rubber store, on the other hand, is vast. It occupies the entire basement of the larger section of the house – of the very much larger section of the house – while the room in which the goods are

[8] See Black Diary, note 14.

(and the two stewards) is about 12 feet square, and all it contains of trade goods could be easily put in one trunk.

The explanation, as furnished through Bell, is this. (It comes I am told from Torrico). When the 'fabrico' is completed, that is to say, the last yield of rubber is delivered up by the Indians for the term, (75 days) for which they have been paid, they all come in to the Section House with it. It is sent down to Chorrera by the launch, and the Indians, who have supplied it, are asked here at Occidente to state what they want 'as advance' for the next term, or fabrico. They go back to their 'chacras' and work (under supervision and direction of this Staff who visit their various settlements in the woods to compel them to acts of tillage) on their 'yuca' or cassara [cassava] patches,[9] and so forth, so as to have their food supplies assured, while their women are retained at the Station to clear up its 'plantations', such as the draggled and disordered sugar cane we see around us here. The goods the Indians have asked for come up in the launch on her return from Chorrera, and are ultimately delivered to the Indians as an 'advance' (not a payment – mark the difference), for which they are held bound to bring in an assigned quantity of rubber.

This is, in brief, Torrico's statement – not all of it – which Bell relates. In addition to the foregoing, Torrico asserted that the Indians here at Occidente, and at all of the Sections, came in of themselves with the rubber, and were not collected or [as] described by Sealy. They gathered voluntarily under the direction of their own capitans on each occasion, and brought the rubber in to the Station; there were no armed bands sent out for them, neither here nor at any other Station. Torrico has been in the Company's service for over a year certainly, as Mr. Gielgud states he was already here at the date of his visit last year. I had been told, incidentally on arrival at Occidente, that Torrico had been only two months here, having come from Para, and this statement seemed to be accepted by Barnes, as well as by myself to cover his service with the Company. We now find we are wrong. ...

Were the condition of things here not so extraordinary no extraordinary compulsion of this arbitrary kind would be called for. The 'justification' of this interference with the Indians' home life that is put forward is indeed the condemnation of the Company's system, and yet Fox, Bell and Gielgud are prepared to swallow it, Not Barnes, I fancy, but he pays so little attention to anything – is obviously so ill and unsuited to the task – that he counts the least of all in local decision, altho' I count more on him at home, when all is closed, and the summing up has to be delivered. ...

* Notes in margin: Get Fox's statement of what Garrido said. Aquiteo Torres came down and passed away.

[9] Cassava, a tuberous edible plant grown in the Americas, is also known as yuca.

FRIDAY, 7TH OCTOBER, 1910. ULTIMO RETIRO.

From Puerto Peruano in 'Veloz' to Ultimo Retiro. Butterfly day. ... It was not Jimenez but the head muchacho, I presume – a nice looking Indian youth, with red painted face, black shirt, blacker hair, and white duck knickers. But down came the redoubtable hero of the headless boy and burnt woman and burnt man of the caquetá Raid of June, 1908. A burly young Ruffian, looks 26 or 30, sturdy, well-built, with that far-off touch of the nigger you see in some of these Peruvian lower grade men, not so much as Dublé has, but still just the touch of it. Rodriguez, with his cruel mouth and glinting eye, had it too. We were all presented by Tizon, and to relieve our feelings we began an elaborate butterfly chase there and then on the sandy bank of the river. They were certainly magnificent specimens, and the soil was aflame with glowing wings, black and yellow of extraordinary size, the glorious blue and white, and swarms of reddish orange, yellow ochre, gamboge and sulphur. Fox got one of the splendid big black and green and yellow. ...

I asked Bishop if Crichley [Crichlow] would speak the truth when interrogated by me, or would he do as Francisco did and lie for the sake of this bribe. Bishop said that Crichley did not want to speak out, that he was anxious to make some money now; that he had been promised a good 'gratification' for his silence, and he was anxious to go home to Barbados with some money. I said I would see about that. That, in any case, his duty was to tell me the truth at all costs. The interrogatory of Fox upon Jiménez continues as I write, Fox asking questions as to 'payment' of Indians – God save us – and the treatment of sick Indians, smallpox cases, and so forth. They segregate them, and the Indians themselves do this – so Tozin [Tizon] translates. (We saw something of this yesterday on the river bank in the measles cases from Atenas.) I took a moment's change, and sent Andokes with the butterfly net to catch the lovely beings that infest this foetid beach. ...

SATURDAY, OCTOBER 8TH, 1910, AT ULTIMO RETIRO.

I found eighteen women with machetes squatting and cleaning the ground, two of them fully grown, stark naked; a third, a girl also naked as when born, and the fifteen remainder (wives of machachos, or from the bush) dressed in the cushuca skirt, with strings of beads or coins. How are these beings paid? not out of this store, surely. Nine of the male Indians have a straw or stick through the nose tendon. All wear fonos, although some of the small boys are naked. Last night at dinner eleven capitans and 'muchachos' sat round the bulwarks looking at us feeding. They were cheery, and seemed in no fear of Jiménez, and Bishop says he has done more with the Indians since Montt left. I heard Tizon say the place had been 'in disorder' when Montt was here, yet Montt is in Atenas. I have determined to tell Crichley that unless he speaks the truth to me in answering my questions, he shall not be permitted to remain in the Company's service, that he is bound to answer with truth questions put to him by a British Consul, and that if I find him lying I shall request Sr. Tizon to dismiss him. Tizon has already volunteered in Chorrera to send away all the Barbados men if I desire it. I consider that this is perfectly fair and just. The man is being bribed by the Company's Chief Agent to lie to the Consular Officer sent to assist these men, and I am fully justified in meeting such disgraceful action by depriving this man of the bribe and continued service at higher wages he counts on as the price of his falsehood. It is his duty to answer truthfully, and if he fails to do this for the sake of the money inducement, then I shall deprive him of this price of corruption, and have him dismissed and sent to Iquitos by next steamer. If he speaks the truth I may ask that he be retained on, with a clear warning that any flogging or illtreatment of Indians by him, no matter who orders it, is illegal; that he must not obey, but must at once inform Sr. Tizon.

I have taken the Store Inventory as well as possible. The 'Commission' went there after questioning Jiménez, and I stood at the door and looked in. They merely glanced at the guns, handled one or two, and came away, but my searching eye and Sherlock Holmes soul did the rest. It would not take 5 minutes to take down every single article, and apprise it too. There is not £5 worth of stuff all told, or anything like it, apart from the guns.

Here is the Inventory:–

27 'guns' and Winchester rifles.

13 old Sniders and Muzzle loaders (6 with Bayonets)

(about) 140 Winchester cartridges.

15 enamel iron 'chambers', 13 with lids, 2 in use.

3 glass candle lamp globes.

(about) 10 enamel iron plates.

1   "   "   jug.

1   "   "   cooking pot.

(about) 50$\frac{1}{4}$ lb. flasks of powder.

  " 75 packets of Matches.

  " 12 cotton Hammocks.

Some drugs of different kinds, one or two tins and paper packets.

3 small rolls of cotton lampwick.

The above to meet the daily and weekly needs of a Station, founded for many years now, 'employing' some fifty or sixty people in one way and another, with cleared ground round it of over a 100 acres, three houses, and, the Devil knows how many concubines. There are surely more concubines than saleable articles in this store, but I suppose these ladies are not saleable. They give their all – like virtue, above price.

I don't know what view the Commission take of their questioning of Jiménez. It endured about $\frac{1}{2}$ an hour, and in my hearing, although I lost words occasionally, and was not listening, and from what I heard it was far from illuminating. Fox did almost all the question[ing], Tizon and sometimes Bell translating to him Jiménez' replies. I heard Fox ask how the rubber was collected, and Jiménez' answer was that the 'blancos' did go out to the house of the capitanes and 'advise' them of when the rubber was due, and bring them in – this twice in the fabrico – except Parvenir, whose rubber went direct to Occidente.

The 'payment' was an 'advance'. The Indians named their goods, and these came up from Chorrera subsequently. Fox asked how 'prices' were fixed? What quantity of rubber was demanded for a gun, say. Jiménez said the Indians did not know prices or quantities; they brought what he told them. He fixed the quantity and prices and decides quantity required accordingly to the 'advance'. No question of any kind was asked as to payment for other services, such as the buildings we see – the clearing, the various services these people are constantly performing.

The Commission are now 'inspecting' outside, and Gielgud taking happy snapshots of interesting natives with painted faces and sticks in their noses. What I should like would be a photograph of <u>all</u> the female staff of the establishment, and then their names, <u>capacities, salaries</u>, and cost to the Company or surrounding Indian population given below each place. Not a difficult thing to do. The place is like a rabbit warren with them, but it will not be done.

As soon as convenient I want to have the Stocks or 'cepo' tested publicly. These are the same Stocks in which Dyall was confined all night by Montt. They have nineteen holes, very small, and I can well believe that to put a big man's legs in here, sit on the heavy beam, and then lock it down on him was veritable torture, as Dyall said, and as his deeply scarred legs showed. I will go in them myself and try and put Bishop and Sealy in! . . .

The Commission, I heard, decided to leave on Tuesday, back to Puerto Peruano by the Launch, and then on foot (7 hours), then on to Entre Rios to 'O'Donnell's[10] country'. To think that a name so great should be dragged so low! That an Irish name of valour, truth, courage, and high-mindedness should be borne by a Peruvian bandit, whose aim is to persecute these wretched Indians, his 'fellow citizens', to rob them of all

[10] See Black Diary, note 130.

they possess, in order to make money from their blood. The only cheering thing is that this Andrios O'Donnell has the best name of the lot – the least scoundrelly record. It is not much, but still in the kingdom of the blind the one-eyed man is king,[11] and it is something here to have it said of you that 'O'Donnell did not kill Indians with his own hands, all the others did.' ...

I went to the Stocks at about 10.30, and tried them on Sealy. They would not nearly close on his legs, the internal measurement being, I think, less than 3", nearer $2\frac{1}{2}$". We put in a sturdy Indian, and they fitted him just. He could move his foot a little up and down, but his leg was thin round ankle. ...

I certainly think the brute-beast Montt ought to be made to pay dearly for having put the unhappy Dyall in this torture-box for a night with his legs lacerated, and then to hang him up to the beam above, by a chain, as Bishop, who stood by, testified aloud to us all. The matter was getting embarrassing. Sr. Tizon, poor man, came along and I walked away.

Another complaint from the Barbadians about their food. Bishop begged me to allow him to give a tin of my meat to a very thin little girl he saw outside working. I said, yes, of course, but he lost sight of her, poor wee soul.

At luncheon we saw a party of women ferried across, and start under one of these scoundrels to prepare the path for the Commission tomorrow, who intend to visit some locality near at hand. Nearly all were women – the man with a gun – the male animal to direct, and the women to work, and these swine of the underworld actually reprove the Indians for that the men don't work their plantations! These pigs who loll in hammocks and wait for the rubber to come in, who never do a hand's turn of work, and could not earn 6d. a day in any decent community, are the lords and masters of this unhappy people – body and soul – and exercise more than feudal tyranny in the name of a great English Company, over a large tract of country inhabited by these gentle, timid beings we see around us, starved and flogged, and humble as dogs that lick the hand that beats them.

After lunch I called Edward Crichley and asked Barnes and Fox to be present while I put questions to him. He spoke out – my injunction of the morning had done its work.

His details of some of the bestiality of Fidel Velarde and Aurelio Rodriguez flogging Indians, men, women and children, the latter extending them in a double 'cepo', one for the legs, the other for the head and arms, a 'cepo' that moved up and down, so that it could fit the stature of children – was revolting. I was glad Fox was present. He did not hear the last part of Crichley's statement, when later I recalled him and interrogated him as to the Expedition to the Caquetá in March–May of this year when Jimenez

[11] The quotation is from Erasmus's *Adages*, book 3.

invaded Colombia, and brought back 21 Indian prisoners and 3 Colombian white men. ...

I am tired now after a very long day of hard work, uninterrupted almost, in much heat, and with a good deal of disgust at the presence of this beast Jimenez at table, and the necessity I am under of being even civil to him, or to any of this gang of dirty cowards. Bruce's laugh that 'he got flogged for not bringing caucho, that's why' was as selfish an exhibition of the inner cur as I have yet seen. He is a sickly, pale, lame youth, flushing easily, with a washed-out skin and a profile and nose like Lefroy,[12] the murderer of my boyhood – just like him. I've been wondering where the resemblance lay – now I have it.

Sealy came to say that I had asked him before at Occidente to point out when we reached Ultimo Retiro the other man who used to flog at Sabana when he was there. 'Here he is,' he said, 'the cook there, Zumaran'. I looked to the kitchen, and saw this undersized underling, in blue pyjamas, one of the gang Bell said yesterday looked 'all cutthroats'. This was poor Sealy's co-executioner before – now our cook. When I look at Sealy's decent, good-natured, black face – a really <u>good</u> darkie's countenance, and see him grinning from ear to ear with delight when I sometimes rub it in to these cowards, in public, as at the Stocks today, I wonder how it was he was saved from sinking altogether to the animal state of his surroundings.

Today at the Stocks there was quite a gathering – unconventional and joking. We began by locking Sealy in, or trying to, his legs distended in the fifth holes, and the stocks would in no wise close on them, not by any manner of means. It was clear that Dyall's story was true of the man sitting on top so as to force the Stocks down on him, and of his agony. I said so that all should hear 'This was not intended for a place of detention, but for an instrument of torture.' The holes would hold only the emaciated legs of these poor Huitotos, whom even the neighbouring tribes call 'mosquito legs'. This was made clear before we finished, by putting in the right leg of the elderly man [Waiteka], and it was just taut, and could move from two to three inches only up and down. It was when he was released he burst out against the Stocks, and showed the floggings all over him in the face of the whole, his injured countenance protesting as much as his words.

The Barbadians enjoyed it, it was first-hand evidence at last – an Indian actually daring to speak out! The man had grasped the situation, and it

[12] R.C. presumably had in mind Baron (Thomas Langlois) Lefroy (1776-1869), who had the reputation of a 'hanging judge'. Antipathy to the judge will have come partly from R.C.'s admiration for Irish rebel John Mitchel, whose *Jail Journal* had been published in Ireland by James Corrigan in 1864. Lefroy had sentenced Mitchel to fourteen years' transportation.

poured out. All were laughing, but in different ways. I was smiling with pleasure that this fearless skeleton[13] had found tongue and the innocent-faced lad beside him, and that these two incontrovertible bottoms with the sign manual of 'Casa Arana' were being flaunted in the faces of the Commission.

I said (to Chase) aloud, and with my finger measuring the required depth. 'Tell him the next time he doesn't bring in enough caucho, and they are going to flog him, to put it [R.C.'s note: i.e. the india-rubber itself to spread it over his posterior & limbs] an inch deep all over his backside and legs, and let them fire away!' All roared, but the thrust went home. The 'staff', with their Idol thus opprobriously made game of and before the Indians too, who had trembled so long in the grip of this monster, did not know whether to smile or protest at this slighting of the Stocks. The latter they dared not do, so they laughed too. I then said 'As we are discussing this instrument of torture — there was the block hole there if they only wanted to detain men — I would suggest — an impertinent intervention perhaps — that the Commission should signalise their visit to Ultimo Retiro by having it publicly burned. That's what I should do if I were in charge here.' All looked grave, only old Fox approved, and he actually brought it forward later on to the members, as an official suggestion, but they thought it 'wiser not' to do anything quite so glaring as to burn the cepo. That would make a flare. Bell said it was to, and would go, and they were to be content with that. The block hole I've not yet described, but shall do so. It lies near the Stocks, but I must return to Sealy's further statement. After telling me of Zumaran being the other flogger at Sabana, when he was there as executioner, he said Jimenez had called Crichley aside this afternoon, after being interrogated by me, and had talked to him apart, and that Crichley would not tell them what Jiménez had said. I asked Bishop if this was so, and he said that Crichley had said that Jiménez asked him to say nothing against him, that he had always treated him well — which was true — and had then gone on to talk about the women of the Station, and had told Crichley to keep a good guard — 'a good eye on them to see that no one interfered with them'. This is exactly what I had been expecting. I told Bishop that he and the other two men were on no account to sleep apart, but all in the room where they are together. The remainder of what Jiménez had said to Crichley, the latter had refused to tell, even to him, Bishop said. He admitted that Jiménez had said more, but refused to say what it was.

We had another tiger interlude just before dinner. Three 'muchachos', or Indians, two with guns, came in to the dining room to see Jiménez. They looked such weird little things (one pale and thin, with his long black

[13] See Black Diary, note 129.

hair draped round his thin mummyish face), and their high staccato, Chinese-like speech, every word cut from its fellow. They were like ghosts in an Opera.

They began excitedly telling Jiménez of their doings, and he laughed, and told us that it was another 'tiger' scare. The head boy had just been stalking a 'paron' (peacock), and was aiming at it up in a tree when a jaguar aimed at him behind. He rose with a yell, fired in the air and leaped after. The jaguar went in one direction and the Indian in the other, and here he happily was, to tell the tale. We are all going out to the forest tomorrow – 2½ hours out – and will take arms, and try for one of these numerous panthers or jaguars – here, of course, called 'tigers'. Poor 'Andokes' (the Camereiro mayor, as I call him) fell off the launch today while it was going up river with the Commission to visit the Chacra, and was nearly lost. He came to the top, however, and was picked up, but is ill tonight. Angry with himself, they say.

I turned in early, very tired with a long day, and tried to sleep to the tread of the sentry pacing the verandah all through the night. The sentry, I believe, is Zamora, the especial looking cut-throat, quite the worst cast of face I think we've struck yet in this Chamber of Horrors' collection of criminals.

SUNDAY, OCTOBER 9TH, 1910. AT ULTIMO RETIRO.

We left for the 'Nation', as they call it, of the Meretas Indians, to see Hevea trees.[14] The whole Commission, Tizon, Jiménez, Bruce, and a train of servants, the cook and empleados, and a lot of press-ganged Indians had gone before. We were to walk 2½ hours through the forest, and the ordinary forest track had been prepared yesterday by the force of women and a few men we had seen going off at lunch.

As we embarked in the 'batalon' to cross the river, two elderly Indian men came down with more camp equipment for us, nude save for their slender fono of white bark cloth. Their sterns were both terribly scarred, indeed the two broad patches on one man's buttocks looked like burns. They were the scars of an extra deep cutting of the lash. All of us saw them, but I broke silence, and said, at large, 'Two very incontrovertible burns, I must say.' These instructive backsides climbed in, and squatted beside us, their elderly owners asking me for a cigarette. 'Chigarro, Chigarro' has become the greeting we get wherever we go, but especially myself, for I give cigarettes with a lavish hand. The poor souls, young and

---

[14] *Hevea brasiliensis*: the Pará rubber tree, which was grown in plantations (on the *Chacaras*).

old, love them, and, God knows, they have little pleasure. Whenever they get a present they stroke one's hand or shoulder affectionately, and say, 'Bigara, bigara' (Good, good). They apply it now universally, and we are constantly hailed with cries of 'Bigara', so I christened them this morning 'the Begorrahs' It sounds <u>exactly</u> like an Irish begorrah. The name has stuck, and Barnes and all of them speak of our poor Indian hosts as the Begorrahs, and we made much play with the word during the day.

As we went along the path we found constant evidence of yesterday's work for our benefit, the rough places made smooth, and, I added, when we noticed this – 'At the expense, I fear, of their smooth places made rough,' – patting my haunches. I am certainly becoming the <u>enfant terrible</u> of the Commission, but I mean to rub these highly instructive backsides well in their faces until they admit that it is the lash behind and not the 'advance' in front that collects each fabrico of rubber.

The path had indeed been smoothed for us – trees felled, saplings and trunks laid over wet spots, and bridges made over many streams with a leana rope[15] banister to hold by. Over three traversings of a large deep river, a tributary of the Igaraparana, we found very large trees felled, and a strong bridge thus made at great labour by these poor people. The road was fully 6 miles long I should say, all through rich forest with many Hevea trees, mostly young saplings, some fine palms, with the cries of birds, toucans and parrots, and the most variegated display of butterfly wings we have yet encountered.

I pointed out more than once, in remarks to those near me, that I could not see how any of this heavy labour of preparing this path for us was to be paid for. It was clear that there was no intention of paying these people, for there was nothing in the Store to do it, and even the pretence of 'feeding' them could scarcely be sustained, seeing the want of food everywhere visible. Perhaps they would assume that these lady workers were to be remunerated with the enamelled iron 'chambers' <u>with</u> lids we had observed in the Store, but even then it was clear you'd have to divide one po between a dozen ladies. I have certainly been nasty today, and have handled my weapons truculently, the enamel iron utensil being so prominent in the tiny Store that it pays the price of obviousness. Crichley, Sealy and Chase came also with us – all armed with Winchesters – as were the 'staff', the cook and the general parade of scoundrels who precede us everywhere. Crichley said once 'This Section used to have plenty of Indians, but it has only a few now – they've been killed mostly.' This was said quite aloud – for general use – but I fancy only Barnes and I, who were leading, heard it.

[15] Liana: a woody vine of the tropical rainforest.

On the way we met a small party coming in under a capitan with a dead monkey, just shot and trussed. This they at once handed to Jiménez, who told them to take it to the Station, and some cassava bread a woman was carrying. These 'gifts' of these poor fugitives, shot by themselves in their own wild forest, or made by their patient wives from their tiny patches of cassava, are another part of the unlimited tribute laid upon them by each of these strongholds of robbery. ...

What we are all doing is clear. To try and save the hideous scandal of a public exposure of what has occurred here, not even in the remote part of, say, 1907, but right up to today, to this very month, in order to save the Company. That the Company as such should be saved neither Tizon nor I think nor care, but the Company is the surest guarantee we can lay hold of for more humane treatment of the Indians, all that are left of them. The destruction during the last few years has been abnormal. This region, bordering on the Japurá has always been, or for a very long time has been, the happy hunting ground of the Portuguese or other enslavers of the Indians. See Lt. Maw's account of what he heard in 1827 when passing down the Amazon from Peru.[16] Then even Portuguese raiding parties went up the Japurá to catch slaves, and the methods he described nearly a century ago are exactly those of Jimenez and this English Company today in 1910. But if you can keep it going, as really an English Company, and not merely as Arana Bros., registered in London, then radical changes can be effected and this disgraceful state of things brought to a more or less speedy ending. The difficulty will be to keep the gang – to prevent the Board from resigning at once. Every pressure that can be brought to bear upon them should be brought by the F.O. and other influences to induce them to hold on even at a loss, so as to repair to some extent the wrong they have innocently helped to inflict on these unhappy, these mercilessly persecuted people. They who have made money from the slavery of the Indians must now be begged, compelled, if it can be, to even lose money to redeem the remnant of the Indians. This is what we are all trying for, Tizon, I think, perhaps more than anyone, save myself, while Gielgud, admitting to the full the moral claim and the dire need, fears that the body of shareholders will kick. So do I. And then there is always Julio Arana himself! He is the danger spot. If he finds he cannot hoodwink any longer the English Company, then he will destroy it and restart the past and actual piracy on even worse lines with the Peruvian Government behind him to wring out the last pound of rubber while one Indian is left alive to procure it in all this stifling wilderness. God help the poor beings – only He can help them. I intend taking a boy home to try and interest the Anti-Slavery people, etc. etc.

[16] See Black Diary, note 160.

and the Missions, so that possibly some of the wealthy people, who are also good people, may, possibly, – who knows? – it is a wild thought – take shares in the Company not to get rubber, but to save Indians. If the Company goes, as I fear <u>must</u> be the case, then all is lost. The last hope of these poor beings disappears for ever, and they would do better to go into their woods for the last time, look around once more, for ever, on their green trees, their blue skies, their rushing rivers, their innumerable woodland signs, and then deliberately and lovingly slay each other. Better far! Die once, and be done with it. Not only do you end it, but you also pay back in the only way left you these scavengers of crime, their atrocious treatment of yourselves. With you all dead and gone these forests are worthless, these thousands of miles of upper Amazon tributaries go back to the wild beasts and the human beasts, who have infested them these 20 years past, go back to their sordid and mean lives in the streets of Peruvian and Colombian towns without rubber and without pelf, and might soon be forced to work for their living. ...

... we saw a lot of Indians on the opposite bank of the river, men with boxes ('Chop boxes') on their backs, carried in the usual fibre slings from the forehead. Poor beings they were, limping along, and sat down to wait for the canoe. We were told they had come from Occidente with more of our food loads we had left behind there – too much for the Launch to bring on. There were about three canoe loads of them, and they were coming in until 6 to 7 p.m. When about a dozen or more had arrived I called Bishop, and we found out that they had been 2 days on the road, and as they looked starved I asked him to enquire what rations they had received at Occidente for this journey. Bishop said 'They've had nothing, sir, can't you see those Indians are starving. They <u>never</u> get any food given for any journey at all – rubber or expeditions – or anything – they've got to find it as best they can, or get it from their friends. That's why they chew the coca.'[17] They say they can go two days without food on the coca.' I said 'Never mind, ask them all the same. So he did, in Huitoto. There was a perfect howl. A 'hugh', and two men turned their scarified bottoms, a boy also, and we saw the most enormous weals and scars I've seen yet. I called Fox and Gielgud, and one of the men, a capitan, who was sitting on the bulwark, told us or rather Bishop with gestures suiting the words, 'We asked Velarde for a tin of sardines for the road, and he told us to eat our private parts,' and he put both hands down there and made pretence of doing what Velarde had done. I was glad I had got Fox and Gielgud and Barnes to be witness of this recital.

[17] The leaves of the South American shrub coca (*Erythroxylum coca*) produce cocaine when chewed. The drug had been used for centuries by the Andean Indians as a stimulant to increase their physical endurance.

I gave these poor starving wretches a tin of meat or fish between every two men. There were over 20 of them, and it made a hole in my supplies, but I never gave food with greater pleasure in my life. They literally wolfed it with the loudest 'begorrahs' I've got yet, and such smiles of delight. All squatted down there and then, all over the verandah, in the door of my room, anywhere two by two, and tore the tins open and swallowed in a brace of shakes, sheeps' tongues, herrings, salmon and other preserved meats. We all enjoyed the spectacle, almost as much as they did. One boy swallowed the greasy paper round a sheep's tongue, inside the tin, and another opened a tin with his teeth. The 'Begorrahs' were one genial flow of eructation. It was only a snack, but was a welcome one and unexpected. The spokesman, a young capitan, gave forth the rest of their charge, against Velarde – that he had 'been frightened' (their very words) when we were there, but now he said he should flog them again, and do as he pleased with them, and hold them under water and drown them. Here again was the same charge uttered by these men, and Tizon only a pace or two away. I was delighted, and Bishop translated for us all with equal pleasure. Fox said it almost made him cry to see them – these poor lacerated, emaciated beings, like children in so many ways, biddable and gentle, and the absolute, entire, slaves of these damnable scoundrels. Gielgud, too, was moved to hearty indignation, the first time I have had the pleasure of hearing him come out with real, unmitigated reproof. He said Velarde ought to be hanged, or handed to these very men and flogged by them till he died. I said I'd like to flog the brute myself, but he was only one of <u>many</u> and the System that had been planted on these poor serfs by Arana & Co. had introduced these ruffians and employed them and their methods for years at highly remunerative terms. It was no use denouncing Velarde as an individual blackguard, it was the entire system of slavery had to go and its substitution by some rational and <u>faintly</u> legal treatment for the Indians. ...

Bishop in the evening brought in a paper on which he had written that an Indian had told him last night that an Indian who had been here in chains and in the Stocks in January last had been shot by order of Montt, the executioner being one Velasquez. I find Velasquez figures on the list of Station hands, but, of course, is not here now, any more than Aquileo Torres, who is 'on the move'. None of these 'racionales' have a stroke of useful or natural work to do, for all their human use the whole lot could go. They are merely the instruments of torture, to bully and oppress and dragoon the peaceful, timid children of the forest.

Jiménez draws a fine percentage of profits here on his 25 tons (mas ou menos) [more or less] of Rubber supplied by the '260 workmen' of his district. I wonder if the 21 Indians brought from far beyond the Japura in Colombia figure among these.

MONDAY, 10TH OCTOBER, 1910 – ULTIMO RETIRO.

Up at 5. Eye (left eye) very sore and swelling again, so that I have to bandage it. Out at 5.30, and saw the poor Indians of last night sweeping the Station! They got rice last night by Gielgud's order. I doubt if anyone would have given them a thought, only my tins and the demonstration they evoked caused so much scandal. If I, a stranger, gave them all this food, valued up here at perhaps 2 pounds (for I gave some fifteen tins), then the people who had press-ganged them and used them like beasts of burden with no thought of paying them, had to give them at least a meal.

They all returned across the river to return to their homes at 7. I gave the Capitan and others some cigarettes, and gave him a couple of flasks of powder, and a bag of shot. His joy was boyish, he fairly hugged it. One boy I saw, and really thought of trying to get home with me to interest the Missions and Anti-Slavery people in the fate of these poor people. If a Mission were started it might help a lot, but it can only come on two conditions – that the Company (I mean the English part of it) is strong enough to crush Arana and dismiss his gang of murderers and put in decent men, and then that the Company itself will consent to carry on – even at a loss, as it must be for some years. Then a Mission here would be first rate, but a Mission with the present System would mean only more victims. ...

TUESDAY, OCTOBER 11TH, 1910.

... Fox is pretty well convinced now. I have been seeking to disabuse his mind this morning on another point. He has been told that the evil system he sees in full swing was a sort of natural and inevitable growth based on the fact that the first 'settlers' had to hold their own against the Indians by terror. These latter would have murdered them and so forth, and so, step by step, this armed abomination grew up as 'a cruel necessity for self defence'. I bore him to my room, read over Arana's statement to the shareholders, in which this lying plea is put out, and asked him if he believed it, and he said 'No, it is untrue.' So I said with the rest of that tale. These men came here not as settlers 'to trade' with the Indians, but to appropriate the Indians. It is not the rubber trees, so much as the Indians they wanted and want. The trees are valueless without the Indians, who, besides getting rubber for them, do everything else these creatures need – feed them, build for them, run for them, and carry for them, and supply them with 'wives' and concubines.

They couldn't get this done by persuasion, so they slew and massacred and enslaved by terror, and that is the whole foundation. What we see today is merely the logical sequence of events – the cowed and entirely subdued Indians, reduced in numbers, hopelessly obedient, with no refuge and no retreat, and no redress. Here, this very year, is this very man, Jiménez, heading a large armed band of the 'Company's servants' far into the republic of Colombia, many days beyond the Caquetá, the indisputed frontier of that State, and putting 3 Colombians in Stocks for 21 days on their own soil, and bringing them and 21 Indians down here as prisoners. These 21 Indians had fled many days' journey to escape from this regime, and they are not saved by flight, even into another so-called civilized country. The whole thing from top to bottom is slavery without law – the most lawless state of things imaginable in this stage of human progress, for these Agents are not savages, but are the highly paid servants of a great English Company – citizens of a civilised State and amenable, so we are told, to an 'Efficient administration of justice'.

I intend taking home, if I can, some of the flogged Indians to convince humane men and women of the dire need for helping these poor people, which incidentally must mean helping the Company.

...We left Ultimo Retiro at about 1.15 p.m. the rain having cleared up. Before leaving I called Crichley again. It was to ask him if the double 'cepo' that Aurelio Rodriguez had used at Santa Catalina for flogging victims raised off the ground, with the more able 'leg stocks' 'so as to fit children' was still in existence, as, if so, we might photograph it. Gielgud and I had been regretting we had not photoed the 'cepo' here, which is such a big one. Crichley said that Rodriguez had had those Stocks destroyed when 'Capt. Whiffen was coming', and then added that it was he (Crichley) had made it 'to the plan of Aurelio Rodriguez'. I said – 'You must be quite a good carpenter then', and he grinned, and said 'I make all the furniture here, sir,' pointing to the strong wooden benches with moveable backs, on which we had been sitting at meals every day. It is for this extra work that Jimenez is giving him 20 soles (£2) per month over his ordinary pay of 50 soles per month. Then, as we were leaving, I said to Crichley in a loud voice, so that all could hear 'Remember, any illegal work, such as flogging Indians or beating them or maltreating them, you are not to perform. It is illegal to ask you and illegal for you to do it, and is a punishable offence, and if you are ordered to do it you must refuse, and at once inform me if I am still here, or if not Sr. Tizon, and write to the Consul in Iquitos.' Everyone heard this, I think, certainly the 'empleados' and Jiménez did, for they were standing close at hand.

Jiménez accompanied us to the beach to wave affectionate farewells with his white military cap. I raised mine to this thrice, triple murderer! And shook hands, too! His face is not so bad – that of a sturdy, rather good-tempered ruffian, strong, healthy, brown and courageous with a thick-set, very strong and sturdy body. He looks well under 30.

I don't know what the Barbadians must think of me – of us all – shaking hands affably with this man whom they saw commit the most appalling crimes, but it will be made clear to these simple dependents later on that <u>we</u> are not so black as this would paint us.

We steamed well down stream to Puerto Peruano, arriving there at 4.34, when we find about 40 Indians – boys and men – sent by O'Donnell from Entre Rios for our baggage. We have some 60 loads I believe, so Bruce tells me, so part of the goods must be left behind. These poor beings were <u>starving</u> – literally starving, as we dined about 7 they sat round on their bare haunches with gleaming eyes and shining, smiling teeth, giving the most hungry looks imaginable at every mouthful. I could not stand it, and by stealth I slipped all the food off my plate as each course was handed me, and collected it up beside me and gave it to two small boys of the group, who divided every morsel with their friends. Tizon ordered them rice and beans, which were boiled subsequently for them.

I turned in very early in the house where I slept before – the two-roomed palm house, and it poured with rain. The 40 Indians and all the others merely slept under these rooms on the ground or on the billets of firewood stored there for the launch. This firewood constantly stored here is another of the tasks laid on these wretched people, without the shadow of any payment.

My eye continues very bad and is bandaged tight over, so that I have only the right eye to see by. Slept fairly well in spite of some very long-legged mosquitos, just like gnats or daddy long-legs. They did not bite, but buzzed.

WEDNESDAY, 12TH OCTOBER.

... As I was ill, and my eye very bad, I did not go to dinner, but lay down right away in this guest room.

Bishop came in the evening and said this brute, Barbolini, who has been the chief flogger of the Indians, had got drunk after dinner and was kicking up a row with him. Barbolini accused him of 'telling on them' to me, and that now we wanted to turn the Peruvians out for the things they had done to the Indians, while he, Bishop, had been as bad as any of them, and had done just as bad things. Bishop said he came to tell me, but that he had told Barbolini he would not talk with him in his actual state.

He added that all he had done he had done under compulsion as already confessed – but he had hidden nothing from me of his own misdeeds, but that he had not even [ever] deliberately killed an Indian. Barbolini, he said, had – he had seen him at <u>Urania</u> long ago (this station is now abandoned) cut off an Indian's head. He had wanted Bishop to do it, and he refused, and then he called a muchacho, and the boy's heart failed him when he had begun to hack the neck, so Barbolini took the mocheto [machete] from him and finished the job. This was long ago, soon after he, Bishop, had joined the Arana gang, probably in 1906.

There is a man named Martin Arana[18] here among the staff who is, so Bishop says, 'a brother of Julio Arana' – I think it means a half-brother (by an unwedded woman); possibly only a cousin. He is a sort of servant – looks after the store, gives out food and cleans lamps etc., also makes cocktails. He has a look, certainly of Lizardo Arana, but is much younger.

There is a circle of fine popuna palms round the house and some very fine bananas.

O'Donnell has been here at Entre Rios seven years. He is now 27 he says, and left Lucia in 1901, when he could have been only 17. He speaks Hiutoto fluently – better than anyone else in the Company's service, so Gielgud and Tizon say. He produced a sketch map of his section this afternoon which is interesting, and which I should much like to copy. It was drawn up by himself in 1908 and shows the 'houses' of each Indian sub-tribe (or 'nation') in his section, with the paths and principal streams. The Cahuniari rises quite close to the north of this, and flows some 250 yards below the house on the east, down through the cleared ground. The bathing place of the blancos is down there – a dressing house by the stream which is 4 feet deep. Even to go down to this stream everyone carries his rifle! It is 'a custom' O'Donnell says – and dates from the days when the Indians used to attack them. 'Before they learned to work – now they are quiet, and very content – muy contentos!' I did not express any doubt. On the map he has places marked four crosses showing where 'los Indios' had burned 'houses of the Columbians' – and then a red patch showing where the 'last rising' took place against him – and another patch quite close to the house – only a few miles away to the north where he had 'fallen into an ambuscade.' I only said 'more power to the Indians', but as he is not an Irishman, in spite of his name, he did not follow.

He has been shot at here while bathing down at the bath house – but that was in the bad days before the Indians took to 'trabajar.' [work] Since they adopted working rubber for him they are very happy and content and don't shoot any more at their patriarchal imported High Chief.

Bell likes O'Donnell, so he told me. I said he seemed the best certainly of a very bad lot.

There are a great number of women here. Indian 'wives' and water girls like those at Occidente – The place is more 'respectable' than Ultimo Retiro – that was the absolute pirate ship without pretence.

[18] See Black Diary, note 131.

Here the plantations, the bananas and palm trees close up to the houses – the evidences of cultivation and the superior appearance and address of O'Donnell certainly create a favourable impression after the recent horrors we have been living with – the snake-like Velarde and the burn 'em alive Jiménez.

ENTRE RIOS FRIDAY, 14TH OCT. 1910.

...The Peruvians I find, hate confrontations of accusers and accused. We Northerners like it. It is the only way of thrashing a matter out and getting to the truth. They prefer letters and secret intrigue behind one's back. The lower class Peruvian half-caste is a cur; the higher class are good like Tizon or the Prefect; while the lowest class, the Indians and Cholas, are fine fellows. They are really Peru, the backbone of the country. It is that 'blanco' type that pulls down the nation, the people with the skins of whiteness only, and certainly not the hearts of Indians. The Zulus were proud of their color, they honoured black, their Chiefs were 'the great, great black one' – a man had a black heart – and we speak of a 'whiteman' meaning an honourable man by it. Here a 'blanco' can mean only a scoundrel, and to the Indian a murderer. These three Barbados men with me have proved themselves far straighter, honester and braver than any Peruvian we have met. They have told the truth, under great stress of fear, (and shame too, I hope) have accused themselves and have manfully stuck to their guns – while the one 'whiteman' the Commission were to rely on (Garrido) and whom they paid £20 a month to, turned tail at the first confrontation and revealed himself a coward and a liar.

Sealy came just now to say that the man Pinedo, here on the staff, was with him at Ultimo Retiro, and was a member of the recent commission to the Caqueta when Crichlow went with Jimenez. Crichlow had declared to me that no one was killed in this raid, and Sealy says that Pinedo has twice, last night and this morning, told him of how Aquileo Torres killed an Indian boy on the road back, and that Jimenez, Crichlow, Reuben Phillips (the other Barbadian on the expedition) and the rest of them saw it done. The boy was tired and Torres called him, and putting the muzzle of his Winchester out to him, told him to blow down the barrel as if for a joke, and when the muzzle was in the boy's mouth he pulled the trigger and killed him. ... Young Rodriquez (who belongs to this section, but is temporarily lent to Occidente) has three wives. All these are taken, by force, or death, or simple appropriation from the surrounding Indian 'nations'. As a rule, an Indian wife is not taken thus, although many cases have been related to me, of Jimenez or Fonseca, or Montt, taking wives by force and killing the husbands who resisted, but as a rule I gather the actual wife of a full grown Indian man is – well, not respected, but left to him. The reason is not solely benevolent respect for the Indian's conjugal rights. Sealy put it quite tersely this afternoon, when telling me of Aguero of Abisinia having nine 'wives' when he was stationed there, and taking as many women as he pleased, just as Whiffen described in his letter to F.O. 'Did he take wives of Indians'? I asked. 'No sir, not their wives'. 'Why not'? I asked. 'Well,' he said 'if you takes an Indian's wife he won't work caucho'. 'But you flog him, you can make him work caucho by flogging'. 'No, not if you takes his wife, he won't work caucho then, you may flog and flog, he will die, some of de Indians loves their wives very much'. What a pitiable people to think of it! The one provision that saves even their wives from the lust of these Satzos [=? <u>Sádicos</u>, Sadists] is the greed of their men, they cannot get the rubber, or as much rubber, if they don't leave the poor hunted Indian man his one wife, the sharer of all his miseries, but the mother of his child.

At dinner we had the chief of the <u>Mimanee</u> [Naimenes] Indians and the capitan of the Inonokomas, who came on the verandah. The latter a very intelligent looking man, with bright piercing eyes. They sat beside O'Donnell before dinner, and he made the capitan take off his soiled and hideous pantaloons and shirt because he said these smelt after the dance. (As a matter of fact, there is no offensive odour from these Indians' skins. They have the most wonderfully clean bodies considering their conditions, and when nude one can stand in the midst of a crowd of them in the hottest hour of the day without perceiving the slightest smell. Their skins are extraordinarily dry, I have not yet seen one perspire, although carrying a heavy load through the forest on an atrocious road. They are weak and frail to the eye and to the leg under the heavy loads, but get along cheerfully and quietly without a word of complaint. As they get scarcely any food and are sent on their marches for days with literally nothing but what they can pick up, it is perhaps no wonder they do not perspire, but it is a marvel they can live and move and carry such weights. They have nothing to exude at the pores, they are chips of this old forest, dried vegetable products rather than flesh and blood.) This gave the Inonikoma capitan his chance. He knew, in a dim way who we all were, and that we were here to 'change things'. That word has gone round. So he stripped at once and stood in his 'fono' and painted bronze limbs, a much finer object, but he turned upon O'Donnell, who was sitting on the bench and delivered his soul. I said to Tizon 'That seems a very intelligent Indian, he can talk quickly and is evidently saying a lot'. None of us knew a word of his rapid speech, save O'Donnell. He tried to stop him, and waved his hand, but the Capitan went on with flashing eyes, and after pointing to his buttocks, now bare, but painted, and extending his hand. It was clear he was saying more than O'Donnell liked. He remarked he was 'very conversador', a great talker, and we laughed agreement, for the Huitoto words, sharp and hard, were pouring out in a continued stream. I felt certain this was an Indian 'witness' at last, one who has got the whole Commission before him, we were all at dinner by this time – and was determined to get a pronouncement from us in the face of O'Donnell. The latter, it was clear, was ill at ease, he said the Indian was saying he was glad to see us (he didn't look it a bit!) and that once he had been O'Donnell's great enemy and had tried to kill him, but that now they were friends and he worked caucho for him and we were to see he got nice things for it. In fact, he was another voluble example of the 'many contentos' [satisfied] Indians. As soon as possible I slipped from the table under pretext of getting a cigarette and told Bishop to come and have a look at the man, and afterwards to find out from him what it was he had really been saying for our benefit. Bishop came to show me a collar of leopard teeth, as a pretext for looking at the man, and I agreed to buy it, another pretext, and when our dinner ended, I waited to hear the result of my stratagem.

It was, as I suspected. He was the spokesman for all. He had said that O'Donnell was working his people to death, that many had died, and now they were all being flogged for not bringing in the rubber put upon them, and they could not work harder than they did, and he wanted the flogging stopped to save his people. This was the gist of his long speech. ...

Bishop, I can see, has no feeling of respect or regard for O'Donnell, he says he is not the worst, perhaps the best of this infernal crew, but that he has flogged and terrorized and <u>caused</u> Indians to be killed for the same pure greed of rubber. I said that I thought Julio Arana was the most guilty of all. I was amazed to see how, at once, the coarse, black face flushed, and he said with vehemence, 'Indeed he is, sir, that's my opinion, and I've thought that always. He knew perfectly what was done here and how the rubber was got, and these men are not so bad as he is'. Fonseca he says is a maniac, a murderous maniac. He relates how, he saw him have 2 Indians taken out of 'cepo' at U. Retiro, two mornings running at 6 a.m. and shot for mere sport by a man called Luiz Silva at Fonseca's order. Fonseca, he said, shouted for this to be done, just like ordering morning coffee, there was no earthly reason for it. The poor wretched Indians were starving in the 'cepo' and for sheer diversion, or as Bishop put it, 'just for pride', he had them killed. This Luiz Silva is now dead, or rather very righteously slain by the Andokes,[19] alongside with Bucelli, in the Caqueta country. He had murdered many Indians, Bishop states, to his knowledge. The shooting of the two unfortunates at Ultimo Retiro by Fonseca's order was in 1906 and soon after, he, Bishop, had come there. Bishop came from Urania (now abandoned) where he had been under Martinengui. This Silva was one of ·

[19] See Black Diary, note 137.

the 'executioners' at Ultimo Retiro, and again, later on, at Occidente, under Fonseca; and at both places Bishop states he saw him flog Indians most brutally, cutting them to pieces.

... O'Donnell says the father of my Muinanes Chief was a 'noted slave dealer with the Brazilians,' but I doubt this. It sounds suspiciously like the indictment formulated against the Boras and other strong tribes who 'won't work', that they are 'cannibals'. It is like Mark Twain's grandfathers – 'Grandfathers are always in the wrong.' The Indian, who is stout enough to resist enslavement, is always in the wrong, and therefore a 'cannibal'.

I have assured Gielgud that some of the nicest people I know on the Congo were cannibals.

O'Donnell is full of Indian lore, and has told us much of the habits of the Indians and their thoughts. I wish I could take it down, but I miss a good deal of his Spanish. He says his grandfather went to Spain from Ireland, and father came from Spain to Peru. I doubt the grandfather. It is probably further back. Still the man is certainly the best by a long way of any agent of the Company we have met, and with seven years of this cruel savagery behind him it is remarkable he has remained so outwardly untouched and with so clear and straightforward an eye. His manner, too, with the Indians is far better, and they seem to have almost an affection for him. Strange that such gentle hearts should be so abused, or rather it is not strange, but, I suppose, human nature. Were these poor savage beings like the Africans, this paltry handful of filibusters and pirates – for the whole gang numbers only about 150 – would have been swept away, after the first few murders. But the simplicity of the Indians and their fatal obedience have been their undoing, and their childish weapons, blow-pipes and toy spears, thrown three at a time in the fingers, are a poor substitute for the African battle spear and axe. The African never feared blood; he liked its flow. These childlike beings, even in their wars, took life secretly and silently with as little flow of blood as is possible. The Winchester rifle in the hands of one desperado can overawe and subdue a whole tribe here, although they are not cowards. Their humble simplicity and humility are more dangerous to them than the weapons of their enslavers.

ENTRE RIOS, SATURDAY, OCTOBER 15TH [(A)]

... The women have been retained at the Station to clear up the plantation, or extend its cultivated area of maize, sugar cane, &c., &c., while the men who returned to their own homes are forced under supervision of the 'rational staff' (the bare-footed, rifle on shoulder, revolver on hip half-castes who draw a salary) to cultivate their patches of cassava. This the

Indian man of himself does not do. It is his woman's task, while he would be hunting or fishing or doing the heavier work.

But the Company objects to the habits and customs of the Indians. They are not civilized – moreover, they would not produce rubber. So the woman of the Indian household is kept at Entre Rios, or Occidente, or Atenas, as the case may be, for a space of from a week to ten days to cultivate the fields of the Company, so that its staff may have cheap food, while her husband, under the 'directions' of a half-breed much more ignorant of agriculture than the wildest Indian in the world, is forced to plant and hoe yucca in order that his body may be fortified against the next fabrico, which begins right away. If this uncongenial task is not performed to the satisfaction of the 'Empleado racionale' sent to his village to chase and hunt him to it, he will not receive his 'payment' (or 'advance' – the terms are synonymous and transposable) for the last fabrico of 40 or 50 or 60 or 70 kilogrammes of rubber he has delivered to the Company – not until he has satisfied this agricultural expert. This seems to me almost the chief refinement of cruelty of this truly devilish system of cruelty. The whole thing is hard to beat, and it has been going on for years – longer than I like to think of, and will go on, I fear, until the last Indian has delivered up his last puesta [consignment of rubber], and, with it, his poor, starved, beflagellated ghost to the God that sent the 'veracucha'[20] to be his moral guide and friend. Alas! poor Peruvian, poor South American Indian! The world thinks the slave trade was killed a century ago! The worst form of slave trade and of slavery – worse in many of its aspects, as I shall show – than anything African savagery gave birth to has been in full swing here for 300 years until the dwindling remnant of a population once numbering millions, is now perishing at the doors of an English Company, under the lash, the chains, the bullet, the machete to give its shareholders a dividend. ...

There are no old people now, I have not seen one old or even elderly man or woman since we reached Chorrera, and I have seen over 1000 Huitotos by now, possibly a tenth or fifteenth of the whole people. The oldest face I have seen is that of a man of the Miriniares tribe who goes with us as a carrier on Sunday, and he is not more than 54. The reason for this is to be found in the story Labadie told me in Iquitos, of Carlos Miranda[21] (now at Sur, only 2 hours from Chorrera) cutting off 'the old woman's' head and holding it up by the hair as 'an example' to the rest. This was because she was 'a bad woman', i.e., gave the younger people bad advice. Bad advice means not to work rubber. Thus the old folk are always the first singled out. Bishop says

[20] R.C. here intends Viracocha, the ancient Andean god who later became a cult figure in the Inca pantheon. According to ancient belief he rose from Lake Titicaca to create the earth, man and the animals, and later the planets.
[21] See Black Diary, note 155.

in the Andokes country,[22] where we go next, the old men and women were killed long ago – all Normand could get hold of. The same thing with the Boras, but these are the boldest and strongest of the Indians the Peruvians have yet had to handle in this part of the Montana. The Boras hit back. 'They don't want to work' is the cry I constantly hear going up like an accusing incense before the Moloch of these forests. ...

ENTRE RIOS, SATURDAY OCTOBER 15TH, 1910.[(B)]

I interviewed Pinedo later on; saw him hanging round and looking at me, so I went out, and as I was not sure of his identity I asked 'Are you Pinedo?' in Spanish and he at once nodded, so I told him to follow me. I had told Bell to come after, and together we took his story. It was all against Aquileo Torres, whom he evidently hated. There were a few moral maxims about treating the Indians kindly thrown in for our benefit, I presume to give us the impression that he disapproved the lash and the cutlass of the ordinary 'rationale'. Anyhow, Torres, according to him, had not only killed the Indians 'boy' by inviting him to blow down the muzzle of his Winchester and then blowing his head off, but had also killed two women, for sheer brutality or sport – all this quite recently. Jimenez had kicked him out from Ultimo Retiro as impossible (the word he used 'botar' means about that), hence his passage through Occidente on 3rd instant. He has evidently a spite against Torres, and is trying to kill two birds with one stone. I told him through Bell I should tell Mr. Tizon, and that he must tell him what he has told us, to which he agreed. We left it there and returned by separate paths as I did not wish, for Pinedo's sake that his companions should suspect he had been giving anything away to us – the intruders who are so manifestly here to upset time-honoured customs.

Bell told Tizon who said he would speak with Pinedo. At lunch we had the Muinanes Chief again. He and a lot of his men and other Indians have been kept back, after the Dance, from returning to their homes to carry our loads to-morrow up to Matanzas. The Muinanes Chief whose name is Hatima, looked through Fox's field-glasses, especially liking the small end which diminishes the object viewed. This, he said, is just what things look like when 'we have taken <u>Una</u> – very clear and distinct and very far off!'[23] This was translated for us by O'Donnell. It shows perception and a comparative mind. A minute later he came out with a much apter remark that caused an appalling silence.

[22] See Black Diary, note 137.
[23] See Black Diary, note 135.

Handling the glasses affectionately, he said, 'I suppose you buy these with the rubber we produce' – O'Donnell translated it too – and I nearly laughed aloud. It was on the tip of my tongue to add, 'Yes, indeed, and this lunch too that we are eating and you get none of –' but I couldn't do it for the sake of Tizon who looked really distressed.

He is very unhappy, I think, at all that is so clearly being revealed to him, and I am sincerely sorry for him, altho' glad to think there is a Peruvian gentleman trying hard to set right all this great wrong, built up by his own countrymen.

I had lots of Indians in the afternoon watching me writing. They come into my room just like Congo men of old and talked to me and smiled. They even bring their biscuits in, or something given them, to eat in peace. I give them lots of cigarettes which they like very much, and everything I can spare from my own tins. Poor starved, flogged and murdered people, how I pity them!

The very idea of keeping back these 40 or 50 men for our long march to Matanzas shows how absolutely enslaved they are. They came to 'a Dance' by special invitation and now they are to wait here – on very short commons – and carry our heavy loads for 10 hours thro' this awful swamp and tree-littered forest, and mighty little food for the road and not a penny of pay or reward at the end of it.

We hope to start early to-morrow. It is the first time (except from Puerto Peruano to this) I have travelled with a caravan of unpaid men; all the years in Africa, bad as I have seen them, I never knew this. ...

MONDAY, OCTOBER 17TH. [(A)]
ON ROAD FROM ENTRE RIOS TO MATANZAS.

... After lunch at the big stream I pushed on with Bishop and Sealy and a few of the quicker Indians. A very heavy thunder-storm broke over us – a rain storm rather – and we got soused. A perfect deluge, but it was cool and delicious, and the road improved too. The Indians plucked instantly palm fronds and big leaves and made themselves quite smart umbrellas – as much to shelter their loads as themselves – although I can well think they do not like the cold sluice on their bare and singularly dry, soft skins. But neither leaves nor true umbrellas availed anything, and I got wet with a Dublin 'brolley' – the first, I'll wager, ever seen in these forests. I was a long way ahead of the rest, and after a clamber over a fallen tree across a dry stream-course – flowing, I am sure, to Caquetá at last – which was filling with the storm, I found myself at the verge of a clearing, and saw the roof of Matanzas or Andokes Station, and the Peruvian flag flying. I decided to wait for the others, rather than go on to meet alone and be civil to this evil-reputationed man, Armando Normand, with whom I wish to have as little and as brief intercourse as possible. The Commission and Tizon arrived about 3.30., perfectly soaked, and we all went on over a knoll into the Station in the midst of the tail of the storm. Found Mr. Normand away at the other Station, where he lives, La China, named capriciously like 'Indostan,' or Abisinia – which is 10 hours away, or, say, close on 30 miles.

He is said to be on a correria [round-up] after Indians. The Staff here are upset at our coming – only heard yesterday we were coming – and they sent off for Normand at once. We are received by a Senor Busta-mante, the second in Command, a pale-eyed man who gives a nasty impression. But he is clean in garb, and that is something after the speci-mens seen in Ultimo Retiro. The usual gang of scoundrels peer round corners, and I catch sight of a black Barbados face, one of the two, Levine or Lane, up here. Levine, I am told, has been here right from the first, with Normand, nearly if not quite six years. What things he must have seen, and what evil things done too during that spell! This place, along with Abisinia, are those which occur most often in the dreadful record of crime and horror compiled by Hardenberg and Normand's name probably more often than that of any other. The Commission and myself have for some time now come to the conclusion that the Hardenberg document is true. The part written by Hardenberg himself certainly is, and I think many of the declarations too. There are obvious exaggerations and mis-statements, and often no doubt actual falsehoods, but on the whole we believe it gives a faithful enough rendering of the class of crime and the evil of the system these men were mixed up in.[24] Nothing in the H. book exceeds in horror the account given by the two B. men of Jiminez burning alive the old Boras woman and the young Boras man in June 1903 – or again, the dreadful series of murders perpetrated by Vasquez only five months ago by the Pama River. Bishop tells me that he firmly believes the stories related of Normand dashing children's brains out against tree stumps and burning them alive. He declares that Donal Francis[25] who was here for nearly two years with Normand at the beginning, has told him more than once of these things, and of the dogs tearing the bodies of the dead to pieces and bringing up an arm or leg to the house to gnaw.

[24] See Black Diary, note 76. Two years later Walter Hardenburg's accounts of atrocities in the Putumayo, which had originally appeared in *Truth* magazine in 1909, were to be published again. Entitled *The Putumayo: The Devil's Paradise*, and edited by C. Reginald Enock, the book included material from R.C.'s Putumayo report. (T.Fisher Unurin, 1912)

[25] R.C. frequently gives preference to the Irish form of Donald – Donal.

Donal Francis, when questioned by me before Tizon and Barnes, had only 'planted yucca and sugar cane' during his year and eight months!

Bishop says he reproached him after that interview as being a coward and as bad as these murderers to lie to me for a bribe – for a 'dirty bribe'. Now, at last here I am in Matanzas, the centre of such dreadful things with one of the very Barbados men who has been through them all to stand the fire. I expect he will lie too, like Donal Francis.

I got Normand's sitting room given to me; it is pasted round with pictures from the 'Graphic', largely dealing with the Russo-Japanese War of 1904. There are also a lot of female midettes [crossed out and replaced by 'cocottes'] taken from some low-class Paris paper and several photos of brutal faced South American people – one in particular I should imagine to be Normand himself 'when a boy' – it looks like a low typed East-end Jew, with fat greasy lips and circular eyes. There are also certificates from The London School of Book-keepers of 1904, giving him a certificate as 'Book-keeper' and a certificate from some senior school of earlier date.

About 5.30 we heard a rifle shot in the woods to South and a murmur of 'Normand', 'Normand' was heard from the boys and servants. It was like the advent of a great warrior!

He arrived a few minutes after – but I did not meet him until dinner. I heard him talking English to Gielgud in the next room and complaining of Chase as having been 'impudent' to him. I had heard the conversation between himself and Chase a few minutes earlier, just across the partition. He had called Chase to bring a candle, and Chase evidently had given it to one of the Indian carriers or boys to take to him, and Normand's voice said, 'Bring it yourself; bring it yourself; aren't you a servant?' Chase had come with heavy foot and in slow voice I heard, 'I am a servant – but' – He was going to add 'not yours' it was clear, but stopped there. I waited until sent for by Tizon's servant to go to dinner, and then was duly presented to the man. He came up, I must say, to all one had read or thought of him, a little being, slim, thin and quite short, say, 5'7" and with a face truly the most repulsive I have ever seen, I think. It was perfectly devilish in its cruelty and evil. I felt as if I were being introduced to a serpent. All through dinner he spoke Spanish only, but whenever by chance a word came to me, I answered in English.

MONDAY 17TH. OCTOBER AT MATANZAS. [(B)]

...I turned in early, being tired and not anxious to see more of Normand than I could help. I have already made up my mind that as soon as Levine, the other B. man arrives from 'La China' I shall return to Entre Rios.

At 2.30 a.m. was wakened by feet pattering round the verandah, and low voices saying at the door of the next room, 'Normand, Normand'. I jumped from bed and went out. A man with a lantern and rifle was guarding a huddle of female figures, five or six of them with bags and road equipment. Some voices shouted down the passage and they all bolted to the room Normand is sleeping in. It was the arrival of the Harem, making for the room where they presumed their sleeping lord was lying. Barnes had been wakened too, and we both turned out and viewed them, and laughed heartily. They looked tiny little things from the glimpse I got. Poor little creatures, pattering all day and night through the forest after this beast. I suppose he set out at once as soon as the messenger reached La China with news of our hourly expected arrival at Matanzas, leaving the household to follow under care of some of the Muchachos of the Guard. ...

AT MATANZAS, MONDAY, [A TUESDAY, IN FACT] 18TH OCTOBER, 1910. [(B)]

... Stanley Lewis after flogging Simona never, he swore, flogged again. In his case he suffered for this refusal. Fonseca beat him and put him in 'cepo', and had it not been for Juan Costanos he might have starved. And here is this big, strong boy [James Chase] stating pretty much the same thing; Levine, he says, does much of the flogging. He has only hit Indians with sticks. He has seen three Indians, however, die from flogging, two here at Matanzas and one at La China, and his account of the death of this last one, a man named Kodihinka, is one of the most atrocious things I have heard yet. It makes me sick to think of it, and it occurred only last month! while we were at Iquitos or Chorrera. This unfortunate man, captured with five others (his wife and child among them) far across the Caqueta in Colombia, was brought down tied up at wrist and elbows for several days' journey to La China. Here they were all flogged, three males and three females. This man was the elder male — the headman of these poor fugitives, who had fled many days to escape the 'advances' of this captivating English Company. They preferred freedom and flight to the gifts lavished upon them for the rubber that we are told they so gladly work in order to obtain these nice things.

So they are pursued. The Commission going after them, headed by this assassin Normand, is actually 21 days engaged on this exploit, six of them days spent in open violation of international law in the territory of another State.

The flogging administered to these 'workers' of the Company on arrival at Normand's house, kills this man. He is put into the cepo alongside the five others, all with bleeding backs and limbs, and there he dies within three days of receiving these lashes. His flesh, according to Lane, stinking and rotten – his wife and child alongside him, pinned like wicked animals with their feet in iron-wood holds. God! what a state of things! And the human beast that did this is telling the Commission across the partition that he has not flogged for three years; that all he does now is to give some of the most recalcitrant 'strokes on the hand with a round piece of wood with holes in it'. My old friend, the Congo 'palmatory' emerged at last![26] As Normand was actually stating this in my hearing, Lane was declaring – unwillingly declaring – that within a month he had seen a man beaten to death, beside five others, three of them women, by the very orders of this man, and giving me the name of the employé, José Cordoba, who had laid on the lash.

I told the Commission immediately after Normand had been dismissed what Lane had declared to me. In the midst of my interrogation of him I heard that Levine had arrived from La China. At lunch I told Tizon that my mind was fully fixed on leaving at day-light for Entre Rios, that I did not wish to stay an hour longer than I could help in this company. In the afternoon I summoned Levine Wastermann [Westerman Leavine]; Levine is his full Barbadian appellation. He is a small-sized, mean-faced negro with a smirk, a face that at once awakens distrust and dislike; a lurking grin always in the eyes, and a weak sloppy mouth. I did not take to him, and it very soon became clear that he was not merely concealing things, but answering direct questions untruthfully. He left Chorrera with Normand on 17th November, 1904, so has been here almost six years. I made no attempt to get a general statement from him concerning this period, but confined myself to putting questions and requiring categoric replies.

. . . After admitting modified flogging, and even a case of shooting an Indian by himself, 'done with orders of the Manager', I asked for particulars of the flogging and death of Kodihinka last month at La China. Here his replies very soon brought him into direct conflict with the statement of Lane. When he had committed himself definitely to the statement that Kodihinka had not died in the cepo, and had died, not from flogging administered in La China, but from the beatings he had received on the road back when in the custody of James Lane and two Muchachos, I called Lane, and confronted the two. I said one or other was lying and I must find out which. I read Lane's replies to my questions about Kodihinka and then Levine's, and the two men faced each other, but only for a moment. Lane adhered to every word of his and openly accused Levine of being a liar. I

[26] R.C. is probably alluding here to the practice, in the Congo, of cutting off the hands of recalcitrant rubber-gathering slaves.

taxed the other with it, and asked if he would now speak the truth. He couldn't face more of it, and gave in – with another lie – that he had forgotten. 'What!' I said, 'forgotten, and only a month ago!' He admitted that Kodikinka had received 30 lashes from José Cordoba. He himself had given '3 cuts'; that he had died in the 'cepo' alongside the other Indians as described by Lane. I asked Mr. Tizon to come in and be present at this confrontation and hear the charge, admitted by both men, and he did this in great distress. Levine, then, in answer to my further questions, admitted he had been employed for six years only at this work, going out with a rifle to hunt Indians, to flog them and maltreat them to bring in rubber, or to flog them for having 'run away', and had done nothing else all this time, except keep guard at night. 'And all this explicitly by the Manager's orders.'

Tizon said it was no use asking Normand – I said apparently not. The matter was clear enough already; no fuller evidence seemed possible to obtain. Here we were on the spot, with Normand a room off (and he could hear what I said), and both these employés of the Company directly charging him before its Chief with ordering these crimes to be committed. I dismissed both Barbados men, on the distinct understanding that they were at once to leave Matanzas. Lane is to accompany me in the morning – Levine to follow with the Commission next day. I refused to allow him to come with me, as I told him I looked upon him as not only a liar, but a cowardly scoundrel. He had said that he gave the '3 cuts' to Kodihinka when the prisoners arrived at La China tied up. Kodihinka, according to him, when he admitted these 'three cuts' was then half moribund. He was tied up and his back cut and bleeding and bruised from the blows he had got on the road from the Muchachos under Lane. It was when in this state that he had given this wretched man three lashes with the twisted tapir hide. 'I give him the cuts, Sir, because he no pay me for a box of matches I give him on de road.'

'I see', I said 'you gave three lashes with his hands tied, his back and limbs bruised and bleeding, and himself, as you say, in a dying condition?' 'Yes, Sir, but it wasn't from these three cuts he died; he died from de beating on the road.'

I told him he was a coward and a scoundrel and that if he were in Barbados he would be hanged for such an act, or for any of the numerous crimes I was now sure he had committed; that to plead Normand's order was no excuse; and that I had a good mind to hand him over to the Prefect at Iquitos for trial there. I said all this before Tizon, Lane and Bishop – this and much more – for I added 'Guilty and contemptible as you are, you are far less guilty than the brute who employed you to do these things for his profit'. When they had gone, Tizon seemed dazed, and said he could not stay in the Company, he could not go on with it. 'To think I am mixed up with this', was his cry. I said that he was honourably mixed up with it, he must stay and do his duty. He had a duty to his country and to these Indians to perform – higher than to the Company, and that he must keep a brave heart and get through with it, and all the moral aid I could give him was his. Wherever I could strengthen his hands he might count on me. He then told me he had always told Normand he was to go, that he had hoped soon to get him away by the very steamer I was going in, but certainly by the next, at end of November. He added that Matanzas Station should be closed right away, and that in time he hoped the Indians there might be induced to come into Entre Rios voluntarily and sell Rubber at a fixed price.

I said this was the only thing to do. The road down to Puerto Peruano was impossible for human transport with such loads as these unfortunates were now compelled to carry, and all this hideous state of crime and outrage on them as well, before they start. He promised me again that the whole staff at Matanzas and La China should go, and go at the very quickest date possible, and the same should be done with Abisinia and Morelia, and also he trusted with Sabana and Santa Catalina. He would confine the sections (save Entre Rios) to the waterway of the Igaraparana and abolish these dreadful inland Posts that could not be inspected or controlled, and would get Mules for the transport from Entre Rios down to Puerto Peruano.

I warmly commended all this and pointed out that in the end it might even mean a financial gain, for the Indians, relieved of this dire pressure of the long marches with enormous burdens, without food, would have more time and greater strength and contentment to collect rubber, and Entre Rios might be made, by wise management, a collecting centre for all the Andokes, and much of the Northern Boras Country. The task before him, I said, was a very hard one, for I feared he would find opposition all round among the 'staffs' and Chiefs of sections, when they realized that the change involved the doing away of their lucrative posts. This man Normand, gets 20% of the gross yields of his district!

What an incentive to crime, this alone! He has the biggest staff of any section, all well-paid, armed ruffians, simply here to terrorize and enslave. Tizon said that Matanzas was not merely wrong, but a 'financial folly'. It had not yielded any profit but was run at a loss! The commission to Normand and the heavy salaries and expenses of keeping it up (as well as the other administrative expenses, for Macedo, too, comes into the Commission account), eat up all the 'profits', and it had been run at a dead loss for some time.

I gather Normand gets only about 8 tons of rubber a year – so he said, I am told – but I have not yet got the figures from any member of the

Commission. They are convinced that he did nothing but lie to them. While Levine's statement was being taken, in the afternoon, a lot of Boras and Andokes Indians were coming in with very heavy loads of rubber. This was Normand's fabrico,[27] the first part of it. He is getting it in now to take down to Puerto P. to ship to Chorrera by the 'Veloz' in a few days. When I had finished with Levine I went out to see the rubber arriving. They came up the hill, men, women and children, largely the two last, staggering under perfectly phenomenal loads. I have never seen such weights carried on roads — and such roads! — in Africa or anywhere else. Lots of the men were Boras, big, fine-looking fellows, with broad faces, very pale skins, almost whitemen indeed, simply bronzed by the sun, and frank open air and manner. Their bodies were slim and graceful, and their bodily strength very remarkable. I tried to carry one load of rubber. Made Chase lift it and put it on my shoulder, Normand standing on. I could not walk three paces with it — literally and truly. My knees gave way and to save my life, I don't think I could have gone 50 yards. Yet here they were, coming in from 8 to 10 hours away, 25 to 30 miles, and with 45 miles of that atrocious path through the forest before them to get to Puerto Peruano, and their only food such as they could bring with them, made by their poor wives who were tottering along under loads of 50, 60, 70 and 80 lbs. The little boys, some of them 5 or 6, without even a 'fono', stark naked, dear little things with soft gentle eyes and long eyelashes were coming along too, often with 30 lbs or more on their tiny backs. I saw one lad, looked about 15, with a boy's frank voice, with a load of fully 75 to 80 lbs. I asked N. for his balance to weigh some of them. He said he had none there, that the rubber was weighed either at La China or at a house in the forest where the Indians had to collect it.

Several loads he admitted had not come in because the bearers were sick. Six were sick and he sent back some of the stronger Boras who had already come in, to bring in these other loads. Not one scrap of food, he admitted, was given to anyone. He had the audacity to tell us that the natives 'preferred their own food'! — that it was so nutritious, and much more 'alimentary' than rice or beans. It consists of rolls of Cassava bread, half cooked and rolled in with the rubber, in leaves, and carried with it in the palm basket, that holds their enormous 'chorisos'.[28] Some of the loads I could not lift at all. I could raise them just off the ground and no more. The Boras men were the finest Indians I've seen yet. Not tall or big really, yet wonderfully graceful and clean limbed. They walked as steadily as machines. Short, quick steps, but the leg never moved or the knee-joint

[27] See Black Diary, note 114.
[28] R.C. here intends *chorizo*, a type of spicy pork sausage; the raw rubber was rolled into large sausage-shaped rolls, hence the allusion.

relaxed. With a big sigh, each man slipped down and slid the load from his back to the ground, releasing the fibre band from his forehead; he sprang up, straight as an arrow, and walked firmly and strongly away. Many of them had fine limbs, strong arms and beautiful thighs and legs, although no-where any remarkable development of muscle. It was simply that they were all over well and perfectly made children of the forest, inheriting ages of its wild free life, until their bodies had grown like the very trees, to be a part and parcel of the soil. They sleep on it naked, walk or run upon it all the day, and never perspire with a load of 100 or 150 lbs. on them. Many of these loads must weigh fully 150–170 lbs, of that I am sure. I hope to weigh some at Entre Rios, and I shall be going down the road with these first fruits of Normand's last fabrico to-morrow.

They are to dance to-night, so he tells us, but it will be entirely off their own bats – for they'll not get a scrap of food or drink from him. There is not even food for us, so Tizon says. He has had to send messages down to Entre Rios for further supplies, some of which arrived this evening by special runner, one of O'Donnell's muchachos, who got in at 4.30 with a load of something to eat and drink. A great many of the men were flogged and showed bad traces of it. One tiny boy child of not more than 8, so small he had no 'fono', but was quite naked had his little backside and thighs covered with scars – broad weals and lashes. An abominable sight. He had a biggish load of rubber too. There must have been fully 30 boys and children carrying, some of them mites of 5 or 6. These latter had only food baskets, the youngest with a load of rubber was 7 I should say, and they ranged on from this up to 10 and 12. One of the big Boras men with raw red scars of a recent flogging, Bustamante hid from us, or tried to. He was taken upstairs with a handkerchief on his bare buttocks. I spoke to several of the men and boys, but all seemed half dazed and wholly frightened, and when I got some to stand for their photos they looked as if under sentence of death. It was impossible to reassure them, as neither Sealy nor Bishop could speak Boras or Andokes.

Normand spent the whole afternoon under the House, arranging the rubber loads for the morrow, and calling over the lists of names. Lane had told me that the 'cepo' had been hidden away on the morning of our arrival, and was lying behind the native house and kitchen covered with leaves. We visited it and found it covered with thatch, in two big pieces, it looked like a double 'cepo' as both parts were quite separate. Lane had also said that the previous evening when word had come that we were on the road, Bustamante himself had hurried the two prisoners away that were in it. He had taken them out to some house in the forest and sent them on, guarded by two 'muchachos', presumably to 'La China'.

I told the Commission of the bare facts of Lane's and Levine's evidence, and took them to see the hidden 'cepo' along with Sr. Tizon.

In the evening at dinner we had quite a farce. Tizon said that neither 'Andokes' nor 'Lincoln', the two local boys he had brought with him, were anxious to stay now in their own country. He had asked both whether they would not like to stay at Matanzas and be near their own people, and both had protested. Normand rose to the occasion. 'That's what I like to hear' he said, 'it shows that civilization is at work'. I said to Barnes out loud, 'This nearly chokes me', and put a piece of bread in my mouth. The whole of us were speechless for a minute, and I was afraid I'd laugh out loud....

Sealy came late to tell me that two of the 'muchachos' who had shot Bucelli, Luiz de Silva, &c. last year, had been kept here with long chains round their necks, and had recently escaped. He was in great excitement, 'They had them down there', pointing to the native house, 'and they got off with the chains, and Levine did not tell you, Sir. They sent after them everywhere, and haven't got them.'

I said, I hoped they would not. I asked if the Indians had any means of getting chains smashed, seeing they had no hammers and chisels, and Bishop, who was standing by, said 'there was never an Indian yet who was long troubled with a chain once he got away. If they have a hatchet or an axe they'll soon get rid of the chain'.

This seemingly is the end of the great Caqueta Rebellion. I've heard several times of the 'four whites murdered by the cannibals'. The two survivors of the killing party I hope are in security and safety somewhere, poor beings. When they killed that party of rascals, they only did what should be done to every single agent and empleado of this damnable Syndicate of murderers, with the single exception of Tizon, who is clearly out of his element here. However, he will have to stay to try and end the lot of them. I hope these two 'muchachos' will keep clear. They are not Andokes or Boras, however, I gather, but Huitotas

FRIDAY, 21ST OCTOBER 1910, AT ENTRE RIOS.

...I set out before Bishop and Sealy and soon overtook the rubber carriers. Poor chaps, they shook hands with me as I passed, and one wretched woman was crying and groaning and spoke to me in Andokes,[29] pointing to her trembling legs and the big load of rubber she had. Some of the boys were awfully nice little chaps, and now that we were alone together, away from the shadow of Matanzas and the eyes of Normand, they were quite cheery and laughed when I patted them and held my hand again and again. A lot of them called me 'Capitan, capitan', and pointed to the stripes and scars over their hips and thighs.

[29] See Black Diary, note 137.

Bishop and Sealy overtook me about one hour out and we passed on rapidly, leaving all the rubber carriers behind and passing my own carriers who had started before me. When about 7 miles out from Matanzas, I heard groans in the pathway ahead and saw a pale smoke stack. I hurried forward and found a boy, a 'muchacho' evidently from his Winchester lying alongside him, stretched on the ground. He had a raging fever and was groaning, and trembling all over. When Bishop came up we questioned him. He said that he was one of the 'muchachos' of Matanzas. He had been sent out 12 days previously without any food to look for the 'wife' of one of the empleados named Negretti, who had run away. He had not found her, had been starving for days, and was now absolutely played out and unable to walk. I stopped then, got some brandy and gave it him, and then when my carriers arrived, I stopped the 'chop box' and got a tin of soup and some biscuits out and heated the soup over the fire and made him drink some. He did not want to, but we made him little by little. He drank a great deal of the tea to quench the raging fever. I rarely have seen a more pitiable sight. At length, after an hour or more, I asked him if he could walk a bit, and if so, I'd try and help him along to the Muinanes house, where I now decided to sleep and give him plenty to eat in the night and morning, so that then he might either return to Matanzas, or if he preferred it, to come on to Entre Rios where I intended to hand him over to Tizon. He said he would try to walk, and so we started. Unfortunately I had let all my carriers go on, they were in a hurry to be off. The boy stumbled a few steps and fell with a groan. This was repeated again and again, and I saw it was useless to attempt to go far with him.

[Deleted heading: ENTRE RIOS
FRIDAY, 21ST OCTOBER, 1910]

So I sent Bishop on to overtake my carriers at first river he could, and get them to stop and light a fire and wait. Then with Lane and Sealy we tried helping this starved being along. He said again and again it was hunger had him, that when he tried to walk the road went away from under his feet and down he fell. At last I got a big Boras man who overtook us with an enormous load of rubber, to lay it down and shoulder the boy. This he did, and carried him up a steep hill and laid him on a bed he made of big leaves he cut. Then, poor chap, he had to trudge back for his huge load of rubber. At last, about 12 noon, I got the boy down to a stream where I found Bishop halted with the two lost men, who fortunately were there with my food supplies. So we had our breakfast. I tried to make the sick boy drink more soup, but I had to force it down his lips. He could do nothing but groan. Soon after he started by himself to try and walk on, and when we broke camp I found him fallen in the track just up the hill at the burnt Muinanes' house which 'Andokes' had told us on the day of our coming had been burnt by Normand. There I was forced, very unwillingly to leave him, as my carriers were far ahead. A rain storm was coming on, so we rigged up a shelter over him of palm fronds and wild banana leaves and I then put my umbrella over him inside this. We promised to send back three of my Indians from the Muinanes house to help him on there. Bishop and Lane said that the Empleado coming behind us at the tail of the rubber caravan who was the very Negretti who had sent the boy out to look for his 'wife' would certainly drive him back to Matanzas. I was afraid of this before they spoke. So I wrote my name on a piece of paper addressing it to Entre Rios – and then, on second thoughts, wrote inside a slip in bad Portuguese to say that the bearer, by name Ramón, was to follow me to Entre Rios. I was in hopes this might serve as a protection if the oncoming man interrogated the poor creature. With this paper and some biscuits and meat I left him, and his last words were to send the Indians quickly, as there would be moonlight, and he would try to get into the Muinanes' house to-night. I then hurried on – hours had been lost, and all hope of reaching Entre Rios was over – We had not gone far, however, when a second case occurred – even worse. The woman who had appealed to me in the morning was unable to go further. She was crying bitterly and trembling all over, and as I came up the most pitiable sounds arose to the poor creature's lips. I knelt beside her and took the load of rubber off her shoulders and the band from her head, and told Bishop to lay it beside the path and cut a cross in the tree it was leaning against. The woman cried still more, and kept saying Normand would kill her, Normand would kill her. She was an Andokes, and have [*sic*] had to do, or try to do the translating. I told him to tell her not to be afraid – that Normand should do nothing with her – that I would be responsible for taking her load away, and that she was to come on with me to the Muinanes' house where I would give her food and medicine and clothes. She was, like most of them, stark naked, and her poor straight back had been battered and beaten. She pointed to her thighs and legs showing the bruises and marks. She seemed to have a severe attack of rheumatism too, and had not a scrap of food. When finally she really understood she was to go on in safety with me she wept still more bitterly and held my hand, pressing it to her forehead again and again. I gave her tea to drink from my bottle, and by this time a lot of the other carriers had arrived and squatted all round – looking on with a sort of hopeless resignation on their faces. Only the small boys – boys all the world over – grinned and laughed.

The woman could hardly walk, and the task of getting her on was a very slow one. She fell several times, and I gave her my walking stick to help her trembling legs. She gave way constantly at the knees and fell. I cried a good deal, I must confess. I was thinking of Mrs. Green and Mrs. Morel if they had been here and could have seen this piteous being – this gentle-voiced woman – a wife and mother – in such a state. Her load had been one of between 50 and 60 lbs, I should think – three fairish 'Chorisos.' Her 'food' for this journey of some 70 miles, (she came from 25 miles beyond Matanzas) down to Puerto Peruano, consisted of a small bundle of palm frond wrapping less than 2 lb. weight of farinba [fariña = cassava flour], with a tiny bottle of 'aji' [chilli pepper] – or notin peppe[r]. This we took from the load and carried on for her. On getting near the Muinanes' house I heard the manguare beating – a welcome sound – and soon after a shot. A minute or two later we met four of the genial 'muchachos' from Entre Rios going up to Matanzas with provisions for Tizon and two letters for him, one from Chorrera and one sent off by O'Donnell that morning at 6 a.m. with the boys. I stopped them and abstracted two bottles of ginger ale, two tins of sausages and a tin of prawns, and wrote a chit to Tizon telling him why, and explaining that I was delayed by these sick people on the road. We were very glad to reach the Muinanes' house at 4 p.m. and the woman fell, a groaning heap, by the fire. I got her, rigged up in pyjamas, on my bed sack, and put a warm coat over her – and several times Sealy fed 'de ole lady,' as he persisted in calling her, with oxtail soup and sausage and biscuits. She eat [*sic*] protestingly, but all the same it went down and would help the poor battered body to revive. She was a woman of some 40 or 45 – and her husband was one of the men who had sat watching me giving her the tea on the road. The Boras and Andokes men and boys and many women – some of them sick too – kept on coming in by twos and threes up to about 7. Then my three Indians, who had been sent back by Sealy to get the sick boy and the three loads of rubber left by 'de old lady', came in empty-handed to say that before they reached the boy they had met Negretti, who turned them back. He said he had already turned the boy back to Andokes. Poor lad – I lay awake thinking of him out in the forest all night. The brute Negretti had told them, they said, the boy belonged to Matanzas, and was not to go down to Entre Rios, so my strategem with the note addressed to myself was in vain. I was grieved and wretched. For all I knew he could not reach Andokes alive – certainly not, unless the food I gave him should later on work some restoration.

The sick woman groaned all night, and some of the other women came for medicine and help. I gave them what I had in the shape of relief, and then the big men, seeing this, came round me with their bruised buttocks and scarified limbs. One big splendid-looking Boras young man – with a broad good-humoured face like an Irishman – had a fearful cut on his left buttock. It was the last scab of what had been a very bad flogging. The flesh for the size of a saucer was black and scarred, and this crown of raw flesh was the size of a florin. I put lanoline and a pad of cotton-wool over it. Many more came for the same treatment. One youth I had already noticed on the road with a bad cut on his back – he said José Cordoba had given it. On the road I gave him my handkerchief to try and keep the strong wood of the palm basket in which his rubber lay from pressing too hard on it. He was grateful, poor soul, a very thin Andokes boy, I think. In the evening he came and showed me many more cuts all over him, fresh ones and raw; one over the shoulder blade. I lanolined all, and with tufts of cotton wool all over him, he and the others roared with laughter. Some had cuts on the feet and shins, these from sticks and trunks. I put plaster on these as well as I could. The man Negretti did not arrive. I lay awake a long time with my revolver loaded, for I thought he might come in and begin abusing the poor woman whose load I had left in the wood, and, if so, I was determined to prevent it at all costs. His hammock came on and some of his muchachos with rifles, but he did not turn up. I was relieved, but could not sleep. I heard the wretched woman groaning and crying all night. At 2 the moon broke through the broken side roof of the house, and I looked round on all the weary forms of these poor men and women. Several of the latter were awake and crying softly; occasionally a man would give a sort of groan of weariness as he moved in his sleep. Some of them awakened and rose from time to time to stir the fires aflame, and then lay down with their backs or feet to the warmth. I was glad of a blanket, and I had put two of my jackets over the sick woman to keep her warm, but these sturdy forms lay naked and almost white in the moonlight and firelight. The Boras are the fairest skinned Indians I have seen yet – some of them are almost white in colour, a very handsome set, and with the children particularly winning, and their forms are graceful in the extreme. One lad of about 15 hung to my heels often during the day – Whenever I came up he ran over and took my hand and held it. This indeed all did whenever I passed them, in the most winning way, men and boys. This boy's name was Doi, he told me. I wrote it in my note book, and he repeated it slowly twice over, laughing all the time. I then tried to find out his tribe, but am not sure if I understood his reply. It was 'Otaniko', and then he said 'Capitan' striking his chest. I gathered that he was one of the people of the Boras Capitan or cacique named Otaniko, although he may have meant that his tribe was the Otaniko one, and he its captain. Several of the Capitanes are boys, I am told. The office is hereditary, like the chieftainship of a clan, although some system of election may enter in to it too. O'Donnell and others have told me of several cases of boys being capitanes, and Bishop, when on the march yesterday from the Muinanes' house into Entre Rios told me of an old woman Capitan he and Robuchon[30]

---

[30] Eugenio Robuchon: French explorer, commissioned by the Peruvian Government to survey the Putumayo. He died mysteriously. His book, intended to

met on the Caqueta in 1906 who was very good to them and gave them food...

I was glad the night passed without trouble from the man Negretti. Bishop and Lane told me that when the Commission were questioning Normand at Matanzas this man had been vapouring before them, and saying that he wished 'the Englishmen' would send for him to question him and he would enjoy insulting them.

I spent thus the night of 19th–20th in some anxiety, for I did not want a row with a low-class brute such as this Empleado was sure to be, and at the same time I was determined to protect the woman.

At 5 a.m. of the morning of the 20th the Boras men and boys and the women with them got up; and, after a warming over the big blaze of the fire, and a handful of cassava bread, without a word they passed away out of the house, each of them getting their enormous loads up and off. They were gone at 5.15 a.m. I stayed on and got coffee and gave some to the two sick women, on top of some of Bishop's Eno's fruit salt, a bottle of which he had bought at Iquitos. I had not made up my mind what to do. At one time I thought of sending back to look for the famished boy, but finally decided to go on to Entre Rios and to leave Lane with a note for Barnes and Tizon explaining about the boy and sick women here – for there were two of them now. I wrote a note to Barnes telling him what I wished done, and then Negretti arrived with the tail of the rubber carriers. There were over 40 of them – mostly women and children. Out of 47 of the rubber people and muchachos then in the house, I counted only 12 men and lads – the rest were women and children. Negretti brought the three pieces of rubber the sick woman had left and threw them down with a vicious snarl, and then came truculently towards me and asked for the rifle of the muchacho I had taken from the starved boy on the road. I gave him this and then asked where the boy was, and he answered at once, a deliberate lie, 'Oh, he's in Matanzas now', and added, to my further enquiry, he had sent a boy to help him. (I found out later that this was absolutely untrue). I then asked if he had seen my umbrella, and he said he had sent it back to Matanzas. (This too I find out is a deliberate lie; Gielgud found the umbrella where I had left it). I then asked if he had not seen the letter I left with the boy, and he said he had not seen it. 'Never saw it.'

The sick woman was lying by the fire, and the other sick woman by another fire, and two more, mere girls, fell beside her groaning. He called out to Lane, whom he gathered that I was leaving behind, to tell Sr.

show that the Putumayo belonged to Peru, was completed by Rey de Castro, a former Peruvian consul at Manaos and close friend of Julio Arana. See *En El Putumayo y sus affluentes*, the diary of Eugenio Robuchon (ed. Rey de Castro), publication made at the expense of the Peruvian Government, 1907.

Normand, who was coming with the rest of the rubber, of these four women and the pieces of rubber he was leaving behind. He then hurried on with his rifle on his shoulder after the rest of the unfortunates who were being hunted down this awful road to Puerto Peruano. What is wanted here is a Hanging Commission with a gallows – not a Commission of botanists and commercial experts. Leaving Lane with the note for Barnes, and with a verbal message to give to Normand if he should attempt to illtreat the woman or scold her for leaving her load, I left at about 7.45 or 8 a.m. I told Lane to say to Normand that the woman was not responsible for leaving her load – that I had taken it from her on finding her sick and unable to proceed, and that if he desired an explanation it was to come from me. Lane promised faithfully to guard the women and feed them throughout the day and to stay there by them till Tizon and the Commission should arrive from Matanzas, which I hoped would be about 4 p.m. I then hurried on, and soon passed the 'human animal' Negretti,[31] as I call him. He is a vicious-looking, thin half-caste from Moyabamba, I should say. A mean ferret face and teeth like a wild animal, and a fierce hungry glare in his eyes. Almost as evil a face as Normand's.

...The whole road along I passed the Boras and Andokes carriers – going slowly and steadily on, often resting against trees or squatting for a moment's pause in this awful track of slush, fallen trees, roots, deep streams to cross by a single log or fallen tree, and all the obstacles a bewildering forest can throw in a track such as this. For me, a famous walker once, and still pretty good on my legs, the route was excessively wearisome. I was bathed in perspiration half an hour after starting, and the constant ducking one's head, or balancing on a slippery pole, or falling over the ankles into the mud, wearied the mind and the attention more even than the body. Here were these men, many of them with loads far over a <u>cwt</u>. on the lightest diet man ever lived on, to get over this path, with no hope of relief before or behind them, and with this human devil and his armed muchachos behind to flog up the stragglers. Every time he appeared in sight it was 'Hiti, Hiti' – 'Get on, get on' and a volley of Boras and Andokes I could not understand. I was so sick of the sight that I hurried past at full speed and did not slacken until I had left the rubber carriers well behind.

I was furious at the whole thing – the most disgraceful form of slavery left among mankind – of that I am certain. Slavery in the interests too, of this miserable gang of cut-throats. Bishop and Sealy told me, as we walked more quietly when we got well ahead, of many things they had seen or knew of. Of Normand Bishop said that nothing related by Hardenberg was untrue. He believed it all. He had not seen Normand kill people during the six weeks he had been with him at Matanzas, but Donal Francis had told

[31] See Black Diary, note 143.

him of the dreadful things he had seen at that section – of the burning alive and the dogs eating the dead... – Young Rodriguez, Bishop says, is to succeed Normand. The boy Lincoln had told him this.[32] Lincoln (who speaks Spanish, and is confidential boy to Torrico at Occidente) said that Normand was to have two more 'fabricos' and then 'Juanito' (Rodriguez' name with everyone) was to be appointed to Matanzas to succeed Normand.

Bishop added that these men were so false even to each other that Normand, believing Juanito was to come after him, had been telling the Indians that Rodriguez would illtreat them dreadfully, so that one 'notin' had already taken to flight. This to ruin Rodriguez' chances from the start of getting a good haul of rubber. There is evidently no honour among these thieves. I said from what I had seen of Rodriguez at Occidente I thought him quite as big a scoundrel as Normand, if that were possible. Bishop laughed, and then told me the following of Rodriguez' conduct once at Sabana. Bishop was there at the time. It was this year in April Rodriguez had come over on a 'visit' to Fonseca, and every morning when he got up he visited the prisoners in the cepo. To these poor Indians he administered sundry cuts with a whip, laughing all the time. This he did for morning sport. As he flogged them he called out 'Here's your tea and coffee – you like tea and coffee – here they are' – and as he lashed them, Bishop said, a big black dog that was there jumped on the man or woman flogged and worried them. Bishop's statement was that the dog 'took bits out of them.' It is too atrocious, and yet one has only to look at these men and the dumb, terrified faces of the Indians when they speak to them to read it all.

...I got on at last to within sight almost of Entre Rios, a shower came and wet me without cooling the air. The road was indescribably bad and I was getting tired. When near the Indian houses 'Huascar',[33] O'Donnell's favourite boy and two others, hove in view with tea, coffee and food sent out by O'Donnell on hearing of my coming. It was very welcome and I was glad of it. We hurried on after this and I plunged into the Cahuinari and sent Sealy up for dry clothes, and while in the river Fox and O'Donnell came down to see me. Sealy had arrived at 12.50, and I got up to the house about 1.20 I should think. I would have been in by 12.30 had I not stayed for the tea and the bathe in the river.

I told Fox of all that had occurred at Matanza and on the road, and of my deep disgust at the slave gang I had seen driven along by the brute Negretti, and the lamentable condition in which many of these wretched people, especially the women, were. I lay down to rest. At 5.15 the long

[32] See Black Diary, note 146.
[33] See Black Diary, note 146.

line of Boras and Andokes carriers – men, women and children, appeared on the path coming up from the Cahuinari, with Negretti the footpad, rifle on shoulder, bringing up the rear. I begged Fox to observe them closely and to take some photos of the children with my camera. This he tried to do, as they arrived, but Negretti appeared and called 'Hi-ti, hi-ti', go on, and the poor beings had to stagger and shamble off through the plantation and on along the road towards Puerto Peruano. It was just 12 hours since I had seen them leave the Muinanes house in the morning, and a 12 hours' march under such loads, upon such roads, with scarcely any food, God alone knows how they do it and live! I was furious with anger, and disgust, and told O'Donnell I thought it brutal and wanton brutality. Here was a big empty Indian house with room for several hundreds of people where they could have passed the night in comfort, and yet they were driven on relentlessly into the forest after such a march. In some ways I think it was the most disgraceful exhibition of brutality I have seen yet. The man Negretti was raging, I could see, at Fox taking photographs of them, he only got two poor ones in the fading light. I have failed to get any photo that will show, I fear, of the lithe, tiny little boys, staggering under 30 or 40 lbs. of rubber. I have seen nothing like this on the Congo, and it is indescribable, and makes me positively ill.

...I turned in very early, very angry and very sad, and now I am trying in the quiet of a day off to write up the happenings of the last three days. What with taking down the depositions by the Barbadians, no light task in point of time, questioning them and trying to check their answers, then looking around me for confirmation or otherwise each day, leaves little time or energy, always with only the night for writing. At night I am very tired, and on the road it is almost impossible to write; the sandflies at Muinanes were a dreadful pest up to about 6 p.m. and then I had the sick Indians, and all my anxiety about the poor famished boy in the forest and the sick woman beside me. If only I could write short-hand, never felt the need as now. So much depends on noting at the time and writing down at the time, leaving as little as possible to memory and the vague chances of recalling correctly, or not recalling at all. Much is lost in any case, and all I can do is to try and record as promptly and as clearly as may be my thoughts, my perception of things and such facts as arise.

I am now quite tired out. I've been writing all day nearly, except when occupied with Fox and O'Donnell, and now by the carriers of Rubber, who turned up belated and footsore from 11 to 1 o'clock and then with Normand's coming. He arrived at about 1 o'clock, we saw him trying to slip past the station over the plantation, $\frac{1}{4}$ of a mile away, but seeing that we had seen him, he left the carriers to go on through the forest and came to us by the Atenas road, which he was cutting across, so as to strike the Puerto road beyond this.

...I must go out to talk to Tizon, Barnes and the rest who arrived very wet from a strong rainfall at 3 p.m. to 3.30. Normand, too, is waiting to try and talk to me. He has already begun with a string of lies, perfectly infantile in one way, but astounding illustrations of impudence and assurance.

It recalls Leopold in the Palace at Brussels in November 1900 – before I had written 'How I found Leopold'.[34] But this hyaena is a poor Leopold. This wretch is only fit for the flogging triangle and then the gallows, and yet he dares to seek me to-day with assurances of his regard for and care for the Indians. ...

ENTRE RIOS
SATURDAY, 22ND OCTOBER 1910.

The interview with Normand yesterday afternoon was really amusing, but it shows the man in a new light and a dangerous one. Most of these criminals I have met here are fools. This man is not. He has courage, courage of a dreadful kind, and cunning. He realises to the full, I can see, the position he is in. He was partly brought up in England and, no doubt, wishes again to go there. He knows perfectly well how such crimes as he has committed during these six years at Andokes are regarded, and how punished in England. He also knows perfectly well that the Barbadians have been illegally employed, and that a share of the responsibility for engaging them as 'laborers' and turning them into criminals might be attributed to him. Not legally of course, but then none of these men are quite sure of law, one way or another. All he knows is that I am out here on an official journey, with an unknown purpose, and that I am obtaining very damaging evidence, both of the system of enslaving the Indians and of the individual crimes of the enslavers, of whom he is one of the worst. He knows perfectly that Lane gave him away first, and then that I compelled Levine to confess all and to accuse him in the presence of Tizon. He is, doubtless, seriously alarmed for his personal safety. Even with such a conscience as he must have, such crimes committed and now, as he fears, going to be exposed by the British Government, possibly himself denounced (for so he will, he fears it must be) he is trying to guard against consequences. The bribing of Levine is one way, the other, the course he adopted yesterday of approaching me to 'disabuse' my mind, as he put it, and not allow me to be deceived, so that I might alter my

[34] On 18 October 1900, whilst in Brussels, R.C. had a private lunch with King Leopold II during which Leopold attempted to discredit the stories of atrocities committed by his administration in the Congo.

'assertions'. However, I will relate the happenings of yesterday, to tell their own story.

I got up late, and tired still. The road the last 4 or 5 miles from the cross roads of Jiminez to Entre Rios is so bad that my feet were swollen. Also they were cut with the roots and spikes of the numberless trees and stumps and a good deal scratched. This, in spite of thick socks and good shoes. The sandfly bites too, had been particularly bad, and both ankles and calves were itching a good deal, as well as my wrists and finger joints. The irritation from these sandflies is worse than from mosquitoes. I had found a huge chigger[35] in a toe of my right foot at Muinanes on the way back on night of 19th, and it too, was sore and raw when I had cut out the bug. This is the first chigger I have had since leaving the Congo. Strange that, in all my time in Brazil, whence this pest came to Africa only in 1868, I have not seen or felt one. Here this insect came, I am sure, when we stopped at the Muinanes house on the way up to Matanzas ... That house is now really a sort of caravan or rest house. The Muinanes family of Hatima, the Chief with me, whose home it was, has moved away from the road on account of Normand's people going and coming from Puerto Peruano. The cassava and plaintains are still around it, but to all intents it is an empty (and partly unroofed) house. As caravans of Andokes and Boras sleep here, they no doubt leave a certain number of chiggers (and other vermin).

I spent the morning of yesterday bathing in the Cahuinari and talking to Fox. I told him of all that we had noticed of things at Matanzas and my experiences on the road. He saw for himself the type of man employed there in the person of the blackguard Negretti. This brute, after having hunted on these weary beings the evening before, had stayed here all night and got good food and rest. He left about 8 a.m. to follow after the rubber men, who must have continued their weary march towards Puerto Peruano very early. Fox and I got talking of many things and suddenly he himself broached a subject that often has been in my mind. The way the Commission are carrying out their investigation. He said they were not proceeding properly at all and he bitterly regretted the absence of Col. Bertie. They needed a President and someone of greater experience to keep them together and collect their work. Barnes had no capacity for it and did nothing. Since he had himself raised the question, I told him I had long since noted this and regretted Col. Bertie's absence fully as much as he. I had suggested, I told him, at Occidente, to both Tizon, and Barnes and Bell that they should telegraph for him or some one else to come out. As things were, they were not a commission at all, and on the few occasions when they met once for an hour, perhaps at each section house to

---

[35] Also known as a jigger: a tropical flea, which burrows under the skin and causes painful swellings.

interrogate the Chief alone, I had noticed that practically all the questions, and certainly answers to the point had come from him. There was no collective action it seemed to me, and no Secretary to take minutes of their proceedings, and no method in their enquiry. All this he said he felt so strongly, and had already made up his mind that he might have to write a separate report. We discussed this quite privately and confidentially and were in full agreement. I advised meeting the Col. as soon as they arrived [holograph insertion (in England)] and getting his advice and help in compiling their report. This, too, had been his idea he said. Barnes had told him he was no good at writing, and moreover Barnes has told me that he is so disgusted that he takes no interest in his part at all. That may be, but then he should not stay on. The whole thing is far too haphazard, each one goes his own easy gait, and were it not for Fox, the collective notes of the party (Barnes, Bell and Gielgud) would not be of the least value. Gielgud, I said to Fox, I frankly could not look upon as a member of the Commission, he stood simply for the Company. Fox agreed, and added 'Didn't the Col. let him know that in Manaos too'! The only cheering thing is, that, as Fox admits, no shadow of doubt exists now in any of their minds as to the reality of the system of slavery we find here. Here they are at one. I said I hoped so, that I could not think any of them, even Gielgud now, would for an instant defend it in any aspect. He said not for an instant, and that if the Company proved powerless to reform, then he should denounce the state of things out here by every means in his power.

We were still discussing these things when some stragglers from the rubber carriers came along up the path from the Cahuinari. I hurried down to try and snapshot them as they passed, but the poor things were so frightened they almost ran, and I lost a fine chance to get one of the tiny boys with a rubber load. The little chap was not more than 6 I should say, a <u>mite</u>, and he fairly bolted with short steps before I could focuss him. I got, however, one or two bigger boys, three in a group, but they were quite big lads, and two of them fat boys as well. Then a lad of perhaps 16, I had seen at Matanzas, the whole afternoon nearly, sitting wearily on the ground, over his load, came along by himself and we called to him and stopped him. – Bishop assisting, I got a better one of him and then I decided to weigh his load. He looked terrified when we laid hands on him and it, and as we could not speak Boras there was no chance of reassuring him. We took him into O'Donnell's store, and he and Fox came down to join me. This boy's load was 37 $\frac{1}{2}$ kilogs. He had no food in the basket, not a scrap. Bishop said all my tins were gone, our last feed with my own carriers on the road and the sick people had finished all. There was only a tin of Libby's Asparagus, the last of those I had got from Cazes in Iquitos. This, I said, was food anyhow and told Bishop to fetch it, and gave it to the boy. O'Donnell said sardines might suit him better. I said yes, and if he liked to give the boy 2 tins of sardines, I'd give him the asparagus. The poor boy looked on with big sad eyes all the time and gave up the asparagus when Martin Arana brought the sardines. I gave him a packet of cigarettes too. He hurried off at a trot almost, when we let him go. The others, who had passed, said Normand and more were behind.

Then just as we were going to breakfast, a weary being with body bent double nearly came up the incline from the road. I watched the slow approach and called Fox. The man came on step by step, and when he reached the shade of the house he fell like dead, he and his load of rubber, and lay groaning. I sent Bishop down, who came saying 'He says he's dying'. I hurried down, he lay inert and almost senseless, only groans coming from his white lips. I took some Irish Whiskey and poured it down his throat and thus got him up, with Bishop, and got him into the store and down on one of O'Donnell's mule rugs hanging there. Fox came down, and we both eyed the piteous spectacle. O'Donnell too. The man was an Andokes too, and O'Donnell said he could not understand. The load was meanwhile brought in by Bishop and Sealy and we weighed it. It was just 50 kilogs, say 111 lbs. and not a scrap of food with it. He had eaten all on the road to this, and was now half dead with hunger, as well as the crushing weight. What infamous cruelty! Both Fox and I were furious and there were tears in our eyes too. At breakfast I felt I could not eat, and at last I apologised to O'Donnell and sent my soup down by Huascar, his boy, to the tired man. He said he would give him food himself, that he never ill-treated 'his Indians' like that, and when he sent them down to P.P. it was only with loads of 30 kilogs at outside, and the whole of the people of the district helped to carry it. I quite believe that the whole of the population of the section is compelled to carry it, but I don't believe that he limits his loads either to 30 kilogs. Bishop told me he had seen just as big loads sent by O'Donnell from this, and the Indians staggering along just the same, O'Donnell having a better cultivated Chacara (all done by the Indians remember) has more food to give away. With regard to this carriage of rubber, it should be borne in mind that it is wholly unremunerated. Neither food nor pay of any description is given for this extra burden, involving these terrible hardships, and exposure and long absence from their own homes and work. No wonder the Indians have no food and no time to cultivate. How one finds such sleek bodies among the Boras I cannot say, except there may be more rubber, there probably is, and so the time spent in collecting is less than in this more peopled and less well-forested Huitoto country.

While we were at breakfast after seeing this poor beggar provided for in some way, another straggler appeared coming up the hill with a huge load. He was not so bad as the last man and managed to get past at a snail's pace. I was moved to go out and call him in too, but did not wish to be too officious, and I feared for the man himself later on when Normand got at him. That beauty was still behind. We had finished breakfast and about 12.30 I noticed a white hat and some Indians over on the other side of the Chacara, making past by a circuit so as to avoid the house. I called Bishop and he said it was Normand. O'Donnell came and Fox and the whole station, and looked to try and make out. O'Donnell got his glasses. The figures appeared and disappeared in the burnt margin of the forest and thus would have to cross our field of vision over a strip of Cassava planting, and O'Donnell said it was Normand passing round to intersect the P.P. road lower down through the forest. He and N. he said were not good friends and had not held any intercourse for 6 months. Still this was the first time N. had ever passed Entre Rios like that, actually leaving the road and going round over the Stumps and through the forest. We could see Muchachos of course, and finally, bringing up the rear, the blue and red costumes of the harem, also of course. The Mrs. Normands appeared to be travelling fast, all were skurrying. The white hat bobbed and bobbed and finally all disappeared into the deep forest beyond the Atenas Road. The thing was a mystery, and it was only when in bed pondering on it all I hit upon the reason for this evasion of us. Just as we thought we had seen the last of N. and that he would flounder through the forest until he struck the P.P. road with the rearguard, we saw the white hat out again, alone, on the Atenas road, and then the figure hurrying down towards us. Soon a couple of rifle shots announced the Paladine [Palatine]'s approach. O'Donnell replied with a revolver volley. These knights of the road all salute each other. Hoping the man would only stay a few minutes I did not remain on the verandah – Lane had turned up shortly after – come in from keeping guard at Muinanes. He said that Normand had arrived first, before the Commission, and had pulled the two coats off the 'old lady', and had ordered her to go to the neighbouring Indian house. He had given her rubber load in pieces to some of the stragglers to bring on. Normand had gone on and slept in the forest. Then the commission and Tizon had arrived and he had given Barnes my note. They had looked for the boy and had given the old woman, who was still there, unable to walk, medicine and food, also the other sick woman.

Normand I found was staying on here, so there was no chance of not seeing him again. The Commission arrived in sections from 3.30 to 4, first Gielgud and then the others. All were soaked, a rain storm in the forest had broken over them, but we had got only the tail of it. Normand came out dressed and cleaned to tea and made up to me at once with a sweeping bow. He began by thanking me elaborately for being so kind to his people on the road and said he wished to explain how it was I came to encounter these cases, as he thought I might have a mistaken impression of his way of dealing with his Indians. Then followed a very contradictory statement, from the famished Muchacho and the 'old lady' to his recent transit across the chacara. Bishop had said he only returned to face us because he saw we had all seen him from the verandah. But as the man spoke to me I saw another intention revealed. His insistence that he wished to 'disabuse' my mind, that I should alter my 'assertions' ('I make no "assertions",' I replied quietly), and his frequent references to the old woman and his regret that I should have thought him capable of illtreating her. Lane had told him, he stated, that I left a message he was not 'to flog her', showed me clearly that he was playing a game. He invited me repeatedly to put any questions to him I wished and he should answer and explain anything he could. He said 'many people don't like us (who the "us" was never transpired), and I do not wish a gentleman in your position to go away with untruthful statements uncorrected. There are bad people, I know, who tell lies about us, and from your message to me by Lane, I am afraid you believe them'. I said that Lane had no message of that kind from me, but only that I was responsible for removing the woman's load, not she, and that as for the beating of her, it was really she herself, poor soul, who, in my hearing, had repeatedly expressed fear of him, Mr. Normand. I said the woman was clearly terrified as well as very ill. 'Oh, no, no, I assure,' he replied, 'she was not at all frightened, not at all. She knew perfectly I would not, I could not touch her. I never illtreat my people. My system is a quite different one, you see. When they are sick I go out to visit them and take them medicine, and when they go like this, carrying rubber, of course, some must fall out because they hurt their feet or get ill (the old woman had 'knocked her leg', that was all) and that is why I came last, as you see, so that I may attend to the sick ones. I carry medicines and spare food with me. I always bring several women carrying food (the Harem! Oh! heavens.) And when I find people like this man here who fell down to-day, you see, I give them this food and make them rest like this and help to divide their loads among the stronger ones. I have left several loads of rubber behind on the road, and by and by the strongest of those who have already gone to Puerto Peruano will be sent to their homes, and after they have had a good time then (he actually used those very words – 'a good time then') they will be sent out, with presents, of course, you see, to take down those other loads, later on, later on.'

This and much more. As regards the starved boy in the forest he had begun with him. This had been without his knowledge. The boy had been sent out to look for the wife of one of the men without his knowledge, (I said Yes, I knew that, as the boy had told me) and the boy had not found the woman and had lost his way coming back from Occidente. Lost his way, and 'got hungry.' I said he was 'Starving', absolutely and literally, and quite unable to move. 'Yes, yes,' he said, 'I heard of that – I knew he was coming, and that he was sick, and I was sending out for him when you so kindly found him and cared for him.' The boy is now 'quite well' and gone to his 'home' at Andokes.

His last touch was perhaps the funniest of all – it was a volunteered explanation of why he had not come directly up to the house here at Entre Rios, but had tried to slip past through the chacara. His rubber people, it seems, always robbed Mr. O'Donnell's fields, so he had given orders that none of his people were ever to pass through this station, but to go round it without spoiling anything. I remarked that fully 150 had passed through the evening before without robbing anything – clearly in defiance of his order that none were to come this way – 'Yes, yes,' he went on, looking two ways at once – 'I never allow them to come this way, that is why, you see, I took all my people round over there, because then they could do no harm, until I saw them past Mr. O'Donnell's fields, and then I came here.'

The Harem had arrived, and now five strong, one of them a <u>child</u>, positively a child, they floated over to Mrs. O'Donnell's quarters, where they were multitudinously received by that household of similar beauties. I nearly said 'But I don't see them carrying the food you speak of, Mr. Normand' – but it really was not worth while. I had listened almost in silence to this tissue of lies and absurdities. The only thing clear was that he was seeking to pose me in a difficulty. If I asked for explanations I'd get them <u>galore</u>, and if I did not, and then persisted in my 'assertions', he could always say he had voluntarily offered to correct the 'mis-statements' I was relying on. Fox came in and listened to the end of our talk, or rather of his talk, and I went away.

SUNDAY, 23RD OCTOBER 1910 AT ENTRE RIOS.

Bishop's letter – just brought to me at 2.35 p.m. tells how he overheard Normand and Leavine plotting together and how Normand told him (Bishop) that Leavine was 'too ill' to return to Entre Rios and that 'the Consul' must do without him. Bishop added that both were going down to Chorrera by land, and he was going to stalk them and stay here till I arrived and warn the remaining Barbados men who were being called in to be questioned by me that their best game was to tell me the truth and the whole truth.

I have read it to Tizon, Gielgud and Fox – and former (who is angry) is at once sending a muchacho to P. Peruano to bring in Levine with a letter to Normand. I said I did not require this to be done. I do not need Levine. I was merely desirous of proving to him the utter dishonesty of these men, and I told him then of Solar's coming to Matanzas with letters from Macedo first as to U. Retiro and Normand's pleasure at Donald Francis refusing to speak out. Also of the attempt to bribe Lane himself the night we arrived at Matanzas. I told him I had been sure from the first when I heard Levine had gone past this without showing that Normand was taking him on to bribe him and that this had been the explanation of his going round this station through the plantation instead of coming by the road past the House. It was to get Lane away without my stopping him here. It was quite clear that he was bribing Lane to retract all he had stated to me in his, Tizon's, presence. Then at Chorrera he and Macedo would further bribe Donald Francis, and bribe or intimidate the Barbados men who might already have arrived there to await my return. I told him I had sent Bishop down to counteract, by his presence, as far as possible, this attempt to suborn these British Subjects. I added that it was, of course very reprehensible action on the part of these high agents of this Company to attempt anything of this kind. 'Yes' he said, 'but it is human nature'. 'Low human nature', I replied. 'That is little', he replied, 'men who are murderers will not think much of being merely dishonest and liars.' I said it was, in one way, a matter of indifference to me as I felt sure he was already as convinced as I of the terrible evils that existed here. He replied, 'Yes, I was convinced before you – not by you – but by my own sources of information.' The messenger was despatched with a written order from Tizon to Normand to send Levine back. I sent also a note for Bishop, acknowledging his letters and saying he was to carry on to Chorrera and follow my instructions and I added that he should tell Donald Francis to be a <u>man</u> and speak the truth when I came down. I asked Tizon if Normand would not open this letter. He said 'No, that was not possible, I might send it in all safety'. I have my doubts, very strong ones, I sealed it with three seals, wrapped it in oiled paper and asked O'Donnell to give it to the muchacho who was to give it <u>only</u> to Bishop himself. We shall see if it reaches him. I am now fully convinced that Normand means danger. I can quite guess what the 'other things' were he said to Bishop, especially after something Lane stated this morning at the end of his replies to my questions. He said that when Normand had spoken to him on the morning of my leaving Matanzas after I had left the station one of the things he said to him was – translating Lane's imperfect English –

'Do you trust these Englishmen? Remember the one who came before and how he failed you. You complained through him and what came of it'. This was the gist of it. I asked Lane – 'What did he mean?' He said 'I don't know, Sir – that's what he say'. This, I fancy, refers to Whiffen. Normand wanted the boy to realise that just as Whiffen had failed in his encounter with Arana, and things had gone on just as these people chose after Whiffen's exposure – so it would be with me. The Barbados men who trusted me would find me a powerless, a broken reed to lean on – that was the intention I imagine.

I have thought it over since writing the above and feel sure that Macedo and Normand will now stick at nothing to save themselves. They are afraid that I am going to inform the Prefect at Iquitos of the things I have seen, etc., and that I am relying on the Barbados men as my evidence. They will, therefore, try to forestall me either by complaining of me even – or else by getting the Arana house in Iquitos to charge the Barbados men (any pretexts would be sufficient for their purpose) and getting them in jail. Once in jail they would rely on being able to force every man of them to retract anything they had stated – and even to say a good deal else that suited the needs of the scoundrels, or they could charge them, the Barbados men, with committing crimes on the Indians. Nothing would be easier, and the witnesses might be the very chiefs of Sections who had compelled these men to those very acts.

...I told Bell and Barnes of my fears as to the plot that is being hatched at Chorrera, and that I had, as a matter of fact, expected that something of this kind would arise sooner or later. Indeed I am surprised it has not come before. Already in Iquitos I told them, I had discussed the possibility of this with Cazes and had told him that I thought it highly probable I should not return to Iquitos, but would get off somewhere in Brazilian territory with all the Barbados men, I might have with me, and wait on the bank of the Solimoes for a down-going steamer to Manaos. I had said then that if I suspected any attempt might be made on the liberty of the Barbados men who had testified truly before me I should not risk their safety by returning to Iquitos with them, but should go straight down to Manaos, by a passing steamer. I now told Bell and Barnes that if, on getting to Chorrera, I saw the likelihood of this game being played I should not return to Iquitos.

At all costs of inconvenience and exposure I would go down the Putumayo on a raft, if necessary. I would not expose those men who had been true to their sense of duty to all the evident risks that might await them in Iquitos. It is I who have put them in peril. Bishop at the outset asked me in Iquitos if there was any 'political' trouble, because he was 'a poor man.' I said that he was to trust in me, that no trouble should come to him and that if it did it would have to fall on my head first.

Both Bell and Barnes agreed with me. I asked them not to say anything about this, it was, perhaps, too soon to anticipate evil, but they knew as well as I did that these scoundrels, now thoroughly alarmed, would stick at nothing. Had I gone to Matanzas alone, I am pretty sure they would have made away with me. I might have 'died of fever' and who would have known? Even Gielgud admitted that this was highly probable. Normand clearly would shrink from no crime to save himself or conceal his infamies. But it is not myself that is in question. It is the whole case against this wrongful system and the hope of reform that we have been planning together.

If the Barbados men should be arrested in Iquitos, I should have to defend them. My first step would be to telegraph home and to ask for legal advice and help. In any case, a 'trial' or imprisonment of the Barbados men would upset the whole apple-cart we have been toilfully dragging through these miry forest tracks. All question of the British Company surviving such a trial and the attendant expenses would be at an end. Our work here would be swept away and the Company with it, and all would again fall into the hands of the Arana gang, and their hired murderers on the Putumayo. More too, the British Government would be involved in nasty questions with the Government of Peru on the imprisoning and trial of the Barbados men. The Peruvian Government, if it found itself committed, by intrigue at Iquitos, to these arrests and prosecutions, would then, right or wrong, to save its face, ensure the conviction of the men as having been guilty of grave crimes on the Indians. The real criminals would all escape, the guilty would survive and, the Company swept away, they would revive their worst forms of pillage and murder to get the last ounce of rubber out of these forests.

That was the position I foresaw as likely to arise on my return to Chorrera, and I wanted them to understand the dangers, and to accord me their full support if, as might become necessary, I should decide not to return to Iquitos but go down the Putumayo with the Barbados men and seek 'reform by flight.' Like Sir Peter Teazle I would leave my character behind me,[36] and I should count on them, the members of the Commission, making quite clear later on why I had taken this course and that they had better come too with their full approval and support as being the best thing to do under the circumstances.

All this is not fantastic conjuring up of dangers. Take only three cases within my knowledge – that of Cyril Atkins, sent down by this very man, Normand, to Iquitos, and who died in jail there, without a trial – of E. Crichlow, confined for 15 months in Iquitos jail on mere letters from Loayza, without one single witness or scrap of personal evidence against him – and finally the case of Brathwaite, that was on while I was in Iquitos, where all the influence of Cazes was powerless to obtain a trial, although the charge against the man was flimsy in the extreme – merely one of disorderly conduct on board one of the river launches, and at the worst of threatening the Captain, while the man alleged the Captain had done more than threaten him. Tizon himself admitted to me only a few days ago (when on the march from P. Peruano here) that in Peru 'they had plenty of law and little justice.'

The Prefect would be probably powerless to intervene. The Casa Arana could get the warrants for arrest from the Court on any sort of pretext

[36] From Richard Brinsley Sheridan: *School for Scandal* (1772) Act 2, Scene 2.

sufficiently backed up by a bribe, and then the Prefect would be powerless in the face of the law. Why, even in civil matters the Iquitos court does as it pleases. Cazes case is one in point, his house surrounded by troops, the British Consulate guarded so that the Consul dare not leave his doors to transact business. The Prefect confessing himself powerless and that, too, in a case where the Aranas were the other parties in the Suit, and the matter was purely a civil one, a case of mere commercial dispute. Finally, as Cazes asserted, the Supreme Court at Lima gave a decision in his favour and the Iquitos Court has quashed it! The Iquitos Court, one of quite inferior jurisdiction, sets aside the Order of the highest Court in the republic and per[s]ists in maintaining a judgment already annulled by law. It is clear that no trial of accused Barbados men in such an environment could be a just one. The witnesses against them would be the very criminals who had compelled them to perform the very acts they would be charged with. I must at all costs, prevent this – even by flight down the Putumayo and the Amazon until I can put these men in safety in Brazilian territory and telegraph home for advice.

My plan then would be, if F.O. sanctioned, to return alone to Iquitos and with Tizon and the Commission behind me convince the Prefect of the true state of things here and of the imperative need for the Government of Peru to intervene promptly and decisively to sweep out all this den of murderers. The Commission would I am sure, back me, and Tizon I hope, too. I shall wait till we reach Chorrera and then tell him all my fears, if I see that Normand and Macedo etc. are intending to carry out the plan I attribute to them, and also my counterplan and claim his full support.

MONDAY, 24TH OCTOBER, 1910. ENTRE RIOS.

Once, I said, the Indians saw one of their murderers hanged and were told it was done for their sakes to save them, they would be with the soldiers as guides, as allies and trackers down. A few good Boras armed with rifles, with the military force of Peru and a military magistrate behind them, would end the correrias and commissions of the Juanitos, Velardes, Montts, and Coy, in a very short time. Something of the kind will have to be done – that I told him – and he sees it well, in his heart. I said, three weeks ago, at Occidente, when we had our last straight talk, that I should strongly urge him to write them for troops and a military magistrate – what in West Africa would have been a District Commissioner. Hanging, I fear, would not be possible – as Peruvian Courts come in and the lawyers – but shooting a few of the scoundrels would be easy enough. Tizon said he would like to do some of it himself. We kept the Commission waiting for dinner with our very protracted yarn, but I am much happier in my mind.

My position is a <u>very</u> difficult one. Here I am quite alone officially, and a heavy official responsibility on me too, to steer clear of all trouble or friction with the Peruvian Government. That I can accomplish, but the situation is an extraordinarily difficult one, for at any moment I may be landed in a row, the end of which no one can see, by any of these guilty men who are now all awake. I am 'the Enemy' because it is only through me and the Barbados men that they fear the truth coming to light. Tizon said they had 'built a wall round him, so that he should not see the truth' – but he had seen it all the same – 'And now', I added, 'we've pulled down the wall altogether and you see clearly, and everyone of them will be against you.' We shall win – not merely against the Normands and Macedos – they are contemptible beings – but against all the bigger intriguers in Iquitos, or wherever they may be. ...

TUESDAY, 25TH OCTOBER, 1910. ENTRE RIOS.

The Commission and Tizon left for Atenas at 8.30 or 9. I staying with O'Donnell. How strange, with this man of Irish name, whose record in any civilized land would consign him a hundred times to the gallows, and yet here I like him actually. We all agree he is the best, and are prepared to forgive his crimes as being part of 'the System' he was engaged to administer. It is the lowest system of slavery in the world, and this man who came here a boy of 20, 7 years ago, has probably sunk less than the others and got his rubber with cleaner hands than any of his neighbours. He is not so low as the system he has worked – that is my apology for him and for my mental attitude towards him. I heard Tizon ask Gielgud how to spell 'gaol-bird', last night. We all smiled and mentally applied it to the agents of this great English Company. I have gone one better, because I called them to-day 'the Excrement of the jails of Peru'.

I am sorry for O'Donnell, as we all are, and really feel that he has not fallen nearly so low as the others; yet if the crimes committed here in Entre Rios, in this far and away best of the Stations, could come to light, what a ghastly record there would be.

The lashes on the limbs of the Indians are far too conspicuous, they tell their horrid tale. Still here I am staying with O'Donnell rather than stay with Montt and I feel a sort of kindly feeling for the man, and a belief that under other direction he would have done well even. As it is he has done well compared to all the men around him, and his Station is a model one among these detestable penitentiaries. Fancy having a jail where the gaolers were all the criminals and the prisoners the innocent and the wronged!

At luncheon to-day, which included Martin Arana, the reputed brother of Julio Arana, O'Donnell told me something of the Indians killing the Colombians in this neighbourhood. I said I had 'great sympathy for the Indians' – and he could only smile.

I have more than sympathy – I would dearly love to arm them, to train them, and drill them to defend themselves against these ruffians. I said to Tizon last night that I only wished this were British territory for a year and with 100 men what pleasure I should take in scouring it clean. Poor chap! he agreed, saying 'Alas! but your Government is a powerful one, and mine is not'. We both agreed that we should have great pleasure in hanging, if needed with our own hands, many of the Company's staff. Tizon said, too, what I have several times averred to Fox and other members of the Commission privately, viz: – that if, by chance, he surprised any of them in the act of flogging an Indian, as this horrid act has been now so revoltingly described to us, he would shoot the man without a moment's hesitation. I told him such had been my intention for sometime back. I did not add that I had loaded my revolver and had it ready on Wednesday last in the Muinanes house, on the road down from Andokes, in case Negretto had arrived in the night and begun to maltreat the sick woman. It is a strange thing perhaps, the only time I have thought even of using a revolver has been against a 'rational' employee of the Company. I have never otherwise had it near me, it has been carried by one of the servants or locked up. I never carried a revolver against African natives, and I certainly shall not begin to do so against these very human South American Indians who are so much gentler and less able to defend themselves. ... The 'muchachos' have been brutalized, and made to behead and shoot, to flog and outrage. They are only another instance of the hopeless obedience of these people. What the white man orders they are only too prone to execute. Their very weapons attest the bloodlessness of their minds and customs. These childish spurs and deadly blowpipe – noiseless, stupefying and not blood-letting. Contrast such a weapon with the battle-axe, the six-foot spear with its 18" blade, or the beheading knives of the African inland tribes. Those robust savages rejoiced in blood-letting, just as the heroic Zulu saw red and well-nigh bathed in it. These soft-voiced soft-eyed, gentle-mouthed people have never slaughtered, they have killed. Even their cannibal feasts, as recounted by Robuchon in 1906,[37] or by Lt Maw in 1827, have never been orgies of blood-letting and seem to have been attended by as little cruelty to the victim as is possible to attach to such a ceremony. Moreover, these feasts do not, in truth, appear to have been banquets at all, and I doubt much if the killing and mastication of an enemy, as described by Robuchon, had anything to do with feeding the

[37] See note 30.

body upon him. It is more like the feeding of the spirit with his spirit; of the heart with his heart; of the soul with his soul.

The subsequent vomit, deliberately provoked, would seem to strongly support my theory that they killed not to eat, so much as to survive.

...If the United States cannot let light into the dark places of S. America then she must stand aside or be swept aside. The Monroe Doctrine is a stumbling-block in the path of humanity. Instead of being the corner-stone of American independence, it is the block on which these criminals behead their victims. If the only great Power in America cannot do her duty, in a matter so vitally concerning America's honour, then the Greater Powers of the World must step in. The Monroe Doctrine has more than served its purpose. It is to-day but the selfish instrument of a grasping diplomacy that, while refusing to act itself, would prevent others capable of action from doing their work. The day the Monroe Doctrine is challenged and Europe protests with shot and shell against this greedy assertion of Yankee ambitions the better for mankind. This blight in the forests of Peru and Bolivia would end to-morrow were it not for the M. doctrine.

TUESDAY, 25TH OCTOBER, 1910. ENTRE RIOS.

I have put down in my Indian notes what O'Donnell told me to-day of the Indians in his district. I wrote a note to John Gordon[38] with the Bridge record of last night.

To-day is a hot day.

Four Boras Indians came down to-day guarded, as usual, by one of the footpads of Andokes Section. This man, a stout mestizo named Villota. The Boras were very light-skinned, a handsome young man and a boy of 12 or 13, each with a load of rubber, and two women – one doubtless the 'wife' of Villota. Both women looked despairing. I gave them a tin of meat. The boy bore brands of flogging all over his nether parts, poor little chap. I photo'd both of them. The young man smiled and shook hands.

WEDNESDAY, 26TH OCTOBER, 1910

...The rubber at Atenas is done up in quite thin 'Chorizos' like the long sausages of a butcher's shop. It is the 'true Putumayo sausage' I am told. As a matter of fact it <u>is</u>. It is the entrails of a people.

Got back to Entre Rios gladly enough despite the terrible downpour – and turned in very early indeed. Our dinner consisted of deer steaks and cassava – very good indeed, but I lay down too soon after it and wakened

[38] See Black Diary, note 148.

at 12 midnight and lay awake most of the night – a prey to the most venomous sandflies. My legs, wrists and hands are now a mass of sores from the scratching.

THURSDAY, 27TH OCTOBER.

Leaving Entre Rios today... I feel quite hopeless in my heart, as I do not think any effective and humane control can be set up. Effort to establish it will, no doubt, be made, and Tizon will do all <u>one</u> man can do; but he is the only honest Peruvian I have met, except the Prefect. One man cannot cleanse this place, and the English Company is only English in name...

...I am on the look out for one lad, named Doi. If I can see him I will try and take him home. I have half a mind to take some of these poor starved beings here to Chorrera, of this Atenas lot. If I were in any authority here I should certainly do so – take the whole lot down and feed them.

FRIDAY – 28TH OCTOBER, 1910.

...After dinner Bishop came with a sort of written Diary of his doings since he left Puerto Peruano. It is not bad for a black man, and is entirely off his own bat. I read it to Tizon after dinner... He says he will settle Normand's little game very soon – that if Normand wants a row he shall have it – and it may be a hanging game for him!

SUNDAY, 30TH OCTOBER, 1910 [(A)]

...Normand left at 2.30 for his Andokes by 'Veloz', and gave me an effusive good-bye – coming to my room to shake hands. He is also to send down a boy – the boy Doi, I saw carrying a heavy load on the road whom I wish to take home if the lad is willing to come. I did not ask him for this. I spoke to Tizon about the boy, who told Macedo and Macedo gave orders to Normand to find the boy and send him to Chorrera as he 'wished to make him a present to someone'! These are Normand's own words. They reveal, innocently – if that word can be applied to such a man – the attitude towards the Indians of these ruffians. 'A present of a man' – fancy it!

I said to Normand that there was no question of this kind, only that if this lad wished to accompany me I should take him. But the position is disgraceful. Here is an entire population, titular freemen in Peruvian law and in the eyes of civilization, who, without question can be sent for, a 100 miles away, and sent down country to be 'given as presents'. If they only knew why I am taking Indians home they would not be so ready to gratify me! They think that they do me a service, and that I may modify my view of them, or that even they will have a hold upon me by saying, subsequently, that I, too, <u>dealt in slaves</u>. If they only knew that I hope to do the Indians a service by choosing two or three good types and getting them introduced to the right circles in Europe whereby to elicit sympathy and help for these people, then they might be far less willing to 'make presents' of these human beings. ...

One lad to-day had a splendid figure – a young Boras boy on one of the launches. I would like to take him, or one like, home for Herbert Ward in Paris. It is a good thought, why not do it? Herbert Ward might help materially in the cause. This Indian world of South America is unknown to Europe. H. W. might help materially with a bronze figure in the nude of a 'Putumayo Indian'.

I will see if I can get hold of any lad or young man willing to go. Bishop said the whole of Entre Rios would have gone with me if I had been able to take them. Several of the carriers of my baggage told him that. There is no question of the Indians gladly going, the question is that the Company's agents will not let them go. Each lad represents some 120–140 kilograms of rubber per annum, at the cost of a Hammock, a shirt and a pantaloon, or put thus – 300 lbs. of Rubber @ 4/- per lb. = £60 sterling – versus Cottons costing 7/6d. The profits are high! ...

SUNDAY, 30TH OCTOBER, 1910. [(B)]

... It must always be borne in mind that the Indian is no party to the contract. He is compelled by brutal and wholly uncontrolled force – by being hunted and caught – by floggings, by chaining up, by long periods of imprisonment and starvation, to agree to 'work' for the Company and then when released from this taming process and this 5/- worth of absolute trash given to him he is hunted and hounded and guarded and flogged and his food robbed and his womenfolk ravished until he brings in from 200 to perhaps 300 times the value of the goods he has been forced to accept.

If he attempts to escape from this commercial obligation, he and his family as defaulting debtors are hunted for days and weeks, the frontier of a neighbouring state being no protection and when found are lucky if they escape with life. The least he can expect is to be flogged until raw, to be again chained up and starved, to be confined in the stocks, in a position of torture for days, weeks and even months. Many Indians have been so kept for months.

... Can any international outcry, and intervention be effective to compel Peru, Bolivia (and Brazil too) to protect their Indian peoples?

I fear not. Still the attempt can be made and with God's help I'll make it.

MONDAY, 31ST OCTOBER, 1910 AT CHORRERA. [(A)]

Up early 5.30. Lovely sunrise flowing over the great pool in a flood of salmon-tinted light. Told Bishop to bring Evelyn Batson to see me at 7.30. He came before 8. He is a fireman now on the Launch 'Huitota' which is going down to-day to St. Julia to bring up the Abisinia fabrico. I presume Aguero will come. Batson's statement is a dreadful one. The man answered every question put to him simply and quietly and with every sign of speaking the truth. It is a horrid record and incidentally throws light on the truth of Crichlow's and Chase's statements, the former's as to his treatment by Aurelio Rodriguez at Santa Catalina in 1898, and the latter's as to the capture of Katindere's wife and the other people on the Pumá a few months ago this year. The state of things at Abisinia must be as bad as ever, the crimes committed by Aguero and his subordinate, Juan Sellar,[*] that Batson knew, are as dreadful as anything ever recorded I think. They include a shocking case of Cannibalism, a man cut up and carried past the house by the Muchachos under Aguero's directions and the limbs taken away to be eaten, and a group of the Pumá prisoners cruelly murdered – three by deliberate starvation and the fourth man shot by Sellar.

Also a woman killed by Armando Blondel at Morelia, by blows of his fist and further the actual shooting of Katendere himself at Abisinia by the Muchachos. This latter incident is like a page of romance. Katendere was the hero of the Boras – the brave captain who resisted and tried to give back blow for blow. Bishop who saw him once, a year ago when he was under Normand at Andokes, says Katendere was a fine, tall, strong young Boras cacique who worked rubber at first but fled from Normand's ill-treatment of him. He it was who shot the scoundrel Bartolomé Zumaeta in May, 1908, at a stream in the Boras country while that villain was directing the washing of rubber.

Since then Katendere has been 'on his keeping' to the hills – as we said once in Ireland – and every effort to kill or capture him failed until this last actual attack of his own on the Station of Abisinia itself. What a pity he did not succeed. ...

[*] R.C.'s note: A mis-spelling. I found later on the man's name was Juan Zellada but the blackmen always pronounced it to me as if it were 'Sellar'.

MONDAY 31ST. OCT. 1910 AT LA CHORRERA. [(B)]

So called 'Whitemen' here would think to apply to a negro – and yet the negro has a better heart and a better conscious [conscience] than they have – and is a far better 'whiteman' at bottom. I told Tizon this, to his secret amazement I think. The <u>Sur</u> fabrico under Carlos Miranda began to arrive just before lunch. He first with a huge dog. He was formally presented to us all by Macedo. He is a fat, gross-looking whiteman, with a fair complexion. I thought, as he shook hands with me, of the 'old woman' in Labadie's statement at Iquitos. That seems a trivial incident now after the more recent first-hand horrors I have had – but it was an atrocious act. The 'old woman' had given 'bad advice' to the Indians. She was a 'wise woman' that counselled them not to work rubber – not to be slaves. So her old head was cut of[f] with a machete and this whiteman who has just shaken hands with us and sits down beside us to lunch, had held it up by the hair to the assembled Indians and told them that that would be their fate if they did not obey him and work Caucho. What a curse there is in those words – to work Caucho.

Fox and I went out to the Store and watched the rubber coming in. Huge loads of it, men, women and children. Dear little bright-eyed boys – tiny girls – mothers with infants – two quite old women and two old men even – almost the very first old people I have seen. Three of the Indian men, too, had beards – stray hairs, it is true, but still beards – one 2" long. These are the first men with hair on the face I have seen. We weighed several loads – one was just 50 kilogs – on a thin spare enough man too. Then I went one better and collared two small boys with their loads and got these weighed first and then the boys themselves.

One mite had a load of 22 kilogs, of rubber on his tiny back and then when put on the balance himself he came to just 25 kos. The next, a little boy whose name he gave as <u>Kaimeni</u>, weighed $29\frac{1}{2}$ himself and was actually carrying $30\frac{1}{2}$ kilogs of rubber! One kilo. more than his own weight. This had been for many miles. The Station of Sur itself is only 2 hours away, but this rubber we were told came from <u>Kaimenes</u> on the way to Encanto – a much greater distance. Fully 100 people came in – more than that I should say – and even as they deposited these enormous loads of rubber in the big Rubber Store they were collared and made to carry off boxes of things and bags for the 'Huitota'. Two birds killed with one stone! They had not time to sit down or get a drink before this further task was put upon them – to load the departing steamer with goods for Abisinia. Fox and I watched this confirmation of so much – it told its own tale, with a sort of grim joy I think.

I sent to the Store for a case of Salmon and distributed tins <u>galore</u> to men, women, boys and <u>mites</u> – also some of my own tins still left from

Iquitos. They clicked their tongues and lips with joy poor souls and I photo'd a good many of them. They are nice bright-looking people – and I picked one dear little chap out and asked if he would come with me. He clasped both my hands, backed up to me and cuddled between my legs and said 'yes'. After much conversation and crowding round of Indians it is fully agreed on, he will go home with me. His father and mother are both dead, both killed by this Rubber curse – and his big brother – a young man – was shot by Montt. Out pat came the story – the boy's Capitan standing by and explaining. The Capitan asked for a present on the agreement – virtually the sale of this child – of a shirt and a pair of trousers which I gave him, and Macedo with great unction made me 'a present' of the boy. The child's name is Omarino[39] and he comes from the Naimenes village, towards El Encanto. He had carried a huge load of rubber down too. I will get him and it weighed to-morrow. The wee chap clung to me often, both hands, and I gave him several tins of Salmon to give to his friends as 'parting gifts'. He [al]so asked for the Salmon – to give away – and I watched him running round and giving those joyous tins – for such they are to these starving folk. Several tins of it went to an elderly woman, who had a mite of a boy nude entirely without 'fono' at all.

...I bathed in afternoon and a boy or young man came and sat on the bank – 'Andokes' and other boys were swimming like fish. This young man is a muchacho of Sur and I had photo'd him along with others as they brought the rubber in. I had noticed him looking at me with a sort of steadfast shyness and as I gave him and others Salmon his face flushed. He now came and eyed me in the same way and when I came out from my swim he followed me up to the house and begged me to take him away with me. Again and again, I called Bishop and he said he would go above all things – to get away! Bishop says the whole country would go if they could get out. This youth is married too! He says, however, his wife has gone to her 'family' and that he will gladly forsake all to get away. He is a fine youth, quite strong and shapely with a true Indian face. I'd gladly take him, but I already have Omarino and Doi is on order from Matanzas, and Tizon says will come. This youth is a bigger boy than either – a married man of 19, probably or 20 and would make a fine type for Herbert Ward[40] in the group I have in my mind for South America. This has been for some time in my thoughts, to enlist Ward (and France) on the side of these poor Indians and to do it through their artistic sense. I'll gladly take the boy if Macedo & Coy. don't kick up too much fuss. Of course they could not <u>lawfully</u> refuse and I could put it that way if I chose, but that would indeed be a challenge!

[39] See Black Diary, note 154.
[40] See Black Diary, note 174.

To actually declare that a Putumayo Indian was free to go and come as he or a civilized man thought right ruat coelum [come what may] rather than that. This youth's name is Arédomi,[41] but he has been called 'Pedro' by these civilizing gentlemen! He has the fine, long strong hair of the Indians, the cartilege of the nose and the nostrils bored for twigs and a handsome face and shapely body. I gave him a pair of pantaloons, and he stripped the old ones off, and stood in his fono – a splendid shape of bronze and I thought of Herbert all the time and how he would rejoice to have the moulding of those shapely limbs in real bronze. I told Arédomi to wait till the morning and I would see if I could take him – Bishop seemed delighted. He has already got the tiny Omarino in harness, getting clothes made for him to carry him as far as Iquitos and he is to sleep in Bishop's hammock to-night, Bishop taking to his cot.

I played four Rubbers of Bridge – won two and lost two. Like Dean Swift I was playing for Arédomi, had I got clear conqueror I was to take him – I had to fight terribly to get this mere tie and so the Bridge did not decide Arédomi's fate. It is really buying the freedom of a slave. I shall not pay in coin or goods for him here – although in some ways even that may be called for, but the expense of conveyance etc. is heavy. My hope is that by getting some of these unknown Indians to Europe I may get powerful people interested in them and so in the fate of the whole race out here in the toils. Harley House and the A.P.S. [Aborigine Protection Society] will help and exploit the boys for all they are worth if it ever comes to raising the question in public campaign against this hellish slavery and extermination ...

TUESDAY 1ST. NOVEMBER 1910 AT LA CHORRERA.

Up early – and saw Arédomi waiting – poor boy...

No time for diary to-day.[42] I swam over to the Island in the early morning at 7 a.m. and then began the Barbados statements right away. Allan Davis has come up too from Abisinia – so I have all men here now, six more to interview and then I am through. Told Tizon of Batson's and Morris' statements... Told him of Normand's setting people on fire and burning them alive as Sidney Morris witnessed it. Perfectly atrocious. Tizon told me all were going. Velarde is down from Occidente to go with me and Normand by next steamer, and Aguero and Fonseca are to go very soon.

[41] See Black Diary, note 154.
[42] See Black Diary, note 129.

...One of the Barbados men who spoke to-day, Augustus Walcott, was shamefully ill-used by Normand at Matanzas at end of 1904 or beginning of 1905 – just after they arrived. He was hung up by his arms tied behind his back for a very long time, and beaten with swords – or machetes. He became unconscious and when let down was ill. Remained ill for a long time and had to be carried down in a hammock to Chorrera. Could not use his arms for two months. ...

WEDNESDAY 2ND NOVEMBER 1910.

The river has risen steadily. It is now fully 5 feet up and the sandbanks are rapidly covering. Did not bath. Saw Arédomi who is cutting firewood and fully decided to take the poor boy with me. Told Bishop I had decided. Carlos Miranda came to bid me good-bye, going back to Sur. Then called James Mapp and got a long statement from him lasting up to 11 a.m. He is one of the first to come here. He saw Velarde have the Indian drowned at Occidente this year – as described by Francisco the Capitan. Saw it with his own eyes – four poor beings were taken down to the river with their hands tied behind their backs and held under water by an Indian acting under Acosta's personal direction until they were filled with water and nearly drowned. One of them struggling to escape got loose from the hold of the Indian and was never seen. With his arms tied, and his 'bowels full of water', as Mapp described it, the poor soul had not much chance. His body was recovered on 24th June at the mouth of the river just below the Station.

I brought Tizon in to hear James Mapp repeat the statement and when he learned that this had actually happened the very day he left Occidente, to go on to Entre Rios he was pale with anger. I was glad of this striking confirmation of the truth of what I have been driving into his soul the last four weeks...The same stories – the same crimes all through – are confirming one another. Quintin had been tied up by Normand and flogged – got 50 lashes and is very ill too – was again beaten by Normand and Bucelli. The marks of the first lashes – 6 years old! – are on him, one dreadful scar across the ribs.

...Poor Quintin, in addition to all the gross ill-treatment done to him by Normand was forced at Santa Catalina to cut off an Indian's head by Rodolfo Rodriguez now second in charge of that Station.

...I measured a fine young Boras Indian to-day come with Aguero 37 $\frac{1}{2}$ inches round bare chest – not inflated – 12$\frac{1}{2}$ round biceps – not distended – 23" round head at forehead. His skin was exceeding fair and he was tall and very well built. I am told some of the Boras are white almost. Some I have seen are as white as a Spaniard or Portuguese.

My little boy Omarino was weighed to-day too; he weighs 25 Kilogs, and the load of rubber he brought in weighed 29 Kilogs!

Arédomi is hanging round Bishop says. They want to take him back to-morrow to carry the 'tula' of one of the Sur empleados who returns.

We shall see. I will ask Macedo in the morning. The poor lad has tasted the hope of liberty. I shall see that he gets away.

THURSDAY, 3RD NOVEMBER, 1910. [(A)]

Arranged early this morning to take Arédomi with me. Sent Bishop with the lad to Macedo who at once consented, so that is happily settled.

...Bishop tells me that another dastardly outrage took place last night under our very eyes. The 'Huitota' with Aguero and Alcosta did not leave till 8 or later. Aguero took one of the poor workwomen here.[43] Macedo gave her to him to swell his Harem. He always has eleven at Abisinia, Chase tells me. This poor woman is a Huitota, one of the local Slave Staff. She used to sweep the Verandah every morning and Fox and I had both noticed her gentle patient face. Bishop says she wept bitterly and begged to stay. She has been working here for years, since her poor Indian husband 'disappeared'.

She had been given, of course, as a wife to some of the Empleados, but these had gone too, or died, and she was for some time working here, sewing, making 'pantaloons', etc. under Mrs. Macedo's direction and performing house tasks and now she is handed over to that degraded infamous wretch to swell his pen of unfortunates.

She begged, Bishop says, to stay and even asked why Aguero, who had so many wives already, should want her. I told Fox, Bell and the others of this fresh outrage and when I am quite certain of all the facts I shall speak to Tizon.

Sent for Donald Francis at last and he came to make his full confession.

...I read him a homily, he apologised humbly, and told me I did not now want his story of wrong-doing, that I knew all and had already received all the information necessary for my mission. He is really sorry and anxious to stand well with me and with his own conscience.

The 'public opinion' of all the other Barbados men has been too much for him. He wants to 'hold up his head' with them. Now he can do it. I don't want criminal evidence against Macedo, it would only add to Tizon's enormous difficulties to add Macedo at once to the black list.

[43] See Black Diary, note 159.

He is perhaps the worst of the lot, as he has been in control and has allowed and stimulated all this dreadful crime, besides the things I know and suspect he has done himself, including the burning alive of the 45 Ocainas Indians here at Chorrera. But Tizon assures me that Macedo too is going, so let him go in peace, for the sake of Tizon's work of cleansing and reform. ...

FRIDAY, NOV. 4TH. 1910.

La Chorrera to Sur.

Commission started to Sur at 7.30. I followed alone with Sealy and Arédomi at 8 and caught them up just entering Sur – an easy $1\frac{1}{2}$ hours' walk, – about $4\frac{1}{2}$ miles, I fancy. Much of the road saplings, fully 30,000 young trees and saplings, felled and laid across for well two miles of the way. Saw a strange orchid – lovely bamboo palm – exquisite thing.

Sur a wretched place – no plantation or food visible, but Miranda says soil is bad and he is removing the Station 40 minutes off to a new chocara he – or rather 'his' Indians – are making. The house a poor place – although better furnished than most and the man himself a more civilized man. James Mapp gives him a good character – better far than most of the others – and the only grave thing I know against him is what Labadie asserts of his cutting the 'old woman's' head off. I fear there is no doubt it is true.

I bathed in the stream and after lunch returned with Sealy and Arédomi, starting at 4 p.m. getting an enormous shower on the way and arriving drenched at Chorrera at 5.30 or so. The river rising steadily and every hour now makes the approach of the 'Liberal' surer.

SATURDAY 5TH. NOVEMBER, 1910

The position of the English Company seems hopeless. To carry out any reform they must smash up the Den of Thieves in Iquitos – that is clear – and yet it is these men who own the Putumayo and the Putumayo Indians and when they see their reign of wholesale plunder threatened, they'll smash the Company and let the English Shareholders whistle for their money. ...

What Gielgud <u>could</u> have been doing in passing <u>such</u> books and <u>such</u> accounts for a firm of London Auditors bangs me. It bangs Banagher. ...

SUNDAY, 6TH. NOVEMBER, 1910.

The three Barbados men, Sydney Morris, Augustus Walcott[44] and Preston Johnson who had gone up to Sabaro to get their things have returned – along with Fonseca. They came down by the Atenas road last evening and I saw them and sent a canoe to bring them over. ...

Yesterday I went carefully through Sealy's, Chase's, Quintin's and James Layne's Statements, reading them out slowly and then getting the men to sign them. This took a good long time.

To-day I have repeated the operation with the three men from Santa Catalina, Preston Johnson, Sydney Morris and Augustus Walcott. I then got them to bring their accounts and have gone into them more thoroughly than has yet been possible. I have compared the prices charged them with those figuring on the Iquitos Invoices of the Company's which I copied yesterday as well as with my own Invoices from Caze's house in Iquitos – and the more I look into the figures, the less I like Macedo's proposal to wipe out the 25%.

It is not good enough. Moreover, the very readiness of the proposal coming from him so instantaneously without the slightest suggestion on my part that anything of the kind should be done makes me suspicious. If he is so ready to give away this money, it is because he fears the question being raised at home. ...

I asked for a sign – and lo! it has come – the most extraordinary utterance – I have been in grave doubt all the afternoon – feeling that by purchasing the present ease of the blackman I might be selling the Indians – giving up the game that is, to some extent, in my hands. And I rose from dinner with this thought heavy on my mind – I left Fonseca and the murderers and the Commission – and walked to the end of the Verandah – far from them, by myself, revolving the whole question and what I should say to Tizon and Macedo to-morrow when they bring me the accounts of the Barbados men with the reductions all round. I said, as I walked the Verandah, to myself, how shall I put it? Shall I accept or say no – and if the latter how say it? The answer of my mind was – 'Say No – say it thus – Say, I am grateful for your offer and thank you for it very sincerely. I appreciate it much and on the men's behalf would gladly accept it, but on full consideration I feel that I am not empowered by my Commission from H.M. Government to accept such a proposal without reference to them. I shall therefore refer your proposal to them in the spirit of goodwill that prompts it – and meantime leave the matter in this state – namely, that you freely offer on behalf of the Company this – and that while thanking you on behalf of the British Subjects to whom it is made, I will beg to be allowed to refer the offer to His Majesty's Government.'

[44] See Black Diary, note 156.

Just as this thought raised itself, I looked up from the Verandah to the <u>eastern</u> sky – and saw, to my amazement, an arc of light across the dark, starless heaven. For a moment I did not realize what it was – then I saw it – a lunar rainbow – a perfect arch of light in the night. The moon was in the West – with stars and a clear sky round her in the East, obscure sky and coming rain – and this wondrous, white, perfect bow spanning the dark. I called Fox, Bell, all of them – everyone came – none had ever before seen such a sight. It was about 7.30 – as near as could be – and as we looked at the perfect arch, curving from forested hill to forested hill right across the Eastern heavens, the rain began to gather over it. It was slowly dissipated – broadening and fading away. We watched it for nearly ten minutes – I take it to be an omen – an omen of peace and augury of good, – that God is still there – looking down on the sins and crimes of the children of men – hating the sin and loving the sinner. He will come yet to these poor beings – and out of the night a voice speaks. I shall not sell the great question of the Indians and their hopes of freedom for this mess of pottage for the handful of blackmen. These shall get their rights, too – but they shall come as rights – freely granted – and I shall not be the agent of silence, but I hope of the voice of freedom.

I have decided – or rather I do feel that this extraordinary sight, coming as it did, when my whole soul is seeking the right path, points the way. It was a direct answer to my question. I think it can only be read one way. Superstition, I suppose – yet are we not all children of a very ancient human mind that has sought in the heavens for its god and read His will in the clouds.

And so to Bridge with my mind made up – and to-morrow alack! instead of peace and smiling Macedo and Tizon – the old uncertainty and suspicion and possibility of trouble at Iquitos. I sacrifice my own ease and the <u>present</u> good of the Barbados men – but so be it. It is in the right cause!

MONDAY, 7 NOV. 1910

...Owing to my long spell of work with the Barbados men to-day is the first day I've had much leisure to write up my diary – and I have missed some incidents of the last few days. For instance, Arédomi's wife – a young girl – has come in and begs to be allowed to go away with him. Arédomi is quite willing to give her up in order to get away. I don't know what to do. I don't want the woman – it is an awful handful to add to the menagerie I am taking down stream – yet I am sorry for her. If I leave her she will be 'all right' Arédomi says with her mother. I daresay she will – but it seems inhuman. If I leave the boy with her he goes back to slavery. Bishop says he would swim away to get off with me – the door of freedom has opened and given him a glance of a life beyond and I have not the heart to shut it. I daresay it will end by the girl going too – in which case I shall leave both at Para to get work there and become free Brazilian citizens. It will be a step up for them indeed. They will soon learn Portuguese and Arédomi can work and earn his living – without fear of the lash, the bullet, the mochet and the cepo.

The Sur Indians of the Naimene and other tribes are fine-looking people – the best Huitotos I've seen. They all smile at me – Arédomi and Omarino have given me a great character – the 'Mare Capitan' – the good chief. ...

To-day an afternoon of fearful heat I took Arédomi up to the hill to the Cataract – and photo'd him in necklace of 'tiger' teeth, armlets of feather plumes and a fono. I also photo'd the falls from the steep cliff above through the dense bushes. We went on to the upper river, to the landing-place and sat there and talked, or tried to talk, I asking him names of things in Huitoto, and he telling me as well as he could. He actually clings to me I can see – poor boy. We saw 14 splendid Araras or Macaws fly slowly by – one alit on a tree quite close with a flash of crimson under-wing. Omarino says he wants to learn to write and came to my room and got a blue lead pencil and covered a sheet of paper with weird signs. ...

TUESDAY, 8TH NOVEMBER, 1910.

...Aredomi brought me a feather head-dress from his house, poor boy it is a gift of gratitude and he went away home to-day to get it.

River dropping fast, it has gone down a good deal, but is still very high. Very weary of this long delay at Chorrera doing nothing.

Not well very.

WEDNESDAY, 9TH NOVEMBER, 1910.

River still dropping. The sand-bank showing out of water a couple of feet at least. Rain yesterday afternoon and a threatening of it to-day and some fell but not enough, I think, to influence the rise or fall of the river. I did nothing all day – am not very well indeed – and I am so sick of this horrid atmosphere of crime. ...

Went out at 4 and watched the mules bringing in the loads of rubber. Every beast is maltreated, and one poor thing with its lips and mouth cut to pieces by the hide thongs passed under the jaw on a slip knot, that has cut near to the bone. Called Barnes and Tizon and made a row. Got out the mule man (Pelayes his name) and told Tizon to see a change made.

Just as we had finished this, heard the people say the 'Liberal' was coming and then at 5.45 she appeared, steaming up – her white mast and funnel showing over the point of land and bushes. We nearly cheered – some of the people did. She, of course, fired off a great rocket into the sky followed by a sound signal that was like the outbreak of a volcano. Saw several passengers on here. She anchored just at 6 p.m. and Bishop came to tell me John Brown of Montserrat – Whiffen's old 'boy', was on board and then brought him up to me with a letter from Barbados Government explaining how it is they came to send him. It is a nuisance – a waste of money – but I suppose cannot be helped. The man is worse than useless now – merely an incumbrance. Told him he had come too late and would have to return at once by the 'Liberal'. A Captain Delgado with a file of Peruvian soldiers on board – going to Encanto I believe – and two fresh 'agents' (God save the mark) for the Company. Have not yet made the acquaintance of any of these folk. The soldiers, poor youths, the Andean hill folk of Peru, the Cholos of the Cordillera – far too good and fine a race to have such disgraceful masters. If only the Monroe Doctrine could be challenged by Germany, and successfully challenged, there would come hope for the hunted Indians and gentle beings of this Continent who have had 400 years of 'Latin civilization' to brood on.

Got lots of letters from home – but none of great interest to me <u>here</u> in these surroundings. Crippen is caught too! but what a farce it seems – a whole world shaken by the pursuit of a man who killed his wife – and here are lots and lots of gentlemen I meet daily at dinner who not only kill their wives, but burn other people's wives alive – or cut their arms and legs off and pull the babies from their breasts to throw in the river or leave to starve in the forest – or dash their brains out against trees. Why should Civilization stand aghast at the crime of a Crippen and turn wearily away when the poor Indians of the Putumayo, or the Bantu of the Congo, turns bloodstained, appalling hands and terrified eyes to those who <u>alone</u> can aid?

I wish I could see some ray of hope. I read letters a bit – wearily and with no interest in anything of home news – except Mrs. Green, Moul [Bill Moule], and a fine little bit of Irish news. . .

THURSDAY, 10TH NOVEMBER, 1910. [(A)]

. . .A Brazilian Negro at Providencia named Pinheiro came and told them of what he had heard Aguero, Blondel, Bruce, etc. saying up at the house and warned them against going on the road. Armando Blondel tried to throw them off the launch by force and make them go but they refused to budge and have come back in her. Solar, they state (the ex-police officer from Iquitos dismissed by Tizon there and now Macedo's lieutenant here) also made disparaging remarks of the Commission (and myself) and said that if any Barbados man stayed on after I left it would be a bad thing for him. He would pay for the rest! Burke, the Engineer, even said lately – Greenidge and Bishop heard him – that if he were a Chief of Section he would have these f — Englishmen shot and he knew one Chief who could do it, Aguero.

I have warned the Commission – particularly as regards Chase and Sealy who will be with them when they go to Abisinia and Morelia. These poor lads might very easily be made away with by a stray Boras or two and then it would be put down to the 'Cannibals'. . . .

THURSDAY, 10TH NOVEMBER, 1910. [(B)]

Dyall reaffirmed categorically his charges against Normand of smashing the two unfortunate men's testicles. He also, incidentally, admitted to Tizon and myself that he had had nine different Indian women given to him by Macedo and other Chiefs during his stay here.

He has one child, a boy of three but the woman now with him is not its mother. Poor Huitota women – what a fate – passed from one to another by these horrid wretches without any voice or question in the matter – as in the case of that unfortunate woman from this that Macedo gave to Aguero a week ago. The whole thing is a pig-stye.

Tizon told me that the Prefect had written to him to say that he had definite news, the Columbian Government was going to invade the Putumayo!

They were making a road from Porto to the upper river and would soon be invading this region. He appeared pleased I thought. I think he sees political kudos in it. He added that he didn't think the Company would have a long lease of life! I told him I had doubt as to my ability to interfere in the proposed settlement of the accounts of the B. [Barbados] men, that I did not think I was authorized to make a settlement here, that was for the Government and the P.A. Coy. to arrange. He said that if the men did not take this offer they might certainly get nothing as the Coy. 'might smash' long before then! This is quite conceivable.

He later shewed me a Power of Attorney he had received from Iquitos giving him full power over the whole business here, to dismiss any employé of 'whatsoever rank and to appoint others and to liquidate and wind up' and take any steps he pleases.

His position is strengthened greatly. On the other hand I don't like his way of viewing the future. He is (I think) already losing sight of the Indians and their future and that of the Coy. in the larger view of a possible conflict with Columbia in which he could play a big part for Peru. There could be a 'victory', an 'extension of the national territory' and things of that kind to fight for, and the poor Indians would be between the Devil and the Deep Sea.

He also showed me a copy of the Comercio of Lima of 10 October containing an article on the 'Indians of the Putumayo' and a forth-coming judicial enquiry to be held by the Iquitos Courts (!) by order of the Peruvian Attorney General.

The article states that the Lima authorities are acting on the evidence raised by M. Deschamps in his letter to the Barcelona press and on the facts alleged by the London Anti-Slavery Society... If there were any hope of this being a real enquiry with a desire to find out the truth and to punish the guilty then it would be for good. I have no such hope. Tizon believes, or affects to believe, that it is meant for an honest effort to protect the Indians. I certainly don't. If any such desire really existed in Peru among the governing class of the country, they would long since have given expression to it much nearer home than on the Putumayo. Are there no oppressed Indians in the Montana save on this tragic river? When the charges were first made in Iquitos now three years ago, why did they not enquire into the matter then? Had they no national honour to safeguard, until it is assailed in the press of the World, and when a very powerful Government has begun to actually take steps on the spot to find out the truth? It is not the truth they seek now – but to suppress the truth being established, to their shame, by others.

I got lots of letters from Monn [E.D. Morel] from Moul[e] and many others. The national Testimonial to him [Morel], Conan Doyle writes to me, amounted to £1,300 early in October and he sees his way to making it far more before the end of the year. Moul[e] has now sailed for the Niger in John Holt's ship.[45] God bless him and old Holt too. I went on board the 'Liberal' and saw Captain Reigada and two 'agricultural experts' the P.A. Coy. had sent out. ...

Read the article in Lima 'El Comercio' of 9 August on the Putumayo Indians. The Fiscal of the Supreme Court of Peru, corresponding to our

[45] *John Holt* (1841–1915): pioneer West African merchant, who traded from Liverpool. His letters from R.C., 27 May 1905–13 February 1913 (Subject: Congo Reform) are in Rhodes House Library, Oxford: MSS Afr. s.1525, Box No. 12, File No. 1. Among other commodities, Holt traded in rubber, and his correspondence includes letters from H. R. Fox Bourne, Secretary of the Aborigines Protection Society, and Travers Buxton, Secretary of the Anti-Slavery Society.

Attorney-General, has ordered the Iquitos Court to open an urgent enquiry into the charges brought against the P.A. Company by the Anti-Slavery Society. He requires a judge to be sent to the spot too. It is based, he states, on the letter from Emil Deschamps, written from Barcelona to the 'Commercio' which that paper published on 7th. Aug. Tizon has shewn this to me as well. It is a good letter – an excellent letter. Tizon tells me privately he has written to the Editor or Proprietor of the Lima 'Comercia' who is his cousin, saying the Government must take action. He is also writing to the Prefect at Iquitos, begging him to come round here as soon as he can. He tells me the Prefect has written to him too – and he begs me to go and see him and speak frankly to him. This I have said I shall do privately. He says it will be a friendly act – an act of goodwill and kindness. Our conversation was long and very friendly – as indeed my conversations with Tizon always are. He has repeated all his former assurances and with emphasis – that the gang at Iquitos must be broken up and Arana eclipsed, and the London Board take complete control. He says the criminals here will fly to Brazil as soon as the Judge appears – and that that will be the best settlement. There they will drift into the Purus and other rivers – to repeat their crimes!...

A very hot day and the afternoon blazing. I walked out to the stream and bathed in the soft brown water of that hillside brook. It is delightful. Talked to some of the Sur Indians down here. They are nice chaps, and several speak Spanish – broken Spanish. The others played bridge after dinner. I walked up and down in the moonlight till near 9.30 and then turned in, reading the latest 'Daily Mails' with their shocking screams against Germany. It is a dreadful little cur of a paper – a regular yapper. The Liberal is repairing her screw shaft. There are over 40 – nearer 50, I should think – Sur Indians down here helping to load her as well as O'Donnell's men – many of whom came to talk to me, saying they were on our caravan to Matanzas.

The Liberal is to leave on Tuesday I am told. That is 15th. and she should be in Iquitos on 24th. The Atahualpa is due to leave Iquitos on 27th., but it will be 30th. before she does so I am sure, so that I may be in Manaos on 4th. or 5th. and Para perhaps on 9th. December.

After that it is hard to say, as I think of going to Barbados, for many reasons and trying to fix up some things there. I see no likelihood of getting home before end of January...

SUNDAY, 13TH. NOVEMBER, 1910. [(A)]

... Borborini [*sic*] will be a nice fellow-passenger for me on the 'Liberal' – knowing that he is dismissed through me and the Barbados men. There will be 16 of them on board – happily – enough to look after themselves. Tizon and I were photographed later on, each to have a picture of the other – by Gielgud.

Borborini, Bishop has already told me, killed two people at Urania long ago when he was there – an Indian he shot and another he cut the head off. How many more he has killed since goodness only knows. He was the principal flogger at Entre Rios up to the date of our arrival there in October – so the Indians told us at Port Peruano.

Tizon told me to-day, in our conversation, he has decided to visit Abisinia and stay there a long time when he starts the real 'trading' venture with the Boras. He says the Colombians are again in the Cahuinari – at the mouth of it – and that the road being made from Pouto to the head of the Putumayo is a serious thing, and the threatened invasion may come off. Several of the Barbados men have Indian 'wives' and children and want to take them away with them. I say it can be done if they marry the women – not otherwise. John Brown is one. Explained situation to him. Again a very hot day, and the river falling steadily. It is now down 7–8 feet from the highest water on Sunday last, I think. That was also the day (or night) of the Lunar Rainbow.

SUNDAY, 13TH. NOVEMBER, 1910. [(B)]

I have told Tizon I shall ask him to distribute the a/cs to the Barbados men to-morrow – and will ask Gielgud to be present. I told him (Tizon) I should be there, but would not counsel the men one way or the other, that I was not here to arbitrate between them and the Co., and that this offer of the Co's was a free one to them which I should leave them quite free to decide on as seemed best to themselves. Miranda came down yesterday and is here to-day. I told Aredomi I could not take his wife, the poor little Indian girl, away with me. I spoke to Miranda about her. Aredomi is quite willing she should stay behind, indeed I think anxious for it. They are only boy and girl – and he does not really care. She is afraid of being taken by one of the empleados of Sur, . . . who has already told her Capitan he would take her. Aredomi explained this to me through Bishop. I asked Miranda to promise (through Bell) that the girl should be safe – and he promised on his honour that he would see no one took her against her will. Aredomi is to 'send for her' – if he elects to become a European – or to return if he wishes it.

Bishop has translated to the girl and he says she is very unhappy. It is not Aredomi she cares about, but simply to get away from the Putumayo too! He says her brother has been in talking to him and saying how much he too, would like to fly. . . .

It is exceedingly hot. I am rather dreading my last day to-morrow and this final settlement by the Barbados men's accounts. I may be wrong in allowing the thing to go through! but I cannot quite see where. If I stand aside and leave Co. and men to deal together it can in no wise tie the hands of the F.O. in any subsequent representations they may wish to make on the grounds of the general ill-treatment of the men.

Then there will remain my few days at Iquitos, when I must be hourly on my guard. I shall not feel safe or happy till I see Tabatinga and the Brazilian flag waving over its mulatto-troop of soldiers. Brazil and freedom are synonymous up here in this benighted region.

The Iquitos letters told me there had been a 'revolution' at Manaos between the Neris and the Bettencourts and that the Federal gunboats had bombarded the town. This on top of the Revolution in Portugal and flight of King Manoel and his Mother to Gibraltar means great news of sorts. Poor Portuguese – they will be out of the frying-pan into the fire. A handful of educated rogues will rob 6,000,000 peasants more cleverly and to a bigger tune than any one-man Show on earth. The Portuguese monarchy was not sufficiently a one-man Show – that was its weakness. Had Dom Carlos' effort at absolutism but carried through and Joao Franco not failed to guard his King, then Portugal to-day might have been on the high-road to financial integrity. She will now lose not only her revenues – 'gone astray' into strange channels – but her African Colonies. These have only been saved to her by the friendship of England. Had England and Germany ever laid their heads together, indifferent to Portuguese feeling, they would have divided the spoils. The influence of the Portuguese Crown secured European friendship – everyone 'liked' the Braganza monarchy. It was old, it was illustrious – the monarchy was coeval with the people, and as long as Portugal kept her King she stood the best chance of keeping her overseas territories. All this friendly feeling will be dissipated to-day. No one will feel the slightest reverence or kindliness for a Portuguese republic run by a gang of half assassins, half card-sharpers. The first serious squabble over natives or any other cause in East or West Africa will bring about the beginning of the end.

I went up the hill with Arédomi and bathed in the river above the rapid. There was a 'batalon' and a balsa or raft there. Many of these Amazon trees will float and when nearly green, for the raft seemed of very fresh timber, all the sappy bark still on the logs. Arédomi and I swam out to it and towed it to the bank where we used it as a sort of wash-board for lathering ourselves. We came back by the swamp and hills behind the house and found an extraordinary caterpillar of pale yellow hairs, with a tufted crown like a cock-a-too. Aredomi said it was poisonous – presumably their irritating spines of yellow downy hair. Borborini, the coward who struck the Indian boy from Sur, is dismissed on the spot, (and by Macedo I hear, to his credit) but will not go away by my 'Liberal' on Tuesday. He returns to pick up his 'wives' (he has two of them, the beast!) and things and will go over to Encanto to catch her next trip when she will go there for the Caraparana rubber. This will save me the unpleasantness of having him on board.

A lovely day, but very hot and poor Fox suffering from asthma. The Commission will come down with me as far as Port Tarma whence they go up to Orienta [*sic*] to Alcortas land. They will then continue to Sabana, I believe, Santo Catolina and Abisinia Sections. The latter is being run at a dead loss so Barnes tells me of 36,000 soles per annum = £3,600! And this money is wasted on a District that is kept going on Murder, Massacre and Cannibalism and every human crime that depraved men can conceive. Played Bridge (Tizon and I partners) and won 2 Rubbers out of three – easily – against Barnes and Gielgud. ...

MONDAY, 14TH NOVEMBER, 1910. [(B)]

After the settling up of the B. men's a/cs I had a long talk with Gielgud, just before lunch. His mental attitude (or moral?) is a strange one. Frankly, at <u>heart</u> I think he is as bad as any of these Peruvian scoundrels. He is a cold-blooded, selfish guzzler, who thinks of himself first and always. He clearly thinks that by the acceptance by the men of this 'bonificacion' [bonus] their mouths are stopped, or the F.O's mouth is stopped as against the Co.

I told him after breakfast that nothing was altered, so far as I was concerned, or the representations I should make to the F.O. as to the treatment of the men. I am glad I am leaving this ghastly hole.

After breakfast an extraordinary thing occurred. Jiménez came with Bruce[46] to translate for him, to ask for an interview. I was sitting by Barnes on the verandah and I said certainly, here now, and sat on, so he began, through Bruce, to say that he learned he was charged in 'Truth' with atrocities &c. and he wanted to disabuse my mind, so that I should stand well with him.

I said that I had nothing to do with what appeared in newspapers and that if an English newspaper had libelled him he had his remedy at law. He said he would take this but that he wanted to stand well with me. I was a 'cavaliero distinguido' [= <u>caballero distinguido</u>, distinguished gentleman] &c. and he did not want me to believe ill of him. Barnes sat listening. O'Donnell and Castro Pol. Adolf Castro Pol and a

---

[46] See Black Diary, note 109.

young Peruvian boy (about 6' tall or more) from Sabana came and sat listening.

Jiménez spoke again and again, there was a clear intention to get me to say that I did not believe Borgos' or 'Truth's' charges against him and accepted his denial. This I refrained entirely from saying. I pointed out I had nothing to do with these matters which concerned him and 'Truth' and the Government of Peru and that while, personally I might even have a good impression of him it was not my business to deal with Truth charges one way or the other. As he persisted to seek an expression of opinion I said 'Very well, as you ask me, I will say quite frankly I <u>cannot</u> carry away a good impression of you. It is not "Truth" alone, but I have heard from many quarters of things you did and while there may be some exaggeration I don't believe all is and I leave you to your conscience. You know what you have done, and if you have done wrong before you may try now to do good.'

I suggested he should bring a libel action against 'Truth' if he thought himself aggrieved, and this he said he should do!

He looked flabbergasted and so did the rest and after some more of the same kind of remarks he shook hands and went. Bruce stayed on to talk to me and he gave the whole show away. He admitted that the whole system of dealing with the Indians was an infamous one, and that if the Indians shot a whiteman they did quite right. All the Chiefs he said had flogged and if any told me they did not they lied. I said I knew that – that the system had been a bad one from the start, and some men were better than others. It was an extraordinary attempt to draw me. Jiménez knows a Peruvian Judge is coming here and he wanted to get a statement made by me in the presence of witnesses, that would have whitewashed him. There is fear all round. I wish I could think that any sincere and honest enquiry by Peru was likely – but I believe the whole thing is simply to whitewash. Tizon is delighted, because he says that it will prove that Peru has acted herself before any foreign pressure was brought to bear upon her! A fine idea – after waiting 3 years and when the fat is in the fire and all is known, – she begins tardily to move.

The truth is all these people are liars – I would not trust one of them – and as I write this late at night this Monday evening, I feel that all the trouble I have dreaded may arise again at Iquitos. Tizon is profoundly afraid of me and of the testimony of the Barbados men. He knows quite well that their evidence, which I hold in written form, seals not only the fate of the Co. for which he does not care very much, but the honour and credit of Peru for which he cares a good deal. It is quite on the cards that he is writing round to the Prefect urging that, on my arrival at Iquitos with these 18 very black witnesses against Peru, they should be questioned, i.e. interrogated by this examining Judge. The method of interrogating would be their own – their very own. The object would also be their very own. To damage these the <u>only</u> witnesses – to obtain discrepancies, denials, recantations, &c., so that the only evidence Peru has to dread should be in her possession before it reaches England that she might play havoc with. I am seriously perturbed. This rushing of a settlement on the Barbados men out here has so clearly been inspired by unworthy motives. I told Tizon I did not wish it. His leg began to jerk – the South American sign of agitation and I told Gielgud – that incomprehensible ass – the same thing, and he said he thought it should be decided on by the Company. They have practically <u>forced</u> a settlement on the men here – involving me as far as they possibly can as an assenting party. The object is clear, that as the men's claims are settled – and in my presence, there remains no ground for representation on their behalf to the Company – or to Peru. Step No. 1 accomplished (as they think) at Chorrera. Step No. 2, the complete robbery of all the evidence of the Barbados men at Iquitos and then Mr. Casement and his 18 very black witnesses to be bowed out of the country. I am in a regular fix.

I spoke to Barnes very late at night and told him of my fears or of my renewed fears. He quite sees their force. He says I cannot break the journey at Javari, or anywhere else, unless the 'passenger' is booked there. That Reigada, the Captain of the 'Liberal', told him that last voyage. So if I leave Chorrera with all my B. men bound to Iquitos they must go. I want to leave them at some place in Brazil and pick them up on the way down river. This I cannot do unless I give notice here and say the men are landing at say the Javari mouth. Then I shall know how I stand or how the intention in regard to the Barbados men stands. I shall say this and test them – and if I see that there is a deliberate intention to <u>compel</u> me to take the men to Iquitos then I shall at least have unmasked the enemy and I can fight openly. I shall then refuse to go by 'Liberal' at all! The raft may again appear floating on the waters of the Igaraparaná! I <u>cannot</u> get down to the Amazon if these people will not assist me. It is 650 miles away and I could not get food even. They would not let me have the 'Huitota' or any means of transport down to the Amazon.

Even the B. men (some of them!) might join the enemy. The crisis of my journey to this accursed river has come, with its gang of villainous ruffians. The 'Liberal' is delayed now until Wednesday 16th., so I shall have to-morrow to prepare for the fight. ...

TUESDAY, 15TH NOVEMBER, 1910, AT LA CHORRERA.

... Burke the Engineer of 'Huitoto' spoke to me after dinner. An amazing story, worthy of the 'goodness' of Alcosta of Oriente. He spoke of

Normand 'dashing children's brains out' as a thing Alcosta had never done. Also he had not allowed his muchachos to eat a man! Also, when one of his 'wives' went wrong with an Indian, he did not shoot her, as Aguero would do, but actually made the man take her. Zumaran at Indostan flogged pieces out of a woman up there. Burke saw her – lumps an inch deep out of her. Also Velarde the same with 2 men. Alcosta is keeping them 'to show the Consul'. Burke admitted, like B. men, everything: A volunteered statement to put himself right with me. He knew that Jiménez had spoken and said 'Of course, everyone knows about Jiménez having killed Indians.' Bruce yesterday actually said that, under the present system, the Indians would not last more than 6 years. I had said 10 years, and he said, 'No, indeed, not 6. When I came here the Company had 10,000 Indians, and it has nothing like that now.'

Two strange avowals to come at this end of my stay. Rats leaving the sinking ship. Seeing that I have won, and know all, they wish to stand well with me. Bruce also said B. Zumaeta had outraged the wife of Katurdore before his eyes while K was in 'cepo', so he shot him.

WEDNESDAY, NOVEMBER 16TH, 1910.

Thank God! I left Chorrera and the Peruvian Amazon Company's 'Estate' today. I am still their involuntary guest on their steamer 'Liberal', with the eighteen Barbados men, four Indian wives of these, and the children of John Brown, Allan Davis, James Mapp and J. Dyall. Dyall made a hard fight to carry off an Indian woman – his tenth 'wife'. He came at 8 a.m. to say the woman Loazza [Loayza] had given him in Encanto refused to be left behind, and insisted on going with him. I went to Tizon who, for reasons I think justifiable, refused to allow her to go. Of course Tizon's refusal is illegal. The Company does not own the people, and only a Government authority could refuse to allow this Indian, or any Indian, to leave. Tizon says that Dyall has no means to support her, which is true; that he refuses to marry her; which is true; and that she is not the mother of his child, which is true. Dyall admits all this, but says the mother of his child was taken from him by Velarde at Occidente, that he has no woman to look after his child, and that, final and best reason, the woman herself wishes to accompany him. The woman came weeping, and protested against staying, and made a regular scene. Tizon was obdurate, and I told Dyall I should not intervene, that I thought Tizon's reasons were good. The woman even tried to get on board the boat, but was turned off on the plank, and made to go ashore. ....

I bade Miranda and O'Donnell special goodbyes, and after a last shake-hands with Tizon, G., Barnes, Bell and Fox, we cleared off the ropes and moved into the stream. Two fearful explosions of sound signals, and we were off. Sealy and Chase had come to bid me a special goodbye, and I saw them last – they, and Francis and Greenidge on the top of the steps waving farewells. We quickly slipped down the still water between the sand bank and the shore and with our nose in the downward current were in a moment swept out of sight. The last thing I saw was by an upward glimpse, the great white cataract pouring into the upper end of the pool. My last view of the scene of such grim tragedy as I believe exists no where else on earth today.

   ...I find Garrido, Gusman and the other employé are at table too with us! In the Sections these 'Perus' are obliged to eat by themselves, and when we came up river Garrido took his meals with Bishop. Bishop and John Brown are at a sidetable on the upper deck, where the servants got their meals before, on the upward voyage; finally, Aredomi and Omarino are on the upper deck too, and a dear little chiviclis[47] that Macedo got for me.

   ...The moon rose bright after a glorious sunset, one of the loveliest I have ever seen. We noticed the brilliant gleam over the tree-top as she rose – a full moon, too. As soon as she was clear of the trees we saw an eclipse[48] was in progress, and as she rose we got a magnificent view of it. A total eclipse by Regada's almanac. The whole visage of the moon was obscured by 8, and then clouds came and covered the subsequent stages.

   I turned in early, but wakened at 2.30 with a glorious moonlight, and the lovely palm-crested forest slipping past silently and softly against a pale blue night sky. I looked long at it, and thought of the fate of the poor Indian tribes, who have been so shamefully captured and enslaved, and murdered here in these lovely regions, by this gang of infernal ruffians. I thought of Katurdore, the brave Boras chief – of all the murdered Indians of these forests; of the incredible and bestial crimes of these infamous men, and wondered at the peace God sheds upon the trees. The forest, with its wild creatures, is happier far than the 'centres of civilisation' these Peruvian and Colombian miscreants have created and floated into a great London Company.

THURSDAY, 17TH NOVEMBER, 1910.

I took the chiviclis into my cabin last night, and it played long with me, and nestled up and chirriped, and then I put it in the nasty cage, and covered it up warm. This morning I made Aredomi take it out to play

[47] The word *chiviclis* has proved untraceable. It is probably a local Amerindian name for the chinchilla, a cavy-like rodent found in Peru. See also diary entry for 17 November below.

[48] See Hugh Casement's opinion, Black Diary, note 172.

with and feed. He and Omarino and Bishop all slept on the upper deck. A lovely morning. The river now is broad and deep, and the banks lower and lower. All suspicion of high land has passed away, and we are in the swampy region near the low, flat shores of the Putumayo. The Captain tells me that he has 66 tons of Rubber aboard, and 35 tons of firewood. ...

4.30 p.m.
Arrived at Pescaria. Here is the blackguard Cerra, Quintyre told me about. The river is lower than when we came up in September last, I think. It is a noble stream and Aredomi and Omarino are looking on a new world. Aredomi says they call it Cottué – the Igaraparana, and Harmia the Putumayo. Where the name Putumayo comes from it is hard to say. Lt. Maw, in 1827, knew nothing of it as applied to the river, but heard of it as a place and as a tribe of Indians. It is probably Quichua, and was doubtless first applied to the Indians of the upper waters, as 'mayo' is the word for water or river in Quichua, I believe. ...

FRIDAY, 18TH NOVEMBER.

...We ... steamed on up to Triunfo, about a mile further up the river. Here ... were several people – three men (so-called Peruvian 'blancos') and a lot of similar-skinned women – the sisters, cousins and aunts, and several Huitoto and other Indian muchachos. The house a veritable pigsty. ...

I landed with Bishop and Aredomi, and took a photo of the place, and of the Sisters, cousins and aunts, promising them copies to their great delight. We bought firewood here, too, and stayed a long time getting it on board. The Captain says there is little or none to be had in Brazil, and he is glad to come up the Yaguas to get it. ...

There was a considerable look of scare on the faces of the three Peruvian 'blancos' up at Triunfo this afternoon when I came into the house. They all knew who I was, because the Recreio man had already addressed me as 'Sr. Consul', and I can't help thinking there is more in the shooting of Fonseca than the simple narrative of Reigada that the boy shot him, because 'some-one told him to'. There has been some of the usual devilment here, too, and these rascals thought, in their ignorant way, (they are all half-castes) that I had come in some way about it. All these people nearly look upon me now as a sort of Enquirer Extraordinary, who has got to the bottom of things.

The Captain tells me that this Fonseca killed here was uncle of the villain now in Sabana. His widow in Iquitos has sold 'the business' here on the Yaguas to the man I saw in the house, Azambriga by name – a Portuguese name.

The skipper tells me queer things. He has now a Huitoto sailor, a strong-limbed, very sturdy chap, about 22 or 23 years of age. This youth 'belongs' to a man named Grosso in Iquitos, but won't stay with him. He came on board to ship as a sailor last time, and Grosso came and wanted the Captain to give him a promissory note for £50 for the boy! Reigada refused, and told him he could take the man to the police if he liked. He said Grosso dared not, because they could not have kept him. He then told Grosso he was going to pay the boy himself, too, not give the wages to him, the Master, and Grosso could only grin.

Reigada admits that there are plenty of Huitoto women and boys who have been sold in Iquitos, that there is always a market for them. I asked how it could be, since they could always claim their freedom, and he only laughed. Men were known to give £40 for a boy or a girl, so he says. He then wanted to tell me of the two Huitoto sailors he had last voyage, when I came up. Neither is with him now. One is staying with the elder pilot, Manuel Lomas, at Punchana. When Reigada paid him off with £6 last trip he asked this boy what he would do with the money, and the boy said he was going to buy 'a cap and a pair of pantaloons.' The skipper then told him the money was sufficient to buy 20 caps and pantaloons, and he only laughed and said he would give it for one of each. So Reigada handed the money to Manuel, and asked him to look after the boy, 'Julio' is his name, and see he was not robbed. He said 'the Jews' in Iquitos would not rob him, as they did all the Indians. The other boy 'belonged' to the present Portmaster of Iquitos, who had got him from the Putumayo somehow or other, but he would not stay with him, and 'came to sea'. He has now gone back to the Portmaster, because he was ill. Bolivar I asked after. He was taken to Iquitos, and ran away there on arrival. Reigada says he wants to be free, and will not return to Putumayo. Pablo Zumaeta tried to get him, but failed, as he cleared out promptly. Well done, Bolivar.

The younger pilot, Simon Pisango, has changed his name to Perez — not Pizarro.

Poor Aredomi is bitten badly by sandflies, and has just been to me for the Colonel's lotion I got in Manaos from the old man before leaving. I rubbed it all over his chest and arms. He is washing up plates on board, and making himself useful, and smiles constantly — very happy...

SATURDAY, 19TH NOVEMBER, 1910. [(A)]

...Lawrence, who has been at Chorrera since 1904, confirms the beatings and floggings of Indians there when loading and unloading the steamers.

The murder of the Ocainas Indians and the burning of them, some not quite dead, took place there in 1903. Bishop says he often heard it spoken of. Rafael Larranga took a leading part in it. The Ocainas were charged with killing Colombians. There is no doubt the Hardenberg papers are in the main true. Here and there details are wrongly given. There are lies and exaggerations, but the main facts and charges are substantially correct. Moreover, hundreds of crimes not recorded there have taken place. Normand, Aguero, Fonseca, Montt, Jiménez, the two Rodriguez brothers and Martinengui, have between them, murdered several thousands of these unhappy beings. There is no doubt of it. Tizon admitted to me in Chorrera last week that the two Rodriguez 'had killed hundreds of Indians', and that Arana gave them 50% of the produce of these two Sections, S. Catalina and Sabana. Normand is again and again charged by the Barbados men with killing many hundreds. Leavine today said 'over 500',; that he had seen 20 Indians killed in five days in Matanzas alone, and the dead bodies eaten by the dogs and stinking round the house, so that he could not eat his food. These seven monsters have probably killed by shooting, flogging, beheading, burning, and got rid of by starvation some 5000 Indians in the last seven years. Barnes said the Indians of the Company numbered 10,000 when he [Normand] came, and there were 'nothing like it now', and he has been here only two or three [five] years at outside. Fonseca has killed hundreds, too, – and Martinengui. The least criminal are probably O'Donnell, Miranda and Alcosta – of the rest it were hard to choose, save that Montt lacked probably the courage of the other monsters. And this is done in the name of civilization and industrial development!

MONDAY, NOVEMBER 21ST. 1910

...4 p.m. We have had quite an interesting day. At 10 a.m. we stopped at a lofty bank on left shore of the river, steep and fully 35 feet above present level, with steps at top. This is Palmares, a line of huts below Belem. Here we got firewood and I went on shore. The two houses at this point were very cozy and well fitted, the most comfortable one could imagine for this locality, and <u>such</u> a people – the soil amazingly rich, everything planted looked gigantic. Sugar cane as thick as one's arm almost, and a great variety of fruits, and Hibiscus flowers, too. A turtle pond, with plenty of turtle, 25 bought this morning, one of the men said. Fine pawpaws, and delicious pink cherry peppers and pineapples as fine as Pernambuco ones. The yucca or cassava very fine too and plenty of hens and chickens, some of which we bought. I saw a couple of lovely green parrots with blue heads, and, of course, their wings quite uncut. They were perched on one of the houses, and very tame. The owner asked £4 each! Then a very fine mutum – a beauty – and he was offered for £2, but I declined. Finally, the 'dono da casa' [man of the house] came down to £1, but I further declined. It was not the price so much as the distance to carry him, and I believe I can get one in Para cheaper.

Everyone nearly on shore enjoying this beautiful natural history store. The forest round was lovely, only a tiny clearing, but each yard of it fruitful. Near the edge of the cliff the grass grew luxuriantly, and there was a patch big enough to feed a cow and sheep or goats. These people might live in absolute clover, if they would only work. They do nothing but rubber. 'The rubber pays for all', just as in the South it is 'coffee pays for all'. There everything needed is bought with money from coffee – here it is pretty much the same, except that even the things needed cannot be bought, so that the money goes in absurd tomfoolery and waste. Then just up above us we can see Belem with its far-famed Church costing £3,000. This corresponds to a nobleman's private chapel at home – without the chaplain. No priest within 1000 miles, and Belem itself is only a one man's place – what in West Africa we should call a 'factory'. I don't object to the Church, however, it shows some mind and soul above the ordinary along this melancholy river, but most of these people, when they have money, waste it on jaunts to Manaos, or on silly things quite unneeded. Houses with no beds, never a book within a week's journey or a school-master, but accordions that cost £10, and a diamond ring, or gold watch chain for flashing down the pretentious sidewalks of Manaos, and often much more paid for much worse there – ladies from Poland. Food at this place is lavished on these people by Nature. I never saw such vegetable profusion, right up to their doors, otherwise they would be starving, for it is not the labour of their hands gives them this...

We left Palmare at 11, and steamed on past Belem at noon. It is a fine clearing, belongs to a man named Mafra[49] of Italian descent, but a Peruvian, like many of these Solimoes magnates. A fine tiled house, and some big iron-roofed stores, and a line of palm-thatched huts for the workpeople – just beyond it a river mouth. Every proprietor here [has] his own river, with a steam launch snugly stowed away. The clearing round the houses a big one, and the famous Church has two towers. The skipper says the priest when he comes here makes a good thing out of it, as Mafra is devout, and has a regular flare up on these bi-annual occasions. He works rubber on this river and another beyond it, which we come to at 12.30. This river is broader, fully 160 yards broad at mouth, and has an 'alvarenga' or lighter anchored in the middle of the mouth. This to receive cargo – goods or rubber – for or from the passing steamers, also to guard

[49] See Black Diary, note 178.

the mouth of Mafra's main 'quebrada' [tributary]. Every 'Estate' its own river, and woe betide the stranger or rubber pirate who intrudes. This one our chief pilot, Manoel Lomas, says he has ascended for 6 hours in a big steam launch, or say 50 miles, at high river. He says Mafra owns Ticuna Indians up it, and they work the rubber. No Brazilian Government launch, I presume, has ever, since the world began, been up this river, and, God knows, what may go on there, in spite of the Church and its two towers out here on the high banks of the Solimoes. Mafra himself may be a godly man, but when it comes to owning Indians in these Amazon forests I fear for the body of the Indian, more even than for the soul of his owner. The great sandbank continues far beyond Belem, bounding our left view up stream for miles. One such bank of soil – for it is not sand but a rich blackish soil – with a thousand Chinamen upon it, would feed a kingdom. There is no felling of timber or clearing required. The great river does that. It just piles up millions of tons of gleaming drift, washed clean and harrowed and shining as the water subsides from the crest, and leaves them stretched out for miles to sun and rain for enough time annually to raise two crops each year. Before the water covers them again they are covered with rich grain, and as each rising river will gradually deposit more silt, the central parts rise annually, and then first the embauba or sloth tree comes, to be gradually followed by all the forest growths until one sandbank turns into an island forest. This island will some day again disappear, mile by mile, tumbling and swirling away with topping trees and ripping leagues of forest into some new opened chasm of the mighty waterway; channels that this year have 60 feet of water, and are the main route for the Liverpool steamers will close up, and become islands the year after. Now as I write, a stretch of fully 4 miles broad of river opens to left and right between the islands. I am sure of this, that in a reorganized South America, when the Monroe doctrine has been challenged by Germany and happily dispatched under her shot and shell, the valley of the Amazon will become one of the greatest granaries of the world. Also, too, I believe it will be peopled with a happy race of men. It supplies practically for the asking all the essentials of human existence, and this in a climate that for an equatorial latitude is superior to anything else in the world. All it needs is the touch of a vanished hand. The Portuguese (and Peruvians and others) have killed off in a shameful and cowardly fashion the aboriginal Indians, who, had the Jesuits gained the day over Pombal and the Colonists,[50] would have today numbered millions. The murderers have put nothing in the place of those whom they destroyed, neither civilization to replace savagery, nor white

[50] Sebastião de Carvalho, marquês de Pombal (1699–1782) Portuguese states-man who sent fresh colonists to the Portuguese settlements in Brazil and fostered trade there by establishing the Companhia do Grão – Pará.

humanity to replace the copper – all they could do and have done was to pull down, not to build up or create. This mighty river, and far beyond its shores of this great continent, awaits the hand of civilization. Four hundred years of the Spaniard at its sources, and 300 years of the Portuguese at its mouth have turned it first into a hell, and then into a desert. No sight could be pleasanter than the flag of Teutonic civilization advancing into this wilderness. The Americans have got their part of America, and it will take them all their time to civilize themselves. Germany, with her 70,000,000 of virile men has much to do for mankind besides giving us music and military shows. Let loose her pent up energies in this Continent, and God help the rats who have gnawed at it so long. Law and order would have meaning then, and justice and labour advancing up this mighty river would subdue the forest and found cities, and realise here in these glorious wastes the glowing words with which Bates closes his book – 'for I hold to the opinion that, although humanity can reach an advanced state of culture only by battling with the inclemencies of nature in high latitudes, it is under the Equator alone that the perfect race of the future attain to complete fruition of man's beautiful heritage – the earth.'

I share Bates' belief, and I believe that the people for the task are 'neither Saxon nor Italian', but our friends the Germans. Not the Americans or Canadians, or anything Latin or Latinized. The curse of this Continent has been its Latinization. With everything in its favour – incomparably ahead of the desolate prairies of the northern America, already peopled by millions of gentle, docile and industrious beings – what have 400 years of 'Latin civilization' done for it? Reduced the many millions of the Andean plateaux to a tenth of their number and to a condition of slavery that is unique among white governing races of the East, and murdered the wilder dwellers of the wilderness in every conceivable barbarous manner – not in order to replace them with white settlers and agriculturists, but solely in order to enslave their survivors in the interest of a handful of sordid, mean-souled and ignorant squatters. And to this has succeeded the pillage of the forests – vegetable filibustering replacing human filibustering, in order that the ignorant mob of Para, Manaos and Iquitos may visit Para or Lima, and indulge the sensual appetite with the vices of both.

TUESDAY, NOVEMBER 22ND. 1910.

We did not arrive at Esperanza until 1 a.m. this morning. I had long since turned in, and had hoped we should lie there until daylight, so as to arrange for the landing of the men. However, the Captain called me to say the young Customs Officer in charge had very willingly allowed the men to land, and to sling their hammocks under the house. This young man came on board ... It was a pleasure to see the frank brown face of a decent looking warm-hearted Brazilian, after the unmitigated murder type I've been accustomed to in the Peruvian Putumayo. He begged me to give directions to the men to make no barneho and not to get drunk. We landed plenty of food for them, and I wrote orders on any down going steamer and to Mr. Derring,[51] the Vice Consul in Manaos, to look after the men on arrival and pay the conveying vessel.

... We stopped at a wooding place on north bank, in the midst of the ancient Loreto, and bought 1500 billets of wood from a Spaniard at 25S/- per 1000. This is £2.10.0 as against £3 (cheapest) in Brazil, but the Captain says the Brazilian wood is better value. The clearing we stopped at is clearly old, the grass short and clipped by 4 head of cattle. No plantation at all, but many popunha palms and with ripe fruit too. We got a lot of these – my little boy Omarino climbed one clean stemmed palm, from which the spires had been removed. He tied my handkerchief round his ankle, and went up in a jiffy. The Brazilian negro, who was at Providencia when Mapp and the other B. men were to be ambushed by Aguero's cannibal muchachos, is on board, going away after five years' service in the Company. He was very busy getting the fruit down from one of the palm trees, cracking jokes all the time. He shinned up an embariba, and then pulled the fruit off the nearest palm with a long stick I passed up to him. ...

I gave the Cholo sailors some cigarettes while they were getting the firewood on board – or rather I gave a packet to one sailor, and he at once distributed all round, keeping only one for himself. They are fine lads, always smiling and willing, and if properly handled by decent white men, would make a splendid race. The owner of the house was away when we arrived, but he returned in time to get payment for his firewood – a Spaniard, the Captain says. I presume he squatted here, as all have done along the river banks. The ancient town of Loretto has quite gone, only two or three scattered huts like this in the forest with here and there the remains of a fruit palm or other planted tree. This Spaniard had two small canoes, the ordinary dugouts of this river, and one rather larger dugout – boat shaped – with gunwale and a palm-thatched pamalcari over the stern. I asked out of curiosity the price of this. He said he had made it himself, and it was not for sale. When asked, however, what its current value was he said £30, and added he had refused £25 for it, offered him in gold. The thing would have been dear in Europe at £4. Here its intrinsic value was much less – for all needed for its making was an axe, saw and adze. The forest gave the timber free for the cutting and the palm for the thatch, the whole of the materials were entirely free, and there was only needed

---

[51] See Black Diary, note 69.

the human labour with the few needed tools. I saw today one of the bits of sandbank planted with yucca or cassava. The plant had shot up splendidly, and all this quite recently grown – only a tiny patch of it. It shows what might be done with this fruitful soil, for this cassava was not two months old I am convinced.

WEDNESDAY, 23RD NOVEMBER, 1910

...Iquitos, which has no church, has a large colony of Jews. It also has a big colony of Chinese, half-castes – that is to say a Chinese cross with the Cholo Indian, and quite a good physical type it is. The Jews are the predominant business factor in Iquitos, and since I have struck this Peruvian Amazon I have solved a riddle that has often puzzled me. In Johannesburg, before the war and probably since it, a Jew was habitually written of in the press and spoken of colloquially as 'a Peruvian'. I never heard an explanation or reason given – now I see its force.

We have stopped once looking for wood, without success. We stayed at quite a pretty beach with a nice little house embowered in a beautiful garden with a high fence round it. The men all landed to get oranges, which, the skipper said, were plentiful. Omarino and I stalked some glorious butterflies – green and black spotted, and a magnificent crimson or scarlet and black barred. We went about it in a half-hearted way – with our fingers. Omarino caught one thus – a white and red, but I let him go at once, and he flew away uninjured. I could not bring myself to crush the little palpitating body between my fingers.

A heavy storm in afternoon – not much wind – but a sultry rainfall. We are due to reach Pebas sometime this evening, so I am told, where we shall stop for firewood. Here, the Captain says, the Yaguas Indians come quite in their original native garb – a dress of Chumbira fibre plaited into a voluminous garment covering the whole body. Tizon gave me one, but I have not seen it worn yet. We shall not reach Pebas by daylight, however, and I fear there will be little or no chance of seeing these Indians. The strange thing is how have they survived and preserved their native customs, and dress, when all elsewhere along these 2,000 miles of river every Indian has merged in garb and external show into the ranks of his so-called civilizers. Generally, this garb is a shirt and dungaree or cotton pants, with a wide, coarse, straw hat. It is singularly unbecoming, and the bronzed, beautiful limbs of these men are so picturesque it is a crime to replace the fono or bleached bark loin cloth with this miserable gear. ...

Reading Harry Johnston's 'Negro in the New World',[52] which I like. He sent me the 'first copy' (so he says) and I find it interesting in the extreme,

[52] See Black Diary, note 120.

and well done. I wrote him a long letter today on the modern slave trade here in S. America, which the great world does not suspect. ...

I saw two Yaguas Indians in their fanciful costume by the dim lantern light on the beach. They were helping our crew with the scantlings [timber cross sections], and carrying enormous beams on board with the utmost ease. I got them brought up on deck in the electric light, and was truly amazed. The costume beats anything I have ever seen. They are bound round the brows with immense streamers behind, and the whole body clothed in this soft rustling fibre. It is all dyed a rich soft terra-cotta red, and the pale, handsome features of these two men looking out from these filaments were a revelation. One was tall, the other shorter, both young and handsome. The faces were exceedingly agreeable and shy and modest. Both looked down on the deck as we examined them. Their skins were coloured too, pink with annatto, I fancy. It looked like African camwood powder.[53] The taller young man might have stood for an Inca prince. Regular features, soft gentle eyes, a beautiful mouth and downcast, pensive glance. I lifted his face twice to try and meet the eyes, but he smiled gently, and looked down again. He had two bunches of red parrot's feathers over the ears. Their two wives were on the beach, and I went to visit them, but they both held down their heads and put up their arms to cover their faces, so I could not do more than glance at them by the lantern – the old man, Ruiz, introducing me in Yaguas. The Captain says these Yaguas are 'free', but the word needs definition here. I presume they are all 'in debt' to this old man Ruiz. He looks 68 or 70 at least and the Captain says was born here at Pebas, and is 'the boss of all the Yaguas'. He is also the 'Governor' of Pebas. When I asked how it was these Indians had not disappeared or merged like the Ticunas and others along the river into the 'civilized' squatter type, Reigada said he did not know, but a minute later the explanation came. There are priests here – a mission of Augustinians, and paid and maintained to some extent by the Peruvian Government, keeps two priests in the Yaguas country, and this has been going on apparently for a very long time. This is, I think, the explanation of the salvation of this noble, graceful tribe... They have been saved by the Missionaries – that seems clear.

...Reigada says that Ruiz is the Governor, and the 'Indians work rubber for him.'

It is like the old sarsaparilla business in Maw's and Hernden's time. If the tribe is untouched, the Peruvian method of 'administration['] is equally so. A century has brought no betterment of method, while on the Putumayo we have Pizarro and the crimes of the fifteenth century in full swing. What a country!

[53] Annatto: a small tropical tree; a yellowish-red dye is obtained from the pulpy outer layer of its seeds. Camwood: a West African tree used to make red dye.

I fear I am going to have an attack of gastritis as in Pará in July, 1908. That awful memory is with me still, and the symptoms that have developed today recall the beginnings of that attack. A nasty bitter taste in my mouth after <u>everything</u> I eat or drink. It doesn't matter what it may be – food or drink, meat, bread, tea or wine – as soon as it is swallowed this acrid, unpleasant taste, as if my mouth were filled with quinine follows. And this, accompanied as it is by the extraordinary irritation of the skin that has arisen since we left the Putumayo, makes me fear very much I am in for another bout of that dreadful infirmity of stomach that laid me low for 3 months in 1908. I shall go to the Doctor of the 'Athualpa' as soon as we arrive, and knock off all meat &c. from tomorrow.

THURSDAY, NOVEMBER 24TH, 1910.

Heavy rain and thunder clouds all along the sky. Great quantities of weed, &c. drifting down, and the river is surely risen much the last few days. I shall be very glad to reach Iquites now, especially as I feel worse today, and fear much that it is a gastric attack. My Pará attack was acute gastritis, and I don't want another. Up here, too, with this long journey before me to get to anything like comfort or care, and to be sick on the 'Athualpa' with a landing in Manaos and worry there over the Barbados men would be the last straw. If we get to Iquitos in time I shall go straight to the Doctor of the 'Athualpa'.

Today is cool. The Cholo sailors are clearing everything up and getting the ship smart for her arrival at the local capital. I looked through Congo letters and others I got on 9th November, and have arranged them for answering when I turn my face down stream, I hope on Sunday next the 27th in 'Athualpa'.

Spent a lazy day, not writing much or doing anything. I played with my little chiviclis in the morning, it is a dear little thing, and will soon be as great a pet as the one we had up the Madeira river in May 1908, which got blown overboard in the tremendous tornado that swept our decks coming down river one afternoon. I keep it warm and cosy in my cabin every night, and early morning Aredomi or Omarino come and take it out, and much of the day I leave it free to play run and chirrup – and eat. ...

I went on shore [at a small settlement called Muruku] with Omarino, & the young pilot Pisango, who is a fine young chap with a handsome pure Indian face. He bought ducks for his home in Iquitos. I merely looked at the houses, three or four scattered along the bank about 100 yards from each other with agreeable garden ground between and around them. I saw bread, fruit [breadfruit], guavas, cocoa, cassava, plantain in great quantity, peppers, maize, sugar-cane and other fruit trees I did not know, all scattered in great confusion mixed up together 'through other', as we say in Ireland. Also, of course, the beautiful popuna palm, called here pifwa, and chontadura in Colombia. ...

One of the young Indians, old Ruiz said, came from 6 days away – the other, the taller and better looking youth, from only 4 hours away. I never saw gentler faces, or more agreeable expressions on any faces than on those of the two young men in their truly extraordinary garb. I shall get Aredomi painted and clothed in it at home, and have him photographed and presented to Dilke and the Anti-Slavery people at a great meeting! That will be an idea to enlist sympathy. ...

FRIDAY, 25TH NOVEMBER, 1910.

Arriving at Iquitos on getting up. ... and at 7 a.m. are abreast of Punchana, the Indian village below Iquitos, where Simon Pisango lives. Its church, too, in ruins! The 'Athualpa' clearly in sight, made fast at the mole [pier] of Booth & Co. Hurrah! I'll welcome the sight of the English flag. I! ever [Even] so, since there is no Irish flag – yet. I am glad to think there is a flag – red and all – that stands today for fair dealing and some chivalry of mind and deed to weaker men.

I have packed up, and all is ready for landing, and today will see my last fight on the Putumayo question. I shall call on the Prefect at 2.30, and then there will be a frank, if confidential, exposing of the situation to him, and I'll make it clear that Peru has got to deal with this hideous evil, or stand the consequences of loss of prestige and reputation, to say nothing of the shutting off of all financial supplies.

I must now put my diary away, and go and stand on the fo'ctle to talk to the skipper.

SATURDAY, NOVEMBER 26TH, 1910.

Landed yesterday at Iquitos, and got all things up to Cazes. Mr. and Mrs. Cazes very well, and took up my quarters in the very hot bedroom of before; Bishop, Aredomi and Omarino to quarters in town I am renting for them. Mrs. C. sniffs at their being here, and suggests a bath. I said the Indians are, generally speaking, much cleaner than whites as regards their bodies. Took both boys to a barber – a Spaniard – to have their hair cut, and my own mop shortened. He was enchanted with their Indian hair – beautiful, long and strong. Received a visit very soon from the Prefect's A.D.C., a young mestizo, who couldn't look me in the eyes, but rapped his knees with his riding whip. Prefect sent complimentary message after my health, &c., and my stay in the Putumayo, &c. I said I should call on him in person tomorrow, or next day. Pablo Zumaeta also called, but I was fortunately out then. Visited Booth & Co. and down to 'Athualpa', to find to my disgust she does not sail until Friday (2nd Dec.) at earliest, and probably not till Sunday, 4th. The s.s. 'Clement' is due to leave Manaos for N. York via Barbados on 9th, and I hope to catch her for Bishop, Brown, and all the men, to get rid of those who are not staying on in Brazil. Visited Reigada on the mole, he was superintending the discharge of the Putumayo 'chorijos' or sausages of vile rubber. All his poor Cholo boys of crew today, he says, got drunk, and he cured them by putting them down the hold and covering them with the hatches battened down – 'to sweat it out', he said. It is a barbarous and infamous method of dealing with men, and I find a favourite one with these Peruvian river skippers. Bishop tells me Zubiaurr,[54] the brute so often mentioned in the H. [Hardenburg] depositions, and who is now Captain of D. Cazes' Launch, the 'Beatriz', put a Peruvian 'down the hold' of the 'Liberal' once, and the man died from suffocation. Nothing was done to Zubiaurr. I can well believe anyone would die from even $\frac{1}{2}$ an hour down the hold of a tiny launch like this – ... there is absolutely no air or breathing hole of any kind once the hatch is on, and iron walls all round, in this climate! The poor Cholo boys were working the rubber when I saw them, having 'sweated it out', and some of them looked pretty pale. I told Reigada that the people who were not afraid to get drunk had conquered the world! – the English, Irish, Scotch, Teutons, and Northerners generally, while the sober races had failed! The man who was not afraid 'to give himself away' had probably a temperament that made for greatness lacking in the more discreet man who feared in vino veritas. When English gentlemen went to bed on their servants' backs, a drunken English Cabinet had smashed France and conquered the world! My homily on the virtues of drink v. sobriety ended. (I said it on purpose, as Reigada had accused 'these Englishmen' – the Commission and myself – of being 'whisky drinkers' and thinking only of that).

I returned to Booth's, and had a cocktail.

Long talk with Cazes about Putumayo – his mental attitude is not a desirable one. Every time he opens his mouth on the subject he shows how very much more he knew about it all than he admitted to the F.O. when asked for information. He was cheek by jowl with Arana in London at that time. He knew of heaps and heaps of things, and yet in his letter to F.O. he pretended that he knew practically nothing – even that Huitoto slaves were bought and sold here in Iquitos. Why, I already know of several. There is the sailor boy Julio on the Liberal this voyage, the property of the present

---

[54] Carlos Zubiabur, one-time captain of the *Liberal*.

Portmaster of the town, who tried to make Reigada sign a bill for £50 when the boy engaged on the Liberal on 1st. October.

Bishop told me yesterday that the woman in the house where he has got a room for himself and John Brown has a Huitoto servant girl, and yesterday morning he heard her tell John Brown that the girl had cost her 500 soles. Brown had known the girl somewhere in the Igaraparana and was asking her about the girl, and she said, 'Yes, I paid £50 for her.'

In the evening (Friday) another long talk with Cazes. I must say he does not inspire much confidence. For instance, he had the effrontery to try and cram down my throat that he often sold goods at Iquitos at below their cost price. This apropos the reform the Commission will suggest that in future all goods shall be bought in England and not in Iquitos. He thinks that 'a possible saving of 10%, at most 15%' might be effected thereby – not more! He adds that the House here in Iquitos (Zumaeta & Co.) do not buy here, even at the cheapest local rates. They make no effort to obtain the best prices locally obtainable. That I had long since guessed. They buy from their friends. He admits that there is an enormous amount of inside swindling in this and other respects, and that the London shareholders don't get a penny out of the Rubber. Every cent goes out here; or to those who have advanced money in one way or another.

As regards the Yaguas Indians, Cazes knows them. Says they are 'nice looking but stupid'.

The old Governor, Ruiz, is a trading client of his, he is godfather to two of Ruiz's children. Cazes does not think the Yaguas are enslaved, but he evidently knows very little about it, and cares less. He did not know that Ruiz's son was established, for instance, up at the head waters of the Yaguas River 6 days from Pebas, although he has such close dealings with the father. He says the present service of rubber is very good for him – plenty of it.

SATURDAY, NOVEMBER 26, 1910.

I went to the Prefect with Cazes as interpreter at 10.15 and stayed till 11.40, a very long interview. I told him much...

He said the Fiscal of the Court, Dr. Cavera,[55] is now Prime Minister of Peru and that the Commission of Justice which is about to sail for the Putumayo will be composed of Dr. Valcarcel (or Balearce?) as Judge, a public officer, troops (public force), officers and a Doctor, that it would leave as [sic] a Government Steamer and be absolutely independent of the

---

[55] Salvador Cavero, Premier of Peru in 1910; his other portfolios were Justice and Public Instruction.

Company, and that he was only awaiting telegraphic instructions from Lucia [Lima] to despatch this Commission, that he would telegraph at once to Lucia [*sic*] to say he had seen me, that I confirmed substantially the worst charges that appeared in Truth, that the crimes alleged were revolting, and that justice must be done. He begged me again and again that there should be no publicity, that I would not write a report for publication, as that would be a 'crushing weight' on the 'guiltless' shoulders of Peru, that the Coy. for its 'criminal negligence' deserved punishment, that the Indians should be protected in future and all possibility of a recurrence of these things removed. His chief fear was that publicity would follow, that H.M. Government would publish facts, my report, answer questions in Parliament, etc., and that would be international obloquy for Peru. Could that be avoided? Could I withhold from F.O. the damning evidence of the Barbados men? Could I omit that from my report? I said No, I could not, that I was bound to report fully, that my instructions were to report on the state in which I found the Barbados men and the nature of their relations to the Company, and all the evidence they laid before me would have to be laid before the S. of S.; but, I said, speaking for myself, I could assure him that there should be no publicity, that as far as I had influence or the humble power to suggest I should beg that the charges involving the welfare of the Peruvian name should in no case be made public, that my idea and wish was, subject, of course, to the permission of the Secretary of State, to write two reports, – one that should deal with the narrower subject of the Barbados men's general treatment by the Company and the causes of complaint they might have against it, that this report should not affront or implicate the Government of Peru, but might – possibly would – be painful reading to the Company. Here he expressed complete satisfaction and interjected, 'True, the Company merits all it will get!'

I then went on: 'But I must faithfully record all the facts laid before me by British subjects, and here, where my report would of necessity deal with these very damaging charges against Peruvian citizens and implicate many individuals of that nationality, I should make it a separate and confidential report, with the permission of the F.O., and I had every hope and every reason to suppose that His Majesty's Government would deal with it as entirely confidential. I said that possibly if the Peruvian Government desired a copy of that confidential report and of the evidence on which I based it, His Majesty's Government would be pleased to communicate it to the Government of Lima, in a wholly friendly and helpful way. That there could be no question of the British Government wishing to wound or affront in any way a friendly country, and that I felt sure in my heart he need not fear a campaign of publicity directed against Peru. But I said there was one danger, if, for example, this Commission of Justice should fail, through one cause or another, from want of evidence and failure to obtain testimony – a possible contingency. Then there might be fear that from other quarters – not from me – public statements would be made. There were others, besides myself, who now knew the facts. He again and again assured me that the Commission should be a real one, that its object was to avenge the wrongs done, to <u>punish the wrongdoers</u> – he repeated this – and to protect the Indians. That it would be some months at its work, and would be a thorough investigation. <u>That it was taking inter-</u><u>preters too.</u> (This is the crucial point. Will the Judge be sincere, and will they get proper interpretation?) He thanked me for talking so frankly, and I said I was saying what I did only to assist him, and his Government, to do right. I promised to send Bishop to him at 10 a.m. on Monday, and he was to put any question he pleased to him. The fat is in the fire!

I put in a last word for the Company and <u>against</u> Julio Arana. I said, that admitting the Company had been to blame, and I, for one, thought they had been sincerely to blame, there were two things to bear in mind. First, that it was better for the Indians and the region that a strong Company should be there, working 'on another road', on humane and sensible lines, than that the district should be abandoned, or given up to petty traders and isolated 'trading' ports. He agreed, and then I said there was a corollary, viz: that Sr. Julio Arana should not be permitted to be supreme in that region. If the Company had erred, it was he who had founded it, knowing the facts, and in all its statements to H.M. Govt. and in its beliefs, it had acted on his advice by his prompting, so that he was much more to blame than the other members of the Board. Therefore, while saving the Company, <u>to do good</u> I thought there should be a limitation of that paramount influence he had personally exercised in the Putumayo. I hope the Prefect guessed all I meant. Cazes, I think, translated this faithfully enough, although I more than once found Cazes saying a great deal more than I asked him to say, and once, <u>certainly,</u> he mistrans-lated what I had said, but it was easy to correct. Several times, I think, Cazes spoke for himself when it should have been for me. However, that is one of the drawbacks of having to try and do through another what I should be able to do myself. Anyhow good only can come from this interview. It will show the Prefect more clearly than he could have realized before the need for making this a <u>real enquiry</u>, and not a sham one, a real Commission of Justice, and not one of white-washing.

I told Cazes of his Captain Zubranio [*sic*] killing the man by putting him down the hold, and I find he knew it already! And, yet, he told the Commission in my hearing in September last that Zubranio was 'such a nice chap', and he knew nothing against him. ...

I told him of Aurelio Rodriguez killing hundreds in Santa Catalina, and of the moveable cepo made by Crichlow at this brute's order. I told him of

Normand killing hundreds and burning them alive, and of Jiménez killing and burning the old woman and the Boras man in June, 1908. I did not mention the names of Sealy, Chase or Donald Francis. Poor chaps, I am sorry for them there! – especially for Francis. I told him of Clifford Quintyre [Quintyne] brutally flogged by Normand, of A. Walcott hung up by the arms until unconscious, of J. Dyall put in the cepo at Ultimo Retiro by Montt, and I assured him that the crimes committed were atrocious, and a disgrace to humanity. He was profoundly impressed, and again and again said that justice should be done. Perhaps the most significant statement he made (apart from his effort to get me to promise I should not lay all the facts before the F.O.) was when he said that when the Peruvian Government had consented to allow the Commission of Enquiry to go in to the Putumayo, and, above all, to allow me, a foreign Consul, to go there in a public capacity, it was because they believed all the charges brought by Hardenberg and 'Truth' were 'chantage' [blackmail] inspired, that they had regarded the whole campaign as a calumny and imposture, and, therefore, attached no importance to it. Had they thought there was any foundation for the charges the Peru Government would never have allowed me to go there and investigate, or have consented to the P.A. Company's Commission. They would themselves have acted – the Government would have sent this Commission of Justice long ago! Now it was due to the spontaneous act of Sr. Savara [*sic*] moved thereto by the letter from Barcelona by E. Deschamps. I could not tell him that it was too late in the day to successfully maintain this attitude. They had had all these dreadful charges made here in Iquitos – witnesses on the spot walking about the streets asking to be interrogated, and nothing had been done....

SUNDAY, 27TH NOVEMBER, 1910.

Started on 'Manati' at 9.40 in heavy rain. The Prefect, his brother, Alejandvo Paz Soldan and a Peruvian Naval Lieutenant, named Bravo,[56] were the foreign guests, and then Brown, Harrison, Sibley, and others of Booth's people, including Captain Kaas of 'Athualpa'. We steamed up river some 25 to 30 miles to a place on right bank called Tarnshiaka, where we landed and visited the (mud) church and were hospitably entertained by the villagers who were delighted to see the Prefect. ...

The Prefect's brother told me (in English) that he had been in the Peruvian Corporation and liked the Indians, especially the Campas, very much. He asked me, too, about the Putumayo, and if the charges in 'Truth' were true, and I said yes in the main and told him one or two things of

[56] See Black Diary, note 182.

what had been declared to me. Also I said that the whole system from top to bottom was undisguised slavery and that the Indians existed only to bring in rubber on the whiteman's terms. He seemed incredulous, but gave me a much better impression than I had first derived from his appearance. ...

I find the Limas [lunar] rainbow we saw at Chorrera on 6th November was seen here, too, by Mr. and Mrs. Cazes, same day and same hour; she says 'about 8 p.m.' Very curious thing indeed! Cazes had noted its clear arc, from horizon to horizon, and says it was very vivid. I am thoroughly tired. I offered to send John Brown and S. Lewis also to the Prefect, and he thanked me much. He begged me to give him any hint I could so that the Commission should now be <u>misled</u> – to put it on the right road.

MONDAY, 28TH NOVEMBER.

...I sent for John Brown and Lewis and told them I wished them to be fully prepared to see the Prefect in the morning. Heavy rain most of the day. I walked towards Punchana late in afternoon, but it was too muddy. Manoel Lomas the Pilot talked to me – he was 'a bit on' – but was very civil and begged me to visit his house.

Cazes told me something of the Dutch-French Company who have been turned back by the Local authorities, and spoke of the disgraceful character of the article in 'El Oriente' which attacked them and threatened them with being lynched. The proprietor of 'El Oriente' and writer of this disgraceful article is Sr. Paredes, a Judge of the Superior Court of Iquitos! On the other hand Cazes says that Dr. Valcarcel the judge going to the Putumayo, is well spoken of locally. He has not been here very long and, as the Prefect said, he hopes that he has few local ties or associations, and is not too deeply in with these people. Cazes told me after dinner that round at his lawyer's he had seen a Memorial (about a year ago) which had been sent to Lima by one of the local Priests, a Spaniard – who had been on the Putumayo.

This Memorial begged the Government to take action. The Priest stated that he could carry on no evangelising or Christian work on the Putumayo, owing to the condition of the Indians and the inhuman treatment they received. I asked Cazes if he would get me a copy of this Memorial and he said he would – but I'll have to press for it. I'll try Vatan, who is a far more reliable little man than Cazes and has a much better head-piece for anything connected with the country and the people. It is clear to me that as I have got in my hands the most damaging evidence and the <u>witnesses</u> too, this Peruvian Judge and the Commission will have to act. They fear exposure above all things. The Prefect confirmed that. He said it would 'crush' Peru – so that practically I have the whip hand of these people – or rather the F.O. has, and it can <u>really</u>, but in a still quite friendly way dictate terms, or at least ensure the cessation of the ill-treatment of the Indians.

TUESDAY, 29TH NOVEMBER, 1910.

I am writing to Mr. Dening[57] or the Vice Consul rather to see that those who are to be repatriated go all by 'Clement'.

. . . back to town and met Vatan and we sat down together. His talk a highly interesting one – First on Putumayo.

He asked if I had found his statement to me made in September was well founded. I said entirely – that things were as he told me. I would say no more. He quite understood. He said he thought nothing would be done – I said I differed – that I believed <u>now</u> much would be done – that I had a firm confidence in a prompt amelioration.

He said that it was only because I had come in an official character that I was allowed out alive! I laughed. He said 'It is true – had you been a mere traveller and had seen these things they would have got [done] away with you up there. Your death would have been put down to Indians – I know what I am talking about.' He went on to say that it was not a moment too soon that I had come on the P.A. Coy's Commission. My coming, he said, would influence things not only on the Putumayo for good, but right through the Department. They would all benefit from it. Now that the truth had been found out – as he knew it <u>had</u> been – something might be hoped for.

. . . He then told me at some length of the failure of the Dutch-French Colonizing Company, and of the disgraceful measures[58] undertaken against them by the Prefect – acting under local excitement. Everyone had been threatened – he himself the Agent of the Syndicate – had been threatened. I told him I had read the article in 'El Oriente' (only today) which referred to them, and it was a disgraceful article.

He gave me many particulars of the Syndicate – its aims and wishes and then of the local hostility. I will draw up a separate Memorandum of all this, as it is useful and throws light on the utter unreliability of the Peruvian authorities, and how essential it is for the betterment of things on the Putumayo that they should be impelled by <u>fear</u>. Honour will not move them. Vatan said to me 'Are you not sanguine in thinking that anything is going to be <u>really</u> done now? These people promise with no

---

[57] See Black Diary, note 69.
[58] See Black Diary, note 198.

intention to fulfil and when you are gone –'. I said nothing more than that the <u>facts</u> were known now and to others besides myself and I hoped and believed that real action would be taken. ...

After dinner I went to Booth's house and walked out with Brown round the Square and to the Merry-go-Round where lots of the Indian lads and young men were enjoying themselves. Saw several of the 'Liberal' crew there.

WEDNESDAY, 30TH NOVEMBER, 1910.

Cazes continuing to pretend that the ill-treatment of Indians in the Putumayo was quite exceptional and took place nowhere else in Peru, I said I could not accept his views – that I preferred to believe the evidence of Von Nordenskjold[59] and of others who all testified as to the slavery (and worse things) of the Indians. I got Von Nordenskjold's letter to the Anti-Slavery people and let him read it and he then said: yes, that is true'! – Amazing – after continually asserting that it was <u>only</u> on the Putumayo, 'the sealed book' as he called it, that these things were possible.

He admits that all Von Nordenskjold asserts is true – that the accounts are falsified – the Indians always 'over-charged on what they take and undercredited on what they bring in'. I told him Nordenskjold's letter did not stand alone and that others had and would testify to the same things, and that if this Peruvian Judge did not do right on the Putumayo the floodgates would be opened. I find Cazes an exceedingly untrustworthy guide to things here. His first concern is his business, and beyond that he pretends to know nothing. The photographer sent back, after repeated requests, my films developed, but has abstracted No.1 – that of 'Bolivar' in chains that I took at Indostan! He refused to print any saying he had been bothered so much. He has had the roll of films (ten 'postcard' films) since 11th or 12th October and by 30th November this is the result! Of course the Company has stolen 'Bolivar'. Cazes says everyone in town knew we had found him in chains, and that I had photo'd him. Duble spoke to him of it as 'regrettable thing that we should have found this man in chains', but that 'satisfactory explanations were given.' Were they? Dan Browne[60] also told me he had heard of it – in the street.

[59] Erland Nordenskjöld (1877–1932): Distinguished Swedish ethnographer with special research interest in native Indian culture of South America. Travelled widely throughout the continent, including Bolivia 1901–2 and Colombia 1908–9, 1913–14.

[60] See Black Diary, note 187.

THURSDAY, 1ST DECEMBER, 1910.

... Heavy rain last night and again this afternoon it passed. I walked about a good deal – went to 'Athualpa' at 4.30, and saw 'Adolfo' starting for Yurimaguas with many passengers. Invited Brown to dinner at Bella Vista, and afterwards we went to the Alhambra to the Cinematograph, where were lots of Indians – all Indians and a few soldiers. Brown told me two interesting things. First, that he believed, too, the Indians were slaves, and in the rivers even close to Iquitos. He said he was sure of it, and that, when a white was killed or 'murdered' by Indians, it was due to his atrocious treatment of them. Within a month, he said, the biggest Cauchero [rubber-trader] in Iquitos, Valdimiro Rodriguez had been killed on the Madredi Dios by 8 Indians. The Indians here knew of it before the papers published it, and he heard them talking of it among themselves on the Plaza before it became general news. This Valdimiro was one of two brothers, Rodriguez, who 'treated' on a big scale in the Ucayali and Maranon and other Rivers. He also told me that Lieut. Bravo, the Peruvian Naval Officer who was with us on Sunday, had told him in strict confidence that the Judge Valcarcel who is going to the Putumayo is <u>not</u> straight, and can be bought. These were Brown's own words. A nice look out. Brown said that the Commission was a sham, sent only because we had already gone to Putumayo and they were trying to save their faces, but that he had few hopes of it doing much. I said nothing, but was glad he told me these things. He tells me there are stocks at Punchana. The Governor there used to be the Schoolmistress! She put an Indian in them one day for beating his wife.

It was a <u>very hot day</u> and the injured wife came and built a palm screen over her husband to shield him from the sun. ...

A letter appeared in last night's 'Loreto Comercial' from Simon Pisango, the young pilot of 'Liberal', bringing grave charges against Reigada of the 'Liberal.' First rate. I <u>am</u> glad. The truth is coming out. I'll get Simon Pisango to come and see me. I have his photos – two of him – in the films the photographer developed, and I gave them to-day to a German to print. As soon as I get the copies I'll go and see Simon and give them to him, and then find out about D. Serrano and the murder in January 1908. D. Brown says there are heaps of Huitoto slaves here in Iquitos – any number, and they are sold. Mrs. Prefect yesterday spoke of the large number of the 'gentle docile' beings here – as servants – and of the duty of the government to protect them. I saw lots to-night at the Alhambra – 'Julio' of the Portmertu for one, and another fine big chap and many young ones. They are all through the town – chiefly girls. Wesdin [Wesche and Co: Inquitos branch of a German business] next door have one – a boy who has been to Germany, and speaks Spanish and German. He, of course, is well cared for. Why on earth cannot this Peruvian Commission of Justice begin by asking here in Iquitos these Huitotos how they came to be brought here – what became of their parents, wives, children, etc. also find out how much was <u>paid</u> for them. A very useful preliminary interrogatory could be conducted in this way if there were any desire to find out the truth.

FRIDAY, 2ND DECEMBER, 1910.

...The truth is that there is not an honest truthful man in the public service or in trade in Iquitos – they are all liars when they are not worse. The straightest men here are young Vatan, David Brown[61] <u>and</u> the Indians.

...The 'Loreto Comercial' of 1 December has telegrams from Lucia saying the ironclads of the Brazilian Navy have mutinied, and, after a futile bombardment of Rio, in which one woman and two children were killed, has put to sea for an unknown destination – This is pleasant news! I wonder how my consulate fared in the bombardment? It seems incredible. A bad beginning for the Presidency of Marshal Hermes da Fonseca!

The 'El Oriente' of to-night has an article on the constant theft of servant boys and girls (<u>menores</u>) [minors] who in 9 cases out of 10 are Huitotos from various people in the town, and mentions two quite recent cases in the house; Roygarda [*sic*] and Zubiani (both Putumayo ship captains). What a confession when one comes to think of it. I will keep the article as further proof.

I walked part of the way to Punchana in the afternoon trying to get 'Julio' the Huitoto off the 'Liberal' to come with me – but the 'road' was too dreadful with mud and water, so I turned back.

In the evening we all went to the Alhambra to the Cinematograph in honour of the Independence of Portugal when the Braganza family freed the country from the Spanish Dynasty in 1640. And the fools celebrating this to-day flaunt their execrable red and green – crude, blood-thirsty colours as one sees them in Iquitos, in vile mercantile cottons – and cheer for the cowardly downfall of a house that led them out of bondage and gave them a historic name and 'national flag' – all of which they will hand over to a gang of mercenary 'politicos' in Lisbon and Oporto. Portugal is less fit to be a republic than Ireland – An Egyptian republic would beat a Portuguese one – certainly a Turkish republic would give it points for intellectual leadership and firmness of mind and courage of heart. Leading

[61] See Black Diary, note 187.

Portuguese are not only robbers but also <u>faineants</u> – the poor people are simple, kind and brave – and as ignorant as the Egyptian fellaheen. An Irish Republic, but better still an Irish state not a republic, if the Protestant and upper classes could be induced to join, would be a fine thing – but with the tenant farmer, the County Councillor and the Dublin Corporation in charge – ahem!

There was not a very big crowd at the Cinematograph. I counted 62 men in uniform – including the band – the so-called military band of Andean Cholos – fine chaps to look at, but the devil to play. The row was infernal – It was like the source of the Maranon – in clash and clatter of falling stones and burying cliffs – I had to fly all 'overtures' and they began and <u>ended</u> every piece. The things shown were of the usual Latin-American type – of the amorous seduction and outraged husband setting – altogether immoral and nasty and the very worst thing to put before an audience mainly composed of young Indians, soldiers and work boys whose natural simplicity can soon be corrupted by what is offered to them thus in the name of the higher civilization. Higher civilization! God save the mark.

A forest Indian's village trip is far finer and more truly civilized than anything in Iquitos I have seen. ...

SATURDAY, 3RD DECEMBER 1910. [(A)]

...Cazes is not at all hopeful of the Peruvian Commission. He said last night he had heard in town it might not even start at all! That it was, in any case, only a blind – got up to hoodwink the British Government and to prevent public disclosures – and that he doubted very much if any of the murderers would even be imprisoned.

Captain Raggada [*sic*] of '<u>Liberal</u>' called on me this afternoon at 2.30 p.m. to thank me for a small visiting case I sent him as a 'recuerdo' [memento] of our voyage. He tells me the 'Liberal' will return to Encanto on Wednesday next 7th December – She is taking 15 Cholos or peons – labouring men from this – to fill vacancies. He says Zumaeta is going to recall all the Chiefs of sections – or all that Gielgud puts on a black list – and that he believes many of them are to come back with him. The 'Liberal' will be at Encanto a long time, and does not expect to be back here until early January.

He spoke in praise of the Commission (<u>our</u> Commission) and said Mr. Zumaeta was very anxious to carry out any suggestions it put forward. What a change!

I am now going out for a walk to Punchana if possible – if the road is not too wet. The Judge Paredes, editor and leader writer of 'El Oriente', is

another of the scoundrels here. This paper is the organ of the Arana gang.
I saw Victor Israel yesterday – looking very wretched indeed. Both Cazes
and David Brown say he is in fear of prosecution over his famous 'Pacaya
Rubber Estate' – the Company is an absolute fraud. He is said to have got
£70,000 out of it. Incredible.

I may be in Para on 16th December – if I keep on board the 'Athualpa'
at Manaos – although I fear I must land there.

SATURDAY 3RD DECEMBER, 1910 – IQUITOS. [(B)]

...I wrote a long letter to Barnes for the information of our Commission,
telling him what I knew and pointing out how he and his colleagues could
influence things for good on the arrival of Dr. Valcarcel. I sent him back
the Hardenberg Documents too – annotated and all. They are a great loss
to me, but I think it only fair that the Commission should have the use of
them under the forthcoming circumstances of this so-called judicial visit to
the Putumayo. I also wrote out a very short Memo: for the Prefect and sent
a copy of it to Barnes for his guidance. In this Memo: I lay particular stress
on the need of good interpretation of what the Indians may say. In the
evening dined with D. Brown and the Booth people, a very stupid, talkless
party – and then I left and walked round the Plaza several times. It was full
of the life of Iquitos – all classes.

SUNDAY, 4TH DECEMBER, 1910.

Out for a walk to the military firing ground with Ignacio Torres[62] as my
guide. Took several photos of the ground and trees and a stream beyond.
Back at 11 – in great heat – and wrote a little in the afternoon altho' it was
stifling. In the evening the Cazes had a bridge party after dinner which
lasted till midnight – and the heat lasted all night. It was really atrocious –
not a breath of air and I lay for hours trying to sleep – and then got up and
wrote, but the mosquitoes stop that game.

MONDAY, 5TH DECEMBER, 1910.

Out for another walk this morning – with the same guide – and first to the
firing ground and beyond it to the forest where plenty of people – men,
women and children go to cut firewood. Nearly all are Indians and some

[62] See Black Diary, note 180.

quite fine types. A lot of soldiers clearing the road and levelling. No officer in charge. All young men from the Andes side – some Ignacio told me from his own home Taropoto. He has been in the army for 8 months and left it in August last. He is now 19½ years old – so he entered it about 18½. He says he is of the 'raca [raza] Espanola' [Spanish race], whereas he is almost a pure Indian and speaks Quechua as his native language I find. What a pity that all these people desire to shake off their Indian birthright and pretend to be part of the race of their oppressors of the people who, according to Raygarda, have left nothing to Peru but their vices.

Some of these young soldiers are very fine chaps – sturdy, well built and with such cheery brown faces and white teeth – and laughing always. So different from the Brazilian type where every man is so self conscious, he would not dare to laugh.

I went on with Ignacio to the Wireless telegraphy station by the bank of the Itaya and took a photo of it – also of the Cholo soldiers at work.

In the afternoon took my tickets for Para. John Browne has decided to stay here – and is entering the Electric Light Company's work at £15. per month. He may be available if the Peruvian Judge wants him as Interpreter – but I fear this Commission of the Peruvian Government is a fraud.

Guzman told Bishop to-day that his second interview with the Prefect had been a longer one and that he had not concealed anything from him. The Prefect wishes him to go back to Putumayo as an Interpreter. He will be better than Viacarra, although I don't expect anything sincere from these people, especially after the revelation of meanness and duplicity displayed in their dealings with the Franco-Dutch Expedition. Two of the Chiefs of this party are going down on the 'Athualpa', and will be able to tell me much privately about it all.

I am convinced the only chance of bringing about a better state of things in the Putumayo is that the Peruvian Government will realise that, if they don't, we will let the world know the truth.

Tonight 'El Oriente' contains a paragraph about a gentleman, referred to as an ex-official, who is stated to have been keeping a man in chains here in Iquitos, and grossly illtreating him. Cazes tells me that the ex-official referred to was once the Commissario of the Napo – nice type of Magistrate! Pablo Zumaeta called on me at 2.30, asking for a list of all the bad people on Putumayo! Said he had been sent by the Prefect. I refused to discuss the matter with him.

TUESDAY, 6TH DECEMBER, 1910. [(A)]

Up early, and packed up all for steamer, and at 9.20 called on Prefect to bid him goodbye, and leave my Memo. Cazes with me. Went to his private house, and found him there, and his brother and wife. He said the Commission would start on the 15th or 20th; it would consist of Dr. Valcarcel, a Secretary, and a small force of not more than 12 soldiers travelling on a small Government launch. Meantime, Duble, I understood him to say, was going up tomorrow on the 'Liberal' to undertake the dismissal of the <u>worst</u> of the Chiefs of Sections – and he mentioned several names, including Normand's, Aguero's, and Fonseca's & Montt's. This is indeed cheering news – the idea of allowing the Chiefs of the incriminated Company to go before the Judge, to arrange all the ground, &, if necessary, terrorize Indians & others. What a farce it is going to be! I had not expected anything quite so bad as this. Evidently the Prefect has allowed himself to be talked over by Pablo Zumaeta and Duble and is practically leaving <u>them</u> control of the <u>cleansing arrangements</u>.[63] It is disgraceful – Well – this will release me from all moral obligation of promise – I said if this Commission did <u>its</u> duty there would be no scandal – but it is not going to attempt it even. Went straight on board and found Rayzada, Zumaeta, the Prefect's brother and his A.D.C. there to bid me goodbye. Zumaeta told Cazes and myself <u>he</u> was going up to La Chorrera tomorrow! The plot thickens.

TUESDAY, 6TH DECEMBER, 1910. [(B)]

He and Duble together will be a nice house party for Christmas. They are evidently going to try and forestall the 'Commission'. What a pack of scoundrels all round – the whole gang! The Prefect's weakness is atrocious too. I thought he was really moved to some perception of the need of independent action – independent and firm action quite regardless of how the Company might feel or wish. Here we find him <u>allowing</u> these two men to precede the Commission by a fortnight and to practically get <u>their</u> witnesses ready. If only Barnes were a stronger man! He is weak as water and there is no one at Chorrera with any capacity for dealing with these rascals – and Tizon will join his countrymen. I begin to think the Hardenburg disclosures will not be in it with those I may some day make or call on Barnes, Fox & Co. to make.

The truth will have to come out – the Peruvian Government is more guilty than the Arana Bros. even, and the only thing to do is to try and move the civilized world to action.

After lots of handshaking and adieux the 'Athualpa' left Iquitos at about 11 a.m. The Wharf was lined with people – and the steps and upper mole and bank outside the Customs barrier. This is the last view I shall ever

[63] See Black Diary, note 191.

have of the Peruvian Amazon – of the Iquitos Indians and their pleasant cheerful faces – of the low line of houses fronting the wide bold sweep of the Maranon as it comes down from its throne in the Andes – the mightiest river upon earth bathing the meanest shores. If only a good race instead of an evil and corrupt people had first come from Europe with the message of change to these long hidden, gentle people.

There are a lot of Cholos going down to Manaos contracted by various 'caucheros' to go up the Purus to the Acre Rubber Swamps. All are young hale boys and men – some almost pure Indians, others Mestizos. I spoke to several. One, a tall lad of nearly six feet says he has engaged himself to 'Don Mario' as his 'patron' for three years – and in any case 'he will make plenty of money.'

So this senseless rush for money goes on – and when they get it they have no notion of spending it, or making happy homes or pleasant lives. Iquitos is a pigstye and yet it gives the Peruvian Government £300,000 a year in Customs dues, and not £2,000 are spent on any public need. One of my latest acts almost was to photograph the thing they are calling a Hospital that the Government at Lima has at length voted £30,000 for. I am told, that sum has already been spent on it – and there is not £1,500 worth of work on it so far.

The only people I regret at Iquitos or elsewhere on the Peruvian Amazon are the Indians – and those in whom the Indian type prevails. Once the Spanish caste gets uppermost all decency disappears; the Indian still preserves some of his originality, morality of mind and gentleness of demeanour and simplicity of heart. My work is over on the Amazon. I have fought a stiff fight, and so far as one man can win it, I have won – but what remains behind no man can see. Anyhow, the party of Englishmen and myself have let daylight in to those dark wastes, and scheme how they may, we have broken the neck of that particular evil. The much bigger question remains – the future of the S. American Indians and Native people generally.

That awaits the challenging of the Monroe Doctrine and the exploring by that fantastic and selfish reservation of a continent – of two continents – for the least capable of mankind. Europe the Mother of Nations, must overflow and here is the field of overflow – waiting the stream of fertilizing life.

Steamed swiftly down river – and so adieu to the Peruvian Amazon.

Further Reading

Most biographical works devoted to Roger Casement have some special contribution to make. Major differences occur, depending for the most part on whether or not their authors had enjoyed access to the original manuscripts of the Black Diaries. The 'watershed' date was 10 August 1959, when these essential primary sources were made available to historians in the Public Record Office.

The first group (those who wrote before the MSS were revealed) are listed in chronological order:

Redmond-Howard, L. G., *Sir Roger Casement: A Character Sketch without Prejudice*, Dublin, Hodges Figgis, 1916 (a booklet published between Casement's arrest and execution).

Gwynn, D., *The Life and Death of Roger Casement*, London, Jonathan Cape, 1930.

Parmiter, G. de C., *Roger Casement*, London, Arthur Barker, 1936.

Mackey, H. O., *The Life and Times of Roger Casement*, Dublin, C. J. Fallon, 1954.

MacColl, R., *Roger Casement, A New Judgment*, London, Hamish Hamilton, 1956.

The second group, also in chronological order, are:

Hyde, M. H., Introduction to *Trial of Sir Roger Casement*, London, William Hodge, 1960. This was one of a number of books in the 'Notable British Trials Series' and another edition of it, of limited scope, had appeared as early as 1917. The editor, G. H. Knott, gave a brief introduction and commented that 'Perhaps no one so notorious was ever so little known in his private life.'

Inglis, B., *Roger Casement*, London, Hodder and Stoughton, 1973.

Reid, B. L., *The Lives of Roger Casement*, New Haven and London, Yale University, 1976.

Sawyer, R., *Casement: The Flawed Hero*, London, Routledge and Kegan Paul, 1984.

Some books have dealt entirely, or almost entirely, with the forgery issue. They are listed alphabetically:

Mackey, H. O., *Roger Casement: The Secret History of the Forged Diaries*, Dublin, Apollo, 1962.

Mackey, H. O., *Roger Casement: The Truth about the Forged Diaries*, Dublin, C. J. Fallon, 1966.

Maloney, W. J., *The Forged Casement Diaries*, Dublin, Talbot, 1936.

Noyes, A., *The Accusing Ghost or Justice for Casement*, London, Victor Gollancz, 1957.

In addition, a strong case for the involvement of a forger was made in the Belfast periodical *Threshold*, Spring–Summer, 1960, by Roger McHugh, in his article 'Casement: The Public Record Office Manuscripts'.

Two of Sir Basil Thomson's accounts of his involvement in Casement's life are to be found in his *Queer People*, London, Hodder and Stoughton, 1922, and *The Scene Changes*, London, Collins, 1939. The recollections of Counsel for the Prisoner were recorded in A. M. Sullivan's autobiography, *The Last Serjeant*, London, Macdonald, 1952; Counsel for the Crown's account is in Birkenhead, The First Earl of, *Famous Trials of History*, London, Hutchinson, 1926. A more reliable Birkenhead assessment is recorded in the 1959 edition of the second earl's biography of his father: *The Life of F. E. Smith, First Earl of Birkenhead*, London, Eyre and Spottiswoode.

Most insights into the attitudes of Casement's friends and foes are scattered about in a multitude of works of reminiscence. One friend, who stuck loyally by him, was H. W. Nevinson, whose impressions appeared in several books, including *Last Changes, Last Chances*, London, Nesbit, 1928. A less sympathetic portrayal was given by Ernest Hambloch in *British Consul: Memories of Thirty Years Service in Europe and Brazil*, London, George G. Harrap, 1938. One articulate collaborator in the German Adventure was Robert Monteith, author of *Casement's Last Adventure*, Chicago, published under the auspices of the Irish People Monthly, 1932 (revised and enlarged edition with foreword by Franz von Papen, Dublin, Michael F. Moynihan, 1953); another was Karl Spindler, who wrote *Gun Running for Casement in the Easter Rebellion*, 1916, Berlin, August Scherl, 1920 (English translation, London, W. Collins, 1921) and *The Mystery of the Casement Ship*, Berlin, Kribe-Verlag, 1931. Spindler's books are not always easy to find, but a comparatively accessible edition of the latter title was published by Anvil Books of Tralee in 1965.

Roger Casement himself should be allowed the last word. Herbert O. Mackey's best contribution to Casement's memory – apart from the work he did to ensure that the Irish hero's remains were removed from Pentonville Prison – was to produce an anthology: *The Crime Against Europe, Writings and Poems of Roger Casement*, Dublin, C. J. Fallon, 1958. It contains the famous Speech from the Dock, made when unanimity was demanded of juries. According to George Bernard Shaw, two jurors stated that, had they heard this speech before retiring to the jury room, the verdict would have been 'not guilty'.

Index